In the Shadow of International Law

In the Shadow of International Law

Secrecy and Regime Change in the Postwar World

MICHAEL POZNANSKY

OXFORD
UNIVERSITY PRESS

Oxford University Press is a department of the University of Oxford. It furthers the University's objective of excellence in research, scholarship, and education by publishing worldwide. Oxford is a registered trade mark of Oxford University Press in the UK and certain other countries.

Published in the United States of America by Oxford University Press
198 Madison Avenue, New York, NY 10016, United States of America.

Library of Congress Cataloging-in-Publication Data
Names: Poznansky, Michael, author.
Title: In the shadow of international law : secrecy and regime change in the postwar world / Michael Poznansky.
Description: New York : Oxford University Press, 2020. |
Based on author's thesis (doctoral-University of Virginia, 2016)
issued under title: Intervention and secrecy in international politics. |
Includes bibliographical references and index.
Identifiers: LCCN 2019048677 (print) | LCCN 2019048678 (ebook) |
ISBN 9780190096595 (hardback) | ISBN 9780190096618 (epub) |
ISBN 9780190096625
Subjects: LCSH: Intervention (International law) | Sovereignty, Violation of, |
Regime change. | Espionage. | Subversive activities. |
United States—Foreign relations—Latin America.
Classification: LCC KZ6368 .P69 2020 (print) |
LCC KZ6368 (ebook) | DDC 327.1/17—dc23
LC record available at https://lccn.loc.gov/2019048677
LC ebook record available at https://lccn.loc.gov/2019048678

1 3 5 7 9 8 6 4 2

Printed by Integrated Books International, United States of America

CONTENTS

ACKNOWLEDGMENTS

One of the most gratifying parts of completing a book is taking stock of all the individuals who lent a helping hand along the way. And there are many. The initial idea for this project originated during my time as a graduate student at the University of Virginia. I owe an enormous debt of gratitude to John Owen, Dale Copeland, Jeff Legro, Jonah Schulhofer-Wohl, and Al Stam for their unwavering support as members of my dissertation committee. Fellow PhD students, including Sarah Andrews, Harrison Frye, Boris Heersink, Roger Herbert, Jeff Jackson, Kenny Lowande, Sam Plapinger, Matt Scroggs, and John York were an invaluable source of inspiration, encouragement, and feedback as well. I also had the privilege of learning from a wide range of first-rate scholars and teachers during my time at Virginia, including John Echeverri-Gent, Paul Freedman, Dan Gingerich, Jeff Jenkins, Jon Kropko, Carol Mershon, Sonal Pandya, Phil Potter, Todd Sechser, Len Schoppa, and David Waldner. All of them played an integral part in helping me think like a social scientist and better understand the world around me.

I was incredibly fortunate to be able to spend the last year of graduate school as a predoctoral research fellow with the International Security Program at the Belfer Center for Science and International Affairs at the Harvard Kennedy School. Steve Miller, Steve Walt, and Sean Lynn-Jones provided much-needed support and feedback. My fellow fellows, including Mark Bell, Zach Kaufman, Julia Macdonald, Evan Perkoski, and Rachel Whitlark, helped make one of the most stressful years of graduate school enjoyable. I also owe thanks to Kelly Greenhill and Jon Caverley for running the Conflict, Security, and Public Policy Working Group. Many of the ideas that appear in these pages were refined during those sessions.

In the fall of 2016, I was lucky enough to land a job as an assistant professor in the Graduate School of Public and International Affairs at the University of Pittsburgh. All of my colleagues in GSPIA have been tremendously supportive from the moment I arrived. I am especially grateful to Luke Condra, Ryan Grauer, Mike Kenney, Ilia Murtazashvili, Erica Owen, Taylor Seybolt, Meredith Wilf, and Phil Williams for offering helpful feedback on the book project at various stages. Colleagues in Political Science, my second home at the university, also provided helpful advice and feedback, including Michaël Aklin, Mike Colaresi, Jonathan Harris, Michael Mackenzie, Burcu Savun, and Will Spaniel.

In July of 2018, I hosted a book workshop in Washington, D.C. with the generous support of Dean John Keeler and GSPIA. I couldn't have asked for a better line-up of participants: Austin Carson, Tanisha Fazal, Josh Rovner, and Elizabeth Saunders. In addition to being some of the kindest political scientists around, they are also among the sharpest. Their constructive suggestions regarding everything from framing to improving the theoretical and empirical claims have greatly improved the manuscript. The end product is infinitely better as a result. I also thank Ryan Baker for taking copious notes throughout the day.

The following individuals provided feedback at different stages of this project, whether by reading drafts or talking through key issues with me: Gary Bass, Jonathan Brown, Zoltán Búzás, Michael Doyle, Jeff Friedman, Loch Johnson, Michael Joseph, Joseph LaPalombara, Kyle Lascurettes, John Mearsheimer, Andrew Moravcsik, Dan Nexon, Lindsey O'Rourke, Emile Simpson, Jeff Taliaferro, Gregory Treverton, Michael Warner, Keren Yarhi-Milo, Philip Zelikow, and participants at Princeton University's CISS Security Studies Colloquium and the University of Pittsburgh's Global Politics Seminar. I also owe a special thanks to Megan Stewart. By happy coincidence, Megan and I went through the book process at the same time. She was a continued source of enthusiasm and encouragement throughout.

I gathered much of the underlying source material for this book at presidential libraries scattered across the country. As anyone who has done archival research knows, the people working in the research rooms are wellsprings of knowledge and invaluable for making the most of any former presidents' sprawling collections. I am grateful to the archivists at the Lyndon B. Johnson Presidential Library, the John F. Kennedy Presidential Library, the Richard M. Nixon Presidential Library, and the Ronald Reagan Presidential Library for their assistance.

I am also grateful to the public servants who were kind enough to let me borrow some of their time so that I could better understand the dynamics of foreign intervention and American foreign policy. In particular, I thank John Helgerson, Richard Kerr, and Robert Kimmit for agreeing to sit for interviews. Their first-hand experience with some of the events discussed in this book provided much-needed context and insights for what I was reading in the archives and elsewhere. I also thank Ashley Deeks, David Priess, and Clyde Taylor for helpful conservations.

Even before submitting my book manuscript to Oxford University Press, every person I spoke with sang Dave McBride's praises. I now know why. Dave is generous with his time and was always on the ball throughout the entire process. I thank him, Emily Mackenzie, and the rest of the OUP team for making my experience a smooth one. I also thank two anonymous reviewers for reading my manuscript with care and providing helpful suggestions for how to improve it. I trust they will see the positive impact their comments had on the final version. I also thank Nate Taylor for designing the fabulous image on the cover. Nate helped bring my vision for the cover to life and handled my incessant questions and comments with grace.

Portions of the argument and evidence contained in this book have previously appeared in Michael Poznansky, "Feigning Compliance: Covert Action and International Law," *International Studies Quarterly* 63(1): 72–84. I thank Oxford University Press for granting permission to reprint that material here.

I owe my deepest debt of gratitude to my family. My parents, Howard and Sheree, have never wavered in their love and support. I wouldn't have reached this stage without them. My sister Amy, my brother-in-law Rob, and my perfect niece Emilia provided laughter and love in equal measure. My future in-laws, Susan and Marc, my future sisters-in-law, Alicia and Hannah, and the entire Ciccone bunch have been great sources of encouragement and humor. Finally, none of this would have been possible without the love and continued support of my fiancé, Zoe. In addition to being a brilliant scientist, a talented musician, and a master of Boggle, she's also the most humble, patient, and thoughtful person I know, always willing to lend an ear as I worked through this or that revision—whether over the dinner table or while driving in the car. I couldn't have asked for a better partner in life if I tried. This book is dedicated to her.

offered a host of meticulous [illegible] manuscript [illegible] ... [illegible] Meredith [illegible] [illegible] guided me with [illegible] and [illegible] [illegible] the entire process [illegible] [illegible] [illegible] [illegible] [illegible] [illegible] [illegible] [illegible] [illegible] [illegible] [illegible] [illegible] [illegible] [illegible] [illegible] [illegible] [illegible] [illegible] suggestions for [illegible] [illegible] [illegible] [illegible] [illegible] [illegible] [illegible] [illegible] [illegible] [illegible] Khalil [illegible] for [illegible] the [illegible] image on the cover [illegible] [illegible] [illegible] [illegible] [illegible] [illegible] [illegible] and [illegible] grace.

[illegible] [illegible] [illegible] [illegible] [illegible] [illegible] [illegible] [illegible] [illegible] [illegible] [illegible] International [illegible] [illegible] [illegible] [illegible] [illegible] [illegible] [illegible] [illegible] University Press [illegible]

1

Introduction

The very word 'secrecy' is repugnant in a free and open society; and we are as a people inherently and historically opposed to secret societies, to secret oaths and to secret proceedings.

—John F. Kennedy on April 27, 1961

Secrecy is a pervasive feature of international politics. Although the late Daniel Patrick Moynihan once quipped that "secrecy is for losers,"[1] most policymakers view it as an essential tool for competing in a self-help world. And compete they have. Leaders keep secrets as they conduct sensitive diplomatic missions abroad,[2] convince reluctant publics to throw their support behind costly wars,[3] surprise foes to achieve tactical advantages on the battlefield,[4] collect sensitive intelligence related to the actions, intentions, and capabilities of sworn enemies,[5] and much more.[6] Even John F. Kennedy, whose statement in the epigraph reflects an ingrained skepticism toward the role of secrecy in a democracy, conceded later in that same speech that exceptions must often be made in matters of national security.[7] If secrecy is indeed for losers, the historical record is littered with them.

[1] Daniel Patrick Moynihan, *Secrecy: The American Experience* (New Haven, CT: Yale University Press, 1998), 1.

[2] Evelyn Goh, "Nixon, Kissinger, and the 'Soviet Card' in the U.S. Opening to China, 1971–1974," *Diplomatic History* 29, no. 3 (2005): 475–502.

[3] Dan Reiter, "Democracy, Deception, and Entry into War," *Security Studies* 21, no. 4 (2012): 594–623; John M. Schuessler, "The Deception Dividend: FDR's Undeclared War," *International Security* 34, no. 4 (2010): 133–165.

[4] Robert Axelrod, "The Rational Timing of Surprise," *World Politics* 31, no. 2 (1979): 228–246; Branislav L. Slantchev, "Feigning Weakness," *International Organization* 64, no. 3 (2010): 357–388.

[5] Michael Warner, "Wanted : A Definition of Intelligence," *Studies in Intelligence* 46, no. 3 (2002): 15–22.

[6] Mary Graham, *Presidents' Secrets: The Use and Abuse of Hidden Power* (New Haven, CT: Yale University Press, 2017).

[7] Speech available at: https://www.jfklibrary.org/Research/Research-Aids/JFK-Speeches/American-Newspaper-Publishers-Association_19610427.aspx See also Sissela Bok, *Secrets: On the Ethics of Concealment and Revelation* (New York: Vintage Books, 1983), 171–209; Alexandra

In the Shadow of International Law. Michael Poznansky, Oxford University Press (2020). © Oxford University Press.
DOI: 10.1093/oso/9780190096595.001.0001

This book investigates one of the most controversial forms of secret statecraft: the use of covert action to overthrow foreign regimes. The central question it asks is why leaders sometimes turn to the so-called quiet option when conducting regime change rather than using overt methods to achieve the same ends. Why leaders might opt for the former instead of the latter is far from obvious.

Take for example America's varied responses to the emergence of leftist regimes in Cuba and the Dominican Republic in the early 1960s. Policymakers felt there were strong incentives to pursue regime change in each case. In the ideological struggle against the Soviet Union, presidents on both sides of the aisle were obsessed with preventing hostile clients from popping up in the Western Hemisphere.[8] Destabilizing and toppling regimes that were sympathetic to communism, or were suspected of harboring such sympathies, was a core tenet of that enterprise. The incentives to act openly seemed equally strong in both instances. Cuba and the Dominican Republic were located squarely in America's sphere of influence. The likelihood that intervention would spark escalation with rivals was low.[9] Additionally, the presidents responsible for these interventions were on record as being committed to combating Soviet influence. An overt display of force would have shown resolve.[10]

And yet, decision makers sought plausible deniability in one case but not the other. In Cuba, the United States trained roughly 1,500 exiles to storm the beaches, start an uprising, and take over the government. America's hand was not supposed to show. The operation, known as the Bay of Pigs, failed miserably on April 17, 1961. Conversely, military intervention in the Dominican Republic in the spring of 1965 was a public spectacle. Over the course of the invasion, Lyndon Johnson deployed upward of 21,000 troops to prevent a communist takeover. Hans Morgenthau captured the puzzling variation across these cases in an article in *Foreign Affairs* roughly fifty years ago: "[E]ven if one takes at face value the official assessment that the revolution of April 1965 was controlled by Cuban communists, it appears incongruous that we intervened massively in the Dominican Republic, whose revolution was, according to our government's

H. Perina, "Black Holes and Open Secrets: The Impact of Covert Action on International Law," *Columbia Journal of Transnational Law* 53, no. 3 (2015): 514.

[8] John M. Owen, *The Clash of Ideas in World Politics: Transnational Networks, States, and Regime Change, 1510–2010* (Princeton: Princeton University Press, 2010), 181–201.

[9] Austin Carson, "Facing Off and Saving Face: Covert Intervention and Escalation Management in the Korean War," *International Organization* 70, no. 1 (2016): 103–131.

[10] Lindsey O'Rourke, *Covert Regime Change: America's Secret Cold War* (Ithaca: Cornell University Press, 2018), 58–60.

assessment of the facts, a mere symptom of the disease, while the disease itself—that is, Cuban communism—is exempt from intervention altogether."[11]

Such behavior is not merely a historical phenomenon. Barack Obama's different approaches to a pair of long-serving dictators at the height of the Arab Spring are instructive. In March 2011, the United States and NATO allies participated in a massive bombing campaign in Libya with the stated aim of halting Muammar Qaddafi's attacks against civilians. Though not pitched as an exercise in regime change, Obama was well aware that by offering protection to the rebels, who themselves were trying to overthrow Qaddafi, this was a likely outcome.[12] Less than a year later, his administration pursued regime change again, this time against Bashar al-Assad in Syria. Unlike the Libya campaign, these efforts were shrouded in secrecy. The CIA-led operation, codenamed Timber Sycamore, entailed quietly funneling arms to the Free Syrian Army with the help of Saudi Arabia and Jordan.[13] Results were limited and Donald Trump pulled the plug in 2017.[14] Both episodes involved humanitarian catastrophes spurred on by brutal dictators with a history of acrimonious relations with the West, making the variation all the more striking. We are thus left with the question we began with, namely why do states undertake regime change covertly in some cases but not in others?

Overview of the Argument

My argument from 30,000 feet is that international law helps explain why leaders often pursue regime change from the shadows. For much of recent history, there was no codified rule prohibiting states from meddling in one another's affairs. While the concept known as nonintervention existed as a norm to varying degrees since the mid-eighteenth century, great powers routinely ignored it. Intrusive, overt interventions were commonplace. This changed in earnest in 1945 when the United Nations Charter enshrined the nonintervention principle—which proscribes unwanted violations of another state's sovereignty—in treaty law. Many regional bodies created afterward adopted similar provisions.

[11] Hans J. Morgenthau, "To Intervene or Not to Intervene," *Foreign Affairs* 45, no. 3 (1967): 433.

[12] Robert A. Pape, "When Duty Calls: A Pragmatic Standard of Humanitarian Intervention," *International Security* 37, no. 1 (2012): 69.

[13] Austin Carson and Michael Poznansky, "The Logic for (Shoddy) U.S. Covert Action in Syria," *War on the Rocks* July 21 (2016).

[14] Greg Jaffe and Adam Entous, "Trump Ends Covert CIA Program to Arm Anti-Assad Rebels in Syria, a Move Sought by Moscow," *Washington Post* July 19 (2017).

In this new environment, prospective interveners were more likely to act openly when they could find one or more legal exemptions to nonintervention; covert action was the preferred method of intervention when they could not.[15] The advent of written guidelines specifying what constituted a legitimate intervention significantly curtailed the range of reasons states could give to justify foreign-imposed regime change. With respect to the UN Charter, which has the broadest applicability, intervening in response to an armed attack or with approval from the Security Council is fair game.[16] Rescuing endangered nationals and acting with the blessing of a regional organization are also typically viewed as permissible.[17] The exemptions laid out in the charters of regional bodies—assuming they contain a nonintervention principle—are also pertinent, at least for interventions in that part of the world.

This gets us some of the way toward a theory of covert regime change but leaves key questions unanswered. We know from the literature that going overt increases the chances of mission success by allowing interveners to more directly control operations and escalate as needed.[18] Why would leaders knowingly avoid using operationally superior overt actions to achieve plausible deniability when they lack legal exemptions? What are the benefits of avoiding flagrant violations of international law?

In brief, covert action helps states retain credibility and evade hypocrisy costs. This is based on the fact that nonintervention represents two things simultaneously. It is both a formal agreement specifying when states can legally violate each other's sovereignty and a moral ideal centered on the notion that all nations, regardless of size, status, or capabilities, should be free from unwanted foreign interference in their internal affairs. States that abrogate formal agreements put their credibility and trustworthiness on the line.[19] Those that violate moral commitments risk looking hypocritical and can damage their character.[20] Figure 1.1 summarizes the logic of the argument.

[15] Vaughn P. Shannon, "Norms Are What States Make of Them: The Political Psychology of Norm Violation," *International Studies Quarterly* 44, no. 2 (2000): 307; Joel H. Westra, *International Law and the Use of Armed Force: The UN Charter and the Major Powers* (London and New York: Routledge, 2007), 51.

[16] Philip Kunig, "Intervention, Prohibition of," *Max Planck Encyclopedia of Public International Law*, 2008.

[17] Kristen E. Eichensehr, "Defending Nationals Abroad: Assessing the Lawfulness of Forcible Hostage Rescues," *Virginia Journal of International Law* 48, no. 2 (2008): 452–484.

[18] O'Rourke, *Covert Regime Change: America's Secret Cold War*, 8.

[19] George W. Downs and Michael A. Jones, "Reputation, Compliance, and International Law," *Journal of Legal Studies* 31 (2002): S96; Robert O. Keohane, *After Hegemony: Cooperation and Discord in the World Political Economy* (Princeton: Princeton University Press, 1984), 105–106.

[20] Martha Finnemore, "Legitimacy, Hypocrisy, and the Social Structure of Unipolarity: Why Being a Unipole Isn't All It's Cracked Up to Be," *World Politics* 61, no. 1 (2009): 58–85; Kelly M. Greenhill, *Weapons of Mass Migration: Forced Displacement, Coercion, and Foreign Policy* (Ithaca,

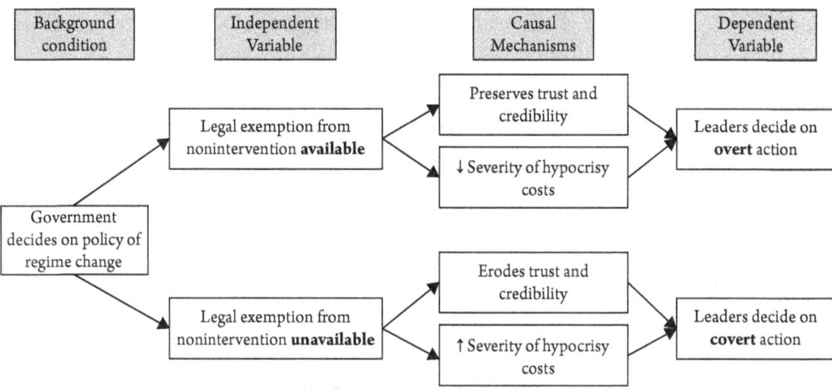

Figure 1.1 Causal Logic of the Argument

The credibility and hypocrisy costs associated with brazen violations of the nonintervention principle are made worse by its status in treaty law. There are a few reasons for this. First, detecting violations of international legal commitments is easier than it is for informal commitments. In the former, pre- and proscribed behavior is articulated in writing. To be sure, legal provisions are often subject to multiple, competing interpretations, and some are clearer than others. Nevertheless, the parameters of what constitutes a violation are less ambiguous than is the case for non-legal agreements. Second, international legal agreements represent the maximal type of commitment a state can make. This markedly raises expectations of how they will behave.[21] Embracing informal rules and norms raises expectations in less dramatic ways. The incentives to hide violations of nonintervention absent a legal exemption should thus be especially strong.

Whether concerns about credibility and hypocrisy costs will induce a state to alter its behavior by turning to covert action depends on many factors, such as regime type or satisfaction with the status quo.[22] As a first cut, this book focuses on U.S. interventions in Latin America during the Cold War. America's efforts to build a rule-based order in the postwar era required committing to agreed-upon

NY: Cornell University Press, 2010); Roseanne McManus and Keren Yarhi-Milo, "The Logic of 'Offstage' Signaling: Domestic Politics, Regime Type, and Major Power-Protégé Relations," *International Organization* 71, no. 4 (2017): 701–733.

[21] Andrew T. Guzman, *How International Law Works: A Rational Choice Theory* (New York: Oxford University Press, 2008), 59; Beth Simmons, *Mobilizing for Human Rights: International Law and Domestic Politics* (New York: Cambridge University Press, 2009), 14.

[22] Miles M. Evers, "On Transgression," *International Studies Quarterly* 61, no. 4 (2017): 786–794; Greenhill, *Weapons of Mass Migration: Forced Displacement, Coercion, and Foreign Policy*, 60–63.

standards of behavior.[23] The desire to project an image of trustworthiness and to credibly signal a commitment to extant rules should have motivated decision makers to hide brazen violations of nonintervention, an agreement they publicly promised to abide by. The liberal order constructed after WWII also involved the endorsement of a wide range of values which enhanced the legitimacy of U.S. leadership.[24] The desire to safeguard America's moral authority meant that leaders should have been keen on hiding violations of nonintervention in its capacity as an ideal they embraced.

Examining U.S. interventions in Latin America during the Cold War has a number of useful properties from a research-design perspective. In terms of the regional focus, many scholars contend that the United States had virtually free rein in the Western Hemisphere.[25] As such, these cases constitute a hard test for my argument. Demonstrating that concerns about violating international law pushed U.S. decision makers to pursue covert action in America's own backyard provides especially strong support. The benefit of focusing on the Cold War is that there are troves of declassified documents which make it possible to tease out the mechanisms of the theory. Nevertheless, Chapter 8 demonstrates that the argument travels across time and space by examining U.S. policy toward Iraq from 1991 to 2003 and Obama's regime-change efforts in Libya and Syria. Although beyond the scope of this project, the conclusion suggests that the argument should apply to countries other than the United States, including liberal democracies and certain great powers.

Definitions

It is important at this stage to define what this book is explaining. *Covert regime change* refers to efforts by one state to alter the domestic authority structures of another state in which the identity of the sponsor is intentionally hidden, ideally

[23] G. John Ikenberry, *Liberal Leviathan: The Origins, Crisis, and Transformation of the American World Order* (Princeton, NJ: Princeton University Press, 2011), 105. See also David A. Lake, *Hierarchy in International Relations* (Ithaca, NY: Cornell University Press, 2009).

[24] Daniel Deudney and G. John Ikenberry, "The Nature and Sources of Liberal International Order," *Review of International Studies* 25, no. 2 (1999): 179–196; Christian Reus-Smit, *American Power and World Order* (Cambridge: Polity Press, 2004); John Gerard Ruggie, *Winning the Peace: America and World Order in the New Era* (New York: Columbia University Press, 1996).

[25] Ikenberry, *Liberal Leviathan: The Origins, Crisis, and Transformation of the American World Order*, 90–91. Even scholars who argue that international law may act as a constraint concede that the costs of violations are lower in major powers' spheres of influence. See Westra, *International Law and the Use of Armed Force: The UN Charter and the Major Powers*, 53.

providing them with plausible deniability.[26] *Overt regime change* is the mirror opposite in one important respect: the intervening state chooses to make their involvement known. Formally, overt regime change refers to efforts by one state to alter the domestic authority structures of another state in which the intervener intentionally acknowledges sponsorship.[27]

The foregoing definitions take a broad view of foreign-imposed regime change. Altering domestic authority structures in a foreign country, whether by overthrowing a sitting government or by installing a new one in cases where authority is ambiguous and contested, qualifies under this definition. That is why both Ronald Reagan's invasion of Grenada and Lyndon Johnson's invasion of the Dominican Republic are treated as instances of the same general phenomenon. In Grenada, Reagan toppled a regime that enjoyed control over the country at the time. In the Dominican Republic, Johnson interfered in a civil war to prevent rebels who had recently taken control of the capital from consolidating power and then worked to install a regime that would be friendlier to U.S. interests.[28] Excluded from this definition, however, are attempts to save wobbling regimes from falling. Given the objective, these interventions are better thought of as regime rescue or maintenance.[29] America's efforts to prop up the South Vietnamese government in the 1960s and early 1970s fall into this category.[30]

Although this book has less to do with the precise tools interveners use to change regimes and more to do with whether or not they choose to keep their identity hidden during an operation, it may be useful to briefly outline the range of activities that interveners might pursue in the service of overt or covert regime change. The most intrusive form of regime change is when an intervener

[26] Whether interveners ultimately fail in this regard and their sponsorship is revealed is interesting but less relevant to the current discussion, which privileges the intent behind an operation. Covert action is also distinct from clandestine operations which prioritize the concealment of the operation itself, not necessarily the sponsor. See Richard C. Gross, "Different Worlds: Unacknowledged Special Operations and Covert Action," *Strategy Research Project: U.S. Army War College*, 2009, https://fas.org/man/eprint/gross.pdf.

[27] The use of "intentional" excludes covert operations in which the sponsor is outed by accident or by discovery of a third party, whether the target state or a rival power.

[28] Existing scholarship also treats this as an instance of regime change. See O'Rourke, *Covert Regime Change: America's Secret Cold War*; Owen, *The Clash of Ideas in World Politics: Transnational Networks, States, and Regime Change, 1510–2010.*

[29] Of note, regime change and regime rescue both qualify as intervention according to Rosenau's classic definition since they aim to change or preserve the political authority of another state and are convention-breaking. More subtle and minimal actions such as the provision of humanitarian aid or diplomatic negotiations would not qualify in this view since they are not typically aimed at influencing political authority structures and do not break conventions. See James N. Rosenau, "Intervention as a Scientific Concept," *Journal of Conflict Resolution* 13, no. 2 (1969): 149–171.

[30] There were, however, several covert regime change efforts that transpired alongside the overt war. See O'Rourke, *Covert Regime Change: America's Secret Cold War*, 158–193.

sends their own armed forces in a ground invasion, imposes a naval blockade, or carries out air strikes. These tactics are only available for overt operations. The size and scope of such endeavors would make it impossible to achieve any semblance of plausible deniability.

Short of large-scale military operations, most regime change tactics can be employed overtly or covertly. Forcible options include openly or secretly stimulating coups d'état, revolutions, and uprisings by providing arms, military hardware, or technical and logistical support to actors working to change a regime. Additionally, states may use a variety of nonforcible means to try to change regimes, ranging from economic sanctions to various diplomatic tools and political action intended to influence elections.[31] While any of these tactics can be used outside the context of regime change, states must make clear their intention to change regimes to qualify for this book.

Why Study Secret Interventions?

Understanding the decision to engage in foreign-imposed regime change using visible or covert means is important for a number of reasons. First, because covert action is defined chiefly by the pursuit of plausible deniability, uncovering its causes provides a window into the kinds of things states worry about when meddling abroad. As suggested previously, covert action imposes nontrivial constraints on interveners.[32] To ensure that operations look homegrown, covert operators often rely on local allies and other indigenous forces to do their bidding. This can introduce principal-agent issues into the mix.[33] Covert operators must also be mindful of the kind and amount of support they are providing. Capable sponsors may only be able to offer equipment and supplies that local actors could have obtained on their own, whether from the black market or prior wars. Asking why great powers would knowingly opt for secret operations despite these inherent limitations provides insights into the factors they account for when contemplating intervention. Existing studies prioritize domestic politics and escalation. This book privileges international law.

[31] Dov H. Levin, "When the Great Power Gets a Vote: The Effects of Great Power Electoral Interventions on Election Results," *International Studies Quarterly* 60, no. 2 (2016): 189–202; O'Rourke, *Covert Regime Change: America's Secret Cold War*, 14–16.

[32] Ibid., 53–57.

[33] William J. Daugherty, *Executive Secrets: Covert Action and the Presidency* (Lexington, KY: The University Press of Kentucky, 2004), 13; Gregory F. Treverton, *Covert Action: The Limits of Intervention in the Postwar World* (New York: Basic Books, Inc., 1987), 118.

Investigating covert intervention is interesting for a related reason: there are very few unqualified success stories. In some cases, the negative consequences were apparent in the short term. The Bay of Pigs pushed Castro closer to the Soviet Union and helped bring about the Cuban Missile Crisis, one of the most dangerous episodes of the Cold War, a year and a half later.[34] In other cases, the fallout from covert operations took decades to manifest. Eisenhower's secret efforts to oust Mohammed Mossadegh in Iran in 1953 provided fuel for the Iranian Revolution in 1979 and remains a source of contention between the two nations.[35] Even when covert intervention worked from the intervener's standpoint, its effects were often devastating for the target country. America's secret interventions in Guatemala in 1954 and Chile in the early 1970s, though successful in ousting unwanted regimes, produced decades of internal strife that wreaked havoc on the populations.[36]

None of this should be taken to mean that overt interventions never end poorly; they can and do. But there are several aspects of covert operations that make them especially likely to go awry. One is that secrecy effectively exempts interveners from the fallout.[37] Should infighting or civil war break out after an intervention, the sponsor may feel little obligation to stabilize the situation. Doing so might betray their involvement. A similar dynamic holds when a brutal autocrat assumes power following a covert operation. The desire for plausible deniability may prevent the sponsor from imposing penalties on new clients who misbehave. Additionally, because covert action short-circuits the marketplace of ideas, the risks of an operation can get swept under the rug.[38] Returning again to the Bay of Pigs, the decision to "exclude . . . many of the most relevant experts" contributed to groupthink.[39] Finally, since covert operations typically require outsourcing, sponsors may be forced to work with local actors who turn on them once the shared enemy is gone. America's relationship with the mujahideen is an example of this. Many of the fighters the United States covertly supported,

[34] Peter Wyden, *Bay of Pigs: The Untold Story* (New York: Simon and Schuster, 1979), 7.

[35] Alexander B. Downes and Lindsey A. O'Rourke, "You Can't Always Get What You Want: Why Foreign-Imposed Regime Change Seldom Improves Interstate Relations," *International Security* 41, no. 2 (2016): 58.

[36] Richard H. Immerman, *The CIA In Guatemala: The Foreign Policy of Intervention* (Austin, TX: University of Texas Press, 1982); Peter Kornbluh, *The Pinochet File: A Declassified Dossier on Atrocity and Accountability* (New York: The New Press, 2003).

[37] O'Rourke, *Covert Regime Change: America's Secret Cold War*, 51.

[38] Ibid., 54.

[39] Irving L. Janis, *Victims of Groupthink: A Psychological Study of Foreign-Policy Decisions and Fiascoes* (Boston, MA: Houghton Mifflin Company, 1972), 32.

directly or indirectly, during the Soviet occupation of Afghanistan in the 1980s became members of terrorist networks like al-Qaeda.[40]

A final reason why the study of covert regime change is interesting centers on its ethical and moral implications. Because these operations rely on secrecy and deception, they are in tension with democratic norms of transparency and openness.[41] Covert action is not debated in public where its merits and viability can be rigorously vetted by different stakeholders.[42] Although accountability is theoretically possible, the barriers are higher in matters of intelligence and national security secrecy.[43] Covert action may also encourage decision makers to ignore or at least downplay diplomatic solutions to crises, especially when overt force is taken off the table. According to political philosopher Charles Beitz, "the low-risk, quick-fix aspect of covert action almost certainly encourages decision makers to commit national power more widely than they would otherwise find it advisable to do."[44]

Contributions

This book contributes to a number of literatures. First, it shines a light on the hidden, illiberal practices that sustained the liberal order the United States helped create in the aftermath of World War II. John Ikenberry, the dean of liberal internationalism, argues that the postwar order is special. For Ikenberry, a core innovation of this enterprise involved the hegemon at the top—the United States—exercising strategic restraint by "acknowledging that there will be limits on the way in which it can exercise power."[45] Not all scholars are convinced. In a recent critique, Patrick Porter points to America's many foreign interventions as evidence that the liberal order is more myth than reality. "Strikingly," he writes, "the Cold War as it was actually conducted and lived—where two superpowers

[40] Steve Coll, *Ghost Wars: The Secret History of the CIA, Afghanistan and Bin Laden, From the Soviet Invasion to September 10, 2001* (New York: Penguin Books, 2004).

[41] Johnson, Loch. *America's Secret Power: The CIA in a Democratic Society*. New York and Oxford: Oxford University Press, 1989; Johnson, Loch. "Covert Action and Accountability: Decision-Making for America's Secret Foreign Policy," *International Studies Quarterly* 33, no. 1 (1989): 81–109; David E. Pozen, "Deep Secrecy," *Stanford Law Review* 62, no. 2 (2010): 285–292.

[42] O'Rourke, *Covert Regime Change: America's Secret Cold War*, 54.

[43] Michael P. Colaresi, *Democracy Declassified: The Secrecy Dilemma in National Security* (Oxford: Oxford University Press, 2014); Joshua Rovner, *Fixing the Facts: National Security and the Politics of Intelligence* (Ithaca: Cornell University Press, 2011), 46–48.

[44] Charles R. Beitz, "Covert Intervention as a Moral Problem," *Ethics and International Affairs* 3, no. 94 (1989): 53.

[45] Ikenberry, *Liberal Leviathan: The Origins, Crisis, and Transformation of the American World Order*, 322.

did not allow rules, sovereignty, multilateralism, and institutions to constrain them when the stakes were high—does not occupy a prominent place in the mytho-history."[46] Others have echoed similar sentiments.[47]

The critics of liberal internationalism are onto something. As a historical matter, it is undeniable that the United States toppled many foreign regimes in violation of its commitment to respect state sovereignty per the dictates of the UN Charter. In this sense, the liberal hegemon was not very restrained. The failure to distinguish between secret and blatant rule violations, though, obscures how decision makers themselves thought about the postwar environment. Self-interest still played a role in U.S. foreign policy. But the desire to promote an order centered on liberalism, transparency, and restraint created incentives to relegate illiberal acts to the covert sphere where they would be less visible and disruptive to this enterprise. Secrecy was a feature of the liberal order, not a bug.

Second, this book advances scholarship on foreign-imposed regime change.[48] International relations scholars have long been interested in why powerful states meddle abroad. Geopolitics,[49] ideology and norms,[50] economic factors,[51] and leaders' causal beliefs[52] are the usual suspects. Most of these studies, however, only focus on visible interventions, neglecting the hidden side of

[46] Patrick Porter, "A World Imagined: Nostalgia and Liberal Order," *CATO Institute* Number 843 (2018): 12.

[47] Graham T. Allison, "The Myth of the Liberal Order," *Foreign Affairs* 97, no. 4 (2018): 124–133.

[48] Melissa Willard-Foster, *Toppling Foreign Governments: The Logic of Regime Change* (Philadelphia: University of Pennsylvania Press, 2019).

[49] Karen A. Feste, *Intervention: Shaping the Global Order* (Westport, CT: Praeger Publishers, 2003), 3; Michael G. Findley and Tze Kwang Teo, "Rethinking Third-Party Interventions into Civil Wars: An Actor-Centric Approach," *Journal of Politics* 68, no. 4 (2006): 828–837; Stephen E. Gent, "Strange Bedfellows: The Strategic Dynamics of Major Power Military Interventions," *Journal of Politics* 69, no. 4 (2007): 1089–1102; Mi Yung Yoon, "Explaining U.S. Intervention in Third World Internal Wars, 1945–1989," *Journal of Conflict Resolution* 41, no. 4 (1997): 594.

[50] Martha Finnemore, *The Purpose of Intervention: Changing Beliefs About the Use of Force* (Ithaca, NY: Cornell University Press, 2003); John M. Owen, "The Foreign Imposition of Domestic Institutions," *International Organization* 56, no. 2 (2002): 375–409; Owen, *The Clash of Ideas in World Politics: Transnational Networks, States, and Regime Change, 1510–2010.* On the promotion of liberalism and democracy in particular, see Jonathan Monten, "The Roots of the Bush Doctrine," *International Security* 29, no. 4 (2005): 112–156; Mark Peceny, *Democracy at the Point of Bayonets* (University Park, PA: The Pennsylvania State University Press, 1999).

[51] Aysegul Aydin, *Foreign Powers and Intervention in Armed Conflicts* (Stanford: Stanford University Press, 2012); Finnemore, *The Purpose of Intervention: Changing Beliefs About the Use of Force*; Benjamin O. Fordham, "Power or Plenty? Economic Interests, Security Concerns, and American Intervention," *International Studies Quarterly* 52, no. 4 (2008): 737–758; Stephen Kinzer, *Overthrow: America's Century of Regime Change from Hawaii to Iraq* (New York: Times Books, 2006).

[52] Elizabeth N. Saunders, *Leaders at War: How Presidents Shape Military Interventions* (Ithaca, NY: Cornell University Press, 2011).

foreign interference.[53] One reason for this is the notion that covert and overt interventions are governed by different data-generating processes. Elizabeth Saunders argues that "[t]he decision process that leads to an overt military intervention requires leaders to weigh a different set of factors and consider a different set of possibilities than the process that governs decisions to undertake covert forms of intervention. Lumping them together would risk comparing apples and oranges."[54] This project joins a growing body of scholarship that pushes back against this assumption, treating the choice to intervene secretly as a direct alternative to overt intervention and theorizing why leaders might opt for one or the other.[55] Covert and overt interventions may be apples and oranges, but they are both fruit.

Despite sharing a similar orientation with these recent works theorizing the causes of covert intervention, this book's focus on international law offers something distinctive. Consider Austin Carson's *Secret Wars: Covert Conflict in International Politics*, which argues that escalation management concerns drive decisions about secrecy.[56] I show that leaders may still turn to covert action when escalation fears are minimal or nonexistent if they are unable to find a legal exemption to nonintervention. Lindsey O'Rourke's *Covert Regime Change: America's Secret Cold War* offers another example. O'Rourke argues that the decision to intervene covertly is shaped by a cost-benefit calculation which includes, among other things, a desire to hide violations of "norms of justified intervention."[57] This captures something important about covert action, but it is underspecified. For instance, it does not distinguish between international legal norms and non-legal norms. Such distinctions matter. As noted, although a nonintervention norm emerged in the mid-eighteenth century, great powers openly violated it for hundreds of years. It was not until nonintervention was codified in international law that states began to think seriously about the benefits of covert violations. Moreover, I show that even if leaders enjoy domestic support, can achieve a quick and decisive victory, and want to signal resolve—O'Rourke's

[53] Owen, *The Clash of Ideas in World Politics: Transnational Networks, States, and Regime Change, 1510–2010*, 275. Finnemore alludes to the relevance of covert action as a consequence of changing norms but does not directly theorize this substitution effect; Finnemore, *The Purpose of Intervention: Changing Beliefs About the Use of Force*, 128.

[54] Saunders, *Leaders at War: How Presidents Shape Military Interventions*, 218.

[55] Austin Carson, *Secret Wars: Covert Conflict in International Politics* (Princeton: Princeton University Press, 2018); O'Rourke, *Covert Regime Change: America's Secret Cold War*; Gregory L. Smith, "Secret but Constrained: The Impact of Elite Opposition on Covert Operations," *International Organization* 73, no. 3 (2019): 685–707.

[56] Carson, *Secret Wars: Covert Conflict in International Politics*.

[57] O'Rourke, *Covert Regime Change: America's Secret Cold War*, 25.

argument for when leaders opt for overt action—they will still act covertly unless they can find a legal exemption to nonintervention.[58]

Third, this book speaks to longstanding debates about whether and how international law influences state behavior.[59] Scholars generally fall into one of two camps. First are the realists who view international law as little more than window dressing.[60] These scholars believe that "legalism . . . provides comforting and delusional justification for policies that are inconsistent with the realities of interest and power."[61] When forced to choose between self-interest and compliance with the law, so this argument goes, states almost always choose the former.[62] In the other camp are liberals and constructivists who take international law more seriously despite meaningful differences in their respective approaches.[63] They tend to believe that international legal commitments can prevent states from indulging their selfish, short-term interests—at least under certain conditions.[64]

I join an emerging literature that challenges the standard dichotomy implicit in this debate wherein states either comply with international laws or ignore them.[65] While the nonintervention principle rarely stopped great powers from intervening to change regimes when it served their interests, concerns about openly violating international legal commitments pushed rule-violating interventions into the covert sphere where they were less likely to succeed. This kind of behavior defies simple categorization. It is clearly not compliance

[58] Ibid., 61–64.

[59] For rare treatments of covert action and international law, see Richard A. Falk, "CIA Covert Action and International Law," *Society* 12 (1975): 39–44; Perina, "Black Holes and Open Secrets: The Impact of Covert Action on International Law"; W. Michael Reisman and James E. Baker, *Regulating Covert Action: Practices, Contexts, and Policies of Covert Coercion Abroad in International and American Law* (New Haven and London: Yale University Press, 1992).

[60] John J. Mearsheimer, "The False Promise of International Institutions," *International Security* 19, no. 3 (1995): 5–49.

[61] Judith Goldstein et al., "Introduction: Legalization and World Politics," *International Organization* 54, no. 3 (2000): 392.

[62] Jack L. Goldsmith and Eric A. Posner, *The Limits of International Law* (Oxford and New York: Oxford University Press, 2005), 13.

[63] Goldstein et al., "Introduction: Legalization and World Politics," 392–393.

[64] Hedley Bull, *The Anarchical Society: A Study of Order in World Politics* (New York: Palgrave Macmillan, 1977), 127–161; Thomas M. Franck, "Legitimacy in the International System," *American Journal of International Law* 82, no. 4 (1988): 705–759; Beth Simmons, "International Law and State Behavior: Commitment and Compliance in International Monetary Affairs," *American Political Science Review* 94, no. 4 (2000): 819–835.

[65] Zoltan Buzas, "Evading International Law: How Agents Comply with the Letter of the Law but Violate Its Purpose," *European Journal of International Relations* 23, no. 4 (2017): 857–883; Zoltan Buzas, "Is the Good News About Law Compliance Good News About Norm Compliance? The Case of Racial Equality," *International Organization* 72, no. 2 (2018): 351–385; Ian Hurd, *How to Do Things with International Law* (Princeton, NJ: Princeton University Press, 2018).

strictly defined, but there is a difference between brazen and hidden violations. The former signals apathy toward international law. The latter represents something more complicated and interesting, namely sensitivity to how others will react to legal deviance and a concomitant effort to manage optics. Because prior studies tend to neglect the covert side of statecraft, these dynamics have largely been overlooked.[66] It is telling that in the *Oxford Handbook of the Use of Force in International Law*, the word *covert* appears just two times.[67] In Ian Hurd's book, *How to Do Things with International Law*, the word does not appear at all.[68]

Roadmap

Chapter 2 traces the evolution of the nonintervention principle from its inception in the mid-eighteenth century to its codification in international law roughly two hundred years later. Before nonintervention was formally codified, great powers ignored the wishes of international lawyers, philosophers, and smaller powers by regularly practicing overt intervention. The primary mode of foreign meddling shifted once nonintervention was enshrined in treaty law. States began to relegate most regime change operations to the covert sphere; overt regime change became the exception. This discussion provides historical context for the remaining chapters, justifies my focus on the postwar period, and provides a basis for examining how changes to the rules governing intervention may influence how states meddle abroad in the future.

Chapter 3 constitutes the theoretical core of the book. It opens by walking through the main alternative explanations to the theory I am developing: escalation management, domestic politics, and nationalism. It then articulates my argument that leaders will pursue regime change openly when they can find a legal exemption to the nonintervention principle and will act covertly otherwise. With the basic framework laid out, I turn to causal mechanisms. The first centers on the idea that states that abrogate formal commitments risk damaging their credibility and trustworthiness. The second mechanism relies on the idea that states that endorse moral principles like nonintervention and then violate them are vulnerable to what Kelly Greenhill calls "hypocrisy costs."[69] I then explain

[66] For an exception, see Westra, *International Law and the Use of Armed Force: The UN Charter and the Major Powers*. Though not about covert action per se, his book flags secrecy as a way to circumvent the rules of the UN Charter.

[67] I used the search function on www.amazon.com. In one case, there is brief reference to an article describing oversight over covert action. In another, the term appears with reference to "covert investigations." See Marc Weller, ed., *The Oxford Handbook of the Use of Force in International Law* (Oxford: Oxford University Press, 2015).

[68] Hurd, *How to Do Things with International Law*.

[69] Greenhill, *Weapons of Mass Migration: Forced Displacement, Coercion, and Foreign Policy*, 52–58.

why these risks are especially salient for the United States given its longstanding commitment to strategic restraint and legitimate leadership. The next section takes up lingering questions, including why leaders do not always opt for covert action and potential issues regarding selection bias. The final two sections discuss my case selection strategy, methodology, and observable implications. The use of archival documents I collected from various presidential libraries combined with interviews I conducted with retired senior government officials allows for comprehensive testing of my argument.

Chapter 4 evaluates my argument in an infamous episode of covert regime change: The Bay of Pigs. The operation to covertly unseat Fidel Castro began under the Eisenhower administration and was carried out by the Kennedy administration. The role of the United States was intended to be shrouded in secrecy. I begin this chapter—and all succeeding empirical chapters—by identifying the kind of evidence we would expect to see if my argument is correct. I then review the historical background, identify the drivers of intervention, and describe the logistics of the failed operation. The next section evaluates my theory using a mix of declassified documents and secondary sources. I argue that the primary constraint holding back decision makers from openly toppling Castro was concern that violating the nonintervention principle without a proper justification would make the United States look hypocritical and undermine its credibility. I also show that decision makers searched for legal exemptions that might have enabled them to intervene openly at reduced risk. Equally important is evidence that senior officials knew they were making operational sacrifices by intervening secretly, a testament to the trade-offs inherent in the covert sphere. Finally, I explain why both general and case-specific competing explanations do a worse job than my theory in explaining the decision to go covert.

Chapter 5 assesses my argument in another prominent episode of covert action during the Cold War: Nixon's intervention in Chile between 1970 and 1973. The specter of Salvador Allende becoming president prompted Nixon to pursue a two-pronged covert action plan. One was intended to prevent Allende from securing the Congressional vote in a runoff using nonviolent means; it failed. The other prong sought his overthrow by destabilizing the country and instigating a military coup. The first part of the chapter provides historical background, discusses the main causes of intervention, and outlines the parameters of the covert operation from late 1970 through Allende's downfall at the hands of Augusto Pinochet on September 11, 1973. The next section draws on documents I collected from the Nixon Presidential Library and secondary sources to show that Nixon, like Eisenhower and Kennedy during the Cuba operation, preferred covert action to avoid brazenly violating the nonintervention principle for fear of incurring hypocrisy costs and damaging America's global credibility. While decision makers never considered a bona fide invasion, I show that they likely would have pursued less intense overt options to overthrow Allende had there been legal exemptions available such as authorization from the Organization of American States (OAS). The chapter concludes by pitting my theory against general and case-specific competing explanations, finding little support for the alternatives.

Chapter 6 is the first of two case studies of overt regime change. In it, I explore Lyndon Johnson's decision to invade the Dominican Republic in 1965. The intervention, which began on April 28, sought to prevent a communist takeover by stopping the constitutionalist forces loyal to Juan Bosch from consolidating power during an incipient civil war. I begin by providing the historical background to Operation Power Pack, identifying the drivers of intervention, and discussing the logistics of the invasion. I then assess my argument using declassified documents I gathered from the Johnson Presidential Library as well as secondary sources. The availability of two legal exemptions enabled the United States to intervene openly. First was the presence of Americans on the island, which decision makers could claim were in clear and present danger. Second was the eventual participation of the OAS, which helped justify the continued U.S. presence until the conflict could be resolved. I also argue that it is plausible Johnson would not have authorized an overt invasion were it not for the availability of these legal exemptions by examining Kennedy's earlier efforts to covertly topple Rafael Trujillo in 1961, as well as several other illustrative episodes. I conclude by showing why general and case-specific alternative explanations perform worse than my theory in this case.

Chapter 7 is the final of four case studies contained in the book. It investigates why Ronald Reagan pursued overt regime change in Grenada in 1983. Plans to topple the New Jewel Movement began in mid-October after the ouster of Prime Minister Maurice Bishop by hardliners in the government and culminated in an invasion on October 25. I begin by going over the historical background, identifying the causes of intervention, and describing the details of the operation. Next, I make the case that Reagan was emboldened to publicly deploy forces by the availability of two legal exemptions that emerged around Bishop's downfall. First was the presence of American medical students on the island. Second was a formal invitation for intervention from the Organization of Eastern Caribbean States and the Governor-General of Grenada, Sir Paul Scoon. Relying on declassified documents I collected from the Reagan Presidential Library, interviews I conducted with former administration officials, and secondary sources, I describe each legal exemption on its own terms, discuss the administration's strategy for selling the entire legal package, and showcase efforts to avoid taking actions that would undermine the offered justification for intervention. I then make the case that an invasion likely would not have occurred without these legal exemptions. In this vein, I provide evidence that Jimmy

Carter authorized covert action in 1979 when no such legal exemptions existed and that the Reagan administration displayed reticence to take open, hostile action against the New Jewel Movement before October 1983. The penultimate section discusses the aftermath of the operation. I posit that the conventional narrative of universal condemnation misses several key points. I conclude by illustrating why general and case-specific alternative explanations fall short.

Chapter 8 is the concluding chapter. The discussion begins by summarizing the theoretical and empirical findings of the book. I then show that my argument extends beyond Latin America and the Cold War by examining variation in U.S. intervention policy toward Iraq from 1991 to 2003, and the Obama administration's different approaches to regime change in Libya and Syria in the so-called Arab Spring. The chapter concludes with a discussion of future research as well as scholarly and policy implications.

2

The Evolution of Nonintervention

This chapter traces the evolution of the nonintervention principle over the last few hundred years. I explore its development from an idea that international lawyers, philosophers, and smaller states promoted but great powers mostly ignored to its codification in the United Nations Charter and subsequent adoption in the charters of regional bodies.[1] This discussion serves several purposes.

First, it sets the stage for the rest of the book by placing the remaining chapters in historical context and justifying my focus on the postwar era as a scope condition. The notion that states interested in regime change would have to factor a codified nonintervention principle into their decision-making calculus is a recent phenomenon. Although nonintervention existed as an idea for centuries, it did not enjoy the status of international law until the mid-twentieth century.[2] Second, my argument that international law is responsible for the lion's share of variation in covert and overt regime change in the postwar period implies that intervention dynamics should have looked different before nonintervention was codified. General patterns of behavior provide preliminary support. Third, this chapter bolsters the idea that non-legal norms are less constraining than legal norms. While many studies that examine nonintervention in one form or another do not draw sharp distinctions between pre- and post-codification,[3] there

[1] J.L. Brierly, *The Law of Nations: An Introduction to the International Law of Peace* (Oxford and New York: Oxford University Press, 1963), 397.

[2] Of course, international law was not invented in 1945. Rules pertaining to ambassadorial immunity, the status of merchant ships in wartime, and the rights and duties of neutral actors, to take a few examples, have existed in some manner for centuries. Sometimes this happened through treaties. Other times it was customary law. See Tanisha M. Fazal, *Wars of Law: Unintended Consequences in the Regulation of Armed Conflict* (Ithaca, NY: Cornell University Press, 2018); Jack L. Goldsmith and Eric A. Posner, *The Limits of International Law* (Oxford and New York: Oxford University Press, 2005). Nonintervention had neither status at the global level before 1945.

[3] Stephen D. Krasner, *Sovereignty: Organized Hypocrisy* (Princeton, NJ: Princeton University Press, 1999); Lindsey O'Rourke, *Covert Regime Change: America's Secret Cold War* (Ithaca, NY: Cornell University Press, 2018).

In the Shadow of International Law. Michael Poznansky, Oxford University Press (2020). © Oxford University Press.
DOI: 10.1093/oso/9780190096595.001.0001

may be good reason to do so. Finally, exploring how changes to nonintervention influenced state behavior in the past provides a basis for evaluating the potential impact of changes to the rules governing intervention in the future. If these rules weaken or change, it could affect how states intervene down the road, a point to which I return in the conclusion.

This chapter is broken into three sections. The first describes the emergence of a nonintervention norm in the eighteenth century and the various reactions to it over the next two centuries. Its champions were lawyers, scholars, and smaller states who were especially susceptible to intervention.[4] Great powers by and large ignored it, making proclamations and creating special provisions that preserved a broad right to intervene when it served the national interest. The second section details the road to codification starting with the United States' acceptance of a nonintervention principle in the Western Hemisphere and ending with its adoption in the UN Charter. This section also walks through the few legal exemptions that permit states to violate nonintervention. The final section discusses the evolution of the nonintervention principle after 1945, including its adoption by some regional organizations, its reaffirmation in UN declarations and resolutions, and the rise of the Responsibility to Protect.

The Birth of a Contested Idea

Notwithstanding the close relationship between sovereignty and nonintervention in today's lexicon, the two did not emerge simultaneously. The system of sovereign states founded in 1648 with the Peace of Westphalia predated the advent of a nonintervention norm by about one hundred years.[5] The first individuals to articulate a right of nonintervention were Christian Wolff, a German philosopher, and Emmerich Vattel, a Swiss international lawyer, in the latter part of the eighteenth century.[6]

Wolff's book *The Law of Nations According to the Scientific Method*, written in 1749, came first. According to Wolff, "no ruler of a state has the right to interfere in the government of another, consequently cannot urge that another should establish anything in its state or do anything, or not do anything, and the government of the ruler of one state is not subject to the decision of the ruler

[4] Krasner, *Sovereignty: Organized Hypocrisy*, 21–22.

[5] Daniel Philpott, *Revolutions in Sovereignty: How Ideas Shaped Modern International Relations* (Princeton, NJ and Oxford: Princeton University Press, 2001), 32.

[6] Hedley Bull, ed., *Intervention in World Politics* (Oxford: Oxford University Press, 1984), 4; Ann Van Wynen Thomas and A.J. Thomas, Jr., *Non-Intervention: The Law and Its Import in the Americas* (Dallas, TX: Southern Methodist University Press, 1956), 5.

of any other state."[7] Though stringent, Wolff's notion of nonintervention was not absolute. For example, he believed in the value of multilateral interventions should a government neglect its duty to protect fundamental human rights.[8] "In the supreme state," Wolff writes, "the nations as a whole have a right to coerce the individual nations, if they should be unwilling to perform their obligation, or show themselves negligent in it."[9] He also makes clear that his conception of a nonintervention principle was consistent with a state's right to use force in self-defense which "belongs to everybody."[10]

Roughly a decade later, Vattel articulated his own version of a nonintervention principle in *The Law of Nations: Or, Principles of the Law of Nature Applied to the Conduct and Affairs of Nations and Sovereigns*: "It is an evident consequence of the liberty and independence of nations, that all have a right to be governed as they think proper, and that no state has the smallest right to interfere in the government of another. Of all the rights that can belong to a nation, sovereignty is, doubtless, the most precious, and that which other nations ought the most scrupulously to respect, if they would not do her an injury."[11] Vattel also identified several exceptions to the otherwise strict norm of nonintervention. First, it was acceptable to intervene on the just side of a civil war to aid an oppressed people against a tyrannical ruler.[12] This did not mean that foreign powers were free "to invite those subjects to revolt who actually pay obedience to their sovereign, though they complain of his government."[13] Encouraging revolt, as opposed to merely assisting one that had broken out, was an abuse of this exception. A second valid reason for disregarding nonintervention was to maintain a balance of power so that no single state became too domineering.[14]

[7] Christian Wolff, *Jus Gentium Methodo Scientifica Pertractatum*, ed. Joseph Drake (Oxford: Clarendon Press, 1934), 131.

[8] R.J. Vincent, *Nonintervention and International Order* (Princeton, NJ: Princeton University Press, 1974), 28.

[9] Wolff, *Jus Gentium Methodo Scientifica Pertractatum*, 14.

[10] Ibid., 139.

[11] Emer De Vattel, *The Law of Nations: Or, Principles of the Law of Nature Applied to the Conduct and Affairs of Nations and Sovereigns*, ed. Bela Kapossy and Richard Whatmore (Indianapolis, IN, 2008), 289. See also Philpott, *Revolutions in Sovereignty: How Ideas Shaped Modern International Relations*, 21.

[12] Krasner, *Sovereignty: Organized Hypocrisy*, 74; Thomas and Thomas, *Non-Intervention: The Law and Its Import in the Americas*, 5–6.

[13] Vattel, *The Law of Nations: Or, Principles of the Law of Nature Applied to the Conduct and Affairs of Nations and Sovereigns*, 291.

[14] Vincent, *Nonintervention and International Order*, 30.

The Nineteenth Century and the Concert of Europe

In some respects, nonintervention gained traction throughout the nineteenth century as a principle states ought to follow.[15] Several prominent thinkers and politicians articulated a variant of it in their writings and speeches. British philosopher John Stuart Mill argued that intervention could only be justified in cases of protracted civil war or to counter an unjustified intervention by another state.[16] Richard Cobden, a high-profile British politician, supported an absolute ban on intervention.[17]

Arguments in favor of nonintervention were also advanced by actors across the Atlantic. Smaller states in Latin America endorsed it at international conferences, including the Congress of Panama in 1826 and the American Congress in 1848.[18] Carlos Calvo, a prominent Argentine scholar, called for a prohibition on intervention in his 1868 book, *Le Droit International*.[19] As Thomas and Thomas put it, "The Calvo Doctrine may be said to be the second American doctrine of non-intervention, the first being the Monroe Doctrine." But unlike the Monroe Doctrine, which sought to "prevent the occupation or control of American territory by non-American states" (chiefly the European powers), the Calvo Doctrine "precludes intervention originating in the collection of international obligations based upon contract or quasi contract or upon delict or quasi delict."[20]

When it came to state practice during the nineteenth century, however, nonintervention languished.[21] Great powers regularly and openly intervened with impunity in the internal affairs of weaker states. Consider the behavior of the major European powers during the Concert of Europe period.[22] The Concert, which began with the Congress of Vienna in 1814–1815 and lasted

[15] Immanuel Kant articulated a nonintervention principle in 1795 but restricted this obligation only to republican governments. See Thomas and Thomas, *Non-Intervention: The Law and Its Import in the Americas*, 7–8.

[16] Michael Walzer, *Just and Unjust Wars: A Moral Argument with Historical Illustrations* (New York: Basic Books, 1977), 87–91.

[17] Vincent, *Nonintervention and International Order*, 54.

[18] Krasner, *Sovereignty: Organized Hypocrisy*, 21; Thomas and Thomas, *Non-Intervention: The Law and Its Import in the Americas*, 55–56.

[19] Amos S. Hershey, "The Calvo and Drago Doctrines," *American Journal of International Law* 1, no. 1 (1907): 27–28.

[20] Thomas and Thomas, *Non-Intervention: The Law and Its Import in the Americas*, 57.

[21] International lawyers at the time recognized as much. See Vincent, *Nonintervention and International Order*, 31–39.

[22] On the Concert of Europe, see Kyle M. Lascurettes, *The Concert of Europe and Great Power Governance Today: What Can the Order of 19th-Century Europe Teach Policymakers About International Order in the 21st Century?* (Santa Monica, CA: RAND Corporation, 2017); Jennifer Mitzen, *Power in Concert: The Nineteenth-Century Origins of Global Governance* (Chicago, IL and London: The University of Chicago Press, 2013).

for decades afterwards, was a novel system intended to manage relations between Great Britain, France, Russia, Prussia, and Austria.[23] According to Henry Kissinger's seminal account, "[t]he issue at Vienna . . . was to create an order in which change could be brought about through a sense of obligation, instead of through an assertion of power."[24] While the treaty establishing this system was considered by its signatories to have the status of international law,[25] they did not adopt anything approximating a nonintervention principle in the spirit of Wolff and Vattel. Their primary concern was focused on process, establishing regular meetings to resolve conflicts. The spheres of influence system that emerged by the early 1820s gave each of the great powers free rein to "unilaterally intervene in polities' affairs within their respective spheres" without violating the tenets of the Concert system.[26]

Even under this arrangement, the five great powers often disagreed about what constituted a legitimate intervention.[27] The autocratic Holy Alliance, comprised of Russia, Prussia, and Austria, fell on one end of the spectrum. For these states, revolutions that threatened the status quo were illegal. Intervening to put them down was deemed acceptable.[28] At the Conference of Troppau in 1820, they declared that, "States which have undergone a change of government due to revolution, the results of which threaten other states, *ipso facto* cease to be members of the European Alliance, and remain excluded from it until their situation gives guarantee for legal order and stability. If, owing to such alterations, immediate danger threatens other states, the parties bind themselves, by peaceful means, or if need be by arms, to bring back the guilty state into the bosom of the Great Alliance."[29]

Britain's approach was more complicated. Castlereagh, one of the architects of the Congress of Vienna, advocated for a principle of nonintervention during a meeting of the great powers at Aix-La-Chapelle in 1818 and again in a State Paper issued on May 5, 1820. Yet, when revolution broke out in Naples two

[23] Martha Finnemore, *The Purpose of Intervention: Changing Beliefs About the Use of Force* (Ithaca: Cornell University Press, 2003), 108–124.

[24] Henry Kissinger, *A World Restored: Metternich, Castlereagh and the Problems of Peace, 1812–22* (Brattleboro, VT: Echo Point Books & Media, 2013), 172.

[25] Finnemore, *The Purpose of Intervention: Changing Beliefs About the Use of Force*, 118–119.

[26] Lascurettes, *The Concert of Europe and Great Power Governance Today: What Can the Order of 19th-Century Europe Teach Policymakers About International Order in the 21st Century?*, 29, ft. 57.

[27] Stanley Hoffman, "The Problem of Intervention," in *Intervention in World Politics*, ed. Hedley Bull (Oxford: Clarendon Press, 1984), 14; Finnemore, *The Purpose of Intervention: Changing Beliefs About the Use of Force*, 119.

[28] Philpott, *Revolutions in Sovereignty: How Ideas Shaped Modern International Relations*, 95.

[29] Thomas and Thomas, *Non-Intervention: The Law and Its Import in the Americas*, 9. See also Mark Raymond, *Social Practices of Rule-Making in World Politics* (New York: Oxford University Press, 2019), 70.

months later he "positively encouraged Austria to act against the Neapolitan rebels unilaterally" in the spirit of maintaining peace in Europe.[30] This was not an isolated episode.[31]

Castlereagh's successors were equally inconsistent in their approach to nonintervention. George Canning, who became Secretary of Foreign Affairs in 1822, initially espoused a strict policy of nonintervention only to intervene openly in Portugal in 1826 and Greece in 1827.[32] Lord Palmerston, the influential British Foreign Secretary throughout the middle of the nineteenth century, was even less committed. Following Austria's intervention in Modena and Parma in 1831, Palmerston chose not to criticize Metternich in order to prevent a conflagration on the continent rather than getting mired in "the abstract and not easily definable principles upon which interference and noninterference should depend."[33] In some cases, Palmerston "was an unapologetic liberal and an interventionist,"[34] using armed force in Portugal and Spain to promote constitutional government.[35] R.J. Vincent summarizes Great Britain's attitude toward the nonintervention principle during this time as follows: "[It] was not an invariable rule but a device to be used when the opportunity presented itself."[36] He continues that, "if the essence of law is that it should have the power to compel an actor in any circumstance against his will, then Britain was not restrained by the rule in this essential sense."[37]

The Era of Big Sticks

The status of nonintervention at the turn of the twentieth century reflected its status in the nineteenth century in many ways. On one side of the spectrum were prominent thinkers and smaller states, especially in Latin America, advocating for the adoption of a nonintervention principle. In 1902, the well-known former minister of foreign affairs from Argentina, Luis Drago, proposed a modified version of the nineteenth-century Calvo Doctrine by arguing against the use of force to collect debts, a common practice at that time.[38] Drago held that such

[30] Vincent, *Nonintervention and International Order*, 78.

[31] Ibid., 83.

[32] Ibid., 84–87.

[33] Ibid., 93.

[34] Lascurettes, *The Concert of Europe and Great Power Governance Today: What Can the Order of 19th-Century Europe Teach Policymakers About International Order in the 21st Century?*, 14.

[35] Vincent, *Nonintervention and International Order*, 93–95.

[36] Ibid., 100.

[37] Ibid., 102.

[38] Thomas and Thomas, *Non-Intervention: The Law and Its Import in the Americas*, 57. See also Krasner, *Sovereignty: Organized Hypocrisy*, 21, 38.

actions were antithetical to the principle of sovereignty and state equality. Only interventions undertaken in the name of self-defense, he claimed, were legitimate.[39] Latin American nations also consistently pressed the issue in regional meetings. For instance, "[a]t the Second Pan-American Conference in 1902–1903, Argentina submitted a version of the Calvo Doctrine, prohibiting extraterritorial intervention (diplomatic or military) to resolve pecuniary disputes and holding that natives and foreigners were equal before the law."[40] A similar proposal was put forward at the Sixth Pan-American Conference in Havana, Cuba in 1928.[41]

As before, great powers ignored these efforts, continuing to downplay calls for the adoption of a binding nonintervention principle. The United States' behavior in the Western Hemisphere is particularly instructive. The 1901 Platt Amendment, which specified the conditions under which the United States would withdraw from Cuba after helping them achieve independence from Spain, paints a stark picture of America's indifference to nonintervention. Article 3 granted the United States "the right to intervene . . . for the maintenance of a government adequate for the protection of life, property, and individual liberty."[42] Three years later, President Theodore Roosevelt effectively extended Article 3's provision to the entire region with the issuance of the Roosevelt Corollary to the Monroe Doctrine.[43] Coming on the heels of the Venezuela Crisis wherein Germany, Great Britain, and Italy blockaded Venezuela's ports after failing to receive debt payments,[44] Roosevelt proclaimed that the United States enjoyed a broad right of intervention to ensure stability:

> If a nation shows that it knows how to act with reasonable efficiency and decency in social and political matters, if it keeps order and pays its obligations, it need fear no interference from the United States. Chronic wrongdoing, or an impotence which results in a general loosening of the

[39] Finnemore, *The Purpose of Intervention: Changing Beliefs About the Use of Force*, 30–31.

[40] Max Paul Friedman and Tom Long, "Soft Balancing in the Americas: Latin American Opposition to U.S. Intervention, 1898–1936," *International Security* 40, no. 1 (2015): 140.

[41] Thomas and Thomas, *Non-Intervention: The Law and Its Import in the Americas*, 59–60. Another important development in 1928 was the signing of the Paris Peace Pact, an agreement among the nations of the world to outlaw war. By this time, however, states had drawn a distinction between intervention and war, as evidenced by America's acceptance of the Peace Pact but rejection of the proposal at Havana, discussed below. On the Peace Pact, see Oona Hathaway and Scott J. Shapiro, *The Internationalists: How a Radical Plan to Outlaw War Remade the World* (New York: Simon and Schuster, 2017).

[42] Quoted in Lars Schoultz, *Beneath the United States: A History of U.S. Policy Toward Latin America* (Cambridge, MA and London: Harvard University Press, 1998), 148.

[43] Thomas and Thomas, *Non-Intervention: The Law and Its Import in the Americas*, 33.

[44] Schoultz, *Beneath the United States: A History of U.S. Policy Toward Latin America*, 180–181.

> ties of civilized society, may in America, as elsewhere, ultimately require intervention by some civilized nation, and in the Western Hemisphere the adherence of the United States to the Monroe Doctrine may force the United States, however reluctantly, in flagrant cases of such wrong-doing or impotence, to the exercise of an international police power.[45]

Given these various amendments and corollaries, it should come as little surprise that the United States regularly torpedoed attempts by Latin American nations and advocates like Luis Drago to explicitly accede to a nonintervention principle. During the 1928 Pan-American Conference in Havana, Secretary of State Charles Evans Hughes "not only refused to adhere to a principle of non-intervention, but sought to justify temporary interposition where necessary to protect the lives and interests of United States citizens in a foreign nation when conditions of anarchy reigned therein."[46] The very fact that the United States blocked such a proposal is telling in and of itself. It suggests that there was at least some sense among policymakers that publicly pledging support for nonintervention would entail nontrivial constraints on their capacity to meddle without consequence in Latin America.

The United States' opposition to nonintervention was also apparent in its actions during this period. According to one estimate, "[b]etween 1901 and 1933, the United States would conduct thirty-five armed interventions in the circum-Caribbean region."[47] This included a raft of regime-change operations. Within the span of one decade, the United States intervened at least nine times to overthrow regimes. Four of these occurred under William Howard Taft's presidency. Perhaps more surprisingly, five of them occurred under the watch of the famous liberal internationalist Woodrow Wilson.[48] Wilson's now-infamous quote from the beginning of his presidency aptly captures how policymakers viewed intervention: "We are friends of constitutional government in America; we are more than its friends, we are its champions. I am going to teach the South American republics to elect good men."[49]

[45] Quoted in Kris James Mitchener and Marc Weidenmier, "Empire, Public Goods, and the Roosevelt Corollary," *The Journal of Economic History* 65, no. 3 (2005): 662.

[46] Thomas and Thomas, *Non-Intervention: The Law and Its Import in the Americas*, 60.

[47] Stephen G. Rabe, "The Johnson Doctrine," *Presidential Studies Quarterly* 36, no. 1 (2006): 50.

[48] See Alexander B. Downes and Jonathan Monten, "Forced to Be Free? Why Foreign-Imposed Regime Change Rarely Leads to Democratization," *International Security* 37, no. 4 (2013): 90–131. Taft's interventions included Nicaragua (1909, 1910), Honduras (1911), and the Dominican Republic (1912). Wilson's included Mexico (1914), the Dominican Republic (1914, 1916), Haiti (1915), and Costa Rica (1919). These kinds of interventions did not stop after Wilson. Calvin Coolidge, for example, intervened in Nicaragua in 1926 to topple the regime there.

[49] Matthew Yglesias, "Woodrow Wilson," *The Atlantic* Jan. 4 (2007), https://www.theatlantic.com/politics/archive/2007/01/woodrow-wilson/41117/.

A quick examination of the League of Nations, Woodrow Wilson's brainchild, drives home the point that great powers were resistant to the idea of relinquishing the right to intervene.[50] To be sure, the League marked a significant advancement in international law in important ways. For the first time, a large group of states agreed to exhaust peaceful means of dispute resolution before resorting to war and created a centralized body to oversee compliance with the Covenant.[51] In Article 15(7), however, member states "reserve[d] to themselves the right to take such action as they shall consider necessary for the maintenance of right and justice."[52] Article 11 allowed states to pick and choose whether events such as revolutions warranted action. This was seen by many observers as the equivalent of the Holy Alliance in the Concert of Europe.[53] As Hathaway and Shapiro conclude, "[t]he League of Nations did not herald the end of the Old World Order. The League was its reprieve."[54]

The Road to Codification

Although the codification of a fully articulated nonintervention principle replete with clear exemptions would await the adoption of the United Nations Charter in 1945, signs that some of the great powers might be moving in this direction, at least in their spheres of influence, were evident by the early 1930s. In his inaugural address delivered on March 4, 1933, Franklin D. Roosevelt committed the United States to being a good neighbor to nations in the Western Hemisphere. "In the field of world policy," Roosevelt proclaimed, "I would dedicate this Nation to the policy of the good neighbor—the neighbor who resolutely respects himself and, because he does so, respects the rights of others—the neighbor who respects his obligations and respects the sanctity of his agreements in and with a world of neighbors."[55]

[50] Ironically, of course, the United States never became a member owing to opposition in the Senate.

[51] Brierly, *The Law of Nations: An Introduction to the International Law of Peace*, 408.

[52] League of Nations, "The Covenant of the League of Nations," The Avalon Project, 1924, http://avalon.law.yale.edu/20th_century/leagcov.asp#art15. See also Vincent, *Nonintervention and International Order*, 297.

[53] Kyle M. Lascurettes, *Orders of Exclusion: Great Powers and the Strategic Sources of Foundational Rules in International Relations* (New York: Oxford University Press, 2020).

[54] Hathaway and Shapiro, *The Internationalists: How a Radical Plan to Outlaw War Remade the World*, 106.

[55] Franklin Delano Roosevelt, "Inaugural Address, March 4, 1933," *World Affairs* 96, no. 1 (1933): 28.

The Roosevelt administration also took tangible steps to signal to Latin America that it was serious about committing to nonintervention. At the Seventh Pan-American Conference in Montevideo, Uruguay in December 1933, Secretary of State Cordell Hull signed the Convention on Rights and Duties of States on behalf of the United States.[56] Most relevant was Article 8, which declared: "No state has the right to intervene in the internal or external affairs of another."[57] While notable, the U.S. delegation attached reservations concerning what such provisions would entail.[58] Three years later at the Inter-American Conference for the Maintenance of Peace in Buenos Aires, Argentina, the United States recommitted to a nonintervention principle, this time without these reservations.[59] In addition to renouncing conquest and the collection of debts by force, the 1936 Buenos Aires Declaration read: "Intervention by one State in the internal or external affairs of another State is condemned."[60]

These developments constituted a sharp break from the past.[61] But several caveats are in order. First, although some call it "remarkable . . . that the United States should bind herself by treaty to the observation of an apparently absolute rule of nonintervention," the protocol's language is notably vague.[62] The use of the word *condemned* produces uncertainty over whether intervention in any circumstance is actually illegal or merely would be frowned upon. The lack of clearly defined exceptions, and the use of stronger legal language elsewhere in the protocol, adds to this ambiguity.[63]

Above and beyond language issues, it is difficult to know what the independent impact of the Buenos Aires Protocol was in practice. For one thing, although there were no major U.S. interventions in the hemisphere during the 1930s,[64] this had a lot to do with the constraints of the Great Depression and the fact that

[56] Vincent, *Nonintervention and International Order*, 115.

[57] "Convention on Rights and Duties of States (Inter-American); December 26, 1933," The Avalon Project, 1933, http://avalon.law.yale.edu/20th_century/intam03.asp.

[58] Ibid.

[59] Vincent, *Nonintervention and International Order*, 115.

[60] "Declaration of Principles of Inter-American Solidarity and Cooperation; December 21, 1936," The Avalon Project, 1936, http://avalon.law.yale.edu/20th_century/intam07.asp. Vincent points out, however, that "the United States left open the option of collective intervention if life and property were threatened by a breakdown of order in a Latin American country." See Vincent, *Nonintervention and International Order*, 129.

[61] Charles G. Fenwick, "The Inter-American Regional System," *American Journal of International Law* 50, no. 1 (1956): 21.

[62] Vincent, *Nonintervention and International Order*, 113.

[63] For instance, the protocol refers to forcible debt collection as "illegal" and "proscribes" territorial conquest.

[64] Downes and Monten, "Forced to Be Free? Why Foreign-Inposed Regime Change Rarely Leads to Democratization."

many Latin American countries were ruled by pro-U.S. autocrats which "made it easier . . . for the United States to behave in a more 'neighborly' fashion while still achieving its principal goals."[65] Moreover, three years after Buenos Aires, World War II was underway and America's attention was fixated on Europe and Asia. When it was over, the United Nations, founded in San Francisco on June 26, 1945, was adopted and established a universal nonintervention principle that remains the primary text for assessing the legality of intervention.[66]

The United Nations Charter

While "the principle of nonintervention between states is nowhere explicit in the [UN] Charter, it is, in the statement of Principles, everywhere implicit."[67] Article 2(4) is the linchpin, articulating what is effectively a nonintervention principle.[68] It reads: "All Members shall refrain in their international relations from the threat or use of force against the territorial integrity or political independence of any state, or in any other manner inconsistent with the Purposes of the United Nations."[69] Attendees at San Francisco unanimously supported its inclusion.[70] Experts view it as "the corner-stone of the Charter system."[71]

It is impossible to come to terms with the Charter's approach to nonintervention without also considering the few exemptions that allow states to disregard Article 2(4) in a given case.[72] The key text in this regard is Article 51, which contains the following: "Nothing in the present Charter shall impair the inherent

[65] Friedman and Long, "Soft Balancing in the Americas: Latin American Opposition to U.S. Intervention, 1898–1936," 148.

[66] For an interesting argument about how the desire to manage escalation following major wars helped laid the groundwork for bodies like the UN, see Austin Carson, *Secret Wars: Covert Conflict in International Politics* (Princeton, NJ: Princeton University Press, 2018), Chapter 3.

[67] Vincent, *Nonintervention and International Order*, 236.

[68] Damrosch, Lori Fisler. "Politics Across Borders: Nonintervention and Nonforcible Influence over Domestic Affairs." *American Journal of International Law* 83, no. 1 (1989): 8.

[69] United Nations, "Charter of the United Nations," 1945, Chapter I, http://www.un.org/en/charter-united-nations/. There is another kind of nonintervention provision in Article 2(7), although the relevant actor prohibited from doing the intervening is the United Nations rather than individual member states. See Thomas M. Franck, *Recourse to Force: State Action against Threats and Armed Attacks* (Cambridge, UK: Cambridge University Press, 2004), 12–13.

[70] Hathaway and Shapiro, *The Internationalists: How a Radical Plan to Outlaw War Remade the World*, 212.

[71] Brierly, *The Law of Nations: An Introduction to the International Law of Peace*, 414.

[72] Josef L. Kunz, "Individual and Collective Self-Defense in Article 51 of the Charter of the United Nations," *American Journal of International Law* 41, no. 4 (1947): 874. Under this framework, non-legal justifications, even if they served liberal ends, were rendered illegal unless linked to a legal exemption. Responsibility to Protect, discussed in the conclusion, is an effort to expand the justifications for intervention to include preventing humanitarian catastrophes.

right of individual or collective self-defence if an armed attack occurs against a Member of the United Nations, until the Security Council has taken measures necessary to maintain international peace and security."[73] Interestingly, this language was not included as part of the original proposal for the UN hammered out by the United States, the Soviet Union, Great Britain, and China in the summer and fall of 1944, known as the Dumbarton Oaks Conversations.[74] The chief advocates of what became Article 51 were states in Latin America. After signing the Act of Chapultepec, a collective security pact, on March 3, 1945, there was concern that the Security Council might impede regional collective action.[75] According to John W. Halderman, "the concept of 'collective self-defense' was incorporated in the Charter primarily for the purpose of enabling regional organizations to take initial action on their own responsibility to deal with aggression without being delayed by United Nations debates or obstructed by possible vetoes in the Security Council."[76]

The most straightforward reading of Article 51 is that states can disregard Article 2(4) if they have been the victim of an actual attack.[77] In such cases, states may respond by using force unilaterally (individual self-defense) or with external assistance (collective self-defense).[78] The latter encompasses operations carried out under the auspices of the UN Security Council, by regional institutions, or even by a loose collection of states. Beyond this straightforward interpretation are a number of complex questions pertaining to what else is tolerable under the UN Charter when it comes to intervention.[79] I will discuss three of the most common ones: anticipatory self-defense, rescuing endangered nationals, and action by regional organizations outside the confines of an armed attack.

[73] United Nations, "Charter of the United Nations," Chapter VII.

[74] *The Yearbook of the United Nations* (United Nations, Lake Success, New York: Department of Public Information, 1947), Part 1, Section 1, Chapter E, 4, https://www.unmultimedia.org/searchers/yearbook/page.jsp?volume=1946-47&page=39&searchType=advanced.

[75] Fenwick, "The Inter-American Regional System," 23–24; Thomas M. Franck, "Who Killed Article 2(4)? Or: Changing Norms Governing the Use of Force by States," *American Journal of International Law* 64, no. 5 (1970): 823.

[76] John W. Halderman, "Regional Enforcement Measures and the United Nations," *Georgetown Law Journal* 52, no. 1 (1963): 94. See also Kunz, "Individual and Collective Self-Defense in Article 51 of the Charter of the United Nations," 872.

[77] For good treatments of the debates surrounding self-defense in the UN Charter, see Christine Gray, *International Law and the Use of Force*, 4th ed. (Oxford: Oxford University Press, 2018), 120–199; Tom Ruys, *"Armed Attack" and Article 51 of the UN Charter: Evolutions in Customary Law and Practice* (Cambridge, UK: Cambridge University Press, 2010).

[78] Loraine Sievers and Sam Daws, *The Procedure of the UN Security Council*, 4th ed. (Oxford: Oxford University Press, 2014), 627.

[79] Rosalyn Higgins, "Intervention and International Law," in *Intervention in World Politics*, ed. Hedley Bull (Oxford: Clarendon Press, 1984), 36–37.

First, legal scholars debate whether Article 51 allows for preemptive action to forestall an imminent attack that has not yet taken place.[80] Some hold that it does, viewing "the reference in Article 51 to an 'inherent right'" as evidence "that the charter's framers intended for a continuation of the broad pre–UN Charter customary right of anticipatory self-defense."[81] The quintessential case articulating a right of anticipatory self-defense comes from the *Caroline* incident of 1837.[82] Others are more skeptical, arguing that an armed attack must have actually occurred before states can legally use force in response under the UN Charter.[83] Perhaps "the best that can be said about the right of self-defense under Article 51 is that it is susceptible [to] varying interpretations; its wording is both ambiguous and confusing. Armed self-defense is definitely permitted against an armed attack, but the picture is hazy as to whether self-defense is permitted against an imminently dangerous aggression."[84] In practice, the perceived legitimacy of appeals to anticipatory self-defense may be determined by whether observers believe that an attack was truly imminent. In this regard, Israel's preemptive action in the Six Day War in 1967 is on firmer legal ground than America's preventive war in Iraq in 2003.[85] More recently, the debate surrounding the legality of President Trump's decision to authorize a lethal drone strike against General Qasem Suleimani, the head of the Quds Force in Iran, has turned in part on whether or not he acted to prevent an imminent attack.

A second question is whether the Charter allows states to use force to protect their own nationals residing abroad, known as the "right to rescue."[86] Many hold

[80] Thomas M. Franck, "The Power of Legitimacy and the Legitimacy of Power: International Law in an Age of Power Disequilibrium," *American Journal of International Law* 100, no. 1 (2006): 101–105.

[81] Anthony Clark Arend, "International Law and the Preemptive Use of Military Force," *The Washington Quarterly* 26, no. 2 (2003): 92. See also Halderman, "Regional Enforcement Measures and the United Nations," 113; Myres S. McDougal, "The Soviet-Cuban Quarantine and Self-Defense," *The American Journal of International Law* 57, no. 3 (1963): 598; A.J. Thomas, Jr. and Ann Van Wynen Thomas, "The Organization of American States and Collective Security," *Southwestern Law Journal* 13, no. 2 (1959): 180.

[82] Craig Forcese, *Destroying the Caroline: The Frontier Raid That Reshaped the Right to War* (Toronto, ON: Irwin Law, 2018).

[83] Michael J. Glennon, "The Fog of Law: Self-Defense, Inherence, and Incoherence in Article 51 of the United Nations Charter," *Harvard Journal of Law and Public Policy* 25, no. 2 (2002): 547; Hans Kelsen, "Collective Security and Collective Self-Defense Under the Charter of the United Nations," *The American Journal of International Law* 42, no. 4 (1948): 783–796.

[84] Thomas and Thomas, "The Organization of American States and Collective Security," 182.

[85] Franck, "Who Killed Article 2(4)? Or: Changing Norms Governing the Use of Force by States," 821; David Wippman, "The Nine Lives of Article 2(4)," *Minnesota Journal of International Law* 16, no. 2 (2007): 398.

[86] This is distinct from the issue of rescuing foreign nationals, which falls within the purview of international humanitarian law and thus exceeds the bounds of what is tolerable under self-defense. See Kristen E. Eichensehr, "Defending Nationals Abroad: Assessing the Lawfulness of Forcible Hostage

that it does.[87] Some scholars reason that this is because intervening to protect nationals has long been recognized as lawful and therefore falls within a state's inherent right of self-defense per Article 51.[88] Others posit that such actions, as long as they are narrowly focused on protecting the intervener's citizens, are not actually in conflict with Article 2(4) which prioritizes violations of territorial and political independence.[89] Regardless, there is consensus that using force to protect nationals must be proportionate to be considered legal.[90] Leaders may thus be able to defend an initial deployment of force to rescue their citizens if there are a sufficient number in imminent danger. Doing anything more would require additional legal justifications.[91] In practice, states have done both, invoking the right to rescue in narrowly defined circumstances and as part of more expansive missions. Israel's raid at Entebbe, Uganda in 1976 to rescue Israeli hostages falls into the former category.[92] So, too, does Jimmy Carter's failed effort to save American hostages in Iran four years later. Both missions were focused squarely on rescuing nationals. More intrusive ventures like Reagan's invasion of Grenada in 1983 or George H.W. Bush's invasion of Panama in 1989 invoked endangered nationals alongside other legal justifications.

A final issue turns on whether international organizations can authorize military operations outside the purview of collective self-defense; that is, to maintain international peace and stability.[93] The UN Security Council is

Rescues," *Virginia Journal of International Law* 48, no. 2 (2008): 452–484; Finnemore, *The Purpose of Intervention: Changing Beliefs About the Use of Force*, 53–54.

[87] Thomas and Thomas, *Non-Intervention: The Law and Its Import in the Americas*, 307. As Kristen Eichensehr points out, "Even states that have not overtly claimed a right to rescue nationals have been reluctant to deny the existence of the right when it has been exercised by others." Criticism of such operations, when they occur, typically has to do with questions over the significance of the threat rather than the right to forcibly rescue nationals itself. See Eichensehr, "Defending Nationals Abroad: Assessing the Lawfulness of Forcible Hostage Rescues," 460.

[88] D.W. Bowett, *Self-Defence in International Law* (Manchester: Manchester University Press, 1958), 92; Eichensehr, "Defending Nationals Abroad: Assessing the Lawfulness of Forcible Hostage Rescues," 461–463.

[89] Richard B. Lillich, "Forcible Self-Help by States to Protect Human Rights," *Iowa Law Review* 53, no. 2 (1967): 336–337.

[90] Bowett, *Self-Defence in International Law*, 93–94; Brierly, *The Law of Nations: An Introduction to the International Law of Peace*, 428; Philip Kunig, "Intervention, Prohibition Of," *Max Planck Encyclopedia of Public International Law*, 2008.

[91] Eichensehr, "Defending Nationals Abroad: Assessing the Lawfulness of Forcible Hostage Rescues," 477–479; Lillich, "Forcible Self-Help by States to Protect Human Rights," 347–349. The legality of rescuing a few nationals as in a hostage situation is more contentious. See Alexandra H. Perina, "Black Holes and Open Secrets: The Impact of Covert Action on International Law," *Columbia Journal of Transnational Law* 53, no. 3 (2015): 568–569.

[92] Higgins, "Intervention and International Law," 39; Ian Hurd, *How to Do Things with International Law* (Princeton, NJ: Princeton University Press, 2018), 72.

[93] Thomas and Thomas, "The Organization of American States and Collective Security," 196–197.

chiefly responsible for sanctioning these kinds of operations. This authority is specified in Articles 39 through 50 of Chapter VII. More interesting perhaps is whether regional bodies, of which there are several, can serve this function.[94] Chapter VIII of the UN Charter, which deals with "Regional Arrangements," offers some guidance. Article 52(1) recognizes the role of regional bodies in maintaining "international peace and security" within their respective regions as long as "such arrangements or agencies and their activities are consistent with the Purposes and Principles of the United Nations." Article 52(2) further notes that these entities "shall make every effort to achieve pacific settlement of local disputes through such regional arrangements or by such regional agencies before referring them to the Security Council."[95] Article 53(1), however, highlights the continued importance of UN machinery: "no enforcement action shall be taken under regional arrangements or by regional agencies without the authorization of the Security Council."[96]

The parameters of what regional organizations can and cannot do legally when it comes to promoting peace and stability has been the subject of debate. One view is that the UN Charter requires regional bodies to seek Security Council authorization whenever they wish to use force outside the context of an armed attack on one of its members.[97] A second view is that the Security Council only needs to be informed in such cases; express approval is unnecessary in this reading.[98] A third is that Security Council approval is not necessary if the regional institution is merely recommending, rather than requiring, member states to act.[99] A final take is that "the relations between the [Security] Council and the regional agencies should be so flexible as to permit these agencies to take effective action for the maintenance of international peace and security in the light of regional conditions and without necessarily bringing regional problems

[94] Franck, "Who Killed Article 2(4)? Or: Changing Norms Governing the Use of Force by States," 822–835. For a recent example of this particular debate, see Reza Nasri, "McCain's UN Charter Confusion," *The National Interest* Aug. 9 (2013).

[95] United Nations, "Charter of the United Nations," Chapter VIII. Some argue, however, that the reference to "enforcement action in Article 53 is not restricted to the use of physical force." See Halderman, "Regional Enforcement Measures and the United Nations," 96.

[96] United Nations, "Charter of the United Nations," Chapter VIII. See also Kenneth W. Abbott and Duncan Snidal, "Why States Act through Formal International Organizations," *Journal of Conflict Resolution* 42, no. 1 (1998): 25; Norman J. Padelford, "Regional Organization and the United Nations," *International Organization* 8, no. 2 (1954): 213.

[97] Thomas and Thomas, "The Organization of American States and Collective Security," 197.

[98] Described in Halderman, "Regional Enforcement Measures and the United Nations," 95.

[99] Abram Chayes, *The Cuban Missile Crisis: International Crises and the Role of Law* (New York and London: Oxford University Press, 1974), 59–61; Halderman, "Regional Enforcement Measures and the United Nations," 97–98; 104.

before a world forum."[100] In general, states have downplayed the first approach, keeping the Security Council apprised without asking permission in some cases and claiming exclusive authority over regional disputes in others.[101]

Although slightly beyond the scope of what I am after, it is worth noting that the UN Charter does not actually define which kinds of groupings count as regional organizations under Chapter VIII.[102] In the part of the world that garners the most attention in the following chapters—Latin America—the Organization of American States readily qualifies. The Organization of American States (OAS), created at the Ninth International Conference of American States in Bogotá, Colombia in 1948, governs inter-American relations and is chiefly responsible for maintaining peace and stability in the Western Hemisphere. Things get more complicated when considering the status of organizations like defensive alliances. According to Abram Chayes, the State Department Legal Advisor under John F. Kennedy, such bodies do not qualify as regional organizations under Chapter VIII.[103] Thomas Franck offers a useful working definition in this regard: "A regional organization is any grouping of states in some defined geographic context with historic, ethnic, or socio-political ties, which habitually acts in concert through permanent institutions to foster unity in a wide range of common concerns."[104]

It is hard to overstate the significance of the framework described in the preceding paragraphs. "For the first time in the history of the Westphalian interstate system," Ian Hurd writes, "war was made explicitly illegal for all states. The Charter subordinates national war decisions beneath a set of legal criteria that distinguish between legality and illegality in war making. It is novel both in its legalization and universality."[105] Of course, the UN Charter system also reified the distinction between great powers and the rest, granting the former special privileges in the Security Council.[106] Even still, "[t]his was," as Michael Byers puts it, "a constitutional moment in international affairs: an anarchic world of self-help and temporary alliances was transformed into a nascent system of

[100] Quoted in Halderman, 106. See also Sievers and Daws, *The Procedure of the UN Security Council*, 627.

[101] Franck, "Who Killed Article 2(4)? Or: Changing Norms Governing the Use of Force by States," 824.

[102] Ibid., 827; Gray, *International Law and the Use of Force*, 411–412.

[103] Chayes, *The Cuban Missile Crisis: International Crises and the Role of Law*, 54.

[104] Franck, "Who Killed Article 2(4)? Or: Changing Norms Governing the Use of Force by States," 832.

[105] Hurd, *How to Do Things with International Law*, 62.

[106] Lascurettes, *Orders of Exclusion: Great Powers and the Strategic Sources of Foundational Rules in International Relations*. See also Mark Mazower, *No Enchanted Palace: The End of Empire and the Ideological Origins of the United Nations* (Princeton and Oxford: Princeton University Press, 2009).

governance."[107] This partly explains why many scholars single out 1945 as such a significant year in international history.[108] For the purposes of this book, it is the moment the nonintervention principle went from an idea propagated by international lawyers and philosophers and adopted selectively by states when it was expedient for them, to a worldwide rule covering all countries in the international system.[109]

Beyond the UN Charter

The nonintervention principle was reaffirmed numerous times in the years following the creation of the United Nations. The OAS was an early adopter.[110] Article 19 of the OAS Charter contains the operative language: "No State or group of States has the right to intervene, directly or indirectly, for any reason whatever, in the internal or external affairs of any other State. The foregoing principle prohibits not only armed force but also any other form of interference or attempted threat against the personality of the State or against its political, economic, and cultural elements."[111] By forbidding both forcible and non-forcible interference, the OAS Charter advances a more restrictive nonintervention principle than is contained in Article 2(4) of the UN Charter.[112] Article 21, which focuses on occupation and conquest, is also relevant: "The territory of a State is inviolable; it may not be the object, even temporarily, of military occupation or of other measures of force taken by another State, directly or indirectly, on any grounds whatever. No territorial acquisitions or special advantages obtained either by force or by other means of coercion shall be recognized."[113]

As with the UN Charter, the OAS Charter's provisions prohibiting intervention are not absolute. There are two main exemptions. The first is Article 22, which permits members to use force in "self-defense in accordance with existing

[107] Michael Byers, "Jumping the Gun," *London Review of Books* 24, no. 14 (2002): 3–5.

[108] For an excellent summary, see Hurd, *How to Do Things with International Law*, 62–66.

[109] Gray, *International Law and the Use of Force*, 9; Ruys, *"Armed Attack" and Article 51 of the UN Charter: Evolutions in Customary Law and Practice*, 11–12.

[110] Thomas and Thomas, *Non-Intervention: The Law and Its Import in the Americas*, 114.

[111] OAS, "Charter of the Organization of American States," 1948, http://www.oas.org/en/sla/dil/inter_american_treaties_A-41_charter_OAS.asp. The text of the OAS Charter has been amended several times since 1948. As such, the numbers attached to the articles referenced here are different from the original; the text is the same.

[112] Thomas and Thomas, *Non-Intervention: The Law and Its Import in the Americas*, 130–141, 409, 415–416. Some have pointed out that it is something of an open question as to whether the UN Charter actually prohibits interventions short of the use or threat of force. See Hurd, *How to Do Things with International Law*, 68.

[113] OAS, "Charter of the Organization of American States," Chapter I.

treaties or in fulfillment thereof." The second is Article 23 which states that, "Measures adopted for the maintenance of peace and security in accordance with existing treaties do not constitute a violation of the principles set forth in Articles 19 and 21."[114]

Whether by coincidence or not, these exemptions neatly map onto core provisions of the Inter-American Treaty of Reciprocal Assistance, a collective security pact signed by the United States and Latin American countries in Rio de Janeiro, Brazil in 1947.[115] Article 3(1) states that "an armed attack by any State against an American State shall be considered as an attack against all the American States and, consequently, each one of the said Contracting Parties undertakes to assist in meeting the attack in the exercise of the inherent right of individual or collective self-defense recognized by Article 51 of the Charter of the United Nations."[116] Article 6 calls for member states, through the Organ of Consultation, to decide on appropriate measures to take "[i]f the inviolability or the integrity of the territory or the sovereignty or political independence of any American State should be affected by an aggression which is not an armed attack or by an extra-continental or intra-continental conflict, or by any other fact or situation [that] might endanger the peace of America."[117] In brief, Articles 22 and 23 of the OAS Charter expressly allowed for what Articles 3(1) and 6 of the Rio Treaty required, respectively.

The nonintervention principle was also reasserted in various UN resolutions and declarations in the years after 1945. The Essentials for Peace Resolution of 1949 and the Peace Through Deeds Resolution in 1950 are among the earliest instances.[118] The former "[c]alls upon every nation . . . [t]o refrain from any threats or acts, direct or indirect, aimed at impairing the freedom, independence or integrity of any State, or at fomenting civil strife and subverting the will of the people in any State."[119] The latter "[condemns] the intervention of a State in the internal affairs of another State for the purpose of changing its legally established government by the threat or use of force" and "[s]olemnly reaffirms that, whatever the weapons used, any aggression, whether committed openly, or by fomenting civil strife in the interest of a foreign Power, or otherwise, is

[114] Ibid.

[115] Vincent, *Nonintervention and International Order*, 195–196.

[116] See also "Inter-American Treaty of Reciprocal Assistance," Department of International Law, OAS, 1947, http://www.oas.org/juridico/english/treaties/b-29.html. Thomas and Thomas, *Non-Intervention: The Law and Its Import in the Americas*, 128–130.

[117] "Inter-American Treaty of Reciprocal Assistance."

[118] Vincent, *Nonintervention and International Order*, 237.

[119] UN General Assembly, "290 (IV). Essentials of Peace," UN Documents, 1949, http://www.un-documents.net/a4r290.htm.

the gravest of all crimes against peace and security throughout the world."[120] According to R.J. Vincent, "[n]either of the resolutions was a conscious exercise in Charter 'gap-filling.' Both were concerned to restate Charter principles and to point them in the direction of that intervention which threatened to undermine them."[121]

Similar resolutions were adopted in the 1960s, 70s, and 80s. The Declaration on the Inadmissibility of Intervention in the Domestic Affairs of States and the Protection of Their Independence and Sovereignty, passed by the UN General Assembly in 1965, defends the significance of nonintervention. It references its codification in various regional bodies such as the OAS, the League of Arab States, and the Organization of African Unity.[122] In so doing, it also appeals to the more expansive version of the nonintervention principle outlined in Article 19 of the OAS Charter, flagging both forcible and non-forcible interventions as being antithetical to UN principles.[123] The Declaration on Principles of International Law concerning Friendly Relations and Co-operation among States in accordance with the Charter of the United Nations[124] from 1970, and the Declaration on the Enhancement of the Effectiveness of the Principle of Refraining from the Threat or Use of Force in International Relations,[125] passed in 1980, followed suit.[126] Although there was some debate about whether these declarations and resolutions had the force of international law or were merely aspirational, there was clear consensus that nonintervention was central to the postwar order.[127]

[120] UN General Assembly, "380(v). Peace Through Deeds," UN Documents, 1950, http://www.un.org/documents/ga/res/5/ares5.htm.

[121] Vincent, *Nonintervention and International Order*, 237–238.

[122] Ibid., 239.

[123] UN General Assembly, "2131 (XX). Declaration on the Inadmissibility of Intervention in the Domestic Affairs of States and the Protection of Their Independence and Sovereignty," UN Documents, 1965, http://www.un-documents.net/a20r2131.htm.

[124] UN General Assembly, "2625 (XXV). Declaration on Principles of International Law Concerning Friendly Relations and Co-Operation among States in Accordance with the Charter of the United Nations," UN Documents, 1970, http://www.un-documents.net/a25r2625.htm.

[125] UN General Assembly, "42/22. Declaration on the Enhancement of the Effectiveness of the Principle of Refraining from the Threat or Use of Force in International Relations," UN Documents, 1987, http://www.un.org/documents/ga/res/42/a42r022.htm.

[126] Nicholas J. Wheeler, *Saving Strangers: Humanitarian Intervention in International Society* (Oxford: Oxford University Press, 2000), 44–45.

[127] Philpott, *Revolutions in Sovereignty: How Ideas Shaped Modern International Relations*, 292, ft. 11; Vincent, *Nonintervention and International Order*, 259–261.

Responsibility to Protect

One of the most recent developments bearing on the nonintervention principle is the rise of Responsibility to Protect, or R2P, which can be traced to the international community's failure to respond to atrocities like the Rwandan genocide in 1994. According to Robert Pape, it "reflects the idea that states have responsibilities to the welfare of their citizens that go beyond ensuring the protection of targeted groups."[128] In a 2012 speech, Kofi Annan argued "that, as a last resort, the international community will be prepared to take collective action, including military force, through the Security Council to protect populations from these crimes."[129] He is referring here to R2P.

While Responsibility to Protect represents another potential exception to nonintervention, there are several factors limiting its applicability. First, and perhaps most importantly, interventions undertaken in the name of R2P are still supposed to receive Security Council authorization. Although the UN Security Council authorized operations under these auspices in Libya and Côte d'Ivoir in 2011, the former episode in particular sparked controversy, with several countries claiming that NATO had exceeded its mandate.[130] This is likely to color future votes on interventions justified on these grounds. Relatedly, although almost all states accept the norm of R2P in principle, there remains significant disagreement when it comes to implementation. Self-interested political calculations combined with the fact that "R2P remains a relatively low priority for most governments" each present significant challenges.[131]

Conclusion

This chapter explored the evolution of the nonintervention principle from its inception to the present. Although nonintervention has been understood as a pillar of Westphalian sovereignty at least since the mid-eighteenth century, great powers often ignored it. For many years, they carved out exceptions for themselves and openly interfered in the internal affairs of smaller states with impunity.

[128] Robert A Pape, "When Duty Calls: A Pragmatic Standard of Humanitarian Intervention," *International Security* 37, no. 1 (2012): 51.

[129] Kofi Annan, "Prevention, Promotion, and Protection: Our Shared Responsibility," *International Coalition for the Responsibility to Protect*, 2012, http://www.responsibilitytoprotect.org/index.php/component/content/article/136-latest-news/4145-kofi-annan-speech-preventin-promotion-and-protection-our-shared-responsibility.

[130] Alex J. Bellamy and Tim Dunne, eds., *The Oxford Handbook of the Responsibility to Protect* (Oxford: Oxford University Press, 2016), 9–10.

[131] Ibid., 13–14.

It was not until the advent of the United Nations that the nonintervention principle became a universally applicable and legally binding provision that applied to all nations, both strong and weak. Obviously, intervention did not magically disappear in 1945. But the primary mode of intervention—at least for some states in the international system—changed. Covert action became much more common.[132]

This discussion provides important historical context for the next chapter which develops a theory that treats international law as responsible for the prevalence of covert intervention in the postwar world. There are undoubtedly factors other than the codification of nonintervention that might also explain the reliance on secrecy, including the advent of nuclear weapons, decolonization and the rise of nationalism, the emergence of bipolarity, and so on. Much of this book is devoted to ruling out these alternatives through particular research design choices and careful process tracing.

[132] States did use secrecy prior to 1945, although most of these operations were some combination of intelligence-gathering missions, secret diplomacy, and competition for territory. Very few involved regime change. For a thorough treatment of early U.S. covert action see Stephen F. Knott, *Secret and Sanctioned: Covert Operations and the American Presidency* (New York: Oxford University Press, 1996). See also Mark J. Rozell, *Executive Privilege: Presidential Power, Secrecy, and Accountability*, 3rd ed. (Lawrence, KS: University Press of Kansas, 2010), 24–38; Abraham Sofaer, "Executive Power and the Control of Information: Practice Under the Framers," *Duke Law Journal* 1, no. 1 (1977): 1–57.

3

The Politics of Secret Interventions

> That's a no-brainer. Of course it's a violation of international law, that's why it's a covert action.[1]
>
> —Al Gore in 1993

This chapter develops a theory that explains how international law influences a prospective intervener's decision to pursue regime change covertly or overtly once a decision to intervene has already been made. The discussion proceeds in five sections. The first describes what the literature has said about why states intervene covertly. The second details the logic of my argument and introduces the two mechanisms underlying it: the avoidance of credibility and hypocrisy costs. Also included in this section is an explanation of why the United States is especially susceptible to these considerations. Third, I take up lingering questions, including why leaders do not always pursue covert action and issues pertaining to selection bias. The fourth section focuses on questions related to research design, including my case selection strategy and methodology. The chapter concludes with observable implications and standards of falsifiability.

Existing Arguments for Covert Intervention

In a general sense, the decision to intervene covertly or overtly is the result of a cost-benefit calculation.[2] The key is to figure out which factor or set of factors decision makers prioritize when deciding between the two. This section examines what scholars have previously said about this issue.

[1] Quoted in Richard A. Clarke, *Against All Enemies: Inside America's War on Terror* (New York: Free Press, 2004).

[2] Lindsey O'Rourke, *Covert Regime Change: America's Secret Cold War* (Ithaca, NY: Cornell University Press, 2018).

In the Shadow of International Law. Michael Poznansky, Oxford University Press (2020). © Oxford University Press.
DOI: 10.1093/oso/9780190096595.001.0001

The Myth of Cost-Effectiveness

A popular explanation for why states turn to covert action is that it is cheaper than overt alternatives.[3] It is thought to provide leaders with a low-cost means of pursuing foreign policy objectives. Former CIA officer William Daugherty argues that covert action as "a foreign policy tool . . . is more flexible and responsive, and often much less costly to the U.S. treasury, than many other options at the chief executive's disposal."[4] Elizabeth Anderson similarly writes that "[c]overt action required little, if any, sacrifice by the American people, and, if done properly, the operations should never become public knowledge. Even when they surfaced, they were viewed by the public as the U.S. 'doing something,' at relatively low cost, both in terms of money and personal sacrifice."[5]

The claim that covert action is attractive because it is cheap has a certain intuitive appeal. When we compare, say, the U.S. invasion of Afghanistan in 2001 to secret support for Kurdish dissidents in Iraq in the 1970s, it is easy to see stark differences in dollar amounts. But this narrative is more misleading than illuminating. Short of a full-scale invasion where there is no viable covert analogue, most actions that can be undertaken overtly can also be done covertly. A state wishing to aid an insurgency can either claim sponsorship, rendering the operation overt, or conceal its hand as in a covert operation. Financially backing a political party in a foreign election can be done loudly or quietly.[6] What is different in each of these scenarios is not the physical act of funding insurgents or propping up a political party, but whether the sponsor intends to make their support known.

An example from the recent past will drive this point home. During the early stages of the Syrian civil war, Obama furnished covert military support to the rebels in their quest to oust Bashar al-Assad.[7] The reason this qualifies as a covert operation has little if anything to do with the fact that the United States was not directly intervening with its own personnel. Instead, the reason turns on the fact that arms were funneled through the CIA and supposed to be untraceable back to the United States.[8] That these weapons had to be sanitized and routed through

[3] O'Rourke, *Covert Regime Change: America's Secret Cold War*, 50–51.

[4] William J. Daugherty, *Executive Secrets: Covert Action and the Presidency* (Lexington, KY: The University Press of Kentucky, 2004), 21–22.

[5] Elizabeth E. Anderson, "The Security Dilemma and Covert Action: The Truman Years," *International Journal of Intelligence and Counterintelligence* 11, no. 4 (1998): 412.

[6] Dov H. Levin, "When the Great Power Gets a Vote: The Effects of Great Power Electoral Interventions on Election Results," *International Studies Quarterly* 60, no. 2 (2016): 189–202.

[7] The provision of aid to the Syrian rebels in their efforts to oust Assad are distinct from the deployment of U.S. personnel to combat ISIS. The latter was an overt operation.

[8] Austin Carson and Michael Poznansky, "The Logic for (Shoddy) U.S. Covert Action in Syria," *War on the Rocks* July 21 (2016) Available at: https://warontherocks.com/2016/07/the-logic-for-shoddy-u-s-covert-action-in-syria/.

third-party countries such as Jordan to achieve plausible deniability meant that it might have actually been cheaper to support the rebels overtly.

Domestic Politics, Escalation, and Nationalism

Three buckets of theories offer more promising accounts for the appeal of covert action: domestic politics, escalation, and nationalism. These serve as the alternative arguments to the framework developed in the next section. The empirical chapters will adjudicate among them.

Let us begin with domestic politics. One set of arguments in this vein is that leaders will turn to secrecy whenever acting openly would trigger a hostile response from their own public.[9] If leaders want to engage in unsavory activities such as installing brutal dictators[10] or going after elected regimes,[11] covert action promises to spare them from the public's wrath. A twist on the domestic politics thesis is that leaders turn to covert intervention because there are fewer institutional hoops to jump through.[12] In the United States, for example, presidents faced minimal restrictions on the use of covert action until the mid-1970s.[13] Even after reforms were enacted, the constraints were still less onerous than for overt action.[14] Such flexibility may be attractive when the public is unwilling to pay for war.[15]

For domestic political arguments, leaders can be expected to shun secrecy when the public is behind them. This can happen for many reasons, including "when media elites support intervention, when the operation adheres to norms

[9] Dan Reiter and Allan C. Stam, *Democracies at War* (Princeton and Oxford: Princeton University Press, 2002), 159–160.

[10] O'Rourke, *Covert Regime Change: America's Secret Cold War*, 61.

[11] Alexander B. Downes and Mary Lauren Lilley, "Overt Peace, Covert War?: Covert Intervention and the Democratic Peace," *Security Studies* 19, no. 2 (2010): 266–306; David P. Forsythe, "Democracy, War, and Covert Action," *Journal of Peace Research* 29, no. 4 (1992): 385–395; Michael Poznansky, "Stasis or Decay? Reconciling Covert War and the Democratic Peace," *International Studies Quarterly* 59, no. 4 (2015): 815–826; Bruce Russett, *Grasping the Democratic Peace: Principles for a Post-Cold War World* (Princeton: Princeton University Press, 1993), 120–124.

[12] David N. Gibbs, "Secrecy and International Relations," *Journal of Peace Research* 32, no. 2 (1995): 213–228.

[13] William Spaniel and Michael Poznansky, "Credible Commitment in Covert Affairs," *American Journal of Political Science* 62, no. 3 (2018): 668–681.

[14] For an argument about the effects of these reforms on decision makers' willingness to covertly overthrow and prop up regimes, see Gregory L. Smith, "Secret but Constrained: The Impact of Elite Opposition on Covert Operations," *International Organization* 73, no. 3 (2019): 685–707.

[15] For arguments about how presidents can use deception to overcome public reticence for overt force, see Dan Reiter, "Democracy, Deception, and Entry into War," *Security Studies* 21, no. 4 (2012): 594–623; John M. Schuessler, "The Deception Dividend: FDR's Undeclared War," *International Security* 34, no. 4 (2010): 133–165.

of justified intervention, or when it is perceived as a defensive response to a clear military threat."[16] If leaders have public opinion on their side, "one of the main rationales for covert conduct—to avoid reputational costs"—disappears.[17] Public support may also reduce the need to circumvent institutional constraints, putting overt action back on the table.

A second set of explanations for covert intervention centers on escalation dynamics.[18] Secrecy may enable rival powers to compete without letting things get out of hand. If a state can hide its sponsorship of an operation such that rivals are none the wiser, they can avoid retaliation entirely. More interesting is when adversaries learn of the perpetrator's actions but choose to keep a tight lip, thereby colluding in the act of secrecy.[19] America's covert efforts to turn communist regimes in Eastern Europe non-communist following World War II—what came to be known as rollback operations—are often held up as the archetypal example of using secrecy to manage escalation.[20]

For escalation-based theories, leaders can be expected to pursue overt intervention when the odds of setting off escalatory spirals are negligible. This may happen in cases where there is "low technological sophistication, [in] local conflicts with no or one-sided outside interest, and if intervening powers are domestically insulated and lack alliance considerations."[21] The upshot is that overt action is most attractive when the target state is located in or near the intervener's sphere of influence. It is also more appealing when the target and its allies lack highly destructive military assets such as nuclear weapons.

A third potential explanation for covert action can be intuited from a well-known risk associated with foreign intervention: inciting a nationalist response.[22] According to Downes and O'Rourke, "in the age of nationalism, occupying powers are often plagued by legitimacy problems that undermine their ability

[16] O'Rourke, *Covert Regime Change: America's Secret Cold War*, 63.

[17] Ibid.

[18] Bruce D. Berkowitz and Allan E. Goodman, "The Logic of Covert Action," *The National Interest* 51 (1998): 38–46; Alexandra H. Perina, "Black Holes and Open Secrets: The Impact of Covert Action on International Law," *Columbia Journal of Transnational Law* 53, no. 3 (2015): 518.

[19] Austin Carson, "Facing Off and Saving Face: Covert Intervention and Escalation Management in the Korean War," *International Organization* 70, no. 1 (2016): 103–131.

[20] Daugherty, *Executive Secrets: Covert Action and the Presidency*, 126; O'Rourke, *Covert Regime Change: America's Secret Cold War*, 125–157.

[21] Carson, "Facing Off and Saving Face: Covert Intervention and Escalation Management in the Korean War," 115.

[22] Robert A. Pape, *Dying to Win: The Strategic Logic of Suicide Terrorism* (New York: Random House Trade Paperbacks, 2005), 79–80.

to effectively govern the target state."[23] Overtly meddling with the domestic authority structures of other states runs up against norms of self-determination and may result in a hostile backlash from the country's population, rallying them around the leader being targeted from without.[24] To the extent that interveners are aware of these risks, concealing efforts to change regimes can be advantageous. I call this alternative the tainted victory thesis.

Existing scholarship on foreign intervention and nationalism identifies several factors that can mute a popular backlash. One is whether the target population agrees on the need for an external intervention. A second is whether the intervener and target population perceive a common threat. A third factor that can stem a nationalist reaction is if the intervener makes a credible promise to withdraw its forces in a timely fashion.[25] When these three conditions are met, secrecy may be deemed unnecessary.

Each of the foregoing explanations has its own limitations. In general, domestic political arguments struggle to explain why leaders would turn to covert action when conditions at home favor a more public response or are at least permissive, which is especially likely in the early stages of a crisis.[26] The variant rooted specifically in democratic peace theory—which holds that elected leaders use secrecy when targeting fellow democracies to avoid the public's wrath—cannot explain covert action against autocracies where mutual norms of trust and respect are absent. Escalation-based theories work best when the target state sits on the doorstep of a powerful rival. They are less useful for explaining the use of covert action against states in the intervener's sphere of influence where the likelihood of clashing with adversaries is lower. Finally, the tainted victory thesis has trouble accounting for the patterns identified in the previous chapter. As shown, the United States intervened openly for decades over the objections of Latin American nations, who routinely made their opposition known. Nationalism was present well before the rise of covert action in the mid-twentieth century. The argument developed in the next section accounts for why leaders might

[23] Alexander B. Downes and Lindsey A. O'Rourke, "You Can't Always Get What You Want: Why Foreign-Imposed Regime Change Seldom Improves Interstate Relations," *International Security* 41, no. 2 (2016): 54.

[24] Alexander B. Downes and Jonathan Monten, "Forced to Be Free? Why Foreign-Imposed Regime Change Rarely Leads to Democratization," *International Security* 37, no. 4 (2013): 97.

[25] David M. Edelstein, "Occupational Hazards: Why Military Occupations Succeed or Fail," *International Security* 29, no. 1 (2004): 49–91. Of note, although Edelstein distinguishes between occupation and intervention, I am assuming that the same set of factors that reduce backlash in the former would operate in the latter.

[26] Matthew A. Baum and Philip B.K. Potter, "The Relationships Between Mass Media, Public Opinion, and Foreign Policy: Toward a Theoretical Synthesis," *Annual Review of Political Science* 11 (2008): 43.

prefer secret intervention even when targeting autocrats in their own backyard with a supportive public. It also accounts for the apparent shift to covert action after 1945 following the advent of the UN Charter.

A Legal Theory of Covert Action

At the most general level, my argument is that leaders will pursue regime change overtly if they can make a credible case they are not in violation of the nonintervention principle. Covert action is the preferred option when they are unable to do so. Like most legal principles, nonintervention is not absolute. Laws typically contain provisions exempting actors from liability for taking an otherwise-proscribed action.[27] Most criminal statutes prohibiting people from killing one another, for example, contain exceptions for using deadly force in self-defense. A similar dynamic applies to nonintervention.[28] A more refined version of my argument, then, is that leaders will pursue regime change overtly when they can locate a legal exemption to the nonintervention principle and will turn to covert action otherwise. The presence or absence of legal exemptions to nonintervention constitutes the independent variable I use to explain variation in covert and overt regime change.

The next step is to specify what qualifies as a legal exemption to the nonintervention principle.[29] This exercise helps guard against tautology wherein a particular justification for intervention is coded as credible simply because a state claimed as much.[30] The most appropriate place to begin is the text of the United Nations Charter which has provided the primary baseline against which interventions are evaluated with respect to their (il)legality for all states in the international system since 1945. Chapter 2 of this book comes in handy here. That discussion showed that the UN Charter did more than simply codify the nonintervention principle; it also laid out the conditions under which states

[27] On reservations, escape clauses, and exit clauses in international law, see Andrew T. Guzman, *How International Law Works: A Rational Choice Theory* (New York: Oxford University Press, 2008), 147–153.

[28] These exemptions fall under the umbrella of *jus ad bellum*, which refers to "the rules concerning *when* force can be used"; Michael J. Glennon, "The Fog of Law: Self-Defense, Inherence, and Incoherence in Article 51 of the United Nations Charter," *Harvard Journal of Law and Public Policy* 25, no. 2 (2002): 551, emphasis in original.

[29] For a summary of these issues, see Robert J. Beck, *The Grenada Invasion: Politics, Law, and Foreign Policy Decisionmaking* (Boulder, CO: Westview Press, 1993), 51–55.

[30] Myres S. McDougal and Richard N. Gardner, "The Veto and the Charter: An Interpretation for Survival," *Yale Law Journal* 60, no. 2 (1951): 262–266.

could legally ignore it. A brief review of that material as it relates to my argument will be useful.

The UN charter contains two broad types of legal exemptions to nonintervention. The first relates to self-defense. Article 51 permits states to intervene individually or collectively if they have been the victim of an armed attack. Article 51's reference to an *inherent* right of self-defense has commonly been interpreted to allow for preemptive action as long as the prospective threat is actually imminent. It is also thought to permit a state's longstanding right to rescue their nationals residing abroad if they are in clear and present danger. The second set of legal exemptions deals with responses to aggression and threats to international peace that fall outside the purview of self-defense. The body with the clearest authority to authorize such interventions is the UN Security Council. Chapter VIII also empowers regional organizations to sanction intervention in certain circumstances.

While we are on the topic of regional organizations, the provisions enumerated in their respective charters—assuming they contain a nonintervention principle—are also relevant, at least for interventions conducted in that part of the world. For example, the OAS, largely echoing language from the UN Charter, allows members to intervene in self-defense or collectively to maintain peace and security. Member states intervening in Latin America should thus factor both the UN and OAS Charters into their decision-making calculus. Readers interested in how exemptions from nonintervention have been understood and operationalized should refer back to the previous chapter.

One question that arises is how many legal exemptions are enough to justify intervention. Whether prospective interveners will appeal to more than one depends partly on availability. As will be discussed in a moment, while flimsy exemptions can easily be invented out of thin air, credible ones cannot. Locating one convincing legal exemption to nonintervention is hard enough in most cases. Finding more than one is even harder. The empirical chapters demonstrate leaders' recognition of this constraint.

A second factor affecting whether states will appeal to more than one legal exemption is the perceived importance of doing so. In some cases, one might suffice. Responding to an armed attack that has already occurred is uniformly accepted on its own as a justifiable reason for disregarding nonintervention and responding in kind. Additional reasons for action may be unnecessary. The same is true of interventions authorized by the UN Security Council. In other cases, invoking multiple, overlapping exemptions to build a stronger legal case for regime change will be preferable. The right to rescue endangered nationals may provide states with an initial rationale for deploying troops to a foreign country but prove insufficient on its own for justifying a more expansive operation to alter the domestic authority structures of the target. Concurrent, or even subsequent, authorization from the Security Council or a regional organization to resolve a crisis could provide such a basis.

Clever Lawyers

Another issue that is important to address is what we might think of as the clever lawyers phenomenon. This is the idea that decision makers can easily generate legal exemptions to nonintervention—or more disingenuously, pretexts, fig leaves, and so on—whenever it suits their interests.[31] In this view, the presence or absence of legal exemptions does not have much, if any, causal power. Instead, they are endogenous to a state's prior decision regarding how they wish to intervene. When officials want to conduct regime change overtly, they simply consult large teams of government lawyers and advance a pretext cloaked in legal language to justify intervention. Conversely, when officials decide they want to go covert owing to concerns about domestic politics, escalation, or nationalism, they refrain from doing so.

The clever lawyers phenomenon rests on the notion that legal pretexts are a dime a dozen. McGeorge Bundy's quip that "Pleikus are like streetcars; if you miss one, another will come along shortly" aptly summarizes this idea.[32] Bundy was referring to the fact that while the Johnson administration used a "Vietcong attack on the U.S. military base located in Pleiku, South Vietnam" to justify Operation Rolling Thunder, this was one of many excuses the United States might have used.[33] In the context of this book, the intuition is that leaders can locate or fabricate intervention pretexts at will.

As appealing as this might be, it has several shortcomings. When it comes to the kinds of exemptions that would render a regime change operation plausibly legal, decision makers should find it hard to invent them out of thin air. This is especially true if they want the stated rationale to be persuasive.[34] To begin with, the fact that documents like the UN Charter outline the few conditions under which states can violate another state's sovereignty means that any justification which falls outside those parameters is likely to be seen as illegitimate.[35] Frank

[31] Robert O. Keohane, "International Relations and International Law: Two Optics," *Harvard International Law Journal* 38, no. 2 (1997): 498.

[32] James B. Blight, Janet M. Lang, and David A. Welch, *Virtual JFK: Vietnam If Kennedy Had Lived* (Lanham, MD: Rowman and Littlefield Publishers, Inc., 2009), 171.

[33] Ronald R. Krebs, "Correspondence: Selling the Market Short? The Marketplace of Ideas and the Iraq War," *International Security* 29, no. 4 (2005): 200, ft. 16.

[34] Joel H. Westra, *International Law and the Use of Armed Force: The UN Charter and the Major Powers* (London and New York: Routledge, 2007), 28.

[35] These dynamics may differ for customary law or codified laws without clear exemptions. All else equal, I expect legal principles with explicit exemption language to be less susceptible to contrived fig leaves.

Schimmelfennig's description of the "limits to strategic manipulation" speaks directly to this issue: "[T]o the extent that the standard of legitimacy is clearly and unambiguously defined as well as internally consistent, it becomes difficult to rhetorically circumvent its practical implications."[36]

Moreover, the barriers to invoking one of the few exemptions to nonintervention that do exist are substantial. With regard to self-defense, interveners must be able to realistically claim that the target has imposed material harm or directly threatened them in some way. While leaders can extend the concept of self-defense beyond a direct armed attack to include things like protecting nationals, the necessity of deploying forces will likely be met with suspicion unless there is a clear and present danger to the intervener's citizens. This could include the outbreak of a civil war and other forms of social unrest that pose a serious and immediate threat to foreign nationals. Merely pointing to the presence of one's citizens abroad absent such danger should not be sufficient to constitute a credible rationale for intervening to rescue.

Gaining authorization from an entity like the UN Security Council should be equally difficult. Because each permanent member has a veto, achieving consensus on the need for regime change will be challenging given the heterogeneity of preferences. Unless the target engages in an action that so offends all of the permanent members such that they can agree on a resolution, the prospective intervener would have to wait for some exogenous event to transpire that could generate agreement. Similar dynamics should operate for regional organizations like the OAS, whose members will be wont to sanction the use of force except in exceptional circumstances. Members of these bodies, especially smaller states, take the nonintervention principle seriously and have a lot to lose by tolerating arbitrary interventions. Coercion or bribery, even by powerful actors like the United States, is unlikely to prove an easy pathway to securing approval for intervention. Moreover, the fact that there are a finite number of organizations that can authorize interventions limits the capacity for forum shopping. In three of the four cases examined here, the United States effectively had one option: the OAS. The UN Security Council was largely disinclined to authorize intervention during the Cold War. In the fourth case, the Grenada invasion, the United States only had one additional option—the Organization of Eastern Caribbean States—to rely on.

Finally, states can always try to justify regime change by eliciting an invitation for intervention from a recently-ousted leader or exile group claiming to be the rightful head of state in an attempt to render legal what would otherwise be an

[36] Frank Schimmelfennig, "The Community Trap: Liberal Norms, Rhetorical Action, and the Eastern Enlargement of the European Union," *International Organization* 55, no. 1 (2001): 65.

illegal action.[37] The challenge, as before, turns on credibility. For such a ploy to be seen as legitimate, at least two conditions must be met. First, the requester must have a genuine claim to power in the state. Second, the invitation must have been offered of their own accord, without coercion. These conditions set a high bar. This is plausibly why, as we will see in the next chapter, the United States in the Bay of Pigs declined to rely on an invitation for intervention from an exile government; it would not have met the first condition. It also helps account for why Soviet interventions in Hungary, Afghanistan, and elsewhere were suspect. The fact that the invitations came from satellites in their informal empire and were engineered by Soviet leadership meant they failed the second condition.[38]

It is reasonable at this point to ask whether states can simply induce a provocation that might result in a credible self-defense claim or move an international organization to act. In theory, the answer is yes. But there are several factors working against such a possibility. First, prospective interveners attempting to create a credible self-defense claim or persuade an international body to sanction intervention would have to willingly put their citizens, military bases, naval vessels, and the like in harm's way. To be sure, there are rare examples of this happening. Two of the most prominent include the Gulf of Tonkin incident in 1964, which Lyndon Johnson used as a precursor to escalation in Vietnam, and FDR provoking the Japanese in 1941 to justify full-blown entry in the fight against Nazi Germany and Imperial Japan. However, in both episodes the stakes were deemed to be extremely high—almost existential—and the provocations were used to shore up domestic support for greater involvement in ongoing conflicts.[39] As the following chapters will make clear, decision makers contemplated similar tactics elsewhere but refrained. Second, the regimes being targeted know that actions they take could be used as pretexts and work to avoid falling into this trap. They are not always successful, as the Grenada case demonstrates, but they can avoid this scenario in some cases, as the Cuba case shows.

One reason the clever lawyers argument has been so popular is how scholars have traditionally gone about assessing the role of pretexts in intervention decisions. Many studies substantiate a version of this thesis by focusing strictly on the fact that leaders usually offer justifications of some kind during overt interventions. In *Sovereignty*, Krasner makes the case, albeit implicitly, that

[37] Under the UN Charter system, incumbent governments willingly inviting violations of their Westphalian sovereignty does not constitute a violation of the nonintervention principle. For a broader discussion of these dynamics, see Stephen D. Krasner, *Sovereignty: Organized Hypocrisy* (Princeton: Princeton University Press, 1999), 22.

[38] Christine Gray, *International Law and the Use of Force*, 4th ed. (Oxford: Oxford University Press, 2018), 15; Tom Ruys, *"Armed Attack" and Article 51 of the UN Charter : Evolutions in Customary Law and Practice* (Cambridge: Cambridge University Press, 2010), 88–91.

[39] John M. Schuessler, *Deceit on the Road to War* (Ithaca, NY: Cornell University Press, 2015).

leaders have easily called up rationales for meddling in another state's domestic authority structures whenever it suited them.[40] The problem with this approach is that we cannot know whether leaders can actually invent credible justifications for violating nonintervention with ease unless we also examine cases of secret interventions. Evidence of decision makers searching for legal exemptions, failing to find at least one, and going covert as a result would support my theoretical expectations. This is especially true when there would be nontrivial strategic benefits to toppling the regime in question. Conversely, if decision makers opted not to bother with any discussion of legal justifications because they already intended to keep their sponsorship of an operation hidden, this would support the counterargument.

At the risk of stating the obvious, there is nothing stopping decision makers from invoking facially implausible pretexts—justifications which stretch the nonintervention principle beyond recognition—to try and defend regime change. But because my argument is that states like the United States seek legal exemptions to nonintervention to avoid incurring hypocrisy costs and to preserve their credibility, believability matters. This also helps explain why states cannot innovate new justifications for intervention to reduce the clash with international law whenever they wish. Unless the justification is widely embraced, it will be of limited use. After the Bay of Pigs, for example, officials decided against trying to redefine what a legitimate intervention was, warning that "[s]uch a doctrine would materially improve the basis for our intervention only if it were generally accepted by the countries of Latin America and elsewhere throughout the free world, and if those countries generally were convinced that the doctrine was applicable to the facts of the Cuba situation."[41]

In the end, whether observers accept the legal justifications interveners offer in a particular case, or whether they evaluate them fairly, is less important for my argument than the intervening state trusting or at least hoping that they will do so.[42] In this respect, the *perceived* availability of a legal exemption is, in

[40] Krasner, *Sovereignty: Organized Hypocrisy*, 69.

[41] "Cuba and Communism in the Hemisphere," *National Security Files, Countries, Cuba, Subjects, Policy - NSC Action No. 2413-C, Papers and Annex I, 5/4/1961 [Folder]; Papers of President Kennedy: National Security Files—Countries, Box 54 [Collection]* (JFK Library, 1961), 14.

[42] Whether the observer is a friend or foe, for example, may impact how legal pretexts are ultimately received. All else equal, adversaries may be less likely to accept legal pretexts from rivals as credible and valid. Although I do not evaluate such claims directly, they are broadly consistent with my contention that preserving trustworthiness and avoiding hypocrisy costs was deemed valuable by U.S. decision makers as a way to lock in continued support by allies and partners. See Cynthia Weber, *Simulating Sovereignty: Intervention, the State, and Symbolic Exchange* (New York: Cambridge University Press, 1995), 5, 16.

practice, the main independent variable of this book.[43] Even still, discussing the dynamics of exemptions in general is important. While my argument, like many others, comes down to perceptions, these perceptions should be reasonable given the information available at the time.[44] There should not be much daylight between what leaders think will be credible and what observers deem credible. That said, there is always room for divergence. This is especially true given that the parameters of nonintervention and their applicability in a particular case are often debatable. Contestation among leaders and lawyers about the relevance and appropriateness of exemptions to a case of regime change may even give states some wiggle room. But there are limits. I still expect decision makers to appeal to jurisprudence, accepted state practice, and popular interpretations of existing legal provisions in both their calculations prior to authorizing an intervention and in their public reasoning in the days afterward.

Causal Pathways

The argument just articulated is the first step in building a legal theory of covert action. However, the claim that leaders are more likely to reach for the quiet option when they lack a legal exemption to the nonintervention principle, and more likely to act openly when they enjoy one, is correlational in nature. The mechanisms or pathways through which these two variables relate to one another to determine outcomes have not been articulated.[45] This is an important undertaking. We know from the existing literature that opting for overt intervention can increase the chances that a mission will succeed relative to covert action by providing more direct control over an operation. It also offers the ability to escalate as needed.[46] Why might leaders knowingly forgo overt options, which are operationally superior, to achieve plausible deniability when they lack legal exemptions to nonintervention? What are the benefits of concealing unwarranted violations of nonintervention?

Covert action allows states to sidestep two distinct costs associated with brazen violations of the nonintervention principle. The first involves the prospect

[43] Kelly M. Greenhill, *Weapons of Mass Migration: Forced Displacement, Coercion, and Foreign Policy* (Ithaca, NY: Cornell University Press, 2010), 57; Westra, *International Law and the Use of Armed Force: The UN Charter and the Major Powers,* 8.

[44] See Dale C. Copeland, *The Origins of Major War* (Ithaca, NY: Cornell University Press, 2000), 31–33.

[45] David Waldner, "What Makes Process Tracing Good? Causal Mechanisms, Causal Inference, and the Completeness Standard in Comparative Politics," in *Process Tracing: From Metaphor to Analytic Tool,* eds. Andrew Bennett and Jeffrey T. Checkel (Cambridge: Cambridge University Press, 2015), 126–152.

[46] O'Rourke, *Covert Regime Change: America's Secret Cold War,* 53–57.

of undermining the credibility of one's propensity for upholding commitments. The second involves the appearance of hypocrisy. The reason nonintervention entails both costs is due to the fact that it is simultaneously a promise to follow specific rules, the commitment component, and an endorsement of a moral principle of state equality, the hypocrisy component. I will address each of these in turn.

One way to think about the nonintervention principle is as a rule or agreement. It is, in short, a formal commitment to behave in specified ways. By signing the UN Charter, states promised to refrain from forcibly interfering in other states' internal affairs unless an international body like the Security Council offered its blessing, there was a credible claim of self-defense, or both.[47] Pursuing regime change in the absence one of these conditions violates this agreed-upon rule.

When couched in these terms, it is apparent why leaders might be reluctant to openly violate the nonintervention principle. States who accede to agreements to follow certain rules can damage their credibility and reputation for trustworthiness by engaging in proscribed activities.[48] According to George Downs and Michael Jones, a popular view in the literature on reputation is that "a major—if not the major—reason why states keep commitments, even those that produce a lower level of returns than expected, is because they fear that any evidence of unreliability will damage their current cooperative relationships and lead other states to reduce their willingness to enter into future agreements."[49] Robert Keohane reaches a similar conclusion. "For reasons of reputation, as well as fear of retaliation and concern about the effects of precedents," he writes, "egoistic governments may follow the rules and principles of international regimes even when myopic self-interest counsels them not to."[50] Covert action enables states to hide inconsistencies between the promises they make (commitments to nonintervention) and the actions they take (regime change in the absence of a legal

[47] Westra, *International Law and the Use of Armed Force: The UN Charter and the Major Powers*, 1–2.

[48] There is an important debate in the reputation literature on whether states develop general reputations for untrustworthiness by violating a single agreement or whether the reputational consequences are limited strictly to the domain in which violations occurred. For a good summary, see George W. Downs and Michael A. Jones, "Reputation, Compliance, and International Law," *Journal of Legal Studies* 31 (2002): S95–114. There is also a debate about whether reputational concerns affect state behavior at all. For an argument on why they do not matter, see Daryl G. Press, *Calculating Credibility: How Leaders Assess Military Threats* (Ithaca, NY: Cornell University Press, 2005). For an argument about how they do, see Alex Weisiger and Keren Yarhi-Milo, "Revisiting Reputation: How Past Actions Matter in International Politics," *International Organization* 69, no. 2 (2015): 473–495.

[49] Downs and Jones, "Reputation, Compliance, and International Law," S96.

[50] Robert O. Keohane, *After Hegemony: Cooperation and Discord in the World Political Economy* (Princeton: Princeton University Press, 1984), 106. See also Abram Chayes and Antonia Handler Chayes, *The New Sovereignty* (Cambridge, MA: Harvard University Press, 1995), 273.

exemption). Put differently, secrecy allows states to appear more trustworthy than they are, thereby protecting their reputation as an actor who keeps their word and abides by prior agreements.

The credibility costs associated with violating international legal commitments are worse than those associated with violations of informal agreements, offering especially strong incentives for states to act covertly when they want to shirk.[51] One reason for this turns on heightened expectations. As Beth Simmons argues, "expectations regarding a particular government's behavior change qualitatively when that government publicly expresses its commitment to be legally bound to a specific set of rules."[52] In the same vein, Andrew Guzman contends that "[a] formal treaty represents the most serious form of commitment not because it is more costly to enter into than other commitments but because it is understood to be a maximal pledge of reputation."[53] It is precisely because international law clearly and explicitly "define[s] the size of the *expectations gap* when governments fail to live up to their provisions" that violations of nonintervention can do even more damage to a state's trustworthiness and credibility than violations of informal, nonbinding agreements.[54]

In addition to increasing the severity of credibility costs, nonintervention's status in treaty law increases the likelihood that violators will incur these costs in the first place. This is because violations of international legal commitments should be easier to detect than violations of informal commitments.[55] In the former, pre- and proscribed behaviors are clearly laid out in writing. In the latter, the parameters of (un)acceptable behavior are more amorphous. States that abrogate legal agreements may thus find it harder to claim they have lived up to agreed-upon terms when they have not. The opposite is true of informal agreements which increases the chances that violators can escape or at least challenge detection and keep their trustworthiness intact.

A second way to think about nonintervention is the endorsement of a moral principle. It represents the idea that all countries should be treated equally. Forcibly altering another state's governance structures is antithetical to this ideal.

[51] This is especially true of treaty law. The same dynamics may be less salient for customary law, which is typically not explicitly written down. See Jack L. Goldsmith and Eric A. Posner, *The Limits of International Law* (Oxford and New York: Oxford University Press, 2005), 21.

[52] Beth Simmons, *Mobilizing for Human Rights: International Law and Domestic Politics* (New York: Cambridge University Press, 2009), 14.

[53] Guzman, *How International Law Works: A Rational Choice Theory*, 59.

[54] Simmons, *Mobilizing for Human Rights: International Law and Domestic Politics*, 14, emphasis in original.

[55] Michael J. Glennon, "How International Rules Die," *Georgetown Law Journal* 93, no. 3 (2005): 955; Peter T. Leeson and Paola A. Suarez, "An Economic Analysis of Magna Carta," *International Review of Law and Economics* 47 (2016): 40–46.

By signing the UN Charter or other regional charters with similar provisions, states signaled their approval of this concept. Subsequently violating it without justification would appear hypocritical. "Hypocrisy," notes Finnemore, "is more than mere inconsistency of deeds with words. Hypocrisy involves deeds that are inconsistent with particular kinds of words—proclamations of moral value and virtue."[56] Violating normatively-infused principles goes beyond trustworthiness and credibility; it speaks to a state's "character and identity."[57]

The costs associated with hypocrisy differ from those accompanying violations of rules or agreements. Whereas trust and credibility are central to the latter, the former has to do with moral standing and perceived genuineness: "We despise and condemn hypocrites because they try to deceive us: they pretend to be better than they are. Hypocrisy leads others to question the authenticity of an actor's . . . moral commitments but also its moral constitution and character."[58] Tangible consequences include naming and shaming campaigns that "expose the distance between discourse and practice. This is embarrassing to many governments, which may try to save face by closing that distance or by making the gap disappear altogether by ending the crisis through concession."[59] Contravening normative commitments may also harm a state's standing in a particular community[60] or the society of states more broadly.[61] Hiding hypocrisy via a successfully concealed covert operation allows states to abrogate commitments to state equality while keeping their moral character intact.

Echoing the discussion of credibility and trust, nonintervention's status in international law exacerbates the hypocrisy problem. First, easing the process of detecting violations means that violators are simply more likely to incur hypocrisy costs.[62] States who make loose pledges to human rights norms, for instance, may face less certain punishment for supporting autocrats given the absence of clear metrics for assessing whether they are acting hypocritically. Committing to nonintervention and toppling regimes without a legal exemption is different

[56] Martha Finnemore, "Legitimacy, Hypocrisy, and the Social Structure of Unipolarity: Why Being a Unipole Isn't All It's Cracked Up to Be," *World Politics* 61, no. 1 (2009): 74.

[57] Ibid.

[58] Ibid.

[59] Quoted in Greenhill, *Weapons of Mass Migration: Forced Displacement, Coercion, and Foreign Policy*, 52. See Margaret E. Keck and Kathryn Sikkink, *Activists Beyond Borders: Advocacy Networks in International Politics* (Ithaca, NY: Cornell University Press, 1998), 24.

[60] See, for example, Schimmelfennig, "The Community Trap: Liberal Norms, Rhetorical Action, and the Eastern Enlargement of the European Union." On the interplay of hypocrisy and legitimation in the context of rising powers, see Stacie Goddard, *When Right Makes Might: Rising Powers and World Order* (Ithaca, NY and London: Cornell University Press, 2018).

[61] Hedley Bull, *The Anarchical Society: A Study of Order in World Politics* (New York: Palgrave Macmillan, 1977).

[62] Glennon, "How International Rules Die," 955.

since the parameters of acceptable behavior are laid out in writing. Moreover, by endorsing a moral principle enshrined in international law, states send strong signals about which values they deem most important. The outrage accompanying violations of codified normative commitments should be especially severe.

Violations of nonintervention may also entail heightened hypocrisy costs for reasons less directly related to international law. All states since 1945, regardless of regime type or capabilities, have enjoyed a right to be free from unwanted interference in their domestic authority structures. Few norms have been as fiercely defended by the international community.[63] This is particularly true of secondary and weaker powers who have the most to gain when states observe nonintervention and the most to lose when they do not.[64] What this means in practice is that brazen violations may result in near-universal condemnation owing to the principle's widespread acceptance and importance to the modern system of sovereignty. The hypocrisy costs imposed on those who violate liberal norms of justified intervention may be confined to the subset of states who also subscribe to those ideals. For example, intervening against elected regimes will likely be viewed as hypocritical by the community of fellow democracies but is unlikely to faze dictatorships who do not observe these same standards.[65]

In sum, because nonintervention is both an endorsement of a moral principle and an agreement to abide by certain rules, states who violate it without a legal exemption not only expose themselves to hypocrisy costs but can also damage the credibility of their commitments. Yet, the two do not always coexist. States frequently make pledges that if broken might tarnish their image as an actor who "reliably upholds its international commitments" but have far less impact on whether they are viewed "as an honorable member of the international community."[66] Arms control treaties and trade deals, neither of which are imbued with any meaningful normative content, readily come to mind. The converse is also true. States can endorse principles that damage their character and moral standing if violated but should have little bearing on whether they can be expected to reliably uphold agreements. Democratic states that espouse liberal values may incur hypocrisy costs for intervening to topple a fellow democracy, but the absence of a formal contract to refrain from engaging in such behavior

[63] Ian Hurd, "Legitimacy and Authority in International Politics," *International Organization* 53, no. 2 (1999): 393.

[64] Martha Finnemore, *The Purpose of Intervention: Changing Beliefs About the Use of Force* (Ithaca, NY: Cornell University Press, 2003), 31.

[65] It is also possible for states that do not subscribe to the rules and norms in question to call out hypocritical behavior of a rival that does in order to embarrass them and undermine their credibility. See, in particular, Greenhill, *Weapons of Mass Migration: Forced Displacement, Coercion, and Foreign Policy*.

[66] Downs and Jones, "Reputation, Compliance, and International Law," S96, ft. 2.

means that these kinds of actions are not as dispositive of whether the violator is viewed as trustworthy. It is the fact that the nonintervention principle sits at the intersection of a formal agreement and an endorsement of a moral principle that is notable here.

At the same time, it is important not to overstate these distinctions. It is possible that states who break commitments lacking a moral dimension may still damage their character to some degree, even though credibility costs are likely to predominate in such cases. Similarly, states that violate their moral commitments may lead others to doubt their credibility even though hypocrisy costs are most salient. Exploring whether the framework developed here explains cases in which there is a non-moral legal commitment or a non-legal moral commitment is an obvious area for future research.

Credibility and Hypocrisy in the American-Led Postwar Order

Even if states who blatantly disregard nonintervention risk damaging their credibility and authenticity, a potential problem remains: not all care.[67] My theory is most likely to apply to states who worry enough about these risks that they are willing to reduce the chances of getting what they want by pursuing regime change covertly even when overt action would be more efficient and effective.

One strategy for figuring out which states satisfy this criterion is to identify general attributes that make some more susceptible to this set of concerns than others. We might expect liberal democracies to be more sensitive to credibility concerns and hypocrisy costs than autocracies.[68] Great powers promoting particular versions of international order predicated on norms of self-determination, anti-colonialism, and the like may also be sensitive to such concerns. [69] In this section, I simply aim to show that the United States since 1945 has cared about these risks given the kind of international order it helped forge in the postwar world. Part of this enterprise entailed commitments to rules and restraint.

[67] Miles M. Evers, "On Transgression," *International Studies Quarterly* 61, no. 4 (2017): 786–794. See also Glennon, "How International Rules Die," 952; Guzman, *How International Law Works: A Rational Choice Theory*, 89.

[68] Greenhill, *Weapons of Mass Migration: Forced Displacement, Coercion, and Foreign Policy*, 60–63; G. John Ikenberry, *After Victory: Institutions, Strategic Restraint, and the Rebuilding of Order After Major Wars* (Princeton: Princeton University Press, 2001), 62.

[69] There may also be times when these concerns are more salient than others. Competition between the U.S. and Soviet Union for new nations during the Cold War, for example, almost certainly increased sensitivity to the kinds of costs discussed here. See Julian Go, *Patterns of Empire: The British and American Empires, 1688 to the Present* (Cambridge: Cambridge University Press, 2011), 149, 152–155.

Another part turned on the legitimacy of American leadership. Seeing whether the argument developed here applies to other interveners is another area ripe for future research.

To substantiate the claim that the United States has been sensitive to hypocrisy and credibility costs since 1945, it will be helpful to first describe the unique nature of the postwar order. Scores of books and articles have been written about America's privileged position in the second half of the twentieth century. A large part of this had to do with its advantages along myriad dimensions of state power. Most impressive was America's economic might.[70] In the aftermath of World War II, U.S. global production represented roughly half of the world total, a figure that diminished slightly as Western Europe and Japan recovered from wartime devastation.[71] In a top-secret State Department paper dated February 24, 1948, George Kennan observed that, "we have about 50% of the world's wealth but only 6.3% of its population . . . . In this situation, we cannot fail to be the object of envy and resentment. Our real task in the coming period is to devise a pattern of relationships which will permit us to maintain this position of disparity without positive detriment to our national security."[72]

The United States also enjoyed military superiority in the first years of the Cold War. Over the course of WWII, "the United States had become the world's leading military power, producing more arms than the Axis states combined and almost three times the amount generated by the Soviet Union."[73] Melvyn Leffler credits economics for this: "America's enormously productive economy bestowed upon the country great military power. . . . Its strategic air force was unrivaled. Its navy dominated the seas. Its aircraft carriers and marine divisions enabled it to project power across the oceans. It held a monopoly over humanity's most intimidating weapon, the atomic bomb. The United States had preponderant power."[74] Similar to the economic domain, America's military edge

[70] Keohane, *After Hegemony: Cooperation and Discord in the World Political Economy*, 139.

[71] Stephen M. Walt, *Taming American Power: The Global Response to U.S. Primacy* (New York: W.W. Norton, 2005), 32. Numbers two and three on the proverbial list of the world's largest economies—the Soviet Union and the United Kingdom, respectively—were each approximately one-fifth the total U.S. economy following World War II, a statistic that also narrowed following the postwar recovery efforts. See Ikenberry, *After Victory: Institutions, Strategic Restraint, and the Rebuilding of Order After Major Wars*, 167.

[72] United States. Department of State, "Report by the Policy Planning Staff," *Foreign Relations of the United States, 1948, General; The United Nations, Volume 1, Part* 2 February 2 (1948).

[73] G. John Ikenberry, *Liberal Leviathan: The Origins, Crisis, and Transformation of the American World Order* (Princeton: Princeton University Press, 2011), 163.

[74] Melvyn P. Leffler, *A Preponderance of Power: National Security, the Truman Administration, and the Cold War* (Stanford: Stanford University Press, 1992), 2.

receded somewhat as the Soviet Union rebuilt its military, increased spending, and tested its first nuclear weapon in 1949.

American dominance was not the only thing that made the postwar order so unique. It was also the *kind* of order decision makers forged. First, the United States created a system of rules intended to govern other states' behavior as well as its own. The desire to maintain a reputation for trustworthiness and credibility should have created strong incentives to hide violations of the nonintervention principle in its capacity as a written agreement the United States had committed to. Second, America positioned itself as the head of a liberal order rooted in norms of self-determination, democracy, human rights, and more. The desire to maintain moral authority and legitimacy should have made covert action an attractive means of pursuing strategic interests without flagrantly violating nonintervention, a normative principle the United States strongly endorsed. The following unpacks each of these dynamics.

Rules and restraint. Some rules and arrangements the United States helped construct after WWII, like the United Nations and the nonintervention principle, were universal in scope and supposed to apply to all states across the globe. Others, like the North Atlantic Treaty Organization and Bretton Woods, were geographically confined.[75] Why the United States pursued denser rule-based arrangements in some parts of the world but not in others has been extensively written about.[76] My concern here is how such efforts impacted U.S. foreign policy with an eye toward intervention in particular.

At the broadest level, it incentivized the United States to exercise restraint, at least in those domains and regions where there were formal rules prescribing and proscribing certain actions. "In seeking a more rule-based order," Ikenberry notes, "the leading state is agreeing to engage in strategic restraint. It is acknowledging that there will be limits on the way in which it can exercise its power."[77] The act of making commitments—to specific rules of conduct in this case—always "entails relinquishing some options, giving up choices, surrendering opportunities, binding oneself. And it works through shifting the expectations of some partner or adversary or even a stranger of how one will behave or react."[78]

[75] Ikenberry, *Liberal Leviathan: The Origins, Crisis, and Transformation of the American World Order*, 90–91.

[76] See, for example, Ikenberry, *After Victory: Institutions, Strategic Restraint, and the Rebuilding of Order After Major Wars*; Peter J. Katzenstein, *A World of Regions: Asia and Europe in the American Imperium* (Ithaca, NY: Cornell University Press, 2005).

[77] Ikenberry, *Liberal Leviathan: The Origins, Crisis, and Transformation of the American World Order*, 105. See also Charles A. Kupchan, *How Enemies Become Friends: The Sources of Stable Peace* (Princeton, NJ and Oxford: Princeton University Press, 2010), 43.

[78] Thomas C. Schelling, *Strategies of Commitment and Other Essays* (Cambridge, MA: Harvard University Press, 2006), vii.

Powerful states like the United States need not sponsor and abide by rules out of the goodness of its heart.[79] There are nontrivial advantages to such an undertaking.[80] First, it lowers the enforcement costs associated with the provision of international order. The less that subordinate states fear arbitrary abuses of power by the leading state, the more likely they are to perceive the order as acceptable.[81] And the more they perceive the order as acceptable, the less eager they are to resist the leading state's initiatives or to embark on a path of neutrality or alignment with geopolitical rivals.[82] This, in turn, reduces the demand to mete out punishment.[83] Second, if the leading state successfully persuades secondary and weaker powers to buy into a system of rule-based arrangements with them sitting at the helm, they can lock in the benefits of such an order even as their power begins to wane.[84]

This discussion buttresses one of the main points of the book, namely that the erosion of credibility and trust accompanying brazen violations of nonintervention is important to the United States because of its commitments to a rule-based order. Unlike some arrangements, the United States does not enjoy special privileges when it comes to the prohibition on interfering in another state's internal affairs without their permission or a viable legal exemption. If decision makers consistently flouted nonintervention, it would signal to allies and partners that they were unwilling to live within the bounds of agreed-upon rules. These states might then begin to doubt America's commitment to restraint in other areas, reducing their willingness to continue buying into the extant order and possibly incentivizing them to hedge by looking for new patrons.[85]

[79] On the compatibility of self-interest and compliance with international law, see Guzman, *How International Law Works: A Rational Choice Theory*, 17.

[80] Keohane, *After Hegemony: Cooperation and Discord in the World Political Economy*, 106.

[81] Michael Mandelbaum, *The Case for Goliath: How America Acts as the World's Government in the 21st Century* (New York: PublicAffairs, 2005), Chapter 4.

[82] Westra, *International Law and the Use of Armed Force: The UN Charter and the Major Powers*, 51–52.

[83] David A. Lake, *Hierarchy in International Relations* (Ithaca, NY: Cornell University Press, 2009), 9; Walt, *Taming American Power: The Global Response to U.S. Primacy*, 160–178. For an argument about the benefits of credible commitments to predictable behavior in the domestic context, see Douglass C. North and Barry R. Weingast, "Constitutions and Commitment: The Evolution of Institutions Governing Public Choice in Seventeenth-Century England," *The Journal of Economic History* 49, no. 4 (1989): 803. For an argument about how violating norms of expected behavior can exacerbate security dilemma dynamics, see Robert Jervis, "Cooperation Under the Security Dilemma," *World Politics* 30, no. 2 (1978): 179. For an argument about the benefits of predictability in the context of international regimes, see Robert Axelrod and Robert O. Keohane, "Achieving Cooperation Under Anarchy: Strategies and Institutions," *World Politics* 38, no. 1 (1985): 234.

[84] Ikenberry, *After Victory: Institutions, Strategic Restraint, and the Rebuilding of Order After Major Wars*, 54–55.

[85] There is also some debate as to whether violations of commitments in one arena signal a willingness to violate commitments in other arenas. The conventional thinking is that they do. For a

Choosing only to pursue regime change openly when it could be legally justified and pursuing secrecy otherwise helps prevent such an outcome.

In light of the foregoing discussion, strategic restraint appears more expansive than previous studies recognize. The predominant view is that America's commitment to a rule-based order was confined to Western Europe and parts of East Asia. "Outside of these two regions," Ikenberry writes, "the United States established a wide variety of patron-client relationships—in many instances, old-style imperial domination."[86] Peter Katzenstein argues that only Western Europe and East Asia were squarely in the U.S. "imperium" by virtue of America's relationship with Germany and Japan.[87] It is certainly true that there were fewer rules constraining the hegemon outside of these two regions. Nevertheless, because the UN Charter was universal in scope, brazen violations of the nonintervention principle anywhere on the globe would work at cross-purposes with America's broader commitment to a rule-based system. This includes regions like Latin America where the United States, despite its label as a quasi-imperial power, recommitted to nonintervention in the OAS Charter.

If an appreciation of how the nonintervention principle fits into the larger enterprise of the American-led international order is important for demonstrating why strategic restraint is more expansive than previously recognized, the frequent use of a quiet option showcases its limits. Strictly focusing on observable behaviors as Ikenberry, Krasner, Lake, and others have done ignores the important role that covert action has played in helping states preserve a public appearance of strategic restraint while simultaneously untying their hands in secret. Secrecy enables states to indulge short-term strategic interests by pursuing regime change when they lack a legal exemption to nonintervention, while at the same time pretending that they are giving up such opportunities for the greater good; that is, a commitment to nonarbitrary behavior. Covert action thus offers leading powers the opportunity to look like they are sending costly signals of restraint even when they are not.

Legitimacy and leadership. Sponsoring a rule-based order and agreeing to live within agreed-upon boundaries does more than reduce smaller powers' fear of domination. It also makes the entire arrangement more legitimate.[88] However,

useful summary, see Downs and Jones, "Reputation, Compliance, and International Law"; Guzman, *How International Law Works: A Rational Choice Theory*, 101–106.

[86] Ikenberry, *Liberal Leviathan: The Origins, Crisis, and Transformation of the American World Order*, 90–91.

[87] Katzenstein, *A World of Regions: Asia and Europe in the American Imperium*, 2–3.

[88] Bruce Cronin, "The Paradox of Hegemony: America's Ambiguous Relationship with the United Nations," *European Journal of International Relations* 7, no. 1 (2001): 113; Ikenberry, *Liberal Leviathan: The Origins, Crisis, and Transformation of the American World Order*, 107; Mandelbaum, *The Case for Goliath: How America Acts as the World's Government in the 21st Century*, 142–143. See also Ian Clark, *Legitimacy in International Society* (Oxford: Oxford University Press, 2005); Thomas

the legitimacy of the U.S.-led order entailed more than just following rules. The content of the principles and norms underpinning the postwar order, and perceptions of America's adherence to them, were crucial ingredients as well. This helps explain why decision makers found it important to avoid damaging the United States' moral character by hiding hypocritical actions, which includes pursuing regime change covertly in the absence of a legal exemption to the nonintervention principle. As with the prior discussion, secrecy has served an underappreciated role in maintaining the legitimacy of the liberal order and America's leadership position within it.

The United States has long viewed itself as a champion of a broad set of universal liberal values and principles.[89] According to Jonathan Monten, "[t]he concept of the United States as agent of historical transformation and liberal change in the international system . . . informs almost the entire history of U.S. foreign policy."[90] Woodrow Wilson famously defended open covenants and self-determination in his Fourteen Points address following the end of hostilities in World War I.[91] Franklin D. Roosevelt's Good Neighbor Policy falls into this tradition as well. These kinds of pronouncements took on new importance as the United States set out to build a liberal international order after World War II. Decision makers "repeatedly justified this enterprise in terms of its conformity with the principles of the UN Charter and its rules forbidding aggression . . . . [D]espite some transgressions, the overall fidelity of the United States to internationalist norms contributed strongly to the legitimacy of U.S. power."[92]

M. Franck, "The Power of Legitimacy and the Legitimacy of Power: International Law in an Age of Power Disequilibrium," *American Journal of International Law* 100, no. 1 (2006): 88–106.

[89] Tony Smith, *America's Mission: The United States and the Worldwide Struggle for Democracy* (Princeton, NJ and Oxford: Princeton University Press, 1994).

[90] Jonathan Monten, "The Roots of the Bush Doctrine," *International Security* 29, no. 4 (2005): 113.

[91] But see Allen Lynch, "Woodrow Wilson and the Principle of 'National Self-Determination': A Reconsideration," *Review of International Studies* 28, no. 2 (2002): 419–436; Trygve Throntveit, "The Fable of the Fourteen Points: Woodrow Wilson and National Self-Determination," *Diplomatic History* 35, no. 3 (2011): 445–481.

[92] Robert W. Tucker and David C. Hendrickson, "The Sources of American Legitimacy," *Foreign Affairs* 83, no. 6 (2004): 21. Part of what drove the U.S. toward a more liberal strategy was the lack of opportunities to engage in old-style colonialism and the rise of anticolonial and nationalist sentiment in the mid-twentieth century. See Go, *Patterns of Empire: The British and American Empires, 1688 to the Present,* 137–145, 157–158. For more on these dynamics, see Daniel Deudney and G. John Ikenberry, "The Nature and Sources of Liberal International Order," *Review of International Studies* 25, no. 2 (1999): 192–195; David C. Hendrickson, "Toward Universal Empire: The Dangerous Quest for Absolute Security," *World Policy Journal* 19, no. 3 (2002): 1–10; John Gerard Ruggie, *Winning the Peace: America and World Order in the New Era* (New York: Columbia University Press, 1996).

Ensuring that participants viewed the existing order and America's position within it as legitimate by living according to certain norms and principles perpetuated U.S. hegemony. According to Christian Reus-Smit, "the hegemon must pursue its interests in a manner consistent with [extant] norms, or the legitimacy of its leadership will fast erode."[93] Legitimate authority induces cooperation "through attraction," or soft power, "rather than coercion or payments."[94] Even some realists recognize the value of legitimacy. As Stephen Walt put it, "if other states regard the dominant state's behavior as generally beneficial and consistent with established moral standards, they will be less likely to fear or resent the asymmetry of power in its favor and less likely to want to undermine it. As the dominant world power," writes Walt, "the United States has much to gain from the perception that its privileged position is legitimate."[95] Writing about the nuclear taboo, Nina Tannenwald argues that one of the reasons U.S. decision makers refrained from using nuclear weapons after Hiroshima and Nagasaki despite a desire to do so in some instances was the negative impact it would have on American leadership.[96]

It follows from this discussion that U.S. decision makers would be keen on avoiding flagrant violations of nonintervention in its capacity as an ideal they formally endorsed.[97] Overtly toppling regimes without a legal exemption signifies that America is indifferent to the notion that states have a right to be free from unwanted violations of Westphalian sovereignty, a principle which it actively promoted in the UN, the OAS, and elsewhere. Hypocrisy of this nature damages the legitimacy of the American-led order and the United States' role as a leader. Hiding such hypocrisy by pursuing covert action promises to deliver the U.S. strategic objectives without doing violence to its moral authority.

A skeptical reader may be quick to point out that America's behavior over the past seventy-plus years has basically been one hypocritical act after another and that concerns about legitimacy are weak drivers of behavior at best and utterly

[93] Christian Reus-Smit, *American Power and World Order* (Cambridge, UK: Polity Press, 2004), 102.

[94] Joseph S. Nye, "Soft Power and American Foreign Policy," *Political Science Quarterly* 119, no. 2 (2004): 256. See also Tom R. Tyler, "Psychological Perspectives on Legitimacy and Legitimation," *Annual Review of Psychology* 57 (2006): 375–400.

[95] Walt, *Taming American Power: The Global Response to U.S. Primacy*, 160–161.

[96] Nina Tannenwald, "The Nuclear Taboo: The United States and the Normative Basis of Nuclear Non-Use," *International Organization* 53, no. 3 (1999): 445.

[97] Violations of norms and principles that are accepted by a given group but that one has not committed to may result in stigma but is not technically hypocrisy. See Rebecca Adler-Nissen, "Stigma Management in International Relations: Transgressive Identities, Norms, and Order in International Society," *International Organization* 68, no. 1 (2014): 143–176; Ayse Zarakol, "What Made the Modern World Hang Together: Socialisation or Stigmatisation?," *International Theory* 6, no. 2 (2014): 311–332.

irrelevant at worst. Despite its commitment to a host of norms such as the rule of law, democracy, and human rights, the skeptic might say, the United States has supported dictatorial regimes, engaged in torture as part of the war on terror, and intervened in a host of cases in ways that show little to no regard for the norm of nonintervention, including in "Cuba, Mexico, Chile, the Dominican Republic, Guatemala, Nicaragua, and elsewhere."[98]

These are valid concerns. If we look a bit closer, though, many of these examples actually support rather than undermine the argument I am making. A common problem with this line of criticism is that it conflates cases in which the United States openly and brazenly departed from its moral obligations with cases in which decision makers tried, even if unsuccessfully, to hide such acts. Consider America's backing for human rights violators; Saudi Arabia is a prime example. Recent research shows that hypocrisy concerns motivated the United States to support autocratic clients "offstage" by using less visible means like arms transfers and military aid rather than defense pacts and high-profile leadership visits.[99] Relatedly, it is noteworthy that while America's use of torture after 9/11 does indeed go against its moral stance on this issue as exemplified by the UN Convention Against Torture, decision makers engaged in these acts at CIA black sites overseas.[100] Their existence was meant to be secret. A similar point applies to the aforementioned list of U.S. interventions, the majority of which were carried out covertly.

The takeaway is that there is a meaningful difference between brazen and hidden hypocrisy. The fact that much of America's hypocritical behavior over the last seventy years has fallen into the latter category is important. At a minimum, it suggests that decision makers often consider how observers will react to acts that contravene America's moral commitments and change their behavior as a result. By overlooking this distinction, we miss the ways in which powerful states balance the pursuit of national security objectives against concerns about legitimacy and leadership. Table 3.1 summarizes the argument regarding the causal mechanisms and their application in the U.S. context.

[98] Walt, *Taming American Power: The Global Response to U.S. Primacy*, 92. Some of these commitments would also qualify as formal agreements, thereby introducing credibility back into the mix.

[99] Roseanne McManus and Keren Yarhi-Milo, "The Logic of 'Offstage' Signaling: Domestic Politics, Regime Type, and Major Power-Protégé Relations," *International Organization* 71, no. 4 (2017): 701–733.

[100] Jamal Barnes, "Black Sites, 'Extraordinary Renditions' and the Legitimacy of the Torture Taboo," *International Politics* 53, no. 2 (2016): 198–219. See also Charlie Savage, "Trump Poised to Lift Ban on C.I.A. 'Black Site' Prisons," *New York Times* Jan. 25 (2017), https://www.nytimes.com/2017/01/25/us/politics/cia-detainee-prisons.html.

Table 3.1. **Credibility, Hypocrisy, and the United States**

View of Nonintervention	*Costs of Violations*	*U.S.-Specific Concerns*
Formal agreement to behave in agreed-upon ways	Undermines trust and credibility of commitments	Antithetical to policy of strategic restraint
Endorsement of a moral and normative principle	Imposes hypocrisy costs and diminishes moral authority	Erodes legitimacy of U.S. leadership role

Before concluding this section, a point of clarification pertaining to audiences is in order. In the argument presented here, it is the reaction of allies and client states to potential violations of the nonintervention principle that U.S. decision makers are most worried about. In the context of the postwar order, these actors are the ones that should be most sensitive to indications that the United States is no longer committed to exercising strategic restraint and legitimate leadership. While the reaction of friendly states within the region where an intervention transpired may take precedence over more distant partners, violations in one part of the world, especially when it involves something as significant as foreign-imposed regime change, should have global ramifications.

Rival states matter as well, albeit less directly. Brazen violations of nonintervention may enable adversaries to call attention to America's hypocrisy and lack of trustworthiness, potentially leading to defections among adherents to the order. Furthermore, these violations potentially set a precedent that makes it harder for the United States to sanction rivals should they engage in similar behavior in the future.

Finally, domestic audiences within the United States itself, while not necessarily indifferent to violations of international law in general, should be less relevant in this context. Previous research has shown that agreements which require governments to make internal adjustments, whether in the form of limiting carbon emissions or curbing human rights abuses, are especially likely to invoke the sensibilities and attention of publics.[101] When it comes to agreements exclusively aimed at governing interstate relations like nonintervention, they may care less relative to the states that would be impacted directly or indirectly.

[101] Xinyuan Dai, "Why Comply? The Domestic Constituency Mechanism," *International Organization* 59, no. 2 (2005): 363–398; Simmons, *Mobilizing for Human Rights: International Law and Domestic Politics.*

Lingering Questions

One lingering question is why, if my argument is right, do decision makers not always pursue covert action? The answer has already been alluded to in several places: it is not a silver bullet. The plausible deniability requirement central to covert operations introduces challenges that are either absent or exist to a lesser degree for overt missions. Interveners who are serious about hiding their sponsorship of an operation almost always have to make choices that curtail effectiveness.

As noted in Chapter 1, covert operations typically require outsourcing to local actors so that the mission looks indigenous. This can create problems of control. Relying on foreign actors who are not directly under the supervision of the intervening state has the potential to create confusion "partly because the chain of command is more ambiguous and less reliable."[102] Moreover, the supported actors may not share the same objectives as the intervening state. Gregory Treverton, the former chairman of the National Intelligence Council, writes that "[t]he link between U.S. intentions and the actions of those foreigners the United States supports is often tenuous at best. They are acting; the United States is only helping. 'Their' purposes may not be 'ours.' . . . Since their relationship to the United States is meant to be secret, the CIA is often in a weak position for compelling them to act to suit American purposes."[103]

Finally, the plausible deniability requirement of covert action means that interveners are limited in the kind of support they can offer. This constraint is vexing for highly capable states like the United States, who may be unable to provide advanced weaponry if they want to keep their involvement secret.[104] As we will see in the next chapter, Bay of Pigs planners opted not to provide Cuban exiles with state-of-the-art aircraft since doing so would have shown America's hand. Instead, they used outdated bombers from WWII that could have reasonably been obtained by the exiles on their own.[105] None of these limitations are relevant when deniability is not a concern.

Another lingering issue has to do with selection bias.[106] This book only examines cases where decision makers have already decided on a policy of

[102] Charles R. Beitz, "Covert Intervention as a Moral Problem," *Ethics and International Affairs* 3, no. 94 (1989): 50.

[103] Gregory F. Treverton, *Covert Action: The Limits of Intervention in the Postwar World* (New York: Basic Books, Inc., 1987), 118.

[104] O'Rourke, *Covert Regime Change: America's Secret Cold War*, 53–54.

[105] Peter Kornbluh, ed., *Bay of Pigs Declassified: The Secret CIA Report on the Invasion of Cuba* (New York: The New Press, 1998), 55–56.

[106] Gary King, Robert O. Keohane, and Sydney Verba, *Designing Social Inquiry: Scientific Inference in Qualitative Research* (Princeton, NJ: Princeton University Press, 1994), 130.

regime change and must make a subsequent choice to conduct an operation covertly or overtly. Because leaders always have the option of doing nothing rather than intervening, I am technically truncating the dependent variable from three potential outcomes to two. The question, then, is whether this impairs my argument.

In order for the exclusion of cases of no intervention to bias the findings, the reasons leaders select into an intervention would also have to affect their decision to use plausibly deniable or attributable means. The literature identifies myriad motives for states to alter domestic authority structures abroad, including geopolitics,[107] ideology,[108] economics,[109] and the beliefs[110] and psychological biases[111] of leaders. The cases demonstrate that many of these factors, especially geopolitics, ideology, and economic considerations, were present across cases of both covert and overt regime change. Though imperfect, this somewhat reduces concerns that the causes of regime change also influenced conduct.[112]

Related to this issue is the question of whether it matters if the causal factors in my framework are also present in cases where there was no intervention. It does not. The presence or absence of legal exemptions is a necessary but insufficient cause of overt and covert regime change. In other words, I accept the possibility that there are cases where legal exemptions were available and leaders

[107] Karen A. Feste, *Intervention: Shaping the Global Order* (Westport, CT: Praeger Publishers, 2003), 3; Michael G. Findley and Tze Kwang Teo, "Rethinking Third-Party Interventions into Civil Wars: An Actor-Centric Approach," *Journal of Politics* 68, no. 4 (2006): 828–837; Stephen E. Gent, "Strange Bedfellows: The Strategic Dynamics of Major Power Military Interventions," *Journal of Politics* 69, no. 4 (2007): 1089–1102; Mi Yung Yoon, "Explaining U.S. Intervention in Third World Internal Wars, 1945–1989," *Journal of Conflict Resolution* 41, no. 4 (1997): 594.

[108] John M. Owen, "The Foreign Imposition of Domestic Institutions," *International Organization* 56, no. 2 (2002): 375–409; John M. Owen, *The Clash of Ideas in World Politics: Transnational Networks, States, and Regime Change, 1510–2010* (Princeton, NJ: Princeton University Press, 2010). On the promotion of liberalism and democracy in particular, see Jonathan Monten, "The Roots of the Bush Doctrine," *International Security* 29, no. 4 (2005): 112–156; Mark Peceny, *Democracy at the Point of Bayonets* (University Park, PA: Pennsylvania State University Press, 1999).

[109] Aysegul Aydin, *Foreign Powers and Intervention in Armed Conflicts* (Stanford, CA: Stanford University Press, 2012); Finnemore, *The Purpose of Intervention: Changing Beliefs About the Use of Force*; Benjamin O. Fordham, "Power or Plenty? Economic Interests, Security Concerns, and American Intervention," *International Studies Quarterly* 52, no. 4 (2008): 737–758; Stephen Kinzer, *Overthrow: America's Century of Regime Change from Hawaii to Iraq* (New York: Times Books, 2006).

[110] Elizabeth N. Saunders, *Leaders at War: How Presidents Shape Military Interventions* (Ithaca, NY: Cornell University Press, 2011).

[111] Jeffrey W. Taliaferro, *Balancing Risks: Great Power Intervention in the Periphery* (Ithaca, NY: Cornell University Press, 2004).

[112] While it is technically possible that the emergence of legal exemptions in cases where leaders were not already planning on intervening could create a desire to do so, I assume that interventions are generally driven by non-legal considerations which, when met, result in a search for fig leaves.

chose not to pursue intervention at all. Similarly, there may be cases where legal exemptions were unavailable and leaders declined to act.[113] There are a host of reasons why either of these outcomes might occur. Decision makers lacking legal exemptions from the nonintervention principle may refrain from intervening rather than going secret if they have no capacity to carry out covert action. It is only problematic for my theory if leaders pursue overt action *in spite of* having no viable legal exemption or if leaders pursue covert action *despite* having a legal exemption they could have appealed to. Either would suggest that factors other than international law were driving secrecy decisions.

Research Design

This section discusses the research design employed in this book. I begin by outlining my case selection strategy and identifying its strengths and limitations. I then discuss the methodology I use to test my theory against alternative arguments and describe the sources I rely on to perform this exercise.

Case Selection

The universe of cases to which my theory applies are regime-change operations, both covert and overt, undertaken against the backdrop of a codified nonintervention principle.[114] In terms of a temporal threshold, I chose 1945 as the relevant starting point. Theoretically I could have selected 1936 after the United States and Latin American nations agreed to a nonintervention pledge in Buenos Aires. There are several reasons why I did not. First, as noted in Chapter 2, while there were no major interventions in this period by the most powerful actor in that region—the United States—this was driven in large part by the lack of domestic appetite for foreign ventures due to the Great Depression and the prevalence of friendly dictators in the region. As Friedman and Long note, this made it fairly easy for the United States to abide by its promise to respect nonintervention.[115] These confounders make it hard to draw inferences about the independent effect of international law. That said, to the extent that this pledge did

[113] For a similar discussion, see O'Rourke, *Covert Regime Change: America's Secret Cold War*, 19.

[114] On the importance of identifying a universe of cases, see Alexander L. George and Andrew Bennett, *Case Studies and Theory Development in the Social Sciences* (Cambridge, MA: Belfer Center for Science and International Affairs, 2005), 69.

[115] Max Paul Friedman and Tom Long, "Soft Balancing in the Americas: Latin American Opposition to U.S. Intervention, 1898–1936," *International Security* 40, no. 1 (2015): 148.

disincentivize overt intervention by the United States against its neighbors, this would be theory-consistent.

Second, and as also noted in Chapter 2, the Buenos Aires declaration—that "[i]ntervention by one State in the internal or external affairs of another State is condemned"—is relatively vague in its parameters. It is not clear whether intervention under any circumstance was outlawed or whether it was merely viewed as a normatively bad thing to do.[116] Although it is impossible to say because it was never tested, it is plausible that this ambiguity would have made it easier for the United States to overtly intervene without being in obvious violation of the agreement.[117] The UN Charter and subsequent regional charters like the OAS offer considerably greater discussion of such words and their meanings. This additional clarity regarding legitimate standards of behavior makes for a tougher test of my theory.

Within these temporal parameters, I focus specifically on regime-change operations carried out by the United States. I argued earlier that the United States should be particularly sensitive to the causal mechanisms underpinning my argument, especially in the postwar world, owing to its interest in showing strategic restraint and safeguarding its leadership position. There are also practical reasons for this focus. Studying any form of secrecy in international politics, whether secret alliances or secret diplomatic initiatives and the like, is challenging because the actors in question are working hard to conceal what has transpired.[118] Covert regime change is no exception. Fortunately, studying America's secret interventions in this period offers an unusually candid window into how leaders made decisions.[119] Government documents older than twenty-five years are subject to mandatory review for potential declassification

[116] The explicit use of legal language in the two principles surrounding this pledge—a proscription on conquest and declaring forcible debt collection illegal—only adds to the confusion surrounding its precise meaning. See "Declaration of Principles of Inter-American Solidarity and Cooperation; December 21, 1936," The Avalon Project, 1936, https://avalon.law.yale.edu/20th_century/intam07.asp.

[117] Abram Chayes and Antonia Handler Chayes, "On Compliance," *International Organization* 47, no. 2 (1993): 188–192.

[118] Jonathan N. Brown and Anthony S. Marcum, "Avoiding Audience Costs: Domestic Political Accountability and Concessions in Crisis Diplomacy," *Security Studies* 20, no. 2 (2011): 141–170; Jonathan N. Brown, "The Sound of Silence: Power, Secrecy, and International Audiences in US Military Basing Negotiations," *Conflict Management and Peace Science* 31, no. 4 (2014): 406–431; Austin Carson and Keren Yarhi-Milo, "Covert Communication: The Intelligibility and Credibility of Signaling in Secret," *Security Studies* 26, no. 1 (2017): 124–156; Keren Yarhi-Milo, "Tying Hands Behind Closed Doors: The Logic and Practice of Secret Reassurance," *Security Studies* 22 (2013): 405–435.

[119] Levin, "When the Great Power Gets a Vote: The Effects of Great Power Electoral Interventions on Election Results," 198; O'Rourke, *Covert Regime Change: America's Secret Cold War*, 2.

and dissemination to the public.[120] The combination of various high-profile Congressional investigations and internal government reports have also uncovered many of the covert operations carried out by the United States, especially during the Cold War (roughly 1947–1989).[121] Relevant examples include the Church Committee investigations in the mid-1970s and the Family Jewels report commissioned by former CIA Director James Schlesinger in 1973 which leaked to the press, among others.[122] Finally, journalistic efforts to identify and expose U.S. covert operations have brought to light much of what officials intended to keep secret.[123]

With this in mind, I test my argument against four cases of U.S.-led regime change in Latin America during the Cold War, two covert and two overt. The cases, in the order they appear, are as follows:

- *Operation ZAPATA*. A covert operation authorized by President Dwight D. Eisenhower in March 1960 and carried out by President John F. Kennedy in April 1961 to covertly overthrow Cuba's revolutionary leader, Fidel Castro.
- *Project FUBELT*. A covert operation authorized by President Richard Nixon which began in the summer of 1970 and ended on September 11, 1973, to covertly overthrow Salvador Allende.
- *Operation Power Pack*. An overt invasion of the Dominican Republic authorized by President Lyndon B. Johnson in April 1965 to prevent leftist rebels from consolidating power and establishing a "second Cuba" after they seized control of Santo Domingo, the capital city.
- *Operation Urgent Fury*. An overt invasion authorized by President Ronald Reagan in October 1983 to forcibly remove the New Jewel Movement from power in Grenada.

I selected these cases for several reasons. First, the Western Hemisphere has useful properties when it comes to testing my argument against alternatives. For starters, it is a least-likely place for observing the constraining effect of

[120] Perina, "Black Holes and Open Secrets: The Impact of Covert Action on International Law," 545–546. This does not mean that documents will necessarily become available after twenty-five years. Relevant agencies may keep documents classified for a much longer period of time for a variety of reasons, including protection of sources and methods. See Executive Order 135206, available at: https://www.cia.gov/library/readingroom/rights/exec_order.

[121] Perina, 546–547.

[122] Brent Durbin, *The CIA and the Politics of US Intelligence Reform* (New York: Cambridge University Press, 2017), 138; John Prados, *The Family Jewels: The CIA, Secrecy, and Presidential Power* (Austin, TX: University of Texas Press, 2013).

[123] Michael F. Joseph and Michael Poznansky, "Media Technology, Covert Action, and the Politics of Exposure," *Journal of Peace Research* 55, no. 3 (2018): 320–335.

international law.[124] It is therefore a hard test for my theory. Scholars tend to flag Latin America as a region where the United States had free rein to do as it pleased.[125] If decision makers worried about hypocrisy and credibility here, my claims will be strengthened. Moreover, escalation-based theories should have less salience than in other, more contested regions owing to the spheres of influence system that characterized the Cold War, making it easier to rule this out as a possibility. Nevertheless, I still evaluate the plausibility of such arguments in all four cases. This is especially important for the Bay of Pigs in light of events that succeeded it, namely the Cuban Missile Crisis. Finally, nationalism should have been particularly salient in Latin America in this period. Chapter 2 detailed the decades-long effort of states and leaders in this part of the world to prevent U.S. interventions. If it can be shown that international legal commitments were as or more important than concerns about stirring up nationalism in the covert cases, this will provide powerful support for my theory. In the overt cases, demonstrating that legal exemptions mattered more than things like common perceptions of a shared threat would also bolster my argument.

Second, these cases exhibit variation on the dependent variable. Ensuring that my theory can explain both covert and overt regime change is important for avoiding a form of selection on the dependent variable, namely a no-variance research design.[126] Although it was the dominant form of U.S. intervention in the Cold War, strictly focusing on covert action might bias my conclusions.[127]

Third, these cases hold constant several possible confounders that might otherwise explain the outcome of interest. All four targets of intervention are situated in the Western Hemisphere, America's sphere of influence, and involved efforts to oust left-leaning regimes. Three of the four cases fall outside of détente, a brief period marked by improved relations between the United States and the Soviet Union in the early- to mid-1970s. The remaining case, the covert operation against Salvador Allende, was first authorized in the pre-détente period, although it continued for several years after.

Fourth, each pair of cases contains variation in the causal beliefs of the presidents, mitigating concerns that such differences are driving decisions. The covert cases involve two "externally focused" presidents (Eisenhower and Nixon), defined as "leaders [who] diagnose threats directly from the foreign and security

[124] George and Bennett, *Case Studies and Theory Development in the Social Sciences*, 121.

[125] Ikenberry, *Liberal Leviathan: The Origins, Crisis, and Transformation of the American World Order*, 90–91.

[126] King, Keohane, and Verba, *Designing Social Inquiry: Scientific Inference in Qualitative Research*, 129–130.

[127] Barbara Geddes, "How the Cases You Choose Affect the Answers You Get: Selection Bias in Comparative Politics," *Political Analysis* 2 (1990): 131–150.

policies of other states regardless of domestic institutions" and one "internally focused" president (Kennedy), or "leaders [who] see a causal connection between threatening or aggressive foreign and security policies and the internal organization of states."[128] The overt action cases involve both an externally focused (Johnson) and an internally focused (Reagan) president.

Despite the benefits of this research design, there are inevitably drawbacks. One is external validity, particularly across space and time. In terms of geography, the fact that the nonintervention principle enshrined in the UN was universal in scope, plus the fact that U.S. decision makers should have been sensitive to brazen violations anywhere on the globe, suggests that the argument should operate beyond Latin America. It is perhaps least applicable when the target country sits directly on the doorstep of a powerful rival. In such cases, escalation concerns may well outweigh considerations of international law.[129] The temporal issue is more complicated. On the one hand, we might expect America's interest in promoting the "New World Order" after the end of the Cold War to render concerns about restraint and legitimacy more salient. On the other hand, it is possible that the disappearance of the Soviet Union lessened the importance of such concerns. All this being said, Chapter 8 provides evidence that the argument indeed travels to other regions and beyond the Cold War period by examining U.S. policy toward Iraq from 1991 to 2003 and Obama's interventions in Libya and Syria.

Another drawback is that while these cases were selected with social science best practices in mind, they give equal emphasis to covert and overt U.S.-led interventions despite the fact that the former predominated in the postwar period.[130] Beyond research design considerations pertaining to variation on the dependent variable, part of the rationale for this decision is that one of the core contributions of the book is showing that international law did not simply incentivize secrecy but also enabled overt action in some cases. Furthermore, both case studies of overt action feature episodes of leaders discreetly attempting regime change in those countries in the absence of legal exemptions. This

[128] Saunders, *Leaders at War: How Presidents Shape Military Interventions*, 5. For more on individual leaders and intervention, see Vaughn P. Shannon and Jonathan W. Keller, "Leadership Style and International Norm Violation: The Case of the Iraq War," *Foreign Policy Analysis* 3, no. 1 (2007): 79–104.

[129] Many observers view the turn to covert action during the joint U.S.–UK operation to overthrow Mohammed Mossadegh in Iran in 1953 being driven by a desire to avoid World War III. See Dale C. Copeland, *Economic Interdependence and War* (Princeton, NJ: Princeton University Press, 2015), 278–282; Francis J. Gavin, "Politics, Power, and U.S. Policy in Iran, 1950–1953," *Journal of Cold War Studies* 1, no. 1 (1999): 59.

[130] See O'Rourke, *Covert Regime Change: America's Secret Cold War*.

provides some semblance of within-case variation that is theory-consistent and elevates the prevalence of covert action overall.

Methodology

In each of the empirical chapters I use process tracing, or the "systematic examination of diagnostic evidence selected and analyzed in light of research questions and hypotheses posed by the investigator."[131] The cases also follow the logic of "structured, focused comparison." They are structured in that I ask a similar set of questions across each pair. They are focused in that I am not "address[ing] all the interesting aspects of a historical event."[132] Rather, I home in on the aspect of each case that allows me to see if my theory offers a more compelling explanation of a specific decision—whether to pursue regime change secretly or openly—than alternative explanations.

Each of the competing arguments I examine posits a different independent variable and mechanism to explain the same outcome. In this sense, they can be considered nonexclusive rivals,[133] or what Sherry Zaks calls coincident hypotheses. In practice, leaders may pursue covert action for many reasons. Showing that international law, credibility, and legitimacy mattered in a particular instance does not prove that escalation, domestic politics, or nationalism were irrelevant. As a result, coincident hypotheses "require different pieces of evidence both for corroboration and invalidation."[134] Identifying confirmatory evidence for one argument neither invalidates nor confirms the alternatives. In each of the cases, then, I look at additional evidence to assess the veracity of rival claims on their own terms.[135]

[131] David Collier, "Understanding Process Tracing," *PS: Political Science & Politics* 44, no. 4 (2011): 823. See also Derek Beach and Rasmus B. Pedersen, *Process-Tracing Methods: Foundations and Guidelines* (Ann Arbor, MI: University of Michigan Press, 2013); Andrew Bennett and Jeffrey T. Checkel, eds., *Process Tracing: From Metaphor to Analytic Tool* (Cambridge: Cambridge University Press, 2015).

[132] George and Bennett, *Case Studies and Theory Development in the Social Sciences*, 70.

[133] See Ingo Rohlfing, "Comparative Hypothesis Testing Via Process Tracing," *Sociological Methods and Research* 43, no. 4 (2014): 606–642.

[134] Sherry Zaks, "Relationships Among Rivals (RAR): A Framework for Analyzing Contending Hypotheses in Process Tracing," *Political Analysis* 25, no. 3 (2017): 351.

[135] There have been significant advances in process tracing with regard to the use of Bayesian methods; see Tasha Fairfield and Andrew E. Charman, "Explicit Bayesian Analysis for Process Tracing: Guidelines, Opportunities, and Caveats," *Political Analysis* 25, no. 3 (2017): 363–380; Macartan Humphreys and Alan M. Jacobs, "Mixing Methods: A Bayesian Approach," *American Political Science Review* 109, no. 4 (2015): 653–673. As Zaks has pointed out, however, such approaches are easiest when the rival explanations under consideration are mutually exclusive, and is much harder in cases where hypotheses are coincident; see Zaks, "Relationships Among Rivals (RAR): A Framework for Analyzing Contending Hypotheses in Process Tracing," 353–355.

In evaluating how my theory fares against alternative explanations, I rely on a wide range of sources. Each chapter draws liberally from prior accounts written by historians and political scientists on the specific episode in question. Additionally, I draw from thousands of pages of declassified documents and other primary sources I gathered from the John F. Kennedy, Lyndon B. Johnson, Richard Nixon, and Ronald Reagan Presidential Libraries as well as numerous online collections—including the CIA's CREST system, the *Foreign Relations of the United States* series, and the *Digital National Security Archives*. I also conducted interviews with former senior officials who offered firsthand insights into how presidents make intervention decisions.[136] These sources allowed me to reconstruct the decision-making process leading up to intervention decisions.

Observable Implications

This section identifies observable implications that will help guide the evaluation of evidence in the following chapters. The first and most important task is to identify the kinds of things I would expect decision makers to say and do if my legal theory of covert action is correct.

At a general level, I expect decision makers to evaluate the existence and credibility of legal exemptions carefully in the lead-up to an intervention decision and to reject operationally superior overt options when none are available. We can think of the former as the *legal evaluation* phase and the latter as the *legal constraint* stage. Showing that such a process transpired across all four cases is important, but it is only half the battle. Getting from congruence to causal explanation requires substantiating the causal mechanisms or the reasons leaders give for following this logic.

In the covert cases, I expect decision makers to search for legal exemptions to the nonintervention principle to justify overt intervention and to come up short. They should also agree to hypothetically pursue overt action if one or more materializes. Some of the most powerful evidence for my theory would be leaders clearly stating that they were sticking with secrecy because a credible exemption was unavailable. Short of that, the mere existence of these discussions in light of the fact that covert action transpired would be highly suggestive. This kind of evidence speaks to the counterfactual.

In terms of validating mechanisms in the two covert cases, decision makers should appeal to the prospect of incurring hypocrisy and credibility costs as

[136] These include the Executive Secretary of the NSC under Reagan (Robert Kimmitt) and the Deputy Director for Analysis at the CIA (John Helgerson) and Deputy Director of the CIA (Richard Kerr), both under George H.W. Bush.

constraints on their ability to openly intervene without a legal exemption to nonintervention. Recognition of hypocrisy costs might take the form of references to moral standing and the legitimacy of the U.S. leadership position. Recognition of credibility concerns might take the form of references to America's commitment to strategic restraint and the rules-based international order.

An interesting question that arises from this discussion is how explicit officials must be about international legal concerns for me to count it as supportive evidence. What happens, for example, if U.S. decision makers appeal to the immorality of regime change without linking it to international law? While such statements would be less compelling than if such concerns were directly tied to the nonintervention principle, the two may be more closely tethered than it first appears. In his recounting of the Cuban Missile Crisis, Abram Chayes, the former Legal Advisor at the State Department, pushes back against the notion that contemporaneous references to the moral costs of attacking Cuba absent explicit discussion of law means that the latter was irrelevant. "It is true," he writes, "that the norm was adduced as a moral not a legal one . . . . No one stood up and said, 'And besides, in addition to being immoral, an air strike is the very kind of conduct forbidden by Article 2(4).' But it is hard to believe that men as familiar as these with the law in general and the specific international-law context of the situation before them could have been unaware or even unmindful of the legal overtones of the moral proposition." Chayes goes on: "Whatever the general relationship between law and morals, it seems to me that at the level of the use of force in the classic sense, as at the level of homicide in domestic law, legal norm and moral precept are two expressions of the same deep human imperative."[137]

With this in mind, the best-case scenario for my theory is still leaders tying discussions of morality, credibility, and prestige to violations of nonintervention. This is particularly valuable since leaders may invoke similar concerns for reasons that have nothing to do with law.[138] Nevertheless, evidence of decision makers generally discussing hypocrisy and credibility independently of nonintervention would still count as suggestive evidence in favor of my argument, especially if there are additional instances in which the two are clearly tied together and alternative sources of the same costs can be ruled out with a reasonable level of confidence. This latter dynamic is important to explore in cases like U.S. intervention Chile, where the fact that the target was a democracy may generate similar concerns about credibility and hypocrisy.

[137] Abram Chayes, *The Cuban Missile Crisis: International Crises and the Role of Law* (New York and London: Oxford University Press, 1974), 39–40.

[138] This is especially true for terms like *prestige* and *credibility*, which may refer to things like mission success or resolve, none of which are germane to the theory I am advancing.

The evidence I would expect to see in the overt cases is different. First, leaders should search for legal exemptions as a means of justifying open intervention and be successful in their pursuit. With one or more of these exemptions in hand, leaders should seek to persuade foreign observers that overt intervention is justifiable according to extant international legal standards. This would include leaning heavily on the given legal justifications and referring to treaty law, precedent, and past practice when framing their rationale. Ideally, they should also reject alternative, non-legal justifications on the grounds that these would not be accepted according to existing standards. Evidence that decision makers might have opted for covert action instead if exemptions were unavailable would be particularly strong evidence in favor of my argument. This may come in the form of deliberations wherein this option is discussed in the hours and days leading up to an intervention or by way of earlier attempts at covert action to accomplish regime change before legal exemptions were available.

The foregoing captures the key observable implications associated with my theory. But there are a number of additional ones that follow from the argument as well. One is that when leaders find a legal exemption to nonintervention, the ensuing operation should be constrained by the justification being offered. Put differently, if leaders use legal exemptions to ameliorate hypocrisy and credibility costs, they should be sensitive to charges that their rationale for intervention is a contrived pretext. The decision-making process during Desert Storm captures this phenomenon. A series of UN Security Council resolutions provided legal cover for the United States to lead a military campaign to expel Saddam Hussein from Kuwait but not to pursue full-scale regime change. This partly explains George H.W. Bush's reluctance to extend the military operation into Iraq despite the fact, as he put it, that "[n]one of us minded if [Saddam] was killed in the course of an air attack."[139] In his joint memoir, Bush writes: "I firmly believed that we should not march into Baghdad. Our stated mission, as codified in UN resolutions, was a simple one—end the aggression, knock Iraq's forces out of Kuwait, and restore Kuwait's leaders. To occupy Iraq would instantly shatter our coalition, turning the whole Arab world against us, and make a broken tyrant into a latter-day Arab hero. It would have taken us way beyond the imprimatur of international law bestowed by the resolutions of the Security Council."[140]

Second, if the primary legal exemption decision makers use to justify an initial deployment of forces is narrow with a short shelf life—rescuing endangered nationals, for instance—I would expect them to search for additional exemptions as a way of maintaining an overt regime change operation. Possibilities include

[139] George Bush and Brent Scowcroft, *A World Transformed* (New York: Alfred A. Knopf, 1998), 463.

[140] Bush and Scowcroft, 464.

authorization from an international organization like the UN or OAS. Relatedly, once the legal exemptions leaders have invoked are no longer relevant, they should revert to covert action if further meddling is desired, or seek out additional exemptions that would justify staying on.[141]

Third, leaders interested in pursuing regime change should weigh relevant legal considerations regardless of whether they are contemplating forcible or nonforcible methods of intervention. However, the legal restrictions on each class of actions may vary by case. This is especially true across regions. Recall from Chapter 2 that the core nonintervention provision pertaining to states in the UN Charter, Article 2(4), only prohibits the use or threat of force without a legal exemption, whereas the OAS Charter also prohibits economic and political meddling. In practice, then, leaders considering regime change in Latin America should search for legal exemptions regardless of whether they are planning to put boots on the ground or destabilize the target's economy. In regions lacking an equivalent to the OAS Charter's broad provision, overt actions short of force may not entail such considerations.

Just as important as outlining the evidence we would expect to see if the theory I am advancing is correct is some discussion of what types of evidence would falsify it.[142] As intimated earlier, overt interventions that do not rely on international legal commitments would be inconsistent with my argument. States openly pursuing regime change in blatant disregard of the nonintervention principle would run counter to claims that international law serves as a constraint on such behavior. In a different vein, if leaders can easily manufacture incidents or crises that they can exploit as legal justification for overt intervention, this would also undermine my argument. The covert cases are particularly useful for evaluating this possibility. Evidence that states could have invented a pretext for overt action but chose to opt for secrecy anyway due to any number of other reasons would be inconsistent with my thesis.

The alternative arguments discussed at the top of this chapter each have their own distinct observable implications. Theories of domestic politics predict that leaders will pursue covert regime change in cases when they anticipate that their own constituencies would disapprove of intervention. Leaders who end up relying on covert action should express concern that openly intervening against a fellow democracy or intervening to install a brutal autocrat, for example, would invite the public's wrath. When states do turn to overt action, this decision should be facilitated by an awareness that the public approves of

[141] A corollary of this is that if leaders begin a covert operation owing to the absence of a legal exemption, they may switch to overt action should one become available.

[142] On the importance of falsifiability, see King, Keohane, and Verba, *Designing Social Inquiry: Scientific Inference in Qualitative Research*, 100–105.

the operation in question. The tainted victory thesis focuses on an entirely different set of factors. In cases of covert regime change, we would expect leaders to voice concern that openly intervening would lead to a backlash from the target's population. References to inciting nationalism and avoiding the appearance of occupation would each qualify. Conversely, if leaders do go overt, they should point to the fact that the population shares their perception of the threat, has expressed recognition that intervention is necessary, and believes that the operation will be short in duration.

Part of my rationale for focusing on U.S. intervention in the Western Hemisphere is to rule out escalation as an explanation for covert action. Nevertheless, it is still worth saying something about the observable implications of this alternative since it shows up as a relevant factor in some of the cases. Escalation-based theories predict that leaders will act covertly whenever they believe that regime change would trigger retaliation of some kind from a powerful rival state. Evidence that leaders pursued secrecy to avoid a direct, or even an indirect, confrontation with an adversary would support this argument. Overt action is most likely when such concerns are muted. Leaders discussing a rival's lack of interest in the state being openly targeted would lend credence to the escalation thesis. So too would evidence that a rival had little capacity to respond to intervention. Table 3.2 offers a summary of my theory's predictions as well those of the alternative arguments.

Table 3.2. **Summary of Theoretical Predictions**

	Legal Theory	*Domestic Politics*	*Tainted Victory*	*Escalation*
Audience being deceived	International audiences	Domestic constituencies	Target population	Geopolitical rivals
Rationale for plausible deniability	Avoid hypocrisy costs and preserve strategic restraint	Avoid punishment at home	Avoid triggering nationalist backlash	Avoid igniting large-scale war
When interveners will go overt	When there exists a legal exemption to nonintervention	When there is public support for intervention	Agreed need for intervention, shared threat, credible promise to leave	When concerns over escalation are low

Conclusion

This chapter developed a theoretical framework to explain why leaders interested in regime change turn to covert action in some cases but not in others. I argued that international law plays an important role in this process. When leaders are able to find legal exemptions to the nonintervention principle, they are more likely to opt for overt regime change. When legal exemptions are unavailable, leaders will instead turn to covert regime change to avoid incurring hypocrisy costs and protect their credibility. A portion of the chapter was devoted to explaining why the United States was particularly susceptible to these dynamics. The next four chapters test this argument empirically.

4

Operation Zapata: Cuba

Operation Zapata was a plan hatched by the Eisenhower administration and carried out by the Kennedy administration to covertly topple Fidel Castro between 1960 and 1961.[1] America's role was supposed to remain secret. Notwithstanding the year-long preparation, the mission was a failure. The Bay of Pigs invasion, as it came to be called, contributed to one of the most dangerous events of the entire twentieth century. According to Peter Wyden, "[i]f Kennedy had not been thoroughly defeated by Castro on the beaches in 1961, Nikita Khrushchev almost certainly would not have dared to precipitate the Cuban Missile Crisis of 1962—the crisis which, in the words of former CIA Director William E. Colby, pushed the world 'as close to Armageddon' as it had ever come."[2]

Much ink has been spilled over the years examining the reasons why the Bay of Pigs failed, ranging from Kennedy's decision to cancel air support for the Cuban exiles at the last minute to obfuscation by various policymakers as well as the failure to subject shared but faulty assumptions to close scrutiny.[3] What existing work has neglected to grapple with directly is why the mission was covert to begin with.[4] Secondary accounts provide some clues. But there exists no

[1] The military's moniker for the operation was Bumpy Road.

[2] Peter Wyden, *Bay of Pigs: The Untold Story* (New York: Simon and Schuster, 1979), 7.

[3] James G. Blight and Peter Kornbluh, eds., *Politics of Illusion: The Bay of Pigs Invasion Reexamined* (Boulder, CO: Lynne Reinner Publishers, 1998); Rebecca R. Friedman, "Crisis Management at the Dead Center: The 1960–1961 Presidential Transition and the Bay of Pigs Fiasco," *Presidential Studies Quarterly* 41, no. 2 (2011): 307–333; Piero Gleijeses, "Ships in the Night: The CIA, the White House and the Bay of Pigs," *Journal of Latin American Studies* 27, no. 1 (1995): 1–42; Richard E. Neustadt and Ernest R. May, *Thinking In Time: The Uses Of History For Decision Makers* (New York: The Free Press, 1986), 134–156; Arthur Schlesinger Jr., *A Thousand Days: John F. Kennedy in the White House* (New York: Mariner Books, 1965); Lucien S. Vandenbroucke, "Anatomy of a Failure: The Decision to Land at the Bay of Pigs," *Political Science Quarterly* 99, no. 3 (1984): 471–491.

[4] An exception is Westra, who devotes part of a chapter to explaining why the Bay of Pigs was covert. See Joel H. Westra, *International Law and the Use of Armed Force: The UN Charter and the Major Powers* (London and New York: Routledge, 2007), 71–77.

In the Shadow of International Law. Michael Poznansky, Oxford University Press (2020). © Oxford University Press.
DOI: 10.1093/oso/9780190096595.001.0001

systematic analysis of the decision to pursue a covert rather than an overt operation. In addition to serving as the first empirical test of my argument, this chapter also fills a void in the historiography of this case.

Such an exercise is all the more important when considering that the decision to go covert was puzzling. As noted at various points, Cuba was in America's sphere of influence. This should have lessened concerns about escalation. An overt intervention would have also signaled resolve. Moreover, decision makers did not have to worry about incurring a hostile reaction from the American public for toppling a fellow democratic regime; Castro's Cuba was a dictatorship at the time. This episode is also a hard test for my argument in light of the conventional wisdom that the United States—for many of the reasons just cited—was unconstrained in the Western Hemisphere.[5] Demonstrating the impact of international law here sets the tone for the empirical chapters that follow.

Before proceeding, it will be helpful to identify the kind of evidence we would expect to see if my theory is correct. First, decision makers should express awareness that toppling Castro without a legal exemption to nonintervention would make the United States appear hypocritical and damage its credibility and trustworthiness. References to America's moral authority and public opinion in the Western Hemisphere and around the globe would serve as an approximation of the former set of concerns. Statements regarding the need to maintain faith in America's commitment to strategic restraint and its obligations in international institutions would approximate the latter. Second, decision makers should search for legal exemptions that would enable them to act openly against Castro at reduced risk and ultimately come up short. Possibilities include the presence of American nationals in imminent danger, attacks on Guantanamo Bay, and authorization from an international body like the UN Security Council or the OAS.

Historical Background

America's interests in Cuba increased markedly in 1898 with the onset of the Spanish American War.[6] After assisting the Cuban people in their struggle for independence, the United States imposed a set of restrictions on their autonomy. The embodiment of this was the Platt Amendment, which gave the United States the right to intervene to ensure the country's independence and protect life,

[5] G. John Ikenberry, *Liberal Leviathan: The Origins, Crisis, and Transformation of the American World Order* (Princeton, NJ: Princeton University Press, 2011), 90–91.

[6] Jonathan Monten, "The Roots of the Bush Doctrine," *International Security* 29, no. 4 (2005): 132–133.

property, and liberty.[7] For years afterward, the relationship between the two nations was dictated by Platt. Overt intervention in 1906 to put down a rebellion was a stark reminder.[8]

Following several tumultuous decades fraught with strife and foreign intervention, Cuba adopted a new constitution in 1940, ushering in twelve years of representative rule. The country's short-lived experiment with democracy ended in 1952 when Cuba's former president, Fulgencio Batista, staged a military coup. U.S. support for the new regime was automatic.[9] The Eisenhower administration "practiced the traditional U.S. policy of supporting Cubans who kept the island secure and stable and protected U.S. investments."[10] Reflexively backing Batista was part of this strategy.

Fidel Castro's first attempt to oust Batista occurred on July 26, 1953. It was unsuccessful. Less than six years later on New Year's Day in 1959, "Castro's forces drove [Batista] into exile and . . . seized control of the government. The Eisenhower administration quickly extended recognition to the fledgling regime, praising its assurances of democratic elections and fundamental freedoms."[11] The honeymoon period did not last long.[12] Two weeks after taking power, Castro announced his intention to set Cuba on a new path, asserting that Platt would no longer govern relations with the United States. "By the end of 1959," Jones writes, "the White House had escalated its efforts, now determined to *remove* Castro either by covert means or, perhaps, by assassination. In December the CIA considered two programs intended to prepare Cubans for paramilitary operations aimed at overthrowing the regime."[13] The rivalry that emerged would color U.S.–Cuban relations for the next half-century.

[7] Stephen G Rabe, "The Johnson Doctrine," *Presidential Studies Quarterly* 36, no. 1 (2006): 50.

[8] Philip W. Bonsal, "Cuba, Castro, and the United States," *Foreign Affairs* 45, no. 2 (1967): 261–262.

[9] Howard Jones, *The Bay of Pigs* (Oxford: Oxford University Press, 2008), 9.

[10] Stephen G Rabe, *Eisenhower and Latin America: The Foreign Policy of Anticommunism* (Chapel Hill, NC and London: The University of North Carolina Press, 1988), 120.

[11] Jones, *The Bay of Pigs*, 10.

[12] Friedman, "Crisis Management at the Dead Center: The 1960–1961 Presidential Transition and the Bay of Pigs Fiasco," 310–311. See also FRUS, "423. Memorandum of Discussion at the 432d Meeting of the National Security Council, Washington, January 14, 1960, 9 a.m.," in *Foreign Relations of the United States, 1958–1960, Cuba, Volume VI*, ed. John P. Glennon (Washington, D.C.: United States Government Printing Office, 1991), https://history.state.gov/historicaldocuments/frus1958-60v06/d423.

[13] Jones, *The Bay of Pigs*, 13, emphasis in original. See also Gaddis Smith, *The Last Years of the Monroe Doctrine: 1945–1993* (New York: Hill and Wang, 1994), 97; Rabe, *Eisenhower and Latin America: The Foreign Policy of Anticommunism*, 127.

Why Intervene in Cuba?

The United States pursued regime change against Castro for several reasons. One was ideological, rooted in the Cold War struggle between communism and liberal democracy.[14] As John Owen notes of this period, "Fidel Castro's regime in Cuba, established in 1959, inspired some of the discontented" across Latin America "to embrace communism, and made others willing to cooperate with communists."[15] Decision makers took notice of these developments.[16] For example, Secretary of State Christian Herter wrote to President Eisenhower on November 5, 1959 stating that "the prolonged continuation of the Castro regime in Cuba in its present form would have serious adverse effects on the United States position in Latin America and corresponding advantages for international Communism."[17]

Perhaps most concerning about Cuba's drift toward communism was the prospect of the Soviet Union gaining a new client so close to the U.S. mainland.[18] According to Gaddis Smith, "[k]eeping Cuba out of the hands of a strong and hostile power was one of the oldest objectives of American foreign policy. The island's size and location—the proverbial '90 miles from our shores'—gave it undeniable strategic significance."[19] The Soviets were aware of these fears.

[14] Vandenbroucke, "Anatomy of a Failure: The Decision to Land at the Bay of Pigs," 472.

[15] John M. Owen, *The Clash of Ideas in World Politics: Transnational Networks, States, and Regime Change, 1510–2010* (Princeton, NJ: Princeton University Press, 2010), 194.

[16] "Memorandum [From Dick Goodwin to McGeorge Bundy, April 26, 1961]," *National Security Files, Countries, Cuba - General, 1/61-4/61 [Folder]; Papers of President Kennedy: National Security Files—Countries, Box 35A [Collection]* (JFK Library, 1961), 1–2; Rabe, *Eisenhower and Latin America: The Foreign Policy of Anticommunism*, 117.

[17] Foreshadowing a point made later in this chapter, Herter concluded his memo by writing that, "In view of special sensitivity of Latin America to United States 'intervention,' I would propose that the existence and substance of this current policy statement be held on a very strict 'need-to-know' basis." See FRUS, "387. Memorandum From the Secretary of State to the President," in *Foreign Relations of the United States, 1958–1960, Cuba, Volume VI*, ed. John P. Glennon (Washington, D.C.: United States Government Printing Office, 1991), https://history.state.gov/historicaldocuments/frus1958-60v06/d387. See also FRUS, "402. Memorandum of Discussion at the 426th Meeting of the National Security Council, Washington, December 1, 1959," in *Foreign Relations of the United States, 1958–1960, Cuba, Volume VI*, ed. John P. Glennon (Washington, D.C.: United States Government Printing Office, 1991), https://history.state.gov/historicaldocuments/frus1958-60v06/d402; FRUS, "408. Memorandum of Discussion at the 428th Meeting of the National Security Council, Washington, December 10, 1959," in *Foreign Relations of the United States, 1958–1960, Cuba, Volume VI*, ed. John P. Glennon (Washington, D.C.: United States Government Printing Office, 1991), https://history.state.gov/historicaldocuments/frus1958-60v06/d408.

[18] "Cuba [February 17, 1961]," *National Security Files, Countries, Cuba - General, 1/61-4/61 [Folder]; Papers of President Kennedy: National Security Files—Countries, Box 35A [Collection]* (JFK Library, 1961), 2.

[19] Smith, *The Last Years of the Monroe Doctrine: 1945–1993*, 91.

They worried that the United States "would take action against an identifiable Communist government in Cuba similar to the action . . . taken in Guatemala" in 1954 against Jacobo Arbenz. To forestall this possibility, "the U.S.S.R. was being very clever in not permitting its interest in Cuba to be openly identified."[20] U.S. apprehension continued to grow anyway.[21] In February 1960, Castro extended recognition to the People's Republic of China and entered into a treaty with the Soviets.[22] On January 27, 1961, the Joint Chiefs of Staff cautioned that, "[u]nless the United States takes immediate and forceful action, there is a great and present danger that Cuba will become permanently established as a part of the Communist Bloc, with disastrous consequences to the security of the Western Hemisphere."[23]

Decision makers were also concerned about the future of America's naval base at Guantanamo Bay.[24] According to Jones, "[f]rom the moment Castro came to power, the United States feared that he would try to nullify or renounce the 1903 treaty granting America's hold on that small piece of land."[25] On January 8, 1960, General Nathan Twining warned: "From a military point of view the problem which Castro poses affects us locally because of our base at Guantanamo and strategically because we may find at our doorstep what, to all intents and purposes, amounts to a Soviet satellite."[26] In short, senior officials all "agreed . . . with the general propositions that Communist control of Cuba—either by the USSR or indirectly—would be intolerable."[27] The seeds of intervention were sown.

[20] FRUS, "402. Memorandum of Discussion at the 426th Meeting of the National Security Council, Washington, December 1, 1959."

[21] FRUS, "456. Memorandum of Discussion at the 435th Meeting of the National Security Council, Washington, February 18, 1960," in *Foreign Relations of the United States, 1958–1960, Cuba, Volume VI*, ed. John P. Glennon (Washington, D.C.: United States Government Printing Office, 1991), https://history.state.gov/historicaldocuments/frus1958-60v06/d456.

[22] Jones, *The Bay of Pigs*, 17.

[23] FRUS, "28. Memorandum From the Joint Chiefs of Staff to Secretary of Defense McNamara," in *Foreign Relations of the United States, 1961–1963, Volume X, Cuba, January 1961–September 1962*, ed. Louis J. Smith (Washington, D.C.: United States Government Printing Office, 1997), https://history.state.gov/historicaldocuments/frus1961-63v10/d28.

[24] FRUS, "383. Memorandum From the Assistant Secretary of State for Inter-American Affairs' Special Assistant (Hill) to the Assistant Secretary of State (Rubottom)," in *Foreign Relations of the United States, 1958–1960, Cuba, Volume VI*, ed. John P. Glennon (Washington, D.C.: United States Government Printing Office, 1991), https://history.state.gov/historicaldocuments/frus1958-60v06/d383.

[25] Jones, *The Bay of Pigs*, 31.

[26] FRUS, "419. Memorandum of Discussion at the Department of State-Joint Chiefs of Staff Meeting, Pentagon, Washington, January 8, 1960, 11:30 a.m.," in *Foreign Relations of the United States, 1958–1960, Cuba, Volume VI*, ed. John P. Glennon (Washington, D.C.: United States Government Printing Office, 1991), https://history.state.gov/historicaldocuments/frus1958-60v06/d419.

[27] FRUS, "421. Memorandum for the Record by Robert F. Packard of the Policy Planning Staff," in *Foreign Relations of the United States, 1958–1960, Cuba, Volume VI*, ed. John P. Glennon

The Plan to Overthrow Castro

Plans to unseat Castro began to take shape in early 1960.[28] The creation of Western Hemisphere Task Force 4 (WH/4) on January 18, 1960 marked a first step. The initial sketch of a secret regime-change operation in Cuba was drafted two months later by the 5412 Committee—the group responsible for handling covert action at the time—and signed by Eisenhower on March 17.[29] The objective was "to bring about the replacement of the Castro regime with one more devoted to the true interests of the Cuban people and more acceptable to the U.S. in such a manner as to avoid any appearance of U.S. intervention."[30] From the beginning, Eisenhower admonished his subordinates to keep a tight lip: "Everyone must be prepared to swear that he has not heard of it."[31]

A core component of the covert operation was a propaganda campaign to discredit Castro and generate support among the opposition in Cuba, Miami, and elsewhere.[32] The United States would transmit messages from a tiny island off the coast of Honduras known as Swan Island. The more complicated part entailed inserting exiles throughout Cuba to prosecute a guerrilla war. Training camps would be set up in the Guatemalan countryside.[33] By August 1960, details were falling into place. As one report noted, "[t]he initial phase of paramilitary operations envisages the development, support and guidance of dissident groups in three areas of Cuba: Pinar del Rio, Escambray and Sierra Maestra. These groups will be organized for concerted guerrilla action against the regime. The second phase will be initiated by a combined sea-air assault by FRD forces on the Isle of Pines coordinated with general guerrilla activity on the main island of Cuba .... The last phase will be [an] air assault on the Havana area with the guerrilla forces in Cuba moving on the ground from these areas into the Havana area also."[34]

(Washington, D.C.: United States Government Printing Office, 1991), https://history.state.gov/historicaldocuments/frus1958-60v06/d421.

[28] Early signs that the U.S. was interested in pursuing the ouster of Castro emerged toward the end of 1959. See Gleijeses, "Ships in the Night: The CIA, the White House and the Bay of Pigs," 3–4. See also FRUS, "454. Memorandum of a Conference With the President, White House, Washington, February 17, 1960, 3:17–3:55 p.m.," in *Foreign Relations of the United States, 1958–1960, Cuba, Volume VI1*, ed. John P. Glennon (Washington, D.C.: United States Government Printing Office, 1991), https://history.state.gov/historicaldocuments/frus1958-60v06/d454.

[29] Friedman, "Crisis Management at the Dead Center: The 1960-1961 Presidential Transition and the Bay of Pigs Fiasco," 311.

[30] Peter Kornbluh, ed., *Bay of Pigs Declassified: The Secret CIA Report on the Invasion of Cuba* (New York: The New Press, 1998), 103.

[31] Gleijeses, "Ships in the Night: The CIA, the White House and the Bay of Pigs," 5.

[32] Kornbluh, *Bay of Pigs Declassified: The Secret CIA Report on the Invasion of Cuba*, 107.

[33] Wyden, *Bay of Pigs: The Untold Story*, 34–35.

[34] Kornbluh, *Bay of Pigs Declassified: The Secret CIA Report on the Invasion of Cuba*, 30.

In just a few months, the idea of parachuting exiles into the mountains of Cuba in the hopes of sparking an insurgency was supplanted by something more ambitious and risky.[35] "On 4 November 1960 WH/4 took formal action to change the course of the project by greatly expanding the size of the Cuban paramilitary unit and redirecting its training along more conventional military lines."[36] This modification came to be known as the Trinidad Plan.[37] It called for a joint amphibious and airborne assault on the island wherein the exiles would arrive by boat "at Trinidad, a shore city in southern Cuba reputed to be a hotbed of opposition to Castro" with concurrent close air support as well as additional ground support from guerrillas already stationed in the Escambray Mountains.[38]

The rationale for the Trinidad concept was outlined in a memo from February 1961. In particular, CIA planners feared that inserting guerrillas into the countryside "would not produce a psychological effect sufficient to precipitate general uprisings or wide-spread revolt among disaffected elements of Castro's armed forces."[39] Several failed attempts to land bands of exiles in Cuba without being captured, combined with challenges in getting requisite supplies to those that actually made it, fueled skepticism.

The last major changes to the covert action plan occurred in mid-March 1961 as John F. Kennedy started to make crucial tweaks. On March 11, he was fully briefed on the Trinidad Plan. Kennedy "rejected [it] as 'too spectacular.' He said, 'This is too much like a World War II invasion.' He preferred a 'quiet' landing, preferably at night, with no basis for any American military intervention."[40] This apprehension resulted in the fateful decision to land the exiles at Bahía de Cochinos, or the Bay of Pigs.[41] The President endorsed the new Zapata

[35] FRUS, "612. Editorial Note," in *Foreign Relations of the United States, 1958–1960, Cuba, Volume VI*, ed. John P. Glennon (Washington, D.C.: United States Government Printing Office, 1991), https://history.state.gov/historicaldocuments/frus1958-60v06/d612.

[36] Kornbluh, *Bay of Pigs Declassified: The Secret CIA Report on the Invasion of Cuba*, 32. See also Schlesinger Jr., *A Thousand Days: John F. Kennedy in the White House*, 234.

[37] Jones, *The Bay of Pigs*, 37–38.

[38] Wyden, *Bay of Pigs: The Untold Story*, 89. See also FRUS, "9. Memorandum From the Chief of WH/4/PM, Central Intelligence Agency (Hawkins) to the Chief of WH/4 of the Directorate for Plans (Esterline)," in *Foreign Relations of the United States, 1961–1963, Volume X, Cuba, January 1961–September 1962*, ed. Louis J. Smith (Washington, D.C.: United States Government Printing Office, 1997), https://history.state.gov/historicaldocuments/frus1961-63v10/d9.

[39] Quoted in Gleijeses, "Ships in the Night: The CIA, the White House and the Bay of Pigs," 10–11.

[40] Wyden, *Bay of Pigs: The Untold Story*, 100. See also FRUS, "61. Paper Prepared in the Central Intelligence Agency," in *Foreign Relations of the United States, 1961–1963, Volume X, Cuba, January 1961–September 1962*, ed. Louis J. Smith (Washington, D.C.: United States Government Printing Office, 1997), https://history.state.gov/historicaldocuments/frus1961-63v10/d61; Schlesinger Jr., *A Thousand Days: John F. Kennedy in the White House*, 242–243.

[41] Neustadt and May, *Thinking In Time: The Uses Of History For Decision Makers*, 142–143; Wyden, *Bay of Pigs: The Untold Story*, 101.

Plan on March 16.[42] Utilizing the Bay of Pigs as a landing site ameliorated many of Kennedy's concerns. One benefit was that it was capable of handling B-26 aircraft, the WWII-era bombers being provided to the exiles. It also had "limited access roads," which would make it harder for Castro's forces to intercept the insurgents, giving them time to establish a beachhead.[43] There were several problems with the landing site, however, at least some of which may not have been presented fully to the president. Chief among them was that it was far away from the Escambrays, making it nearly impossible for the exiles to retreat into the mountains if need be or even to receive support from the existing guerrillas operating there.[44]

The invasion was carried out on April 17, 1961. Castro learned that the exiles were coming beforehand, eliminating any element of surprise. His more advanced T-33 fighter jets outmatched the outdated B-26 bombers. Most of the anti-Castro forces were killed or captured during the initial landing. Why the operation failed, while important in its own right, is not relevant for present purposes. Most important is why the plan was covert at all. It is to this question I now turn.

Confronting Legal Constraints

The Eisenhower Years

From the beginning, decision makers in the Eisenhower administration, including the president himself, recognized the risks of openly intervening against Castro. International legal considerations were front and center.[45] On January 23, 1960, less than two months before the first covert action plan was authorized, Eisenhower complained "he is finding that dictators devoted to fomenting disorder can have a terrible influence on our affairs. Except for the existence of the OAS and its abhorrence of intervention, we would have to be thinking already of

[42] FRUS, "66. Editorial Note," in *Foreign Relations of the United States, 1961–1963, Volume X, Cuba, January 1961–September 1962*, ed. Louis J. Smith (Washington, D.C.: United States Government Printing Office, 1997), https://history.state.gov/historicaldocuments/frus1961-63v10/d66.

[43] Friedman, "Crisis Management at the Dead Center: The 1960–1961 Presidential Transition and the Bay of Pigs Fiasco," 326.

[44] Wyden, *Bay of Pigs: The Untold Story*, 101–102.

[45] Rabe, *Eisenhower and Latin America: The Foreign Policy of Anticommunism*, 166. See also FRUS, "464. Memorandum From Edward E. Rice of the Policy Planning Staff to the Assistant Secretary of State for Policy Planning (Smith)," in *Foreign Relations of the United States, 1958–1960, Cuba, Volume VI*, ed. John P. Glennon (Washington, D.C.: United States Government Printing Office, 1991), https://history.state.gov/historicaldocuments/frus1958-60v06/d464.

building up our force at Guantanamo."[46] During a press conference on January 26, Eisenhower "restated U.S. policy toward Cuba," wherein he referenced this issue explicitly. The first item on the list was "[s]trict adherence to the 'policy of nonintervention in the domestic affairs of other countries, including Cuba.' "[47] When analyzed side by side, these comments paint a picture of a president sensitive to the ramifications of openly disregarding nonintervention, which the United States had embraced in various international charters and which Latin American countries took seriously. Absent these constraints, overt action might well have been on the table.

One month later, Admiral Arleigh Burke, the Chief of Naval Operations, penned a memo outlining the pros and cons of a range of proposals for unseating Castro. Burke opened by declaring that "[t]he Castro movement in Cuba is a vehicle by which international communism appears to be gaining a foothold in the Western Hemisphere. If the present trend continues, it will soon be too late for the United States to stem the Soviet incursion into this hemisphere."[48] He then drew attention to the main constraint on America's ability to forcibly respond to the threat: "The United States is bound by treaties which commit it to seek settlement of hemispheric dispute by peaceful means."[49]

In addition to pointing out America's treaty commitment to refrain from forcible interference unless sanctioned by other Latin American nations, Burke also discussed the benefits and risks of specific intervention strategies. The memo identifies three: (1) multilateral intervention through the OAS, (2) unilateral overt intervention, and (3) unilateral covert action. Consistent with my theoretical expectations, the benefits of the first option were that "[i]t would be in consonance with our national policy and our treaty commitments under the OAS" and "would reassure the Free World and the Latin American States of U.S. willingness to live up to commitments." The downsides were that the OAS was unlikely to support such a venture and the prospect that it might

[46] FRUS, "434. Memorandum of a Conference With the President, White House, Washington, January 23, 1960, 8:27–9:50 a.m.," in *Foreign Relations of the United States, 1958–1960, Cuba, Volume VI*, ed. John P. Glennon (Washington, D.C.: United States Government Printing Office, 1991), https://history.state.gov/historicaldocuments/frus1958-60v06/d434.

[47] FRUS, "438. Editorial Note," in *Foreign Relations of the United States, 1958–1960, Cuba, Volume VI*, ed. John P. Glennon (Washington, D.C.: United States Government Printing Office, 1991), https://history.state.gov/historicaldocuments/frus1958-60v06/d438.

[48] FRUS, "466. Letter From the Chief of Naval Operations (Burke) to the Under Secretary of State for Political Affairs (Merchant)," in *Foreign Relations of the United States, 1958–1960, Cuba, Volume VI*, ed. John P. Glennon (Washington, D.C.: United States Government Printing Office, 1991), https://history.state.gov/historicaldocuments/frus1958-60v06/d466.

[49] Ibid.

eventually require a vote at the UN Security Council where the Soviets would almost certainly veto the proposal.

The benefits of unilateral overt action against Castro included showing America's continued commitment to the Monroe Doctrine, "serv[ing] notice to the world that the U.S. will not tolerate the establishment of a communist or communist 'front' regime in the Western Hemisphere." But the costs were deemed significant. Burke argued that "(a) It would violate our OAS commitment to seek settlement by peaceful means; (b) It would lead to charges of aggression against the U.S., both in the OAS and in the United Nations, with the resulting possibility of UN and OAS action against the U.S.; (c) It would prove that the U.S. is not willing to abide by its treaties if U.S. interests dictate otherwise; (d) It could isolate the U.S. from other American states; and (e) It would violate the principle of non-intervention." The third option, unilateral covert action, promised to circumvent many of these risks. The "U.S. would not be charged with aggression," Burke wrote, and "[i]f carried out successfully, Free World and Latin American opinion would be favorable to the U.S." The challenge with this plan was that "[t]here is no certainty of success" and "[t]he effort might well come too late."[50]

It is notable that Burke's concerns about unilateral overt action did not have anything to do with America's physical ability to act against Castro. To the contrary, he believed "[t]he U.S. has the capability to seize Cuba by direct military action, and after a consolidation period, cause the establishment of a friendly, non-communist government."[51] Moreover, Burke was known for having hardline views, rendering his attentiveness to international legal concerns all the more striking.[52]

Burke's proposal was given a boost when it was embraced by the Joint Chiefs of Staff and presented to Secretary of Defense Thomas Gates on March 2, 1960. The memo to Gates first pointed out that Cuba had become a direct threat to the United States under Castro owing to its drift toward "International Communism" and that "the United States should, therefore, initiate now a program of positive action to re-establish a stable, friendly, non-communist government in Cuba."[53] To achieve these aims, the Joint Chiefs then put forward Burke's paper, arguing that it would advance the cause of removing Castro from power and "contribute

[50] Ibid.

[51] Ibid.

[52] Wyden, *Bay of Pigs: The Untold Story*, 25.

[53] FRUS, "468. Memorandum From the Joint Chiefs of Staff to the Secretary of Defense (Gates)," in *Foreign Relations of the United States, 1958–1960, Cuba, Volume VI*, ed. John P. Glennon (Washington, D.C.: United States Government Printing Office, 1991), https://history.state.gov/historicaldocuments/frus1958-60v06/d468.

to any future action that may be required to reduce unrest and thwart the establishment of International Communism in Latin America." The memo concluded by recommending to the Secretary of Defense that it be taken up at the next National Security Council (NSC) meeting.[54]

Eisenhower's National Security Advisor, Gordon Gray, ultimately decided not to raise Burke's proposal at the March 10 meeting, but it was not because of major differences of opinion.[55] Rather, it was because there were already plans in the works to remove Castro quietly for the very same reasons Burke had homed in on. Gray's briefing notes from a meeting of the Planning Board of the NSC convened two days earlier on March 8 are informative. They began by enumerating America's priorities vis-à-vis Castro. First and second were geostrategic: "Denial of Cuba to the influence and control of hostile interests" and "[t]he Guantanamo Naval Base." Third was "[t]he effect our Cuban policy has on other Latin American countries, i.e., a possible loss of U.S. prestige and encouragement of other revolutionary groups on the one hand, or a possible favorable reaction to our policy of non intervention and restraint." Later in his notes, Gray points out that the NSC Planning Board "concluded that no overt action against the Castro regime would, at the present time, be in U.S. interests" in part because of "the obligations we have to the OAS and the need of having its support for any measures taken" and "the effect on world opinion."[56] This last point mirrors Burke's concerns about the negative reactions in the region and around the world to unprovoked U.S. intervention.

The day after the NSC Planning Board met, Assistant Secretary Rubottom wrote to Secretary Herter summarizing the State Department's views on Cuba and Castro. He made clear that "there is no disagreement between the Departments and agencies concerned about our basic approach to Cuba—that the Castro regime is a threat to our security interests and the achievement of our objectives in Latin America, that there is no reasonable hope that the Castro

[54] Ibid.

[55] FRUS, "473. Memorandum From the Assistant Secretary of State for Inter-American Affairs (Rubottom) to the Secretary of State," in *Foreign Relations of the United States, 1958–1960, Cuba, Volume VI,* ed. John P. Glennon (Washington, D.C.: United States Government Printing Office, 1991), https://history.state.gov/historicaldocuments/frus1958-60v06/d473.

[56] FRUS, "472. Editorial Note," in *Foreign Relations of the United States, 1958–1960, Cuba, Volume VI,* ed. John P. Glennon (Washington, D.C.: United States Government Printing Office, 1991), https://history.state.gov/historicaldocuments/frus1958-60v06/d472. The additional reasons, which included the "absence of any apparent alternative to the present government" and that "it would tend to solidify Castro's support" are taken up in the section on alternative explanations. See also FRUS, "475. Letter From the Under Secretary of State for Political Affairs (Merchant) to the Chief of Naval Operations (Burke)," in *Foreign Relations of the United States, 1958–1960, Cuba, Volume VI,* ed. John P. Glennon (Washington, D.C.: United States Government Printing Office, 1991), https://history.state.gov/historicaldocuments/frus1958-60v06/d475.

regime will voluntarily reverse the policies which run counter to our interests and objectives, and that consequently we seek a change in Cuba *with the minimum damage to U.S. prestige and interests in the hemisphere and elsewhere in the Free World*."[57] Rubottom's warning to Herter about the need to keep ongoing plans to resist Castro secret speaks to the ways international legal concerns shape U.S. policy: "In view of the fact that any action tending to cause a change in Cuba is subject to being construed in Latin America and elsewhere as 'intervention,' it remains highly important that our approach to the Cuban problem and our plans to achieve the desired result be held as strictly as possible on a 'need-to-know' basis and especially the circulation of papers within the Government tending to imply that the United States seeks a change."[58]

The evidence presented so far shows that the Eisenhower administration was sensitive to the fact that openly intervening against Castro would undermine faith in America's commitment to nonintervention and international institutions generally and would sour regional and global opinion of the United States.[59] Many studies of the Bay of Pigs overlook these documents, focusing primarily on the Kennedy period.[60] This is understandable to an extent. Kennedy had a chance to shut the program down. Nonetheless, identifying the factors that led the original authors of the plan to pursue secrecy is important for fully understanding what happened. With this in mind, we can evaluate how members of

[57] Here, Rubuttom appears to be using the term *prestige* differently than the way Gray used it in his briefing notes cited above. For Gray, prestige appears to refer to America's willingness to stand up to communism. For Rubottom, it appears to refer to America's reputation for upholding its commitments.

[58] FRUS, "473. Memorandum From the Assistant Secretary of State for Inter-American Affairs (Rubottom) to the Secretary of State."

[59] Assistant Secretary Rubottom noted in a meeting on June 27, 1960 that "unilateral intervention" against Castro "would turn the clock back 27 years." He went on to note that "it would cause incalculable loss in the hemisphere"; FRUS, 536. Memorandum of a Conference, Department of State, Washington, June 27, 1960," in *Foreign Relations of the United States, 1958–1960, Cuba, Volume VI*, ed. John P. Glennon (Washington, D.C.: United States Government Printing Office, 1991), https://history.state.gov/historicaldocuments/frus1958-60v06/d536. A memo from Rubottom to Secretary Herter on August 11 recognized just how negatively Latin American countries would react to unilateral U.S. intervention against Castro; FRUS, "574. Memorandum From the Assistant Secretary of State for Inter-American Affairs (Rubottom) to the Secretary of State," in *Foreign Relations of the United States, 1958–1960, Cuba, Volume VI*, ed. John P. Glennon (Washington, D.C.: United States Government Printing Office, 1991), https://history.state.gov/historicaldocuments/frus1958-60v06/d574.

[60] Friedman, "Crisis Management at the Dead Center: The 1960–1961 Presidential Transition and the Bay of Pigs Fiasco"; Irving L. Janis, *Victims of Groupthink: A Psychological Study of Foreign-Policy Decisions and Fiascoes* (Boston, MA: Houghton Mifflin Company, 1972), 14–49. For exceptions, see Gleijeses, "Ships in the Night: The CIA, the White House and the Bay of Pigs"; Wyden, *Bay of Pigs: The Untold Story*.

the Kennedy administration thought about the risks associated with overt intervention against Castro. As will become clear, their concerns mirrored those from the Eisenhower period.

The Kennedy Years

On February 15, 1961, less than a month after Kennedy authorized the continuation of the Castro operation and roughly one month before the switch from Trinidad to Zapata, Assistant Secretary of State Thomas Mann sent a memo to his boss, Secretary of State Dean Rusk, offering his personal assessment of the plan at that time. He was largely opposed, doubting that a popular uprising would materialize. Assuming this was correct, Mann argued that "we would be faced with the alternative of a) abandoning the brigade to its fate, which would cost us dearly in prestige and respect or b) attempting execution of the plan to move the brigade into the mountains as guerrillas, which would pose a prolonged problem of air drops or supplies or c) overt U.S. military intervention."

Mann's subsequent discussion of why the operation would be so risky echo the concerns of Admiral Burke and others: "Execution of the proposed plan would be in violation of Article 2, paragraph 4, and Article 51 of the Charter of the United Nations, Articles 18 and 25 of the Charter of the Organization of American States, and Article 1 of the Rio Treaty, which, in general, proscribe the use of armed force with the sole exception of the right of self-defense 'if an armed attack occurs.'" In addition to the operational issues raised in the previous paragraph, Mann also feared that "the proposal comes closer to being a military invasion than a covert operation of the Guatemala type," which presumably would expose the United States to all of the risks that incentivized the turn to covert action in the first place. "At best," Mann warned, "our moral posture throughout the hemisphere would be impaired. At worst, the effect on our position of hemispheric leadership would be catastrophic."[61] It is reasonable to conclude from this memo that Mann was not averse to pursuing regime change against Castro per se. His comparison to the Guatemala operation suggests that his main concern was the visibility of the plan under consideration and the attendant risks of unwanted exposure.[62]

[61] FRUS, "45. Memorandum From the Assistant Secretary of State for Inter-American Affairs (Mann) to Secretary of State Rusk," in *Foreign Relations of the United States, 1961–1963, Volume X, Cuba, January 1961–September 1962*, ed. Louis J. Smith (Washington, D.C.: United States Government Printing Office, 1997), https://history.state.gov/historicaldocuments/frus1961-63v10/d45.

[62] Wyden, *Bay of Pigs: The Untold Story*, 74.

Mann had another opportunity to express concern about intervening in such a way that might expose America's hand at the White House on March 11. This was the meeting where CIA planners pitched the Trinidad plan to Kennedy and were told to make the operation quieter. Mann concurred with Kennedy's decision "on behalf of the State Department. To avoid anti-American reaction in the United Nations and Latin America, he wanted American sponsorship thoroughly concealed. He particularly opposed Trinidad because its airstrip could not handle B-26s; there would be no way to maintain the fiction that the planes operated from Cuban bases."[63] This was consistent with State's desire "to be in a position to deny that the attacks had come from either the United States, Guatemala, or Nicaragua . . . [so as not] to alienate other Latin American nations by directly assaulting a fellow OAS member."[64] At the end of the March 11 meeting, Kennedy "said the problem seemed to be: the smaller the political risk, the greater was the military risk, and vice versa. The two risks should be brought into better balance."[65] Since Trinidad was heavier on political liabilities, the result was an operation that minimized those at the expense of effectiveness.

Four days later, Kennedy's national security advisor, McGeorge Bundy, wrote to the president indicating that "CIA will present a revised plan for the Cuban operation. They have done a remarkable job of reframing the landing plan so as to make it unspectacular and quiet, and plausibly Cuban in its essentials."[66] The remainder of Bundy's memo is devoted to discussing the logistics of ensuring that Castro's air force could be sufficiently immobilized subject to the constraint that the operation would have to appear homegrown. "The question in my mind," Bundy wondered, "is whether we cannot solve this problem by having the air strike come some little time before the invasion. A group of patriotic airplanes flying from Nicaraguan bases might knock out Castro's Air Force in a single day without anyone knowing (for some time) where they came from, and with nothing to prove that it was not an interior rebellion by the Cuban Air Force . . . . *Then the invasion could come as a separate enterprise, and neither the air strike nor the quiet landing of patriots would in itself give Castro anything to take to the United Nations.*" He concluded by stating that, "I have been a skeptic about [Deputy Director of Plans Richard] Bissell's operation, but now I think we are

[63] Wyden, 100. See also "General Lemnitzer," *National Security Files, Countries, Cuba - Subjects, Para-Military Study Group, Taylor Report Part II, Meetings 17-18 [Folder]; Papers of President Kennedy: National Security Files—Countries, Box 61A [Collection]* (JFK Library, 1961), 10.

[64] Jones, *The Bay of Pigs*, 51.

[65] Wyden, *Bay of Pigs: The Untold Story*, 101.

[66] FRUS, "64. Memorandum From the President's Special Assistant for National Security Affairs (Bundy) to President Kennedy," in *Foreign Relations of the United States, 1961–1963, Volume X, Cuba, January 1961–September 1962*, ed. Louis J. Smith (Washington, D.C.: United States Government Printing Office, 1997), https://history.state.gov/historicaldocuments/frus1961-63v10/d64.

on the edge of a good answer. I also think Bissell and [Colonel Jack] Hawkins have done an honorable job of meeting the proper criticisms and cautions of the Department of State."[67] Bundy's concern thus stemmed from whether the United States would be hauled before the UN for an unprovoked attack against a sovereign regime. The revised plan partially allayed these fears.

Two weeks later on March 31, 1961, Under Secretary of State Chester Bowles sent a memo to Secretary Rusk expressing reservations about the proposal to depose Castro.[68] Bowles conceded at the outset that he was "not a wholly objective judge of the practical aspects." He continued, "my concern stems from a deep personal conviction that our national interests are poorly served by a covert operation of this kind at a time when our new President is effectively appealing to world opinion on the basis of high principle. Even in our imperfect world, the differences which distinguish us from the Russians are of vital importance. This is true not only in a moral sense but in the practical effect of these differences on our capacity to rally the non-Communist world [on] behalf of our traditional democratic objectives." Bowles was careful to make clear that he was not "overlook[ing] the ruthless nature of the struggle in which we are involved" but still felt that "[i]n sponsoring the Cuban operation . . . we would be deliberately violating the fundamental obligations we assumed in the Act of Bogota establishing the Organization of American States." His worries in this regard were not confined to Latin America. "More generally," Bowles wrote, "the United States is the leading force in and substantial beneficiary of a network of treaties and alliances stretching around the world. That these treaty obligations should be recognized as binding in law and conscience is the condition not only of a lawful and orderly world, but of the mobilization of our own power. We cannot expect the benefits of this regime of treaties if we are unwilling to accept the limitations it imposes upon our freedom to act."[69]

At first blush, Bowles seems critical of any operation with the goal of removing Castro by force, not simply an overt one. If we look closer, however, the nature of his objections is actually similar to Mann's. "Those most familiar with the Cuban

[67] Ibid.

[68] As scholars have pointed out, Rusk apparently never passed on Bowles' memo to President Kennedy. Even if this particular memo did not reach the president's ears, however, the concerns Bowles expresses are entirely consistent with those of his colleagues, concerns that did reach the president's ears. See Janis, *Victims of Groupthink: A Psychological Study of Foreign-Policy Decisions and Fiascoes*, 42; Schlesinger Jr., *A Thousand Days: John F. Kennedy in the White House*, 250–251; Wyden, *Bay of Pigs: The Untold Story*, 121.

[69] FRUS, "75. Memorandum From the Under Secretary of State (Bowles) to Secretary of State Rusk," in *Foreign Relations of the United States, 1961–1963, Volume X, Cuba, January 1961–September 1962*, ed. Louis J. Smith (Washington, D.C.: United States Government Printing Office, 1997), https://history.state.gov/historicaldocuments/frus1961-63v10/d75.

operation," he argued, "seem to agree that as the venture is now planned, the chances of success are not greater than one out of three . . . . The one way we can reduce the risk is by a sharply increased commitment of direct American support . . . . If the operation appears to be a failure in its early stages, the pressure on us to scrap our self-imposed restriction on direct American involvement will be difficult to resist, and our own responsibility correspondingly increased."[70] In short, Bowles worried that if the current plan looked like it would fail—which he thought was likely—the administration would face pressure to get more openly involved, exposing the United States to charges of hypocrisy and damaging its credibility and trustworthiness in the region and beyond.

On April 5, Arthur Schlesinger, Kennedy's Special Assistant, followed up with the president to clarify his stance on the operation.[71] Schlesinger had been asked about it at a White House meeting the day before and was dissatisfied with his initial reply.[72] "My brief answer," he now explained, "is that I am in favor of a continuation and expansion of the present approach to Cuba—i.e., quiet infiltration of anti-Castro exiles into Cuba and subsequent support through air drops." But he opposed "[t]he beachhead operation" which constituted "a change of phase in our Cuban policy. If entirely successful, it would have the highly beneficial result of getting rid of the Castro regime. If we could achieve this by a swift, surgical stroke, I would be for it. But in present circumstances the operation seems to me to involve many hazards; and on balance . . . I am against it."[73]

The reasons why Schlesinger opposed the joint amphibious/air operation began with his belief that "[n]o matter how 'Cuban' the equipment and personnel, the US will be held accountable for the operation, and our prestige will be committed to its success." Additionally, "[s]ince the Castro regime is presumably too strong to be toppled by a single landing, the operation will turn into a protracted struggle" which would "create increasing pressure on us to guarantee the success of the operation through ever more intense and overt involvement." [74] In other

[70] Ibid.

[71] Schlesinger Jr., *A Thousand Days: John F. Kennedy in the White House*, 252–253.

[72] Declassified summary notes of the April 4 meeting at the White House generated general consensus for continuing ahead with the operation, although Secretary Rusk "expressed opposition to the plan"; FRUS, "80. Editorial Note," in *Foreign Relations of the United States, 1961–1963, Volume X, Cuba, January 1961–September 1962,* ed. Louis J. Smith (Washington, D.C.: United States Government Printing Office, 1997), https://history.state.gov/historicaldocuments/frus1961-63v10/d80. This conflicts with Wyden's account, who argues that "Rusk stayed 'closer to abstention than to a ringing affirmative.' " See Wyden, *Bay of Pigs: The Untold Story*, 148.

[73] FRUS, "81. Memorandum From the President's Special Assistant (Schlesinger) to President Kennedy," in *Foreign Relations of the United States, 1961–1963, Volume X, Cuba, January 1961–September 1962,* ed. Louis J. Smith (Washington, D.C.: United States Government Printing Office, 1997), https://history.state.gov/historicaldocuments/frus1961-63v10/d81.

[74] Ibid.

words, Schlesinger did not think the reformulated plan would remain covert.[75] His assessment of the risks should be familiar by now, reflecting statements from Burke, Mann, Bowles, and others: "The protraction of the struggle will give the Soviet Union a magnificent opportunity to wage political warfare. Cuba will become our Hungary; and, since our pretensions to international good behavior have been greater than those of the Russians, we would be more damaged by Hungary than they were (and they were considerably damaged)."[76]

Schlesinger's specific reference to the Soviet Union's invasion of Hungary five years earlier is worth unpacking. Nikita Khrushchev justified a crackdown on the Hungarian revolution and the overthrow of Imre Nagy's regime by relying on a flimsy request for intervention from a manufactured provisional government.[77] The invasion was widely condemned by the international community. Schlesinger's desire to avoid falling into the same trap in Cuba is significant in light of the fact that, as discussed later in the chapter, decision makers contemplated doing something similar—that is, using a request from an exiled government as a pretext for intervention—but ultimately refrained from doing so.

It is also worth reiterating that Schlesinger, an ostensible dove, was not opposed in principle to regime change against Castro. According to Wyden, "the encouragement of an exile effort to oust Castro did not bother him; there was historical precedent for backing refugees against dictatorships back home."[78] Rather, Schlesinger's concerns turned on the feeling that the new operational concept would implicate the United States with severe consequences: "If we admit involvement, we admit action taken in violation of the basic characters of the hemisphere and of the United Nations. If we justify such violations by pleading a higher law, we place ourselves thereafter on the same moral plane as the Soviet Union. If we deny involvement, few will believe us . . . . Whatever we do, the effect will be to spoil the new US image—the image of intelligence, reasonableness and honest firmness which has already had such an extraordinary effect in changing world opinion about the US and increasing world confidence in US methods and purposes."[79] In a subsequent memo on April 10, one week before the operation began, Schlesinger warned that "much of the world will interpret" a U.S.-backed invasion against Castro "as calculated aggression against a small nation in defiance both of treaty obligations and of the international

[75] Jones, *The Bay of Pigs*, 67; Schlesinger Jr., *A Thousand Days: John F. Kennedy in the White House*, 253–255.

[76] FRUS, "81. Memorandum From the President's Special Assistant (Schlesinger) to President Kennedy."

[77] Hans J. Morgenthau, "To Intervene or Not to Intervene," *Foreign Affairs* 45, no. 3 (1967): 429.

[78] Wyden, *Bay of Pigs: The Untold Story*, 151.

[79] FRUS, "81. Memorandum From the President's Special Assistant (Schlesinger) to President Kennedy."

standards we have repeatedly asserted against the Communist World. . . . In short, for many people the easiest explanation of our action will be as a reversion to economic imperialism of the pre-World War I, Platt-Amendment, big-stick, gunboat-diplomacy kind."[80]

To recap, the main concern expressed by senior officials in both the Eisenhower and Kennedy administrations turned on the prospect of undermining perceptions of America's commitment to strategic restraint and doing irreparable harm to its moral authority by brazenly violating the nonintervention principle. When senior policymakers raised objections to the covert action plan in its various iterations, they almost always did so on the grounds that the operation was too noisy and would expose the United States to the kinds of costs that had driven them to pursue secrecy and plausible deniability. Kennedy was especially sensitive to these concerns. Moving the landing site from Trinidad to the Bay of Pigs was a conscious effort to reduce the political risks of the operation. Like Bundy, Schlesinger at one point "praised the 'skill and care' that had gone into 'Cubanizing the operation and doing nothing which would be inconsistent with a spontaneous Cuban effort.' "[81]

Although less informative than the declassified record, Kennedy's public remarks before and after the disastrous invasion bear the marks of a president sensitive to international legal constraints. In a press conference on April 12, five days before D-Day, he proclaimed that, "[t]here will not be, under any conditions, an intervention in Cuba by the United States Armed Forces. . . . The basic issue in Cuba is not one between the United States and Cuba. It is between the Cubans themselves."[82]

Several days after the invasion, Kennedy delivered a speech reiterating that "any unilateral American intervention in the absence of an external attack upon ourselves or an ally would have been contrary to our traditions and to our international obligations." He did, however, go on to declare that the United States' respect for nonintervention was not absolute and that he would be willing to break with it in the event of clear outside interference, presumably by the Soviet Union: "But let the record show that our restraint is not inexhaustible. Should it ever appear that the inter-American doctrine of non-interference merely conceals or excuses a policy of non-action—if the nations of this Hemisphere should fail

[80] FRUS, "86. Memorandum From the President's Special Assistant (Schlesinger) to President Kennedy," in *Foreign Relations of the United States, 1961–1963, Volume X, Cuba, January 1961–September 1962*, ed. Louis J. Smith (Washington, D.C.: United States Government Printing Office, 1997), https://history.state.gov/historicaldocuments/frus1961-63v10/d86. See also Vandenbroucke, "Anatomy of a Failure: The Decision to Land at the Bay of Pigs," 472.

[81] Wyden, *Bay of Pigs: The Untold Story*, 160.

[82] Schlesinger Jr., *A Thousand Days: John F. Kennedy in the White House*, 262; ellipsis in original.

to meet their commitments against outside Communist penetration—then I want it clearly understood that this government will not hesitate in meeting its primary obligations which are to the security of this nation."[83] Perhaps this was a serious threat. Kennedy's unwillingness to pursue overt action in the months prior, though, suggests that it was probably cheap talk. This is bolstered by the fact that while decision makers discussed various plans for overthrowing Castro in the weeks after the Bay of Pigs, they continued to emphasize the risks outlined in this section.[84]

Legal Evaluation: Coming Up Short

An important aspect of this episode is how senior decision makers discussed the conditions under which they would be willing to support overt action against Castro. If my argument is right, legal exemptions to nonintervention should have been front and center. This is indeed what the declassified documents show. Not only did decision makers weigh the prospect of locating exogenously derived legal exemptions, they also raised the possibility of fabricating them. But this is only part of the story. Smoking-gun evidence would also include these same officials explicitly noting that they were forced to stick with covert action because legal exemptions, real or contrived, were unavailable. Unfortunately, this kind of evidence is harder to come by. Short of this, the fact that decision makers pursued covert action knowing it was less likely to succeed, discussed in the next section, is telling. Were legal exemptions available, it is reasonable to assume that decision makers would have used them as cover for pursuing a more effective overt operation to overthrow Fidel Castro.

A common thread running through deliberations about Castro was a willingness to use overt force to protect American lives and the U.S. naval base at Guantanamo Bay. During an NSC meeting on January 14, 1960, Eisenhower told the group that "an attack on Guantanamo would be an occasion for action against Cuba."[85] Roughly one year later on January 3, 1961, the Assistant Deputy

[83] John F. Kennedy, "Bay of Pigs Invasion," *C-Span* April 20 (1961), https://www.c-span.org/video/?192032-1/bay-pigs-invasion. See also Schlesinger Jr., *A Thousand Days: John F. Kennedy in the White House*, 287–288.

[84] "Plan for Cuba," *National Security Files, Countries, Cuba, Subjects - Policy, 4/24/61-4/27/61 & Undated [Folder]; Papers of President Kennedy: National Security Files—Countries, Box 54 [Collection]* (JFK Library, 1961), 2–3, 8.

[85] FRUS, "423. Memorandum of Discussion at the 432d Meeting of the National Security Council, Washington, January 14, 1960, 9 a.m." See also FRUS, "483. Memorandum of Discussion at the 437th Meeting of the National Security Council, Washington, March 17, 1960, 10 a.m.," in *Foreign Relations of the United States, 1958–1960, Cuba, Volume VI*, ed. John P. Glennon (Washington, D.C.: United States Government Printing Office, 1991), https://history.state.gov/

Director of Plans at the CIA and Richard Bissell's right-hand man, Tracy Barnes, summarized the consensus of a high-level gathering which included Secretary of State Herter, Secretary of Defense Gates, CIA Director Allen Dulles, Deputy Director of Plans Bissell, and others, as follows: "The tone of the meeting was clearly in support of overt introduction of U.S. forces if any steps were taken by the Cubans either to harm American citizens or to attack or damage official U.S. property (e.g. Guantanamo)."[86] Ten days later on January 13, Whiting Willauer, the U.S. Ambassador to Costa Rica at the time, similarly wrote: "There is one military contingency plan which will have to be ready for use if Castro should start slaughtering Americans. This would be a purely military plan and would include military occupation. General Gray noted that such a plan already exists and is being revived."[87]

In addition to discussing the prospect of openly wielding force against Castro if he started targeting Americans or attacking the base at Guantanamo, decision makers contemplated whether they could speed things along by inventing a self-defense claim. According to Jones, "[s]ome Washington officials pushed for direct American military intervention, even if it entailed manufacturing an incident as justification.... In response to a State Department request, the Defense Department prepared a study of possible military actions, including a fabricated Cuban attack on Guantanamo that required an appropriate U.S. response. Propaganda could manipulate world opinion or make the facts so 'muddled' that U.S. forces could hit the island under the guise of self-defense."[88]

historicaldocuments/frus1958-60v06/d483; FRUS, "585. Memorandum of Discussion at the Department of State-Joint Chiefs of Staff Meeting, Pentagon, Washington, September 30, 1960, 11 a.m.," in *Foreign Relations of the United States, 1958–1960, Cuba, Volume VI*, ed. John P. Glennon (Washington, D.C.: United States Government Printing Office, 1991), https://history.state.gov/historicaldocuments/frus1958-60v06/d581S.

[86] FRUS, "3. Memorandum for the Record," in *Foreign Relations of the United States, 1961–1963, Volume X, Cuba, January 1961–September 1962*, ed. Louis J. Smith (Washington, D.C.: United States Government Printing Office, 1997), https://history.state.gov/historicaldocuments/frus1961-63v10/d3.

[87] FRUS, "18. Memorandum of Conversation," in *Foreign Relations of the United States, 1961–1963, Volume X, Cuba, January 1961–September 1962*, ed. Louis J. Smith (Washington, D.C.: United States Government Printing Office, 1997), https://history.state.gov/historicaldocuments/frus1961-63v10/d18. There was some discussion, however, about whether an attack on Guantanamo would justify a full-scale assault against Castro or whether it would simply require a more limited response to defend the naval base; FRUS, "608. Memorandum of Discussion at the 466th Meeting of the National Security Council, Washington, November 7, 1960, 8:30–10:14 a.m.," in *Foreign Relations of the United States, 1958–1960, Cuba, Volume VI*, ed. John P. Glennon (Washington, D.C.: United States Government Printing Office, 1991), https://history.state.gov/historicaldocuments/frus1958-60v06/d608.

[88] Jones, *The Bay of Pigs*, 43. See also Rabe, *Eisenhower and Latin America: The Foreign Policy of Anticommunism*, 172.

A staff study prepared in the Defense Department on January 16, 1961, whose purpose was "[t]o evaluate possible military courses of action to overthrow the Castro Government in Cuba in the event currently planned political and paramilitary operations are determined to be inadequate," similarly stated that overt action would be justifiable "if Castro attacked Guantanamo Bay or if such an attack were 'staged.'" Assuming this were possible, and "[w]ith prior propaganda effort by the U.S., Free World opinion could be sufficiently swayed, or the facts sufficiently 'muddled', that U.S. unilateral action in response to such an attack, actual or 'staged' would have less impact on U.S. prestige in the Free World."[89] Castro knew this was a possibility. On April 24, he addressed the Guantanamo Bay issue directly in a public speech: "We wish to avoid giving [the United States] a pretext for intervention .... We said that we would never want to obtain the base by force, only through international law."[90]

Waiting for a self-defense claim or fabricating one were not the only conditions policymakers discussed as being sufficient to warrant overt action against Castro. Another was gaining support through the OAS.[91] At an NSC meeting on March 10, 1960, Eisenhower remarked that "we could do almost anything if we had the support of the OAS."[92] One possibility was to invoke the Caracas Declaration of Solidarity, signed in 1954, which affirmed the region's commitment to combating communism.[93] During a meeting of the Special Group of the NSC on March 14, 1960, Director Dulles observed that the large presence of communists in Cuba "might not be disadvantageous because it would facilitate multilateral action by the OAS."[94] In a White House meeting three days later, Gordon Gray "asked whether OAS support will only be forthcoming if

[89] FRUS, "19. Staff Study Prepared in the Department of Defense," in *Foreign Relations of the United States, 1961–1963, Volume X, Cuba, January 1961–September 1962*, ed. Louis J. Smith (Washington, D.C.: United States Government Printing Office, 1997), https://history.state.gov/historicaldocuments/frus1961-63v10/d19.

[90] "Cuban Daily Summary [April 24, 1961]," *Papers of Robert F. Kennedy - Attorney General's Papers: National Security Classified File - 71-4-16-24, Cuban Daily Summary, Section 1:1/30/61-5/31/61, Folder 1 of 2 [Folder]; Attorney General Files, Box 201 [Collection]* (JFK Library, 1961), 1.

[91] Gleijeses, "Ships in the Night: The CIA, the White House and the Bay of Pigs," 5. For a lengthy discussion of the process through which this would work, see FRUS, "540. Memorandum Prepared in the Department of State," in *Foreign Relations of the United States, 1958–1960, Cuba, Volume VI*, ed. John P. Glennon (Washington, D.C.: United States Government Printing Office, 1991), https://history.state.gov/historicaldocuments/frus1958-60v06/d540.

[92] FRUS, "474. Memorandum of Discussion at the 436th Meeting of the National Security Council, Washington, March 10, 1960," in *Foreign Relations of the United States, 1958–1960, Cuba, Volume VI*, ed. John P. Glennon (Washington, D.C.: United States Government Printing Office, 1991), https://history.state.gov/historicaldocuments/frus1958-60v06/d474.

[93] See http://avalon.law.yale.edu/20th_century/intam10.asp.

[94] Wyden, *Bay of Pigs: The Untold Story*, 25.

the Cubans actually attack Americans on the island," to which Roy Rubottom replied "that the OAS might be brought to act prior to such an attack on the basis of Castro being tied up with international communism." Eisenhower then wondered aloud "whether we have to base it on the word 'communism' or whether we couldn't base it on dictatorship, confiscation, threats to life etc." Then–Vice President Richard Nixon "thought the Caracas Resolution was based on the term 'international communism.' "[95]

Ideas about how to get the OAS to authorize collective action against Castro also included the possibility that Cuba might attack other nations. Chester Bowles, whom we met earlier as a strong opponent of acting against Castro in any way that could be traced to the United States, wrote in his March 31 memo to Rusk that "[a]nother possibility is that Castro, once he has created sufficient military power, will move against a neighboring area, such as Haiti, the Dominican Republic, or perhaps into Central America. If this occurs, we can move to block him with whatever force is required, presumably through the Organization of American States and with the full support of the people in Latin America and elsewhere."[96] Put differently, he believed that repelling an invasion by Castro against his neighbors would be compatible with America's formal and normative commitments to nonintervention.

Similar to the discussion of self-defense exemptions, decision makers also talked about the prospect of fabricating an international incident involving an attack on one of Cuba's neighbors as a means of legitimizing overt intervention.[97]

[95] FRUS, "486. Memorandum of a Conference With the President, White House, Washington, March 17, 1960, 2:30 p.m.," in *Foreign Relations of the United States, 1958–1960, Cuba, Volume VI*, ed. John P. Glennon (Washington, D.C.: United States Government Printing Office, 1991), https://history.state.gov/historicaldocuments/frus1958-60v06/d486. Interestingly, in a meeting two months earlier, Assistant Secretary Rubottom noted that intervening under the auspices of "the Caracas Resolution and the OAS would be preferable to action under the Monroe Doctrine," signifying that decision makers prioritized regional institutions over the longstanding Monroe Doctrine which was in effect a unilateral policy. See FRUS, "423. Memorandum of Discussion at the 432d Meeting of the National Security Council, Washington, January 14, 1960, 9 a.m." For further discussion of Caracas, see FRUS, "459. Memorandum From the Assistant Secretary of State for Inter-American Affairs' Special Assistant (Hill) to the Assistant Secretary of State (Rubottom)," in *Foreign Relations of the United States, 1958–1960, Cuba, Volume VI*, ed. John P. Glennon (Washington, D.C.: United States Government Printing Office, 1991), https://history.state.gov/historicaldocuments/frus1958-60v06/d459. For the intelligence community's assessment of why communists in Cuba might move slowly to avoid invoking Caracas, see FRUS, "531. National Intelligence Estimate," in *Foreign Relations of the United States, 1958–1960, Cuba, Volume VI*, ed. John P. Glennon (Washington, D.C.: United States Government Printing Office, 1991), https://history.state.gov/historicaldocuments/frus1958-60v06/d531.

[96] FRUS, "75. Memorandum From the Under Secretary of State (Bowles) to Secretary of State Rusk."

[97] It was deemed unlikely that Castro would do this on his own. See "Memorandum for the National Security Council - Subject: U.S. Policy Toward Cuba," *National Security Files, Countries,*

In a memo to Kennedy dated February 11, 1961, Schlesinger posed the following question: "Would it not be possible to induce Castro to take offensive action first? He has already launched expeditions against Panama and against the Dominican Republic. One can conceive a black operation in, say, Haiti which might in time lure Castro into sending a few boatloads of men on to a Haitian beach in what could be portrayed as an effort to overthrow the Haitian regime. If only Castro could be induced to commit an offensive act, then the moral issue would be clouded, and the anti-US campaign would be hobbled from the start."[98] Although Schlesinger does not directly mention the OAS or the Security Council in these remarks, it is clear that his conception of what constitutes a legitimate intervention included an assault on one of Cuba's neighbors by Castro, which would be perceived as more acceptable by America's friends and allies.

One of the more creative options decision makers considered to excuse overt force against Castro was to recognize the exiles as the legitimate government and subsequently come to their rescue.[99] Two senior operators intimately involved with the planning of the Bay of Pigs operation wrote on January 4, 1961 that "the lodgement established by our force can be used as the site for establishment of a provisional government which can be recognized by the United States, and hopefully by other American states, and given overt military assistance. The way will then be paved for United States military intervention aimed at pacification of Cuba, and this will result in the prompt overthrow of the Castro government."[100] An analogous strategy was discussed in a high-level meeting on January 22. Secretary Rusk wrote that, "what we needed was a 'fig leaf.' A Cuban provisional government on the Isle of Pines, for example, could sink Soviet ships carrying supplies to Castro with less danger than would be the case with direct

Cuba, Subjects - Policy-NSC Action No. 2413-c - Papers and Annex I, 5/4/61 [Folder]; Papers of President Kennedy: National Security Files—Countries, Box 54 [Collection] (JFK Library, 1961), 1.

[98] FRUS, "43. Memorandum From the President's Special Assistant (Schlesinger) to President Kennedy," in *Foreign Relations of the United States, 1961–1963, Volume X, Cuba, January 1961–September 1962*, ed. Louis J. Smith (Washington, D.C.: United States Government Printing Office, 1997), https://history.state.gov/historicaldocuments/frus1961-63v10/d43. See also Jones, *The Bay of Pigs*, 52–53.

[99] Gleijeses, "Ships in the Night: The CIA, the White House and the Bay of Pigs," 34. This could not merely be done by declaring that the U.S. recognized an alternative government to Cuba prior to anti-Castro opposition establishing a foothold on the island itself; FRUS, "619. Memorandum From the Legal Adviser (Hager) to the Under Secretary of State for Political Affairs (Merchant)," in *Foreign Relations of the United States, 1958–1960, Cuba, Volume VI*, ed. John P. Glennon (Washington, D.C.: United States Government Printing Office, 1991), https://history.state.gov/historicaldocuments/frus1958-60v06/d619; FRUS, "18. Memorandum of Conversation."

[100] FRUS, "9. Memorandum From the Chief of WH/4/PM, Central Intelligence Agency (Hawkins) to the Chief of WH/4 of the Directorate for Plans (Esterline)."

involvement of U.S. forces."[101] A CIA memo four days later argued along similar lines: "[A]ssuming that the provisional government had been recognized by the United States, there would appear to be a basis for an overt, open U.S. initiative to institute a military occupation of the island by a composite OAS force in order to put a stop to the civil war."[102] Parenthetically, this is akin to what happened in the Dominican Republic in 1965, discussed in Chapter 6. Given how events transpired in this case, however, it does not appear that any of these possibilities came to fruition.

Trade-Offs

The final piece to the Bay of Pigs puzzle is showing that decision makers knew they were making operational sacrifices by acting covertly. Demonstrating that policymakers chose secrecy with eyes wide open showcases the power of international legal constraints. Using the quiet option to avoid brazenly violating nonintervention despite the higher risks of failure is powerful evidence that decision makers take credibility concerns and hypocrisy costs seriously. It also highlights covert action's complexities. By pursuing secrecy, interveners are giving up the operational advantages of overt action to hide their complicity in an operation. My argument is not that decision makers thought covert action had zero chance of achieving success.[103] The point is rather that they knew it was less likely to succeed relative to overt action, an option that was off the table for political reasons.[104]

[101] FRUS, "24. Memorandum of Conversation," in *Foreign Relations of the United States, 1961–1963, Volume X, Cuba, January 1961–September 1962*, ed. Louis J. Smith (Washington, D.C.: United States Government Printing Office, 1997), https://history.state.gov/historicaldocuments/frus1961-63v10/d24. See also "Memorandum for the President [From McGeorge Bundy, February 18, 1961]," *National Security Files, Countries, Cuba - General, 1/61-4/61 [Folder]; Papers of President Kennedy: National Security Files—Countries, Box 35A [Collection]* (JFK Library, 1961).

[102] FRUS, "27. Memorandum Prepared in the Central Intelligence Agency," in *Foreign Relations of the United States, 1961–1963, Volume X, Cuba, January 1961–September 1962*, ed. Louis J. Smith (Washington, D.C.: United States Government Printing Office, 1997), https://history.state.gov/historicaldocuments/frus1961-63v10/d27.

[103] Some were actually optimistic about its chances of success. See "Evaluation by Colonel Hawkins on 13 April 1961," *National Security Files, Countries, Cuba - Subjects: Exiles, 1961 [Folder]; Papers of President Kennedy: National Security Files—Countries, Box 48 [Collection]* (JFK Library, 1961).

[104] Indeed, decision makers realized that the only way to guarantee success in an effort to topple Castro was for the U.S. to overtly intervene. See FRUS, "20. Memorandum for the Files," in *Foreign Relations of the United States, 1961–1963, Volume X, Cuba, January 1961–September 1962*, ed. Louis J. Smith (Washington, D.C.: United States Government Printing Office, 1997), https://history.state.gov/historicaldocuments/frus1961-63v10/d20. There was, however, a divergence of opinion between the CIA and Defense Department on the one hand and the State Department on the other

One of the clearest and most forceful statements testifying to the operational sacrifice decision makers were making by seeking plausible deniability comes from the chief architect of the operation, Richard Bissell. In the aftermath of the failed invasion, the Inspector General of the CIA, General Lyman Kirkpatrick, was tasked with writing a postmortem of what went wrong. His report was scathing. It faulted the CIA for poor organization, treating the Cuban exiles like puppets, overestimating the odds that the invasion would spark resistance, and more. Bissell drafted a lengthy response with the help of Tracy Barnes. The description of the tension between the plausible deniability requirement imposed by the White House and the desire to make the operation as effective as possible is illuminating. "Inherent in this situation," Bissell remarked, "was a clear conflict between two goals, a conflict of the sort familiar in recent American history. One objective was that . . . the Castro regime should be overthrown. The other was that the political and moral posture of the United States before the world at large should not be impaired. The basic method of resolving this conflict of objectives that was resorted to was that of attempting to carry out actions against Castro in such a manner that the official responsibility of the U.S. Government could be disclaimed."[105]

Bissell is putting his finger on the key challenge facing both Eisenhower and Kennedy. The United States wanted Castro gone. The most efficient way to accomplish this would be to deploy overt military forces. But the United States also wanted to circumvent the political costs associated with an unprovoked attack on Castro. In the end, decision makers privileged the latter set of concerns over the former. Bissell describes this exact trade-off later in his reply: "If complete deniability had been consistent with maximum effectiveness, there would theoretically have remained no conflict of goals but in fact this could not be (and never is) the case. The most effective way to have organized operations against the Castro regime, even if they would have been carried out exclusively by Cubans, would have been to do so perfectly openly, on the largest scale and with the best equipment feasible. Practically every departure from this pattern of behavior imposed operational difficulties and reduced effectiveness."[106]

There is further evidence from the weeks and months leading up to the invasion that decision makers knew they would have to make operational sacrifices

about the efficacy of the covert plan. See "Memorandum for the President [From McGeorge Bundy, Feburary 8, 1961]," *National Security Files, Countries, Cuba - General, 1/61-4/61 [Folder]; Papers of President Kennedy: National Security Files—Countries, Box 35A [Collection]* (JFK Library, 1961).

[105] Kornbluh, *Bay of Pigs Declassified: The Secret CIA Report on the Invasion of Cuba*, 141.

[106] Kornbluh, 141. See also "Some Preliminary Administrative Lessons of the Cuban Expedition [April 24, 1961]," *National Security Files, Countries, Cuba - General, 1/61-4/61 [Folder]; Papers of President Kennedy: National Security Files—Countries, Box 35A [Collection]* (JFK Library, 1961), 1–4.

which limited the chances of success if the mission was to remain plausibly deniable. One instance comes from Kennedy's first briefing of the plan on January 28, 1961: "The meeting began with a description of the present situation in Cuba by the Director of Central Intelligence. The judgment expressed without dissent was that Cuba is now for practical purposes a Communist-controlled state." After walking through the covert measures the United States had taken so far, the memo concluded that, "[t]he present estimate of the Department of Defense is that no course of action currently authorized by the United States Government will be effective in reaching the agreed national goal of overthrowing the Castro regime."[107]

One of the clearest examples of where U.S. decision makers were forced to make operational sacrifices in the interest of plausible deniability was in the kinds of equipment they provided to the Cuban rebels. As the Inspector General's postmortem contends, "[i]nsistence on adhering to the formalities imposed by a non-attributability which no longer existed produced absurdities and created obstacles and delays. For example, the use of obsolete and inadequate B-26 aircraft, instead of the more efficient A-5s originally requested, was a concession to non-attributability which hampered the operation severely."[108] Additional examples include not providing a requested surgical tent or a particular kind of rifle, since these items could have been traced back to the United States. Most infamous was the last-minute decision to cancel airstrikes for when the exiles were landing on the beaches. In sum, even if U.S. decision makers thought the covert operation had some chance of success, it is clear that the plausible deniability requirement curtailed the mission's odds of actually working. As the operation was collapsing in mid-April, former Secretary of State Dean Acheson wryly told Kennedy that "[i]t doesn't take Price Waterhouse to tell you that 1,500 Cubans aren't as good as 25,000."[109]

Although slightly beyond the scope of what I am after, this discussion sheds light on an unanswered question: Why did Eisenhower, and especially Kennedy, stick with covert action once it became clear that outsiders knew about the operation? News stories detailing U.S. efforts were frequently plastered in major

[107] FRUS, "30. Memorandum of Discussion," in *Foreign Relations of the United States, 1961–1963, Volume X, Cuba, January 1961–September 1962*, ed. Louis J. Smith (Washington, D.C.: United States Government Printing Office, 1997), https://history.state.gov/historicaldocuments/frus1961-63v10/d30. There is some evidence to suggest that the Joint of Chiefs of staff were not fully read into the CIA's plans. Nevertheless, Kennedy was briefed on their findings, which suggests that he was aware of the possibility that the plan had a lower chance of success than a full-blown overt operation. See Wyden, *Bay of Pigs: The Untold Story*, 86–92.

[108] Kornbluh, *Bay of Pigs Declassified: The Secret CIA Report on the Invasion of Cuba*, 55–56.

[109] Kornbluh, 2.

news outlets. At one point, Kennedy complained that, "Castro doesn't need agents over here. All he has to do is read our papers. It's all laid out for him."[110]

Bissell tackles this issue head-on in his response to the Inspector General's report: "That it did become 'overt' in the sense that there was extensive public discussion of the preparations for invasion and that the military action was widely attributed to the United States Government, both before and after it took place, there can be no doubt." He then asks, "[w]hy . . . would anyone continue to regard the involvement of the United States as plausibly deniable and why was the undertaking not converted into an overt operation . . . ? The answer to the first part of this question is that up to and through the invasion itself the operation remained to an extraordinary degree *technically* deniable." Bissell also notes that "no one in the Executive Branch was ready at any point until after the defeat to officially avow U.S. support."[111] The various attempts to lighten the U.S. footprint at the expense of effectiveness indicates that decision makers thought such efforts would still offer some semblance of deniability for the United States, reducing the perceived need to either come clean or abandon the operation entirely.[112]

Arthur Schlesinger provides a similar rationale in his memoir when discussing why Kennedy decided to proceed with the invasion despite the political risks. "So far as the operation itself was concerned," Schlesinger writes, "[Kennedy] felt . . . that he had successfully pared it down from a grandiose amphibious assault to a mass infiltration."[113] Moving the operation from Trinidad to the Bay of Pigs and canceling the airstrikes at the last minute as the exiles landed were all decisions made to further ensure plausible deniability despite the fact they impeded the likelihood of success.

[110] Wyden, *Bay of Pigs: The Untold Story*, 155.

[111] Kornbluh, *Bay of Pigs Declassified: The Secret CIA Report on the Invasion of Cuba*, 142–143, emphasis in original. See also "Cuba [February 17, 1961]," 5.

[112] "Cuba [From Tracy Barnes to Arthur Schlesinger, April 11, 1961]," *National Security Files, Countries, Cuba - Subjects: Intelligence Material, 1961 [Folder]; Papers of President Kennedy: National Security Files—Countries, Box 51 [Collection]* (JFK Library, 1961), 1–2. After the operation failed, CIA Director Dulles acknowledged he could have made clearer to Kennedy that plausible deniability had been compromised as early as November, 1960. See "Memorandum for Record: Paramilitary Study Group Meeting [At the Pentagon Twenty-First Meeting, May 30, 1961]," *National Security Files, Countries, Cuba - Subjects, Para-Military Study Group, Taylor Report Part II - Meeting 21 [Folder]; Papers of President Kennedy: National Security Files—Countries, Box 61A [Collection]* (JFK Library, 1961), 8–9.

[113] Schlesinger Jr., *A Thousand Days: John F. Kennedy in the White House*, 257.

Competing Explanations

It will be useful at this point to take up several alternative explanations to the one presented here. Some of these are based on arguments that emerge from the literature on covert action described in Chapter 3. Others are more idiosyncratic and have to do with this case specifically.

One possibility is that Eisenhower authorized covert action against Castro which Kennedy then reauthorized because of concerns that overt intervention would invite escalation with the Soviet Union. This explanation has obvious appeal. A year and a half after the Bay of Pigs debacle, the United States and the Soviet Union squared off in the Cuban Missile Crisis, bringing the two superpowers to the brink of nuclear war.[114] It is tempting to view these harrowing thirteen days in October 1962 as emblematic of the prospect that any U.S. intervention in Cuba during the Cold War might have spiraled into World War III. The problem is that this mischaracterizes the state of Soviet–Cuban relations—or at the very least, U.S. decision makers' perceptions of these relations—in the months leading up to April 17, 1961.

Although decision makers' interest in overthrowing Castro emanated from fears that he would turn Cuba into a Soviet satellite, they saw their actions as a preventative measure. The relationship between the two communist countries in 1960 and early 1961 was nascent, though the window for action was closing.[115] A Special National Intelligence estimate from March 22, 1960 concluded: "Should the Castro regime be threatened, the USSR would probably do what it could to support it. However, the USSR would not hesitate to write off the Castro regime before involving itself in a direct military confrontation with the US over Cuba, or, at least during the present state of Soviet policy, in a major diplomatic crisis with the US."[116] This is significant. Not only did the intelligence community believe the Soviets would not risk a military confrontation with the United States over Cuba; they also thought the Soviets would not even risk a diplomatic spat. Senior decision makers in both the United States and Soviet Union echoed similar sentiments. Arthur Schlesinger's April 5 memo to Kennedy downplayed escalation risks: "I must say, however, that I question the

[114] Graham T. Allison, "Conceptual Models and the Cuban Missile Crisis," *American Political Science Review* 63, no. 3 (1969): 689–718.

[115] Some scholars note that Khrushchev made clear to the U.S. that he was ready to lend support to the Castro regime if the U.S. attempted intervention, although the documents outlined here suggest that senior officials did not take these threats seriously. On this point, see Jones, *The Bay of Pigs*, 18.

[116] FRUS, "491. Special National Intelligence Estimate," in *Foreign Relations of the United States, 1958–1960, Cuba, Volume VI*, ed. John P. Glennon (Washington, D.C.: United States Government Printing Office, 1991), https://history.state.gov/historicaldocuments/frus1958-60v06/d491.

view that this operation would have serious substantive effect on Soviet policy. My guess is that the Soviet Union regards Cuba as in our domain and is rather surprised that we have not taken action before this to rid ourselves of Castro."[117] Evidence from the other side lends credence to Schlesinger's conclusion. Oleg Daroussenkov, a Soviet specialist on Cuba from that period, writes: "[I]n reality, the real cooperation of the Soviet military with Cuba begins after the Bay of Pigs. In a way, the Bay of Pigs invasion speeded up everything immensely. There was a big hurry to arm the Cubans before the Americans invaded."[118] This point is crucial. It suggests that relations between Castro and the Soviets strengthened as a result of the Bay of Pigs invasion. Escalation concerns surely increased afterward.[119]

While the Cuban Missile Crisis itself is beyond the scope of this book, it is worth noting that international law played an underappreciated role in shaping Kennedy's response here as well. This is all the more surprising given the overwhelming concerns about escalation. On Friday, October 19, 1962, the Executive Committee—the ad hoc group of senior officials tasked with formulating responses to the crisis—specifically requested an assessment of the legal implications of the proposed naval blockade, or quarantine, as it came to be known. Deputy Legal Advisor Leonard Meeker raised the prospect that this action might be seen as a violation of Article 2(4). Although "there were several recognized exceptions to this prohibition" including self-defense and Security Council authorization, he feared that neither option was feasible. The former was not credible, and the latter would be stymied by a Soviet veto. He pointed out, though, that OAS authorization under the auspices of the Rio Treaty, which they eventually got, might render the quarantine legal.[120] Robert Kennedy argues in his book on the crisis, "it was the vote of the Organization of American States that gave a legal basis for the quarantine . . . [which] changed our position from that of an outlaw acting in violation of international law into a country acting in accordance with twenty allies legally protecting their position."[121]

[117] FRUS, "81. Memorandum From the President's Special Assistant (Schlesinger) to President Kennedy." In his personal memoir of his time in the Kennedy administration, Schlesinger admits at one point that he might have underestimated "the possibility of Soviet reprisals against West Berlin." It is worth reiterating, though, that my theory emphasizes what senior decision makers thought at the time they made particular decisions. Assessments after the fact, though insightful, are less important. See Schlesinger Jr., *A Thousand Days: John F. Kennedy in the White House*, 253.

[118] James G. Blight and Peter Kornbluh, eds., *Politics of Illusion: The Bay of Pigs Invasion Reexamined* (Boulder, CO: Lynne Reinner Publishers, Inc., 1998), 37.

[119] In fact, Cuban–Soviet relations were strengthened greatly as a result of the failed Bay of Pigs invasion; Smith, *The Last Years of the Monroe Doctrine: 1945–1993*, 103.

[120] Abram Chayes, *The Cuban Missile Crisis: International Crises and the Role of Law* (New York and London: Oxford University Press, 1974), 15–16.

[121] Ibid., 16–17.

A second set of alternative explanations focuses on the role that domestic politics might have played in incentivizing Eisenhower and Kennedy to rely on covert action. We can easily dispense with the variant rooted in democratic peace theory.[122] Cuba was not a democracy at the time of intervention. Although Castro rode to power on a popular revolution, he did not hold elections, did not tolerate a free press, and jailed political opponents. During Castro's visit to the United States in April 1959, Nixon asked the new Cuban leader "why he didn't hold free elections." Castro supposedly responded that "[t]he people of Cuba don't want free elections; they produce bad government." Nixon then asked "why he didn't give fair trials to his opponents," to which Castro replied, "[t]he people of Cuba don't want them to have fair trials. They want them shot as quickly as possible."[123] Mutual respect for shared democracy and norms of peaceful dispute resolution was not an impediment to overt action.

Even if arguments rooted in the democratic peace do not apply here, it is possible that decision makers pursued covert action because they feared the U.S. public would have generally disapproved of overt action to topple Castro. To begin with, the most frequently voiced concern related to the prospect of overt regime change in Cuba was potential backlash from foreign audiences, who would view brazen violations of the nonintervention principle as a broken promise and evidence of American hypocrisy. Although it is conceivable that domestic audiences also cared about such things, decision makers seemed not to have noticed if they did. There is also circumstantial evidence suggesting that domestic audiences supported more open and aggressive action. One study from the mid-1960s found that a majority of those surveyed in a poll supported America's overarching foreign policy toward Cuba. The question read: "Do you approve or disapprove of the way the United States government has dealt with Fidel Castro and his government in Cuba?" In total, 55% approved, 28% disapproved, and 17% had no opinion.[124] Obviously, a poll taken from after the Bay of Pigs invasion leaves much to be desired. Even so, the fact that there seems to have been an appetite for hardline policies against Cuba implies that concerns about a hostile reaction from the American public was not an impediment to overt action. Indeed, Kennedy himself remarked at one point after the operation

[122] Bruce Russett, *Grasping the Democratic Peace: Principles for a Post-Cold War World* (Princeton: Princeton University Press, 1993).

[123] Wyden, *Bay of Pigs: The Untold Story*, 28.

[124] William C. Rogers, Barbara Stuhler, and Donald Koenig, "A Comparison of Informed and General Public Opinion on U.S. Foreign Policy," *The Public Opinion Quarterly* 31, no. 2 (1967): 248. The poll ran from August 1960 to September 1961. This question was asked just after the Bay of Pigs. Of note, a panel of "'experts'—educators, business and professional people, organization leaders, journalists, ministers, and political leaders" more strongly disapproved of U.S. policy toward Cuba at 73%.

went awry that, "if I had gone further, [the American public] would have liked me even more."[125]

A third alternative explanation, the tainted victory thesis, enjoys some support. Declassified documents show that part of why decision makers worried about overt intervention in Cuba was that "it would tend to solidify Castro's support—indeed, Castro may be trying to provoke such action."[126] Compounding this problem were concerns that if the United States openly installed a new government, they might have to stay for an extended period or leave prematurely: "Unless we were indefinitely to occupy Cuba militarily, the only solution to the Cuban problem is necessarily the emergence of a Cuban leadership willing to and capable of governing the country along lines acceptable to the Cuban people and along lines consistent with basic U.S. policy with respect to Latin America. This will take time. On the one hand, it is doubtful that any Cuban Government which resulted from U.S. armed or other overt intervention could long survive our withdrawal."[127]

The challenge for theories focused on nationalism is the fact that decision makers were ready to dispense with secrecy if they could locate or manufacture a legal exemption. The tainted victory thesis suggests that states should only be willing to go overt if they can persuade the population of the need for intervention in response to a shared threat and credibly signal that the operation would be short. None of these items were raised by decision makers.

Although it does not fit neatly into one of the three buckets of alternative explanations discussed so far, O'Rourke's study of covert regime change argues that policymakers are more likely to disregard secrecy and choose overt action instead "when they face significant time pressure to act." The imperative to act quickly before a window of opportunity closes is even more salient when states also want to "send a strong signal of their resolve to diffuse a regional crisis."[128] Both of these factors were present here, and yet decision makers pursued covert action anyway.[129] Admiral Arleigh Burke's memo from February 26, 1960, is a case in point. Recall his concern that "[i]f the present trend continues, it will soon be too late for the United States to stem the Soviet incursion into this hemisphere," as well as his belief that acting openly and forcefully, albeit unilaterally, had the benefit of "serv[ing] notice to the world that the U.S. will not tolerate

[125] Schlesinger Jr., *A Thousand Days: John F. Kennedy in the White House*, 292.

[126] FRUS, "472. Editorial Note."

[127] FRUS, "475. Letter From the Under Secretary of State for Political Affairs (Merchant) to the Chief of Naval Operations (Burke)."

[128] Lindsey O'Rourke, *Covert Regime Change: America's Secret Cold War* (Ithaca, NY: Cornell University Press, 2018), 63.

[129] Westra, *International Law and the Use of Armed Force: The UN Charter and the Major Powers*, 71–72.

the establishment of a communist or communist 'front' regime in the Western Hemisphere."[130] In March 1960, the NSC's Planning Board also discussed how the prospect of allowing Castro to remain in power could damage U.S. prestige and embolden revolutionary groups in the region.[131] These sentiments, combined with the evidence from the previous section demonstrating that decision makers knew that covert action was less likely than overt action to deliver regime change, undermine this alternative explanation.

There is a final, case-specific alternative that might help explain the United States' decision to pursue covert action against Castro, particularly Eisenhower's initial decision for secrecy. This explanation, which we might think of as the "learning thesis," goes something like this. Decision makers discovered that secrecy works based on earlier efforts at covert regime change throughout the 1950s such as the operations against Mossadegh in Iran in 1953 and Arbenz in Guatemala in 1954. Emboldened by these successes, senior officials in the Eisenhower administration thought they could exploit covert action for the same purposes in Cuba against Castro with relative ease.[132]

The learning thesis provides a partial explanation for why decision makers were attracted to covert action early on.[133] Bissell conceded as much: "Unquestionably, Castillo Armas in Guatemala"—the CIA-installed dictator that ousted Arbenz—"was an analogy and a precedent."[134] As the evidence presented in this chapter shows, however, officials were aware they were making nontrivial sacrifices by opting for secrecy. Unlike in Iran and Guatemala, Castro came to power on the heels of a popular revolution, rendering it difficult to remove him short of an invasion. Decision makers' persistent desire for plausible deniability was also driven more by concerns about preserving America's reputation and the health of international order and less by the view that covert action would be an easy, quick-fix solution to a thorny problem.

[130] FRUS, "466. Letter From the Chief of Naval Operations (Burke) to the Under Secretary of State for Political Affairs (Merchant)."

[131] FRUS, "473. Memorandum From the Assistant Secretary of State for Inter-American Affairs (Rubottom) to the Secretary of State."

[132] Wyden, *Bay of Pigs: The Untold Story*, 20.

[133] For an argument in support of this view, see Vandenbroucke, "Anatomy of a Failure: The Decision to Land at the Bay of Pigs," 474. For a more skeptical take, see Gleijeses, "Ships in the Night: The CIA, the White House and the Bay of Pigs," 40–41.

[134] Kornbluh, *Bay of Pigs Declassified: The Secret CIA Report on the Invasion of Cuba*, 152.

Conclusion

The Bay of Pigs provides considerable support for the theory developed in this book. The United States' commitment to the nonintervention principle in the UN and OAS charters constrained its ability to openly topple Castro without incurring significant costs. Decision makers worried that pursuing overt regime change without a legal exemption would damage America's moral authority and undermine faith in its commitment to restraint in light of prior promises. It is notable that this set of concerns won out over the perceived benefits of intervention, which included ridding the Western Hemisphere of a potential Soviet client so close to the continental United States. Ironically, the failed covert invasion sped up the very thing decision makers were trying to prevent.

International law also proved more salient than alternative considerations. Although it is hard to imagine given what transpired during the Cuban Missile Crisis, concerns about escalation were low in the lead-up to the Bay of Pigs. Domestic politics were not an impediment either. If anything, the evidence suggests that the public would have likely supported a more public operation. The tainted victory thesis enjoys some support. Decision makers worried that overt regime change would rally the Cuban population around Castro. But the fact that decision makers were willing to pursue overt intervention if they could locate or create a legal exemption to nonintervention, including an attack by Castro on Guantanamo Bay or on American citizens, is not predicted by this argument, which privileges persuading the population of the need for a short intervention to address a common threat.

5

Project FUBELT and Track II: Chile

On the morning of September 11, 1973, bombs rained down on La Moneda, Chile's presidential palace. Salvador Allende, the first self-avowed Marxist to be elected head of state in the Western Hemisphere, was inside. Rather than risk capture, he took his own life. His death marked the beginning of nearly two decades of repressive rule under General Augusto Pinochet. In the years preceding Allende's overthrow, Richard Nixon led a sustained campaign from the shadows to get of rid him.

There are several reasons why this case is useful for evaluating my argument. As previously mentioned, interventions in the Western Hemisphere pose a hard test since scholars often assume the United States was free to do as it pleased there.[1] This case, which involves the Cold War's most prominent adherents to *Realpolitik*, is especially difficult. Richard Nixon and Henry Kissinger are renowned for their commitment to power politics over ideology.[2] This disposition affected their foreign policy on a range of issues, from arms control[3] to the decision to seek rapprochement with China in the early 1970s.[4] Showing that international law played a role in preventing these hard-nosed realists from openly pursuing regime change against Allende, a leader they reviled and feared would encourage other revolutionaries throughout Latin America to follow suit, would be a powerful boon to my argument.

This case also differs from the Bay of Pigs in ways that demonstrate the generalizability of my theory. First, whereas Castro's Cuba was a dictatorship, Salvador

[1] G. John Ikenberry, *Liberal Leviathan: The Origins, Crisis, and Transformation of the American World Order* (Princeton, NJ: Princeton University Press, 2011), 27.

[2] Thomas A. Schwartz, "Henry Kissinger: Realism, Domestic Politics, and the Struggle Against Exceptionalism in American Foreign Policy," *Diplomacy & Statecraft* 22, no. 1 (2011): 121–141.

[3] Francis J. Gavin, "Nuclear Nixon: Ironies, Puzzles, and the Triumph of Realpolitik," in *Nixon in the World : American Foreign Relations, 1969–1977*, ed. Fred Logevall and Andrew Preston (Oxford and New York: Oxford University Press, 2008), 126–145.

[4] Bruce Jentleson, *The Peacemakers: Leadership Lessons from Twentieth-Century Statesmanship* (New York: W. W. Norton, 2018), 4–30.

In the Shadow of International Law. Michael Poznansky, Oxford University Press (2020). © Oxford University Press.
DOI: 10.1093/oso/9780190096595.001.0001

Allende came to power through elections. This episode thus offers an important test of a legal theory of covert action in a case that should be an easy win for arguments that focus on Chile's status as a democracy as the decisive factor.[5]

Second, the two cases took place in different contexts. Although relations between the superpowers were tense in the lead-up to the Bay of Pigs, the United States was not embroiled in any major overseas conflicts at the time. The height of the Berlin Crisis, which increased tensions and resulted in the building of the Berlin Wall, transpired months after the failed attempt to depose Castro.[6] By contrast, this episode occurred when the United States was mired in the Vietnam War, which was going poorly by 1970.[7] Although technically directed at Asia, the Guam Doctrine, wherein Nixon declared that the United States would avoid future "Vietnams," reinforced the lack of appetite for new military ventures.[8] The notion that covert action against Allende was attractive simply due to these constraints is appealing. As this chapter will show, however, while the Nixon administration did not consider invading Chile, they still weighed and ultimately rejected alternative overt options for removing Allende given America's commitment to nonintervention. These included destabilizing sanctions and expelling Chile from the OAS. Decision makers were not drawn to covert action merely because there were no viable overt options. There were, but international legal commitments took them off the table.

Despite some differences with the last chapter, the evidence we would expect to see if my argument is correct is similar. First, decision makers should exhibit concerns about intervening overtly against Allende without a legal exemption that would justify a violation of the nonintervention principle. Statements demonstrating a desire to preserve the credibility of American commitments and safeguard the legitimacy of U.S. leadership would support my argument. Second, decision makers should have unsuccessfully searched for legal exemptions that would have made overt regime change less risky. This would include authorization for intervention from the UN Security Council or the OAS, or a credible a self-defense claim such as the presence of Americans in imminent danger.

[5] Alexander B. Downes and Mary Lauren Lilley, "Overt Peace, Covert War?: Covert Intervention and the Democratic Peace," *Security Studies* 19, no. 2 (2010): 266–306; Lindsey O'Rourke, *Covert Regime Change: America's Secret Cold War* (Ithaca, NY: Cornell University Press, 2018), 51–52; Bruce Russett, *Grasping the Democratic Peace: Principles for a Post-Cold War World* (Princeton, NJ: Princeton University Press, 1993), 120–124.

[6] Although the crisis had been brewing since at least 1958, it reached its zenith in the summer of 1961. See Kevin W. Dean, "'We Seek Peace, But We Shall Not Surrender': JFK's Use of Juxtaposition for Rhetorical Success in the Berlin Crisis," *Presidential Studies Quarterly* 21, no. 3 (1991): 531–544.

[7] Gregory A. Daddis, *Withdrawal: Reassessing America's Final Years in Vietnam* (New York: Oxford University Press, 2017).

[8] J.L.S. Girling, "The Guam Doctrine," *International Affairs* 46, no. 1 (1970): 48–62.

Before proceeding, it is worth noting that there is a longstanding debate about the impact of U.S. meddling on Allende's downfall relative to Chile's own internal politics.[9] Because my goal is to explore the Nixon administration's decision to intervene covertly, I draw heavily from declassified U.S. government documents, and so the narrative may give the appearance of endorsing the former view.[10] That is not my intention. Whether U.S. interference was more consequential than domestic political forces is an important question but ultimately beyond the purview of this chapter. The aim here is simply to uncover the reasons why Nixon acted as he did. Readers should bear this in mind throughout.

Historical Background

Chile gained its independence from Spain in 1818. For the next century and a half, it enjoyed a special status among Latin America countries. Between 1818 and 1973, "Chile underwent only three brief interruptions of its democratic tradition."[11] The four decades preceding Pinochet's coup were defined by constitutional rule, democratic elections, and peaceful transitions of power.

The figure at the center of this story, Salvador Allende, first came onto Washington's radar in 1958. It was a presidential election year in Chile. Allende, representing a socialist coalition, was locked in a tight race with Jorge Alessandri, the right-wing candidate.[12] Alessandri narrowly won. This episode, combined with the Cuban Revolution in 1959, caused the United States to reevaluate its unwavering support for the far right.[13] And so the Alliance for Progress, a Kennedy administration initiative aimed at strengthening cooperation with Latin

[9] James Lockhart, *Chile, the CIA and the Cold War: A Transatlantic Perspective* (Edinburgh: Edinburgh University Press, 2019); William D. Rogers and Kenneth Maxwell, "Fleeing the Chilean Coup: The Debate Over U.S. Complicity," *Foreign Affairs* 83, no. 1 (2004): 160–165.

[10] On the way in which the use of declassified government documents can give the appearance of greater causal weight to one actor relative to other forces in this case, see Kenneth Maxwell, "The Other 9/11: The United States and Chile, 1973," *Foreign Affairs* 82, no. 6 (2003): 147–151.

[11] United States Senate, "Covert Action in Chile 1963–1973," *Staff Report of the Select Committee to Study Governmental Operations With Respect To Intelligence Activities, 94th Congress, First Session.* (Washington, D.C.: U.S. Government Printing Office, 1975), 3, http://www.intelligence.senate.gov/sites/default/files/94chile.pdf.

[12] Kristian Gustafson, *Hostile Intent: U.S. Covert Operations in Chile, 1964-1974* (Washington, D.C.: Potomac Books, Inc., 2007), 21; Jonathan Haslam, *The Nixon Administration and the Death of Allende's Chile: A Case of Assisted Suicide* (London and New York: Verso, 2005), 10; Sigmund, *The Overthrow of Allende and the Politics of Chile, 1964–1976*, 25.

[13] Peter Kornbluh, *The Pinochet File: A Declassified Dossier on Atrocity and Accountability* (New York: The New Press, 2003), 3.

American countries by promoting economic growth and prosperity throughout the hemisphere, was born.[14] Chile was the crown jewel of this initiative.[15]

Allende pursued his second bid for president in 1964. This time he squared off against Eduardo Frei, a left-of-center Christian Democrat backed by the United States. According to one estimate, the millions of dollars the CIA pumped into Frei's campaign comprised roughly fifty percent of his total expenditures. The CIA also disseminated propaganda aimed at discrediting Allende and his coalition.[16] In the end, Frei was victorious.[17] For years afterward, the United States continued to bolster the moderate left and middle class in Chile. Frei and the Christian Democrats (PDC) were the big winners of these efforts.[18] The Soviet Union did similar things for socialist and communist parties.[19]

The last time the United States indirectly faced off against Salvador Allende was during the 1970 presidential elections, held on September 4. It was a three-way race between Allende for Unidad Popular (UP), Radomiro Tomic for the PDC, and Jorgé Alessandri, functionally representing the National Party.[20] As in the past two elections, the United States tried to prevent Allende from winning. But rather than supporting either of his competitors, the CIA engaged in a spoiling operation.[21] This involved propaganda aimed at harming the UP, financial and logistical support to the Christian Democrats, and attempts to bribe Chilean legislators to vote against Allende in case there was a Congressional runoff between the top two vote earners.[22] Although Allende ended up winning the most votes, Alessandri came in a close second, triggering the runoff on

[14] Gustafson, *Hostile Intent: U.S. Covert Operations in Chile, 1964–1974*, 25–26.

[15] Sigmund, *The Overthrow of Allende and the Politics of Chile, 1964–1976*, 27.

[16] Kornbluh, *The Pinochet File : A Declassified Dossier on Atrocity and Accountability*, 4.

[17] Gustafson, *Hostile Intent: U.S. Covert Operations in Chile, 1964–1974*, 47–48.

[18] Kornbluh, *The Pinochet File : A Declassified Dossier on Atrocity and Accountability*, 5–6.

[19] Haslam, *The Nixon Administration and the Death of Allende's Chile: A Case of Assisted Suicide*, 13–14.

[20] Michael Poznansky, "Stasis or Decay? Reconciling Covert War and the Democratic Peace," *International Studies Quarterly* 59, no. 4 (2015): 822.

[21] FRUS, "A Spoiling Operation: The 1970 Chilean Presidential Election, January 1–September 4, 1970," in *Foreign Relations of the United States, 1969–1976, Volume XXI, Chile, 1969–1973*, ed. James McElveen and James Siekmeier (Washington, D.C.: United States Government Printing Office, 2014), https://history.state.gov/historicaldocuments/frus1969-76v21/ch2.

[22] FRUS, "29. Memorandum for the 40 Committee," in *Foreign Relations of the United States, 1969–1976, Volume XXI, Chile, 1969–1973*, ed. James McElveen and James Siekmeier (Washington, D.C.: United States Government Printing Office, 2014), https://history.state.gov/historicaldocuments/frus1969-76v21/d29; "Political Action Related to 1970 Chilean Presidential Election [For the 40 Committee, March 5, 1970]," *Country Files—Latin America, Chile Wrap-Up and Post-Mortem, March 1971, The President (1 of 3) [Folder]; National Security Council Files, Henry A. Kissinger Office Files, Country Files-Latin America, Box 128 [Collection]* (Nixon Presidential Library, 1970), 1–14.

October 24.[23] Most observers expected Congress to choose Allende since he had secured the most votes in the initial contest, which is precisely what they did. In November, Salvador Allende Gossens was inaugurated president of Chile.[24]

Allende confronted challenges on several fronts. Externally, the United States was trying to overthrow him. Internally, high inflation, food shortages, and protests contributed to his political plight.[25] Allende also faced challenges from the military.[26] First in the fall of 1972, and then again in the summer of 1973, he formed two emergency cabinets composed of senior officers in an effort to placate the armed forces. The move only politicized Chile's military further.[27] Rumors of a coup began to spread soon afterward and picked up steam in late August after the constitutionally oriented commander-in-chief of the armed forces, General Carlos Prats, resigned in the wake of a smear campaign against him.[28] The eventual decision to launch a coup was made on September 7 by General Gustavo Leigh of the Air Force and General Augusto Pinochet of the Army.[29] Allende was overthrown four days later on September 11.[30] Pinochet quickly consolidated power, bringing strongman rule to Chile.[31]

[23] Tomic received just 27.8% of the vote. See "The Situation Following the Chilean Presidential Election [September 7, 1970]," *Country Files—Chile Volume II, 01 Jan '70—Nov '70 (2 of 4) [Folder]; National Security Council Files, Country Files-Latin America, Boxes 771-779 [Collection]* (Nixon Presidential Library, 1970), 1.

[24] Downes and Lilley, "Overt Peace, Covert War?: Covert Intervention and the Democratic Peace," 290.

[25] Haslam, *The Nixon Administration and the Death of Allende's Chile: A Case of Assisted Suicide*, 107–126. See also "Chile: Conciliation, Confrontation, or Coup? [April 4, 1972]," *SRG Meeting—Chile, 4/11/72 (1 of 2)[Folder]; Senior Review Group Meetings, SRG Meeting Chile 4/11/72 (1 of 2) to SRG Meeting Korea/UN 8/9/72, Box H-064 [Collection]* (Nixon Presidential Library, 1972), 2; "Next Steps Options on Chile [April 4, 1972]," *SRG Meeting—Chile, 4/11/72 (1 of 2)[Folder]; Senior Review Group Meetings, SRG Meeting Chile 4/11/72 (1 of 2) to SRG Meeting Korea/UN 8/9/72, Box H-064 [Collection]* (Nixon Presidential Library, 1972), 1–14.

[26] "Chile: Conciliation, Confrontation, or Coup? [April 4, 1972]," 5–6.

[27] Gustafson, *Hostile Intent: U.S. Covert Operations in Chile, 1964–1974*, 205–207.

[28] Sigmund, *The Overthrow of Allende and the Politics of Chile, 1964–1976*, 231–232. See also "Contingency Paper for Chile Ad Hoc Working Group [August 24, 1973]," *NSSM 97 (1 of 3) [Folder]; National Security Study Memorandums, NSSM 94 to NSSM 97 (3 of 3), Box H-172 [Collection]* (Nixon Presidential Library, 1973), 1.

[29] Gustafson, *Hostile Intent: U.S. Covert Operations in Chile, 1964–1974*, 211.

[30] Poznansky, "Stasis or Decay? Reconciling Covert War and the Democratic Peace," 823.

[31] Kornbluh, *The Pinochet File : A Declassified Dossier on Atrocity and Accountability*. For a summary of the immediate aftermath of the coup, including efforts by the United States to support the Christian Democrats in one of the major signs that decision makers believed politics might return to normal, see Gustafson, *Hostile Intent: U.S. Covert Operations in Chile, 1964–1974*, 227–236.

Why Intervene in Chile?

Decision makers did not believe that Chile, even under Allende, would pose a direct threat to the United States. An intelligence memo produced three days after the September 4 election concluded that "[t]he U.S. has no vital national interests within Chile . . . . The world military balance of power would not be significantly altered by an Allende government."[32] Senior officials pointed out that even if the Soviets used Chile to project power throughout the Western Hemisphere, "this in itself would not constitute a mortal threat to the United States."[33] What, then, pushed Nixon to intervene?

One concern was how Allende's election would shape the broader politics of the region. The fact that he had come to power through the ballot box was particularly troubling to decision makers.[34] National Security Study Memorandum (NSSM) 97, published in August 1970, stated: "a. Hemispheric cohesion would be threatened by the challenge that an Allende government would pose to the OAS, and by the reactions that it would create in other countries . . . b. An Allende victory would represent a definite psychological setback to the U.S. and a definite psychological advance for the Marxist idea."[35] If a self-avowed Marxist could win elections and get away with it in Chile, so the thinking went, this might inspire others across Latin America to follow suit.

An October 16 strategy paper reiterated many of these concerns: "An Allende Government is likely to lead opposition to U.S. influence in the Western Hemisphere and to promote policies counter to ours in the region . . . It is likely

[32] "The Situation Following the Chilean Presidential Election [September 7, 1970]," 9. See also "Strategy Toward Chile [October 16, 1970]," *Senior Review Group—Chile (NSSM 97) 10/17/70 [Folder]; Senior Review Group Meetings, Joint SRG-WSAG Meeting Filed Under WSAG 10/9/1970 (Empty) to Senior Review Group Middle East 10/29/70, Box H-048 [Collection]* (Nixon Presidential Library, 1970), 1.

[33] "Strategy Toward Chile [October 16, 1970]," 1–2.

[34] FRUS, "150. Minutes of a Meeting of the Senior Review Group," in *Foreign Relations of the United States, 1969–1976, Volume XXI, Chile, 1969–1973*, ed. James McElveen and James Siekmeier (Washington, D.C.: United States Government Printing Office, 2014), https://history.state.gov/historicaldocuments/frus1969-76v21/d150; "HAK Talking Points on Chile [NSC Meeting, November 6, 1970]," *NSC Meeting—Chile, 11/6/1970 [Folder]; National Security Council Meetings, NSC Meeting—Defense Budget 8/19/70 (1 of 2) to NSC Meeting—NATO and MBFR 11/19/70 (3 of 4), Box H-029 [Collection]* (Nixon Presidential Library, 1970), 1–3; "NSC Meeting, November 6—Chile [From Henry Kissinger to Richard Nixon, November 5, 1970]," *NSC Meeting—Chile, 11/6/1970 [Folder]; National Security Council Meetings, NSC Meeting—Defense Budget 8/19/70 (1 of 2) to NSC Meeting—NATO and MBFR 11/19/70 (3 of 4), Box H-029 [Collection]* (Nixon Presidential Library, 1970), 1.

[35] Kornbluh, *The Pinochet File : A Declassified Dossier on Atrocity and Accountability*, 8. See also United States Senate, "Covert Action in Chile 1963–1973," 47–48.

to seek the elimination of U.S. influence and authority in the Hemisphere." The paper also points out that Allende might "seek linkages to the Soviet Union, Cuba and the socialist world and . . . constitute a potential entry point and base for these countries' influence and activities" while "encourag[ing] elements opposed to the United States in other Latin American countries."[36]

Not all officials believed the doom and gloom. A memo from Viron Vaky, Henry Kissinger's top aide on Latin America, wondered: "Is Allende a mortal threat to the US? It is hard to argue this. Is he a serious problem that would cost us a great deal? Certainly. Is it inevitable that he will consolidate his power? He has a very good chance; but it is far from inevitable or that if he does that he will be a success. Does an Allende government start . . . South American dominoes? Unlikely; the impact of a Marxist state in the rest of Latin America is containable."[37] An assessment from the State Department's Bureau of Intelligence and Research poured more cold water on the prospects of a communist takeover, noting that "the rise of a Soviet-type regime in Chile under the leadership of the Chilean Communist Party seems far-fetched, partly for the following reasons: a) the checkered history of Communists in coalitions in the post-World War II period, b) the long-standing fractious relationship between Chilean Communists and Socialists, and c) the erosion of Soviet authority in the Communist movement leading to ambiguities concerning the nature of a Marxist-Leninist state."[38]

Kissinger, Nixon's all-important National Security Advisor, was less sanguine in his evaluation. He outlined his chief concerns in a memo to the president on November 5, 1970:

> "*The election of Allende as President of Chile poses for us one of the most serious challenges ever faced in this hemisphere.* Your decision as to what to do about it may be the most historic and difficult foreign affairs decision you will have to make this year, for what happens in Chile over the next six to twelve months will have ramifications that will go far beyond just US-Chilean relations. They will have an effect on what happens in the rest of Latin America and the developing world; on what our future

[36] "Strategy Toward Chile [October 16, 1970]," 1–2.

[37] FRUS, "86. Memorandum From Viron P. Vaky of the National Security Council Staff to the President's Assistant for National Security Affairs (Kissinger)," in *Foreign Relations of the United States, 1969–1976, Volume XXI, Chile, 1969–1973*, ed. James McElveen and James Siekmeier (Washington, D.C.: United States Government Printing Office, 2014), https://history.state.gov/historicaldocuments/frus1969-76v21/d86.

[38] "Chile: Is Allende the Prelude to a Communist Victory? [October 1, 1970]," *Senior Review Group—Chile (NSSM 97) 10/14/70 [Folder]; Senior Review Group Meetings, Joint SRG-WSAG Meeting Filed Under WSAG 10/9/1970 (Empty) to Senior Review Group Middle East 10/29/70, Box H-048 [Collection]* (Nixon Presidential Library, 1970), i.

> position will be in the hemisphere; and on the larger world picture, including our relations with the USSR. They will even affect our own conception of what our role in the world is."[39]

As we know from what transpired, Kissinger won the day. Over the course of three years, the Nixon administration worked assiduously but quietly to remove Allende. The next section details these covert efforts. The subsequent section explains why plausible deniability was deemed valuable.

The Plan to Overthrow Allende

The covert operation against Allende unfolded in several stages.[40] The first spanned from the September 4 election to the October 24 runoff. It was comprised of two prongs, known as Track I and Track II.[41] Track I was an extension of the spoiling operations leading up to the 1970 election[42] but also included ploys decision makers referred to as "Rube Goldberg" schemes.[43] The Frei reelection gambit was the most prominent. It hinged on Alessandri being confirmed by Congress in the runoff, forming a military cabinet, and resigning.

[39] FRUS, "172. Memorandum From the President's Assistant for National Security Affairs (Kissinger) to President Nixon," in *Foreign Relations of the United States, 1969–1976, Volume XXI, Chile, 1969–1973*, ed. James McElveen and James Siekmeier (Washington, D.C.: United States Government Printing Office, 2014), emphasis in original, https://history.state.gov/historicaldocuments/frus1969-76v21/d172.

[40] Downes and Lilley, "Overt Peace, Covert War?: Covert Intervention and the Democratic Peace," 285–287.

[41] "Action in Support of U.S. Posture Towards Chile," *Senior Review Group—Chile (NSSM 97) 10/17/70 [Folder]; Senior Review Group Meetings, Joint SRG-WSAG Meeting Filed Under WSAG 10/9/1970 (Empty) to Senior Review Group Middle East 10/29/70, Box H-048 [Collection]* (Nixon Presidential Library, 1970), 1–3; United States Senate, "Covert Action in Chile 1963–1973," 23–26. See also United States. Central Intelligence Agency, *CIA Activities in Chile*, 2000, https://www.cia.gov/library/reports/general-reports-1/chile/.

[42] Poznansky, "Stasis or Decay? Reconciling Covert War and the Democratic Peace," 822. The actual planning for Track I—strategies for the September 4 to October 24 period—begun earlier in the summer after the publication of NSSM 97. See Gustafson, *Hostile Intent: U.S. Covert Operations in Chile, 1964–1974*, 105–106.

[43] FRUS, "99. Telegram From the Embassy in Chile to the Department of State," in *Foreign Relations of the United States, 1969–1976, Volume XXI, Chile, 1969–1973*, ed. James McElveen and James Siekmeier (Washington, D.C.: United States Government Printing Office, 2014), https://history.state.gov/historicaldocuments/frus1969-76v21/d99; FRUS, "102. Backchannel Message From the Ambassador to Chile (Korry) to the President's Assistant for National Security Affairs (Kissinger)," in *Foreign Relations of the United States, 1969–1976, Volume XXI, Chile, 1969–1973*, ed. James McElveen and James Siekmeier (Washington, D.C.: United States Government Printing Office, 2014), https://history.state.gov/historicaldocuments/frus1969-76v21/d102.

This would trigger new elections, allowing Eduardo Frei to run again and hopefully win. The gambit was abandoned after it became clear Alessandri's chances of succeeding in the runoff were slim to none. An additional ploy called for Frei to dismiss his cabinet and replace them with senior military officers, appoint an acting president, leave Chile, and allow the military to retain control until new elections could be held.[44] This plan never got off the ground either.[45]

Whereas Track I sought to prevent Allende from taking office via the election gambit and other nonviolent schemes, Track II—codenamed Operation FUBELT—focused on stimulating a violent coup by working with factions in the Chilean military. Details of these efforts were highly restricted. Edward Korry, the U.S. Ambassador to Chile, was kept out of the loop, as were others.[46]

Even before Chileans cast their ballots on September 4, there were hints the United States might try to instigate a coup in the event of an Allende victory. A covert annex to NSSM 97, written a month before the 1970 election, provided an early blueprint. According to Peter Kornbluh, "[a] secret CIA supplement titled 'Extreme Option—Overthrow Allende,' addressed the assumptions, advantages, and disadvantages of attempting to foster a military coup." Plausible deniability was key to the enterprise: "This option assumes that every effort would be made to ensure that the role of the United States was not revealed, and so would require that the action be effected through Chilean institutions, Chileans and third-country nationals . . . . Successful U.S. involvement with a Chilean military coup would almost certainly permanently relieve us of the possibility of an Allende government in Chile."[47]

Discussions of spearheading a coup through the Chilean military picked up in tempo after the first phase of the presidential elections. On September 8 during a meeting of the 40 Committee—the group responsible for reviewing covert actions at the time—several senior officials, including CIA Director Richard Helms, discussed the feasibility of such an option. Kissinger requested "a cold-blooded assessment of: (1) the pros and cons and problems and prospects involved should a Chilean military coup be organized now with U.S. assistance, and (2) the pros and cons and problems and prospects involved in organizing an effective

[44] Kornbluh, *The Pinochet File : A Declassified Dossier on Atrocity and Accountability*, 12–13. See also FRUS, "107. Telegram From the Central Intelligence Agency to the Station in Chile," in *Foreign Relations of the United States, 1969–1976, Volume XXI, Chile, 1969–1973*, ed. James McElveen and James Siekmeier (Washington, D.C.: United States Government Printing Office, 2014), https://history.state.gov/historicaldocuments/frus1969-76v21/d107.

[45] Downes and Lilley, "Overt Peace, Covert War?: Covert Intervention and the Democratic Peace," 291. The intelligence community's estimate of the chances that this gambit would succeed were slim. See "The Situation Following the Chilean Presidential Election [September 7, 1970]," 3.

[46] Kornbluh, *The Pinochet File : A Declassified Dossier on Atrocity and Accountability*, 14.

[47] Ibid., 8–9.

future Chilean opposition to Allende."[48] The head of the Western Hemisphere Division at the CIA, William Broe, sent a note to the CIA Station Chief in Santiago the following day. In it, Broe argued that "[t]he only prospect with any chance of success whatsoever is a military *golpe* either before or immediately after Allende's assumption of power."[49]

Plans to engineer a coup received a boost on September 15 during a meeting involving Nixon, Kissinger, Helms, and Attorney General John Mitchell. Helms' handwritten notes capture the broad strokes of what was discussed: "1 in 10 chance perhaps, but save Chile!; worth spending; not concerned risks involved; no involvement of embassy; $10,000,000 available, more if necessary; full-time job—best men we have; game plan; make the economy scream; 48 hours for plan of action."[50] Helms relayed the message to his aides the next day. Soon after, a Special Task Force was created.[51] The CIA's plan involved three components: "(1) identify, contact, and collect intelligence on coup-minded officers; (2) inform them that the U.S. was committed to 'full support in coup' short of sending the marines; and (3) foster the creation of 'a coup climate by propaganda, disinformation and terrorist activities' to provide a stimulus and pretext for the military to move."[52]

The culmination of Track II was the Viaux solution. General Roberto Viaux had been forced into early retirement after unsuccessfully attempting to oust Frei in 1969.[53] The CIA first contacted him on October 5, 1970.[54] Concerns quickly emerged that Viaux would either be unable to successfully launch a coup or that he would move prematurely. In mid-October, officials urged him to hold off for the time being.[55] Viaux ignored them and proceeded with a plan

[48] Ibid., 45–46.

[49] Ibid., 10.

[50] FRUS, "93. Editorial Note," in *Foreign Relations of the United States, 1969–1976, Volume XXI, Chile, 1969–1973*, ed. James McElveen and James Siekmeier (Washington, D.C.: United States Government Printing Office, 2014), https://history.state.gov/historicaldocuments/frus1969-76v21/d93.

[51] Kornbluh, *The Pinochet File : A Declassified Dossier on Atrocity and Accountability*, 2. See also FRUS, "94. Memorandum for the Record," in *Foreign Relations of the United States, 1969–1976, Volume XXI, Chile, 1969–1973*, ed. James McElveen and James Siekmeier (Washington, D.C.: United States Government Printing Office, 2014), https://history.state.gov/historicaldocuments/frus1969-76v21/d94.

[52] Kornbluh, *The Pinochet File : A Declassified Dossier on Atrocity and Accountability*, 14.

[53] Haslam, *The Nixon Administration and the Death of Allende's Chile: A Case of Assisted Suicide*, 43.

[54] Gustafson, *Hostile Intent: U.S. Covert Operations in Chile, 1964–1974*, 122.

[55] Maxwell, "The Other 9/11: The United States and Chile, 1973"; FRUS, "154. Telegram From the Central Intelligence Agency to the Station in Chile," in *Foreign Relations of the United States, 1969–1976, Volume XXI, Chile, 1969–1973*, ed. James McElveen and James Siekmeier (Washington, D.C.: United States Government Printing Office, 2014), https://history.state.gov/historicaldocuments/frus1969-76v21/d154.

to kidnap General René Schneider as a prelude to taking over the government.[56] Schneider, the commander-in-chief of the armed forces, was seen as an impediment given his constitutionalist fealties.[57] After several botched attempts, he was murdered on the way to military headquarters on October 22. Viaux and his co-conspirators were thrown in jail.[58] Two days later, Allende became president.

"After the failure of Project FUBELT," Kornbluh writes, "U.S. policymakers adjusted their strategy; but the goal of bringing Allende down remained. Rather than a small group of covert operatives trying to stimulate a military move in a short period of time, most of the U.S. government would now be involved in a long-term, expanded effort to destabilize the Chilean government—economically, politically, and militarily."[59] National Security Decision Memorandum 93, drafted in November 1970, outlined the broad contours of the approach using coded language: "The President has decided that (1) the public posture of the United States will be correct but cool . . . but that (2) the United States will seek to maximize pressures on the Allende government to prevent its consolidation and limit its ability to implement policies contrary to U.S. and hemisphere interests."[60] Although not stated here explicitly, helping to bring about Allende's downfall was the takeaway message.[61]

In many respects, this second phase offered a broader attack surface. Economic turmoil and squabbles within Allende's coalition created a host of problems for him.[62] The Nixon administration exploited these and other weaknesses. During municipal elections in April 1971 and congressional elections in March 1973, millions of dollars were funneled to moderate parties and candidates contesting Unidad Popular.[63] The CIA also carried out a campaign to spread chaos. They fomented truckers' strikes, supported right-wing militias like Patria Y Libertada who were engaged in violence, financially supported *El Mercurio*—one of Chile's largest right-wing newspapers at the time—in a propaganda campaign to discredit Allende, and (re)established contacts within the Chilean military to

[56] Gustafson, *Hostile Intent: U.S. Covert Operations in Chile, 1964–1974*, 127–128.

[57] The U.S. role in the plot that led to Schneider's murder has been a source of contention. See Kornbluh, *The Pinochet File : A Declassified Dossier on Atrocity and Accountability*, 29–35. For additional discussion of Schneider's constitutionalist predilections, see Haslam, *The Nixon Administration and the Death of Allende's Chile: A Case of Assisted Suicide*, 47.

[58] Gustafson, *Hostile Intent: U.S. Covert Operations in Chile, 1964–1974*, 129–130.

[59] Kornbluh, *The Pinochet File : A Declassified Dossier on Atrocity and Accountability*, 79–80.

[60] "National Security Decision Memorandum 93 [November 9, 1970]," *NSC H-Files: Policy Papers—NSDM 93 (1 of 2) [Folder]; National Security Decision Memorandums, NSDM 90 to NSDM 94, Box H220 [Collection]* (Nixon Presidential Library, 1970), 1.

[61] I thank Peter Kornbluh for pointing me to these distinctions.

[62] Kornbluh, *The Pinochet File : A Declassified Dossier on Atrocity and Accountability*, 86.

[63] United States Senate, "Covert Action in Chile 1963–1973," 28–29.

identify potential coup plotters.[64] Although the CIA had some inclination that a coup was imminent before it happened in 1973, they did not play a direct role in the operation itself.[65]

Confronting Legal Constraints

A persistent theme running through the declassified documents is a desire to avoid damaging America's moral authority and credibility by pursuing any operation against Allende that risked revealing U.S. complicity. The covert annex to NSSM 97 from August 1970 referenced earlier captures these sentiments: "An unsuccessful attempt, involving as it probably would revelation of U.S. participation, would have grave consequences for our relations with Chile, in the hemisphere, in the United States and elsewhere around the world."[66] A CIA report dated September 8, 1970, expresses similar concerns. According to the authors, "if the USG's role in such an activity were exposed, it could seriously damage US prestige and credibility both in Chile and elsewhere in the hemisphere."[67] Although these concerns are not directly tied to nonintervention, they are nevertheless suggestive.

Viron Vaky elaborated on these points in a memo to Kissinger prior to the September election. He first summarized the options for dealing with Allende, relaying the CIA's conclusion that the prospects of a coup were slim and that the Frei reelection gambit was the best choice. Vaky's analysis leaves little doubt that he believed the risks of getting caught interfering in Chile, even in nonviolent schemes, were significant: "The biggest danger is exposure of US involvement. This would wreck our credibility, solidify anti-U.S. sentiment in Chile in a permanent way, create an adverse reaction in the rest of Latin America and the world and perhaps domestically. Exposure of US involvement with an effort that failed would be disastrous; it would be this Administration's Bay of Pigs." He then linked these concerns to commitments the United States had made in the

[64] Kornbluh, *The Pinochet File : A Declassified Dossier on Atrocity and Accountability*, 90–96.

[65] As the Church Committee puts it: "[A]lthough the purpose was information-gathering, the United States maintained links to the group most likely to overthrow the new president. To do was to walk a tightrope; the distinction between collecting information and exercising influence was inherently hard to maintain. Since the Chilean military perceived its actions to be contingent to some degree on the attitude of the U.S. government, those possibilities for exercising influence scarcely would have had to be consciously manipulated"; United States Senate, "Covert Action in Chile 1963–1973," 6.

[66] Kornbluh, *The Pinochet File : A Declassified Dossier on Atrocity and Accountability*, 8–9.

[67] Quoted in Downes and Lilley, "Overt Peace, Covert War?: Covert Intervention and the Democratic Peace," 294.

past. "What we propose," he argued, "is patently a violation of our own principles and policy tenets. Moralism aside, this has practical operational consequences. Are they rhetoric or do they have meaning? If these principles have any meaning, we normally depart from them only to meet the gravest threat to us, e.g., to our survival."[68] Here again, the lack of specificity regarding the source of these concerns—in particular, whether they are rooted in America's commitment to nonintervention or something else—renders this suggestive.

As an interesting aside, Peter Kornbluh uses this document as evidence that Vaky was acting somewhat courageously by pointing out the folly of targeting Allende in violation of America's promises and values.[69] But Vaky's views are more complicated upon closer inspection. For instance, Kornbluh omits his suggestion, contained later in the same memo, that while a coup was infeasible as of September 14, 1970, "[the U.S.] should keep [its] lines open and broadened into the military. An opportunity may open up later." Vaky also advised Kissinger that the Frei reelection gambit be allowed to continue "but with the utmost discretion and tact and with absolute minimum USG involvement."[70] What we see here is a senior decision maker attempting to balance the benefits of targeting Allende against the damage the United States might do to its credibility and moral authority if they got caught. What we do not see is wholesale opposition to any form of foreign intervention in Chile.

The evidence presented so far only offers imperfect support for my argument. Attentiveness to U.S. credibility and moral authority, and a general fear of damaging relations in Latin America and across the globe, are consistent with the mechanisms my framework identifies. Because these documents do not explicitly tie such concerns to brazen violations of nonintervention, however, they leave something to be desired. The references to America's "principles and policy tenets" are indicative but not quite specific enough. Fortunately, there are additional documents which show that America's past commitment to nonintervention in particular was one of the main factors driving these concerns.

For starters, a report from the NSC's Interdepartmental Group for Inter-American Affairs, written in March 1971, offers a window into how the Nixon administration thought about the nonintervention principle in general terms. A section on the "Inter-American System" spelled out the benefits of participating in fora like the OAS. These included fostering solidarity among nations in the Western Hemisphere, helping to jointly resolve collective problems,

[68] FRUS, "86. Memorandum From Viron P. Vaky of the National Security Council Staff to the President's Assistant for National Security Affairs (Kissinger)."

[69] Kornbluh, *The Pinochet File : A Declassified Dossier on Atrocity and Accountability*, 11.

[70] FRUS, "86. Memorandum From Viron P. Vaky of the National Security Council Staff to the President's Assistant for National Security Affairs (Kissinger)."

and offering security from external threats. Given this, the thinking went, "withdrawal would represent a shattering reversal of U.S. policy and efforts built up over more than 80 years of history. President Nixon emphasized our 'firm commitment to the Inter-American system . . . as exemplified by the OAS.' "[71]

Even more relevant for the current discussion is an elaboration of the obligations America assumed by joining this group: "While recognizing the advantages of U.S. participation in the Inter-American system, we also recognize there are certain liabilities and certain inherent restraints on U.S. freedom of action, including: a. In accepting the principles of non-intervention and of collective action in the fields of peace and security, the U.S. has placed a voluntary restraint on its freedom to take unilateral action in these fields, e.g. under the Monroe Doctrine."[72] The authors note that Latin American countries view this as "an obvious improvement over the self-appointed U.S. role under the Monroe Doctrine" and "value the restraint on the exercise of preponderant U.S. power and the acceptance by the U.S. of the principle of non-intervention."[73] Finally, the report makes clear that the United States need not entirely refrain from pursuing its interests "unilaterally if necessary," but that "this residual responsibility must be exercised with great restraint in the light of our obligations under international law and in view of Latin American sensitivity to unilateral U.S. action and intervention."[74]

The foregoing shows that the Nixon administration generally took America's commitment to the nonintervention principle seriously, especially in the OAS Charter, and appreciated the risks associated with blatantly disregarding it. These concerns also played a direct role in shaping how decision makers thought about the pros and cons of different regime change options against Allende in particular.

On September 14, 1970, Winston Lord, an NSC staffer and a special advisor to Kissinger, wrote a memo linking U.S. actions in Chile to the ongoing war in Vietnam: "There are many powerful arguments against U.S. meddling in the Chilean internal scene to thwart an Allende victory in the congressional runoff . . . [including] the risk of exposure and the damage to our policy throughout Latin America, doubts whether effective actions are possible, the general

[71] "Review of U.S. Policy Toward Latin America: Response to National Security Memorandum 108 [Chapter on The Inter-American System]," *SRG Meeting—Latin America/Caribbean, 8/17/71 (3 of 3) [Folder]; Senior Review Group Meetings—SRG Meeting-Latin America/Caribbean 8/17/71 (1 of 3) to SRG Meeting-Cease-Fire 10/1/71, Box H-059 [Collection]* (Nixon Presidential Library, 1971), 1–2.

[72] "Review of U.S. Policy Toward Latin America: Response to National Security Memorandum 108 [Chapter on The Inter-American System]," 2.

[73] Ibid., 3–4.

[74] Ibid., 4.

repugnance of our trying to arrange the political structure of another country, etc." He believed that "[r]evelation of our directly moving to reverse the unpalatable electoral outcome in Chile would make a mockery of our stance on South Vietnam, would make hollow the following tenets of our policy: We are for *self-determination* of the South Vietnamese people without *foreign interference*; We think this can best be accomplished through *free elections; We will abide by the outcome* of elections, even if this means Communist influence or control."[75] In short, Lord is arguing that if the United States got caught pursuing regime change in Chile, it would undermine perceptions of America's fealty to nonintervention and have broad ripple effects. As we will see in the next chapter, officials in the Johnson administration were similarly concerned that observers would view an invasion of the Dominican Republic as indicative of America's indifference to nonintervention with consequences in Vietnam.

One of the most illuminating documents is the aforementioned memo Kissinger wrote to Nixon on November 5, 1970.[76] His assessment of the situation was bleak: "While events in Chile pose these potentially very adverse consequences for us, *they are taking a form which makes them extremely difficult for us to deal with or offset,* and which in fact poses *some very painful dilemmas for us.*"[77] Kissinger's depiction of these dilemmas speak to the heart of this book's argument. "We are strongly on record in support of self-determination and respect for free election[s]," he argued. "*[Y]ou are firmly on record for non-intervention in the internal affairs of this hemisphere and of accepting nations 'as they are.'* It would therefore be very costly for us to act in ways that appear to violate those principles, and Latin Americans and others in the world will view our policy as a test of the credibility of our rhetoric." Later in the memo, he wondered whether it was desirable "to do something to prevent [Allende] from consolidating himself now when we know he is weaker than he will ever be and when he obviously fears our pressure and hostility." For Kissinger, the advantage of this approach was that Allende would inevitably align Chile with countries in the Soviet camp. One of the risks, though, was that it could "*[damage] our credibility in the eyes of*

[75] FRUS, "87. Memorandum From Winston Lord of the National Security Council Staff to the President's Assistant for National Security Affairs (Kissinger)," in *Foreign Relations of the United States, 1969–1976, Volume XXI, Chile, 1969–1973*, ed. James McElveen and James Siekmeier (Washington, D.C.: United States Government Printing Office, 2014), emphasis in original, https://history.state.gov/historicaldocuments/frus1969-76v21/d87.

[76] A day later, a document containing Kissinger's talking points for the November 6 NSC meeting reiterated each of the same themes that appear below. See "HAK Talking Points on Chile [NSC Meeting, November 6, 1970]," 1–12.

[77] FRUS, "172. Memorandum From the President's Assistant for National Security Affairs (Kissinger) to President Nixon," emphasis in original.

the rest of the world as interventionist . . . and perhaps [fail] to prevent his consolidation anyway."[78]

Several aspects of this memo stand out. First, the sheer fact that Kissinger flagged America's pledges to nonintervention as a constraint on their capacity to openly pursue regime change against Allende and his sensitivity to the United States' credibility and image abroad is significant. His concerns echo the arguments contained in the NSC report from March 1971, which highlighted the Nixon team's continued support for the OAS and the risks of unilaterally intervening in contravention of America's legal obligations. In terms of smoking-gun evidence, this is about as close as it gets.

Second, the timing of the memo is notable. Most of the documents presented in this section were drawn from the period before Chile's presidential elections and the congressional runoff when time pressures were acute. Kissinger wrote this memo in the weeks after Allende was officially selected as president of Chile. If there was ever a moment when U.S. decision makers might have reconsidered their approach toward Allende, this was it. And yet, they did not. To the contrary, the administration continued to behave as my theory would predict, even after the time pressure to act was diminished following the election.

Third, the fact that it was Henry Kissinger uttering these concerns is important. As many have pointed out, Kissinger held a unique status in the Nixon administration.[79] In the context of U.S. policy toward Allende and Chile specifically, "briefing the president was the job of Kissinger alone. 'Kissinger's determination to monopolize all contact with the new president' [even] caused troubles."[80] Given his special role, we can be more confident than usual that the views Kissinger expressed here were directly shaping U.S. foreign policy toward Chile and Allende.

Fourth, the fact that Kissinger was a hard-nosed realist makes his sensitivity to things like the nonintervention principle all the more surprising. My claim is not that Kissinger internalized the importance of nonintervention, self-determination, and the like. I am agnostic about this. Rather, what stands out is the fact that someone like him felt hamstrung by commitments to nonintervention.

Finally, there is evidence that Kissinger had earlier entertained the question of whether the United States should bother worrying about getting caught

[78] Ibid., emphasis added.

[79] Jussi M. Hanhimaki, *The Flawed Architect: Henry Kissinger and American Foreign Policy* (Oxford and New York: Oxford University Press, 2004); Joshua Rovner, *Fixing the Facts: National Security and the Politics of Intelligence* (Ithaca: Cornell University Press, 2011), 90; Jeremy Suri, *Henry Kissinger and the American Century* (Cambridge, MA: The Belknap Press of Harvard University Press, 2007).

[80] Gustafson, *Hostile Intent: U.S. Covert Operations in Chile, 1964–1974*, 86–87.

pursuing regime change against Allende. In a meeting of the Senior Review Group on October 29, 1970, Kissinger said: "Let me ask a cynical question. Do we care whether we are blamed if our action succeeds in getting rid of [Allende]? Certainly, if he goes, people will say, 'Those damned Americans!' "[81] It is apparent from his subsequent memo and talking points that the administration's eventual answer to this question was yes, they cared.

As the preceding discussion makes clear, a major reason decision makers were reluctant to pursue overt regime change against Allende was their fear that openly violating America's commitment to nonintervention would damage its credibility and moral authority. Kornbluh, echoing the through line of this book, places these concerns in the context of the postwar legal order: "Nixon's bald directive [to secretly overthrow Allende] was neither unparalleled nor unprecedented. Throughout the nineteenth and early twentieth-century history of U.S. policy toward Latin America, presidents frequently authorized overt military efforts to remove governments deemed undesirable to U.S. economic and political interests. After the signing of the United Nations charter in 194[5], which highlighted nonintervention and respect for national sovereignty, the White House made ever-greater use of the newly created Central Intelligence Agency to assert U.S. hegemonic designs."[82] The theory developed in this book provides a framework for understanding how these dynamics played out in Chile.

Legal Evaluation and Options Short of War

Decision makers never seriously discussed overtly invading Chile as a live option. While not stated anywhere explicitly, the reasons for this likely included a failing war in Vietnam and the lack of appetite for new large-scale military ventures. On its face, this might seem like it poses problems for my argument. If officials simply pursued covert action given the lack of viable overt alternatives, the legal theory I am offering might be unnecessary. There is reason to doubt this is what happened. The previous section partially refuted this notion already by showing that decision makers were not just attracted to secrecy given their desire to avoid becoming embroiled in another war. Instead, they were sensitive to America's commitment to nonintervention and wanted to avoid incurring

[81] FRUS, "169. Minutes of a Meeting of the Senior Review Group," in *Foreign Relations of the United States, 1969–1976, Volume XXI, Chile, 1969–1973*, ed. James McElveen and James Siekmeier (Washington, D.C.: United States Government Printing Office, 2014), https://history.state.gov/historicaldocuments/frus1969-76v21/d169.

[82] Kornbluh, *The Pinochet File : A Declassified Dossier on Atrocity and Accountability*, 2–3.

hypocrisy and credibility costs by openly violating it. This section goes one step further. I show that decision makers discussed numerous overt options short of a military offensive with the stated goal of regime change. This helps demonstrate that leaders faced a real choice between covert and overt action even though they did not consider sending the Marines to Santiago. I also show that when officials evaluated these options, the issue of whether they could find legal cover was front and center.

Before proceeding, though, it may be worth briefly revisiting a point made in Chapter 2 about the relationship between nonintervention and regime-change operations not involving force. Technically speaking, the overt policies discussed below are not covered under Article 2(4) of the UN Charter, which emphasizes forcible interference. However, the version of nonintervention contained in the OAS Charter explicitly encompasses non-forcible activities. As the following will make clear, decision makers were aware of these legal constraints. Parenthetically, the fact that overt military force was the main alternative to covert action in the Bay of Pigs probably helps explain why decision makers routinely referenced both the OAS *and* the UN charters.

Keeping this in mind, the first step is to show that decision makers contemplated pursuing overt options short of a full-fledged invasion and, equally important, that they had regime change on the brain. The evidence bears this out. Consider a strategy document produced on October 16, 1970, following a Senior Review Group meeting which outlined a series of policy options for achieving regime change in Chile. One of them involved exclusively covert means, the benefits of which mirror the discussion from the previous section.[83] Another option was an "[o]vertly hostile, hard line" approach. According to the report, "[t]his option assumes Allende is automatically our implacable enemy. *It aims at his overthrow, and certainly at his failure, by using all possible pressure to isolate and hamper him, and it would make that unambiguously clear to everyone*. Possible program lines are sketched below. These could be shaded harder or softer depending on how many of these measures we used."[84] This approach included a range of politically oriented policies like isolating Allende from the OAS, as well as a host of economic tools to destabilize the Chilean economy such as cutting off aid and investment.

After Allende became president, decision makers continued to discuss the stakes associated with pursuing policies akin to the overtly hostile approach described in the strategy document. In his November 5 memo to Nixon, Kissinger raised the "hostile approach"—the preferred option of the Defense

[83] "Strategy Toward Chile [October 16, 1970]," 6–9.

[84] Ibid., 4, emphasis added.

Department, the CIA, and some officials in the State Department—as one of several courses of action the United States might take. One version, which was eventually rejected in favor of a quieter but equally antagonistic solution, would demonstrate overt hostility toward Allende by: "(1) initiating punitive measures, such as terminating aid or economic embargo; (2) making every effort to rally international support of this position; and (3) declaring and publicizing our concern and hostility."[85] Kissinger did not explicitly use the language of regime change. He opted for euphemisms instead, for example, "prevent him from consolidating himself *now* when he is at his weakest."[86]

When Kissinger briefed his counterparts at an NSC meeting on November 6, they were less timid about articulating the true aims of these policies. After agreeing with Kissinger's assessment that Allende would turn Chile into a communist state and consolidate power, Secretary of State Rogers argued that "[i]f we have to be hostile, we want to do it right and bring him down." His hangup with the overt options turned on their political ramifications in Latin America. Secretary of Defense Melvin Laird concurred. "I agree with Bill Rogers," he said. "We have to do everything we can to hurt him and bring him down, but we must retain an outward posture that is correct." Later in the meeting, Under Secretary of State John Irwin echoed similar sentiments: "The problem is how to bring about [Allende's] downfall."[87]

When policymakers evaluated the feasibility of overtly hostile options in subsequent memos, they homed in on the challenges of gaining legal cover as a means of justifying such action, the benefits that would accrue if they could secure exemptions, and the risks if they could not. A lengthy report approved by the Ad Hoc Inter-Agency Working Group in December 1970, intended for the Senior Review Group at Kissinger's request, is instructive.[88] One of the issues discussed was whether the United States could gain OAS support for sanctions against Allende. The report began by pointing out that when they had sponsored sanctions against members in the past, they "[were] tied directly to

[85] FRUS, "172. Memorandum From the President's Assistant for National Security Affairs (Kissinger) to President Nixon."

[86] Ibid., emphasis in original.

[87] "Memorandum of Conversation—NSC Meeting—Chile (NSSM 97) [November 6, 1970]," *NSC Meeting—Chile, 11/6/1970 [Folder]; National Security Council Meetings, NSC Meeting—Defense Budget 8/19/70 (1 of 2) to NSC Meeting—NATO and MBFR 11/19/70 (3 of 4), Box H-029 [Collection]* (Nixon Presidential Library, 1970), 2–3.

[88] The fact that the Inter-Agency Working Group was intended for the Senior Review Group—which had explicitly raised the prospect of bringing Allende down as evidenced by the October 16 strategy document—is a strong indicator that the non-forcible overt actions outlined in their report were tied to the ultimate goal of regime change.

interventionism" by the target.[89] Those imposed against the Dominican Republic in 1960 followed Rafael Trujillo's aggression against Venezuela. Sanctions levied against Castro in 1962 and 1964 were justified on similar grounds.

The issue for decision makers was that Allende's behavior did not rise to this level: "[He] is currently maintaining that he will respect the principle of non-intervention and as yet there are no clear signs that his government is engaged in subversive activities in other countries . . . . Allende will probably attempt to avoid the interventionist label so as to minimize the chances of confrontations with neighboring countries and the application of OAS sanctions." Although officials realized that they could "[a]ttempt to organize support for sanctions against Chile as soon as there is reiteration by Allende of his advocacy of revolution in the hemisphere," they made clear that without "concrete evidence of actual interventionist activities" it would "alienate many of our Latin American supporters," among other risks. Waiting for tangible evidence would "project a favorable image of restraint" and "have a reasonably good chance of winning the necessary two-thirds majority of Rio Treaty signatories."[90] These remarks are similar to a point contained in an options paper the Executive Secretary of the National Security Council sent to Kissinger prior to an NSC meeting on November 6: "we will be in the strongest position within Chile and the hemisphere if it is clear that sanctions that we take against Chile are in reaction to what the Allende government *does* rather than to what we fear it *may* do."[91]

The Inter-Agency report also discussed the conditions under which the United States could isolate Allende by challenging Chile's status as an OAS member. Allende had initially promised to leave the regional body during the 1970 presidential campaign but reversed course once in office.[92] The problem for the Nixon administration was that "an attempt to exclude Chile from the OAS . . . in the absence of clear grounds and gross provocation by Chile, would be most unlikely to win sufficient support. Such an effort would, in addition, be highly divisive; would, if sponsored by the U.S., be a decisive and dramatic act of open hostility toward Chile; would alienate many of our Latin American

[89] "A Study of Options for U.S. Strategy Concerning Chile's Future Participation in the Organization of American States [December 4, 1970]," *NSSM 97 (1 of 3) [Folder]; National Security Study Memorandums, NSSM 94 to NSSM 97 (3 of 3), Box H-172 [Collection]* (Nixon Presidential Library, 1970), 11.

[90] "A Study of Options for U.S. Strategy Concerning Chile's Future Participation in the Organization of American States [December 4, 1970]," 11–15.

[91] "Options Paper for NSC: Chile [November 3, 1970]," *NSC Meeting—Chile, 11/6/1970 [Folder]; National Security Council Meetings, NSC Meeting—Defense Budget 8/19/70 (1 of 2) to NSC Meeting—NATO and MBFR 11/19/70 (3 of 4), Box H-029 [Collection]* (Nixon Presidential Library, 1970), 5–6, emphasis in original.

[92] Sigmund, *The Overthrow of Allende and the Politics of Chile, 1964–1976*, 131.

supporters; and would project an unfavorable public image." Officials also believed, however, that "[t]his current negative prospect would be altered in direct proportion to the clarity, extent and blatancy of Chilean actions inimical to the interests of OAS members other than the U.S., particularly acts of intervention."[93]

This same report also argued that one of the best chances for securing OAS backing for overtly hostile actions against Allende was if Soviet military bases were discovered in Chile. The explicit use of legal language is noteworthy and betrays an eagerness to gain adequate cover:

> If Soviet military facilities affecting hemispheric security were to be established in Chile, the OAS, while not the focal point of our actions, would nevertheless play an important role. In the above eventuality, we judge Soviet and Chilean actions would be viewed with such seriousness in the hemisphere as to assure in all probability a two-thirds majority for the adoption of appropriate measures commensurate with the threat. Just as in the 1962 Cuban missile crisis, in which United States action received unanimous support of the OAS member states, the OAS Council, under authority of the Rio Treaty, could provide useful legal justification and political support for our actions.[94]

As this makes clear, officials believed that targeting Allende under the auspices of the OAS and Rio Treaty in response to a breach of regional security would be a game changer. Whether or not they envisioned full-scale intervention to overthrow Allende or something else is hard to say from this document alone. The phrase "appropriate measures" is vague. But the subsequent reference to U.S. actions during the Cuban Missile Crisis—which involved a naval blockade or "quarantine" to use the official parlance of the Kennedy administration—indicate that the authors had military action of some kind in mind.[95]

Given how events played out, it seems none of these scenarios came to pass, thereby limiting what the United States could do overtly within the confines of its treaty obligations and commitments to nonintervention. Kissinger's assessment of the situation from after the Chilean congressional runoff proved

[93] "A Study of Options for U.S. Strategy Concerning Chile's Future Participation in the Organization of American States [December 4, 1970]," 5.

[94] Ibid., 26.

[95] In the Cuban Missile Crisis, the U.S. received OAS backing to implement a naval quarantine around Cuba with the aim of forcing the Soviets to remove nuclear weapons. See Abram Chayes, *The Cuban Missile Crisis: International Crises and the Role of Law* (New York and London: Oxford University Press, 1974), 16–17.

prescient: "Allende's government is likely to move along lines that will make it very difficult to marshal international or hemisphere censure of him—he is most likely to appear as an 'independent' socialist country rather than a Soviet satellite or 'Communist government.'"[96]

Trade-Offs

This section shows that the Nixon administration appreciated the sacrifices they were making by opting for plausibly deniable action against Allende. The fact that they stuck with the quiet option knowing that an overt operation of some kind would have been more likely to result in his overthrow is testament to the importance they accorded to protecting America's credibility and moral authority.

One of the challenges confronting the Nixon administration in its efforts to covertly stimulate a coup had to do with finding the right people for the job. Recall from Chapter 3 that covert operations frequently require outsourcing to local actors who may not share the same objectives or sense of urgency as the intervener. This can create obstacles when it comes to achieving an objective. Part of the problem in Chile was that those most likely to carry out a coup, senior military officers, had a constitutionalist bent. CIA Director Helms' earlier comment from a 40 Committee meeting about the "apolitical history" of Chile's military being an impediment to coup plotting speaks to this issue. Kissinger, who was also present at this meeting, "voiced his 'considerable skepticism that once Allende is in the presidency there w[ould] be anyone capable of organizing any real counterforce against him.'"[97]

A cable from CIA headquarters on October 16 affirms the challenges of trying to plot a coup covertly: "It is firm and continuing policy that Allende be overthrown by a coup. [While] [i]t would be much preferable to have this transpire prior to 24 October . . . efforts in this regard will continue vigorously beyond this date." The cable goes on to emphasize "that these actions be implemented clandestinely and securely so that the USG and American hand be well hidden" and points out that "this imposes upon us a high degree of selectivity in making military contacts and dictates that these contacts be made in the most secure manner."[98] While I was unable to find evidence that decision makers ever considered overtly stimulating a coup—probably because

[96] FRUS, "172. Memorandum From the President's Assistant for National Security Affairs (Kissinger) to President Nixon."

[97] Kornbluh, *The Pinochet File : A Declassified Dossier on Atrocity and Accountability*, 9.

[98] Ibid., 64–65.

they would never have been able to legally justify it—doing so in secret clearly imposed limitations, as this document makes clear. Without a plausible deniability requirement, they may well have been able to scour the Chilean military to determine which officers would be most effective and then provide them with all the resources they needed.[99]

More generally, the Nixon administration confronted the challenge of how much support they could provide for the various schemes to unseat Allende without betraying U.S. involvement. Vaky's memo to Kissinger on September 14, in which he outlined the CIA's assessment of options for preventing Allende from winning the runoff, touches on this issue: "[T]here are limits to what we can do acceptably. It is not a question of just adding more effort and money. Our capacity to succeed is simply not a function of how much effort we put in, and the greater our involvement the sharper the danger of exposure."[100] Vaky's sentiment here is similar to the one Richard Bissell expressed in his response to the scathing postmortem from the CIA's Inspector General after the Bay of Pigs fiasco. Devoting more resources to increase the chances of success can have the effect of reducing the prospect of concealing the sponsor's hand. These constraints are not relevant when plausible deniability is not an issue.

On October 5, Vaky updated Kissinger on the available options in the lead-up to the October 24 runoff. "In my own view," he wrote, "there is now no chance that anything will happen which we can either stimulate or support to prevent Allende's election [on] October 24 . . . . I think we are kidding ourselves to believe there are any more gambits that we can work. Not even economic deterioration is likely to achieve such a dramatic turn-around in less than three weeks." Vaky's next sentence touches on the central theme of this section: "*Unless we are prepared to intervene overtly and physically in Chile we had better start planning for an Allende election and how we deal with that situation.*"[101] The limitations imposed by the requirements of covert action, namely that the U.S. hand not show, are evident in these remarks.

[99] Though a rare occurrence, foreign powers openly supporting coups is not unprecedented. France, for example, did it in the Central African Republic in 1979. See "Bokassa Successor Says Dictator Killed Children in April Massacre," *New York Times* Sept. 24 (1979), https://www.nytimes.com/1979/09/24/archives/bokassa-successor-says-dictator-killed-children-in-april-massacre.html.

[100] FRUS, "86. Memorandum From Viron P. Vaky of the National Security Council Staff to the President's Assistant for National Security Affairs (Kissinger)."

[101] FRUS, "134. Memorandum From Viron P. Vaky of the National Security Council Staff to the President's Assistant for National Security Affairs (Kissinger)," in *Foreign Relations of the United States, 1969–1976, Volume XXI, Chile, 1969–1973*, ed. James McElveen and James Siekmeier (Washington, D.C.: United States Government Printing Office, 2014), https://history.state.gov/historicaldocuments/frus1969-76v21/d134.

A briefing memo for Secretary Rogers dated November 3 from two senior State Department officials indicates continued appreciation of the U.S. government's limited ability to overthrow Allende shy of an invasion after he won in the runoff. The administration, they argued, had to operate under "a realistic assessment of U.S. capability to influence the situation there." They continued by pointing out that "developments in Chile will be primarily controlled by the Allende government and by its reactions to internal pressures. U.S. overt and covert capabilities to force the course of events positively in our favor, *short of the use of armed force*, are marginal at best."[102]

Of course, Allende was eventually deposed. And regardless of whether the United States had a direct hand in it, it is unarguable that they helped create conditions conducive to a "coup climate."[103] Nevertheless, the fact remains that decision makers stuck with a policy they knew was less efficacious than overt alternatives in the interest of hiding their role. Simply because we know with hindsight that a coup transpired three years after they began these efforts does not change this fact.

Competing Explanations

This section considers a number of competing explanations. One is that decision makers were driven to pursue regime change secretly in Chile for fear that overt intervention would trigger escalation with the Soviet Union. This thesis falls short on several fronts. Of the hundreds of declassified documents examined for this chapter, none indicated that decision makers worried about direct confrontation with the Soviets as they weighed the costs and benefits of different strategies for regime change in Chile. To paraphrase Donald Rumsfeld, the absence of evidence of escalation concerns does not mean that such evidence is absent, but it is still noteworthy.

Evidence from the Soviet side lends further support to the notion that escalation concerns were not salient in this case. Although the Soviet Union financially backed Allende and his party, they knew their capacity to prevent him from

[102] FRUS, "171. Briefing Memorandum From the Acting Assistant Secretary of State for Inter-American Affairs (Hurwitch) and the Director of the Policy Planning Staff (Hartman) to Secretary of State Rogers," in *Foreign Relations of the United States, 1969–1976, Volume XXI, Chile, 1969–1973*, ed. James McElveen and James Siekmeier (Washington, D.C.: United States Government Printing Office, 2014), emphasis added, https://history.state.gov/historicaldocuments/frus1969-76v21/d171.

[103] Kornbluh, *The Pinochet File : A Declassified Dossier on Atrocity and Accountability*, 16–22.

being ousted was limited.[104] Reports coming in through the CIA at the time confirmed as much. Yuri Andropov, chairman of the KGB, purportedly conceded at one point that "Latin America is a sphere of special U.S. interests. The U.S. has permitted us to act in Poland and Czechoslovakia. We must remember this. Our policy in Latin America must be cautious."[105] Chilean politicians appreciated these constraints as well. Jacques Chonchol Chait, the official responsible for enacting agrarian reform during the Allende years, put it this way: "At the time of the appearance of UP the situation had changed. We were witness to a degree of rapprochement between the Great Powers. Peaceful co-existence was entering a phase of intense diplomatic and economic activity with a view to normalising relations between the United States and the Soviet Union and to finding for each the means of respecting the sphere of influence of the other."[106]

A second set of alternative arguments looks to domestic politics. One variant, democratic peace theory, must be taken more seriously than it was in the last chapter. Unlike Castro's Cuba, Chile was democratic when the United States intervened. From the time Eduardo Frei was elected in 1964 until Allende's overthrow in 1973, Chile enjoyed a high score on the Polity IV index, which ranks countries on a 20-point scale from most autocratic (-10) to most democratic (+10).[107] Senior decision makers shared these assessments.[108] As Kissinger stated at one point, "Allende was elected legally, the first Marxist government ever to come to power by free elections. He has legitimacy in the eyes of Chileans and most of the world; there is nothing we can do to deny him that legitimacy or claim that he does not have it."[109]

The fact that the United States covertly targeted a country they recognized as democratic is not enough on its own to substantiate democratic peace theory. One would also need to show that senior officials opted for secrecy specifically because of Chile's status as a democracy and, just as importantly, that the audience they wanted to deceive was the American public. The evidence on this score is mixed. On the one hand, Allende's election at the ballot box

[104] For a comprehensive study of secret Soviet and Cuban involvement in Chile during this period, see Kristian Gustafson and Christopher Andrew, "The Other Hidden Hand: Soviet and Cuban Intelligence in Allende's Chile," *Intelligence and National Security* 33, no. 3 (2018): 407–421.

[105] Quoted in Gustafson, *Hostile Intent: U.S. Covert Operations in Chile, 1964–1974*, 207.

[106] Quoted in Haslam, *The Nixon Administration and the Death of Allende's Chile: A Case of Assisted Suicide*, 154–155.

[107] Monty G. Marshall, Ted Robert Gurr, and Keith Jaggers, "Polity IV Project: Political Regime Characteristics and Transitions, 1800–2009. Dataset Users' Manual," *Center for Systemic Peace*, 2010.

[108] Downes and Lilley, "Overt Peace, Covert War?: Covert Intervention and the Democratic Peace," 290–293.

[109] FRUS, "172. Memorandum From the President's Assistant for National Security Affairs (Kissinger) to President Nixon."

was certainly relevant. In a phone call with Kissinger on September 14, 1970, Secretary Rogers warned: "After all we've said about elections, if the first time a Communist wins the U.S. tries to prevent the constitutional process from coming into play we will look very bad."[110] The problem is that the U.S. public was not the audience officials were most concerned about. Rather, they cared most about foreign reactions. According to Downes and Lilley, the record in this case is "filled with discussions of the negative repercussions for the U.S.'s reputation in Latin America and the wider world of openly working to overthrow Allende."[111]

While not fully supportive of the democratic peace, decision makers' concern that overthrowing an elected leader would damage America's credibility and image abroad raises interesting questions for my argument, which prioritizes international law as a key driver of these types of concerns. To be clear, the nonintervention principle need not be the only commitment states worry about violating to qualify as being relevant. It might actually be more surprising if officials completely disregarded the fact that Allende was elected when weighing various intervention options against him.[112] Nevertheless, there are several reasons to suspect that nonintervention took precedence over concerns about democracy.

First, some policymakers viewed America's past pledges to respect elections as subordinate to broader commitments to nonintervention. Winston Lord's memo, cited previously, wherein he situated respect for election outcomes as a logical consequence of nonintervention, offers a good example. It is likely that Kissinger also had a similar conception in mind. His description of free elections as part and parcel of America's commitment to self-determination, a corollary of nonintervention and a core part of the UN Charter, is suggestive. Second, comparing the evidence in this case to the previous chapter supports this point. In the Bay of Pigs, pledges to respect elections were irrelevant since Cuba was

[110] FRUS, "88. Transcript of a Telephone Conversation Between Secretary of State Rogers and the President's Assistant for National Security Affairs (Kissinger)," in *Foreign Relations of the United States, 1969–1976, Volume XXI, Chile, 1969–1973*, ed. James McElveen and James Siekmeier (Washington, D.C.: United States Government Printing Office, 2014), https://history.state.gov/historicaldocuments/frus1969-76v21/d88. See also FRUS, "171. Briefing Memorandum From the Acting Assistant Secretary of State for Inter-American Affairs (Hurwitch) and the Director of the Policy Planning Staff (Hartman) to Secretary of State Rogers." It is interesting to note that decision makers did not draw distinctions between Western-style liberal democracy and Allende's brand of democratic socialism in these assessments. Rather, the fact that he was elected took precedence over these differences, at least with respect to the implications of intervention.

[111] Downes and Lilley, "Overt Peace, Covert War?: Covert Intervention and the Democratic Peace," 294.

[112] For a general argument about norms and covert action, see O'Rourke, *Covert Regime Change: America's Secret Cold War*.

not a democracy. Nevertheless, the absence of legal exemptions to nonintervention was sufficient to drive decision makers underground. Although it is necessary to examine more cases before drawing firm conclusions, based on these two chapters we can tentatively posit that commitments to free elections on their own are not a necessary condition of covert action for the United States. Third and finally, I showed earlier that decision makers were willing to embrace overtly hostile policies against Allende if they could garner legal cover for such actions; Chile's status as a democracy was orthogonal.

A broader argument rooted in domestic politics holds that Nixon intervened covertly against Allende because the American public would have disapproved for reasons other than Chile's status as a democracy. The available evidence does not support this explanation. If anything, it points in the opposite direction. Declassified records show that leaders worried that the American public and Congress would react negatively if the United States did not act *more* forcefully.

One concern in this vein was that Nixon would be personally blamed for allowing a second Cuba to emerge in the Western Hemisphere. As we will see in the next chapter, Johnson had this same concern in the lead-up to the Dominican invasion. A declassified memo from November 3, 1970, argues that despite the positive press coverage up through that time, "[a]s the actions of the Allende government become more overtly hostile to U.S. interests . . . we may expect adverse reaction by some sectors of the U.S. public, press, and Congress to the 'establishment of another communist government in the hemisphere,' with consequent pressures on U.S. policy."[113] Some officials worried that this kind of criticism would negatively affect Nixon's chances of securing reelection in 1972.[114] If domestic politics were the determining factor, decision makers might well have pursued overt regime change against Allende. The fact that they did not is problematic for this argument.

The tainted victory thesis enjoys some support in this case. There was concern that overt aggression against Allende would trigger popular backlash. The strategy document from October 16 mentioned above argued that hostile action against Allende in which the U.S. role was known "would galvanize Latin American nationalism and make it Allende's greatest ally. It would almost surely unify Chileans on this ground and give Allende an argument to resist us; it will antagonize the rest of the Hemisphere because of its image of 'intervention.' " Quieter approaches were deemed beneficial partly because they "avoid[ed] the pitfall of public confrontation, the 'David and Goliath' syndrome" and

[113] "Options Paper for NSC: Chile [November 3, 1970]," 3. See also "Memorandum of Conversation—NSC Meeting—Chile (NSSM 97) [November 6, 1970]," 2.

[114] Downes and Lilley, "Overt Peace, Covert War?: Covert Intervention and the Democratic Peace," 296.

"recognize[d] the need to be on the right side of nationalism."[115] Kissinger's oft-cited November 5 memo also invokes the threat of nationalism as a liability of overt intervention. It would, he noted, "giv[e] [Allende] the nationalistic issue as a weapon to entrench himself" and "[turn] nationalism and latent fear of US domination in the rest of Latin America into violent and intense opposition to us."[116]

As in the previous chapter, the fact that decision makers were seemingly willing to pursue overtly hostile policies to topple Allende if they could secure legal exemptions is not predicted by the tainted victory thesis. I was unable to find evidence of Nixon administration officials discussing the need to persuade the Chilean population that short-term interference was necessary to address a common threat. Rather, their main considerations turned on how to persuade audiences in Latin America and around the world that they were behaving in conformity with existing international legal commitments.

A final alternative explanation worth evaluating, also taken up in the last chapter, turns on the idea that decision makers are more likely to pursue overt action when there is significant time pressure to act and a perceived need to signal resolve. Both factors were present in this case. And yet, the Nixon administration opted for covert action anyway. In terms of time pressure, the moment leading up to the election of Salvador Allende was particularly acute. Unlike in Cuba, where decision makers could only speculate about how much time they had before Castro fully consolidated power, elections impose tangible deadlines. Decision makers' interest in moving before the congressional runoff on October 24 exemplifies this. Even still, they stuck with covert schemes they knew had a limited chance of working due to legal constraints. This runs counter to the notion that proverbial closing windows push leaders toward overt options. Time pressures obviously lessened after Allende won the presidency in late October.

The perceived need to signal resolve was also salient. Decision makers expressed concern that inaction would show weakness to allies and adversaries but opted for covert action against Allende anyway. Kissinger warned the president at one point that "our failure to react to this situation risks being perceived in Latin America and in Europe as indifference or impotence in the face of clearly adverse developments in a region long considered our sphere of influence."[117] During a meeting at the White House the next day at 9:40 a.m., Nixon talked at length about the risks of sitting idly by while Allende remained in power. Concerns about U.S. resolve were palpable:

[115] "Strategy Toward Chile [October 16, 1970]," 8–9.

[116] FRUS, "172. Memorandum From the President's Assistant for National Security Affairs (Kissinger) to President Nixon."

[117] Ibid.

> If Chile moves as we expect and is able to get away with it—our public posture is important here—it gives courage to others who are sitting on the fence in Latin America . . . . This is not the same as Europe—with Tito and Ceaucescu—where we have to get along and no change is possible. Latin America is not gone, and we want to keep it. Our Cuban policy must not be changed. It costs the Russians a lot; we want it to continue to cost. Chile is gone too—he isn't going to mellow . . . . No impression should be permitted in Latin America that they can get away with this, that it's safe to go this way. All over the world it's too much the fashion to kick us around. We are not sensitive but our reactions must be coldly proper . . . . We can't put up with 'Give Americans hell but pray they don't go away.' There must be times when we should and must react, not because we want to hurt them but to show we can't be kicked around.[118]

Despite this, Nixon concluded the United States "must be proper on the surface with Allende, but otherwise we will be tough. He is not going to change; only self-interests will affect him."[119] The evidence thus points in the opposite direction of what we would expect if concern about demonstrating resolve was decisive.

Conclusion

The Nixon administration's efforts to quietly topple Salvador Allende in Chile lends support to a legal theory of covert action. Although an overt invasion was never seriously considered, decision makers faced a real choice between overtly hostile policies aimed at bringing down Allende and a covert campaign to accomplish the same thing. The reason they chose the latter conforms with this book's expectations. Decision makers feared that brazenly violating nonintervention would damage America's position of leadership and commitment to restraint, both of which are observable implications of my two mechanisms. The fact that Nixon and Kissinger, two of the Cold War's most well-known realists, were sensitive to these concerns showcases the reach of this book's framework.

My theory also outperformed alternative explanations. Unlike in the Bay of Pigs, escalation played virtually no role in this case. Although more relevant, domestic politics did not fare particularly well either. Key details run counter to

[118] "Memorandum of Conversation—NSC Meeting—Chile (NSSM 97) [November 6, 1970]," 4–5.

[119] Ibid., 5.

democratic peace theory's expectations. Moreover, there is evidence that Nixon was concerned that he might be blamed for letting Chile go communist and chose to pursue a second-best covert option anyway. The tainted victory thesis performed slightly better, helping to account for one of the perceived benefits of plausible deniability but failing when it comes to predicting when decision makers would be willing to pursue regime change overtly.

6

Operation Power Pack: Dominican Republic

Lyndon B. Johnson's invasion of the Dominican Republic in 1965 marked the first large-scale overt U.S. intervention in Latin America in over three decades. The purpose of the operation, codenamed Power Pack, was to prevent the country from going communist after the reigning junta had been forced out of the capital by rebels loyal to Juan Bosch, the exiled former president of the country. This chapter identifies the factors incentivizing Johnson to openly deploy upwards of 21,000 troops at a time when American involvement in Vietnam was ramping up.

The kind of evidence we would expect to see if my argument is correct is different than what we saw in the two covert cases. To begin with, we would expect the Johnson administration to have, and appeal to, one or more legal exemptions to the nonintervention principle. This would include a credible self-defense claim such as the need to protect U.S. nationals in clear and present danger or authorization for intervention from an international body like the UN Security Council or the Organization of American States. Particularly powerful evidence would include public and private statements of how these legal exemptions satisfied America's obligations under international law.

Given how this case unfolded, it is challenging to validate the implied counterfactual, namely that Johnson would have opted for the quiet option if credible legal exemptions were unavailable. The difficulty here is that exemptions *were* available as soon as the crisis broke out, meaning that the bulk of available documents were devoted to how best to exploit them to justify overt intervention.

This notwithstanding, there are several pieces of evidence to suggest that things might have turned out differently if legal exemptions were unavailable. First, before the OAS officially got involved in the Dominican crisis, some officials discussed the possibility of discreetly supporting the junta in its efforts to reclaim power. Second, the United States pursued covert regime change against

In the Shadow of International Law. Michael Poznansky, Oxford University Press (2020). © Oxford University Press.
DOI: 10.1093/oso/9780190096595.001.0001

Rafael Trujillo four years before Power Pack due to concerns about hypocrisy and credibility costs emanating from what would have amounted to a brazen violation of nonintervention. As in the previous two chapters, officials discussed the prospect of going overt if they could secure a legal exemption. Finally, the Johnson administration reverted to covert action during the June 1966 elections after the United States withdrew its forces. Though discussed only briefly, these episodes provide important within-case variation.

Historical Background

The Dominican Republic gained independence in 1844.[1] For decades afterward, the country was plagued with instability and crises.[2] At the turn of the twentieth century, Theodore Roosevelt intervened with the purpose of occupying their custom houses and assuming responsibility for their finances.[3] The next major episode of U.S. military intervention happened in 1916 when Woodrow Wilson landed Marines to quell a civil war. American forces stayed for the next eight years.[4]

From 1930 until 1961, Rafael Trujillo ruled the Dominican Republic.[5] He had a close relationship with the United States for most of his tenure. Trujillo's participation in World War II alongside Allied forces helped ensure that U.S. presidents turned a blind eye to his brutality at home. But American deference did not last forever.[6] Things began to change in the late 1950s when, as noted in the previous chapter, decision makers reassessed their unqualified support for right-wing dictators.[7] In 1960, the United States imposed sanctions on the Dominican Republic in conjunction with the

[1] Russell Crandall, *Gunboat Democracy: U.S. Intervention in the Dominican Republic, Grenada, and Panama* (Lanham, MD: Rowman and Littlefield Publishers, Inc., 2006), 39.

[2] Piero Gleijeses, *The Dominican Crisis: The 1965 Constitutionalist Revolt and American Intervention* (Baltimore, MD and London: The Johns Hopkins University Press, 1978), 8–13.

[3] David A. Lake, *Hierarchy in International Relations* (Ithaca, NY: Cornell University Press, 2009), 4.

[4] Abraham F. Lowenthal, *The Dominican Intervention* (Baltimore and London: The Johns Hopkins University Press, 1995), 9.

[5] On Trujillo's rise to power, see Gleijeses, *The Dominican Crisis: The 1965 Constitutionalist Revolt and American Intervention*, 20–29; Jonathan Hartlyn, *The Struggle for Democratic Politics in the Dominican Republic* (Chapel Hill, NC and London: The University of North Carolina Press, 1998), 39–42.

[6] Hartlyn, 43–45.

[7] Crandall, *Gunboat Democracy: U.S. Intervention in the Dominican Republic, Grenada, and Panama*, 47.

OAS.[8] In May 1961, Trujillo was assassinated with covert support from the Kennedy administration.[9]

Joaquín Balaguer took over after Trujillo's death. He was removed in January of 1962 and replaced by a Council of State until elections were held later that year.[10] In early 1963, Juan Bosch was sworn in as the country's first popularly elected leader in over thirty years.[11] Then–Vice President Johnson attended the inauguration.[12] Bosch immediately confronted challenges, alienating groups on both sides of the political spectrum.[13] His inability to carry out reforms angered his own supporters. Tolerance for communists and an unwillingness to compromise angered the right.[14] In September 1963, Bosch was ousted in a coup.[15] Donald Reid Cabral emerged as the new leader.[16] After initially cutting ties with the junta, the United States extended recognition and resumed normal relations, appointing W. Tapley Bennett as Ambassador in early 1964.[17] Cabral's tenure

[8] Jerome Slater, *Intervention and Negotiation: The United States and the Dominican Revolution* (New York, Evanston, IL, and London: Harper & Row, Publishers, 1970), 8. See also "Background Information," *National Security Files, Countries, Dominican Republic—General, 1/61-6/61 [Folder]; National Security Files—Countries—Dominican Republic, General, 1/61-6/61—Dominican Republic, Subjects: Murphy Trip, 8/61-5/63, Box 66 [Collection]* (JFK Library, 1961), 1–2.

[9] Crandall, *Gunboat Democracy: U.S. Intervention in the Dominican Republic, Grenada, and Panama*, 48.

[10] G. Pope Atkins and Larman C. Wilson, *The Dominican Republic and the United States: From Imperialism to Transnationalism* (Athens, GA and London: The University of Georgia Press, 1998), 127; Crandall, *Gunboat Democracy: U.S. Intervention in the Dominican Republic, Grenada, and Panama*, 48–49.

[11] Stephen G Rabe, "The Johnson Doctrine," *Presidential Studies Quarterly* 36, no. 1 (2006): 55.

[12] Elizabeth N. Saunders, *Leaders at War: How Presidents Shape Military Interventions* (Ithaca, NY: Cornell University Press, 2011), 157.

[13] John Bartlow Martin, the U.S. Ambassador to the Dominican Republic at the time, provided a lengthy summary of these challenges on April 28, 1963; "Bosch's First Two Months [from John Bartlow Martin, April 28, 1963]," *National Security Files, Countries, Dominican Republic—General, 4/63-5/63 [Folder]; National Security Files—Countries—Dominican Republic, General, 1/61-6/61—Dominican Republic, Subjects: Murphy Trip, 8/61-5/63, Box 66 [Collection]* (JFK Library, 1963), 1–8. See also "President Bosch and Internal Security in the Dominican Republic [CIA Memorandum, June 7, 1963]," *National Security Files, Countries, Dominican Republic—General, 6/1/63-6/13/63 [Folder]; National Security Files—Countries—Dominican Republic, General, 1/61-6/61—Dominican Republic, Subjects: Murphy Trip, 8/61-5/63, Box 66 [Collection]* (JFK Library, 1963), 1–10.

[14] Lyndon B. Johnson, *The Vantage Point: Perspectives of the Presidency, 1963-1969* (New York: Holt, Rinehart and Winston, 1971), 189.

[15] Slater, *Intervention and Negotiation: The United States and the Dominican Revolution*, 14–15.

[16] Gleijeses, *The Dominican Crisis: The 1965 Constitutionalist Revolt and American Intervention*, 115–116.

[17] Atkins and Wilson, *The Dominican Republic and the United States: From Imperialism to Transnationalism*, 130–131.

was also marked by poor governance.[18] On April 24, 1965, elements loyal to Bosch overthrew his regime, triggering a civil war that pitted the "constitutionalist" rebels against the "loyalists" of the recently ousted junta.[19] The pro-Bosch contingent distributed weapons to civilians throughout Santo Domingo, the country's capital.[20]

The U.S. government was caught off guard. Bennett was out of town visiting his sick mother. William B. Connett, the chargé d'affaires, was in charge.[21] In a cable to Washington on April 26, he wrote that "[p]robably nothing short of major U.S. involvement could prevent Bosch's return at this stage."[22] Such an action, he warned, "would have extremely serious implications for our foreign relations and particularly serious repercussions in Latin America. We could be cast in role of interventionist power opposing popular revolution of democratic elements overthrowing unpopular unconstitutional regime."[23] That same day, Johnson told Thomas Mann, the Assistant Secretary of State for Inter-American Affairs, "[w]e are going to have to really set up that government down there, run it and stabilize it some way or another. This Bosch is no good. I was down there."[24]

Two days later on April 28, Bennett, who was back in the country, sent a cable to Washington with a CRITIC designation, indicating the highest level

[18] FRUS, "1. Special National Intelligence Estimate," in *Foreign Relations of the United States, 1964–1968, Volume XXXII, Dominican Republic; Cuba; Haiti; Guyana*, ed. Daniel Lawler and Carolyn Yee (Washington, D.C.: United States Government Printing Office, 2005), https://history.state.gov/historicaldocuments/frus1964-68v32/d1; FRUS, "17. Airgram From the Embassy in the Dominican Republic to the Department of State," in *Foreign Relations of the United States, 1964–1968, Volume XXXII, Dominican Republic; Cuba; Haiti; Guyana*, ed. Daniel Lawler and Carolyn Yee (Washington, D.C.: United States Government Printing Office, 2005), https://history.state.gov/historicaldocuments/frus1964-68v32/d17.

[19] Saunders, *Leaders at War: How Presidents Shape Military Interventions*, 156.

[20] "The Dominican Conflict," *National Security File, National Security Council History—Dominican Crisis, 1965—Bowdler to Rostow Memo [Folder]; National Security Council Histories, Dominican Crisis 1965, Box 8 [Collection]* (LBJ Library, n.d.), 4–5.

[21] Gleijeses, *The Dominican Crisis: The 1965 Constitutionalist Revolt and American Intervention*, 177–182.

[22] "Incoming Telegram [Joint State/Defense Message, April 26, 1965, 10:08 a.m.]," *National Security File, National Security Council History—Dominican Crisis, 1965—Incoming State Cables, April 24-May 4, 1965 (1 of 4) [Folder]; National Security Council Histories, Dominican Crisis 1965, Box 4 (1 of 2) [Collection]* (LBJ Library, 1965), 1.

[23] "Incoming Telegram [Joint State/Defense Message, April 26, 1965, 10:08 a.m.]," 1–2.

[24] FRUS, "22. Telephone Conversation Between the Under Secretary of State for Economic Affairs (Mann) and President Johnson," in *Foreign Relations of the United States, 1964–1968, Volume XXXII, Dominican Republic; Cuba; Haiti; Guyana*, ed. Daniel Lawler and Carolyn Yee (Washington, D.C.: United States Government Printing Office, 2005), https://history.state.gov/historicaldocuments/frus1964-68v32/d22.

of urgency: "Country Team unanimously of opinion that, now that we have request from military junta for assistance, time has come to land the Marines. American lives are in danger . . . I recommend immediate landing."[25] Soon after, a few hundred Marines were deployed with the ostensible aim of rescuing American and other foreign nationals.[26] Officials hoped "the mere presence of U.S. troops would 'strengthen the will' of the loyalist forces and perhaps lead to a negotiated settlement."[27] These hopes were quickly dashed. Bennett warned of the Dominican Republic becoming a second Cuba and recommended a larger deployment.[28] Johnson obliged. Over the course of the next few days, the United States significantly expanded its military presence. On May 6, the OAS created an Inter-American Peace Force (IAPF) to end the civil war.[29] Around this time, the loyalists established the Government of National Reconciliation led by General Antonio Imbert. The rebels created a Constitutional Government headed by Colonel Caamaño Deno.[30]

In June, the OAS established a three-person mission known as the Ad Hoc Committee with representatives from the United States, Brazil, and El Salvador to help establish a caretaker government.[31] A few months later, García Godoy

[25] FRUS, "32. Telegram From the Embassy in the Dominican Republic to the Director of the National Security Agency (Carter)," in *Foreign Relations of the United States, 1964–1968, Volume XXXII, Dominican Republic; Cuba; Haiti; Guyana*, ed. Daniel Lawler and Carolyn Yee (Washington, D.C.: United States Government Printing Office, 2005), https://history.state.gov/historicaldocuments/frus1964-68v32/d32. Interestingly, Bennett penned a cable to Washington earlier that day wherein he noted that he did not think landing U.S. troops was necessary despite a request from a member of the loyalist junta for these purposes. See "Incoming Telegram [Joint State-Defense Message, April 28, 1965, 3:16 p.m.]," *National Security File, National Security Council History—Dominican Crisis, 1965—Incoming State Cables, April 24-May 4, 1965 (2 of 4) [Folder]; National Security Council Histories, Dominican Crisis 1965, Box 4 (1 of 2) [Collection]* (LBJ Library, 1965), 1.

[26] "The Dominican Conflict," 8–11.

[27] Saunders, *Leaders at War: How Presidents Shape Military Interventions*, 158.

[28] "Incoming Telegram [Joint State/Defense Message, April 28, 1965, 7:52 p.m.]," *National Security File, National Security Council History—Dominican Crisis, 1965—Incoming State Cables, April 24-May 4, 1965 (2 of 4) [Folder]; National Security Council Histories, Dominican Crisis 1965, Box 4 (1 of 2) [Collection]* (LBJ Library, 1965), 1.

[29] Atkins and Wilson, *The Dominican Republic and the United States: From Imperialism to Transnationalism*, 138.

[30] "Military Operations in the Dominican Republic," *National Security File, National Security Council History—Dominican Crisis, 1965, State-DOD-OAS—Chronologies and Narratives (5 of 5) [Folder]; National Security Council Histories, Dominican Crisis 1965, Box 7 (2 of 2) [Collection]* (LBJ Library, n.d.), 6.

[31] Crandall, *Gunboat Democracy: U.S. Intervention in the Dominican Republic, Grenada, and Panama*, 84–85.

took over as provisional president.[32] In late-September, Bosch returned to the Dominican Republic from exile in Puerto Rico.[33] Elections were held the following year. Balaguer, who was covertly aided by the United States, won with 57% of the vote, beating Bosch and Rafael Bonnelly of the National Integration Movement.[34]

Why Intervene in the Dominican Republic?

The Johnson administration's main motivation for intervening in the Dominican Republic was fear of a communist takeover.[35] Decision makers worried that the country would become another Soviet client if Bosch returned to power. Although they did not think Bosch himself was a communist, they worried he would tolerate and be overrun by them.[36] Most senior officials shared this sentiment.[37]

Such concerns were evident from the first days of the crisis. Bennett's CRITIC cable suggested the United States "intervene to prevent another Cuba from arising out of the ashes of this uncontrollable situation."[38] A CIA memo dated April 29 stated: "Early in the present insurrection it became apparent that the well-organized Dominican communists and associated e[x]tremists were committing their full resources to the rebel effort. . . . The well-armed mobs now resisting the hard-pressed loyalist forces in the city are largely controlled by the communists and other extremists." It went on to argue that "[w]hile there is no evidence that the Castro regime is directly involved in the current

[32] Gleijeses, *The Dominican Crisis: The 1965 Constitutionalist Revolt and American Intervention*, 273–277.

[33] Crandall, *Gunboat Democracy: U.S. Intervention in the Dominican Republic, Grenada, and Panama*, 88.

[34] Lindsey O'Rourke, *Covert Regime Change: America's Secret Cold War* (Ithaca, NY: Cornell University Press, 2018), 219–221.

[35] Tanisha M. Fazal, *State Death: The Politics and Geography of Conquest, Occupation, and Annexation* (Princeton, NJ: Princeton University Press, 2007), 198–203. This fear dates back to the Trujillo period, where decision makers sought to prevent a communist regime from replacing him. See "Memorandum for McGeorge Bundy: The White House," *National Security Files, Countries, Dominican Republic—General, 1/61-6/61 [Folder]; National Security Files—Countries—Dominican Republic, General, 1/61-6/61—Dominican Republic, Subjects: Murphy Trip, 8/61-5/63, Box 66 [Collection]* (JFK Library, 1961), 1.

[36] Crandall, *Gunboat Democracy: U.S. Intervention in the Dominican Republic, Grenada, and Panama*, 59–60; Daniel I. Papermaster, "A Case Study of the Effect of International Law on Foreign Policy Decisionmaking: The United States Intervention in the Dominican Republic in 1965," *Texas International Law Journal* 24, no. 3 (1989): 467; Rabe, "The Johnson Doctrine," 54–55.

[37] Slater, *Intervention and Negotiation: The United States and the Dominican Revolution*, 37.

[38] Johnson, *The Vantage Point: Perspectives of the Presidency, 1963–1969*, 197.

insurrection, it is nevertheless clear that Cuban trained Dominican extremists are taking an active part."[39] Intelligence reports from the week after the invasion further described the communist presence among the constitutionalists. One from May 7 observed: "[T]he prospect at the time of US intervention clearly was one in which a movement increasingly under the influence of Castroites and other Communists was threatening to gain the ascendency in the Dominican Republic."[40] Another memo several days later stated that, "[t]his situation is made to order for radical agitations, and it is clear that both pro-Bosch and Communist elements in the rebel movement are attempting to exploit it."[41]

Whether decision makers' concerns were overblown is a fair question.[42] Regardless, it is clear that the Johnson administration—rightly or wrongly—took the threat seriously.[43] And it was not only U.S. officials that thought a communist takeover was a real possibility in April 1965. For example, "the five Latin American members of the OAS investigating commission unanimously reported that, had the United States not intervened, the revolution could have been converted into a communist insurrection."[44] While four of the members were rightist regimes, one of them, Columbia, was not.[45] Another piece of illustrative evidence comes from an intelligence memo dated May 23, wherein Silvestre Antonio Guzman, a member of Bosch's party who would go on to become president in the late 1970s, "acknowledged the important role of communists in the 'constitutionalist camp.' "[46]

[39] "Involvement of Cuban-Trained or Foreign Communist Supported Rebels in the Dominican Insurrection [From CIA to State, April 29, 1965]," *National Security File, Country File—Dominican Republic, Volume 1, Cables—6/64-4/65 (3 of 3) [Folder]; National Security File—Country File, Latin America-Dominican Republic, Box 38 (1 of 2) [Collection]* (LBJ Library, 1965), 1.

[40] "The Communist Role in the Dominican Revolt [May 7, 1965]," *National Security File, National Security Council History—Dominican Crisis, 1965—1965 Background Documents (4 of 6) [Folder]; National Security Council Histories, Dominican Crisis 1965, Box 7 (1 of 2) [Collection]* (LBJ Library, 1965), i.

[41] "The Situation in the Interior of the Dominican Republic [May 14, 1965]," *National Security File, Country File—Dominican Republic, Volume 5—5/19/65-5/31/65 (5 of 5) [Folder]; National Security File, Country File—Latin America-Dominican Republic, Box 40 [Collection]* (LBJ Library, 1965), i.

[42] Fazal, *State Death: The Politics and Geography of Conquest, Occupation, and Annexation*, 202–3; Gleijeses, *The Dominican Crisis: The 1965 Constitutionalist Revolt and American Intervention.*

[43] Crandall, *Gunboat Democracy: U.S. Intervention in the Dominican Republic, Grenada, and Panama*, 37.

[44] Papermaster, "A Case Study of the Effect of International Law on Foreign Policy Decisionmaking: The United States Intervention in the Dominican Republic in 1965," 483.

[45] Slater, *Intervention and Negotiation: The United States and the Dominican Revolution*, 37–38.

[46] "Acknowledgment of Silvestre Antonio Guzman and Former Rebel Captain Pedro A. Ricart That There Are Communists Involved in the Rebel Movement [May 23, 1965]," *National Security File, Country File—Dominican Republic, Volume 5—5/19/65-5/31/65 (3 of 5) [Folder]; National*

The Logistics of Power Pack

Operation Power Pack evolved and expanded over the course of several days and weeks. A day after fighting broke out on April 25, the Joint Chiefs of Staff ordered ships to be sent to Santo Domingo in the event that American citizens had to be evacuated. According to declassified notes from the time, "[t]he force was to remain offshore, out of sight, to avoid the appearance of intervention."[47] One day later, the 82nd Airborne was placed on high alert.[48] They were "unofficially warned at 10:00 P.M. and then, at midnight, formally alerted to ready one brigade (2,253 men) for possible action."[49]

American involvement escalated quickly following Bennett's dire cable to Washington on April 28. Hours after the ambassador sent warning, Johnson "ordered troops to land in the Dominican Republic to protect Americans and to reinforce the embassy guard. During the night, over 500 Marines were flown ashore by helicopters. They established a safety perimeter around the Ambassador Hotel to protect American and other foreign national evacuees, and also set up a helicopter evacuation area."[50] Lieutenant General Bruce Palmer of the Army was placed in charge of American forces.[51]

On April 30, the OAS called for a ceasefire between the opposing forces.[52] An International Safety Zone (ISZ) was established the next day, "encompassing an area of about three square miles . . . located in the southwestern portion of Santo Domingo . . . [and] contain[ing] most of the embassies and the Ambassador Hotel."[53] Around this same time, additional Marines as well as members of the 82nd Airborne secured the San Isidro Airfield in the eastern part of Santo Domingo and moved west along the highway. They safeguarded the Duarte Bridge connecting the two halves of the capital and eventually linked up with

Security File, Country File—Latin America-Dominican Republic, Box 40 [Collection] (LBJ Library, 1965), 1.

[47] "Military Operations in the Dominican Republic," 1.

[48] "Build-up of U.S. Forces in the Dominican Republic [from Robert McNamara to Lyndon Johnson, May 26, 1965]," *National Security File, Country File—Dominican Republic, Volume 5—5/19/65-5/31/65 (4 of 5) [Folder]; National Security File, Country File—Latin America-Dominican Republic, Box 40 [Collection]* (LBJ Library, 1965), 1.

[49] Lowenthal, *The Dominican Intervention*, 88–89.

[50] "Military Operations in the Dominican Republic," 3.

[51] Saunders, *Leaders at War: How Presidents Shape Military Interventions*, 160.

[52] "The Dominican Conflict," 30.

[53] "Military Operations in the Dominican Republic," 5. Initially, it was called the international neutral zone of refuge. It was later named the International Security Zone. See Lowenthal, *The Dominican Intervention*, 115.

forces in the International Safety Zone to establish a corridor.[54] Once the IAPF was established on May 6, U.S. forces were placed under its command.[55] At the height of the invasion in late May, there were roughly 21,000 American troops deployed to the Dominican Republic, "half as many as were serving in Vietnam" at the time.[56] By late June, fifty percent of U.S. forces had returned home.[57]

Legal Evaluation

The legal exemptions the Johnson administration relied on to defend overt intervention manifested in roughly two stages.[58] The first covers the onset of the civil war, wherein the presence of American nationals was used to justify the initial deployment of U.S. forces. The second stage covers the days afterward when the OAS got involved, beginning with calls for the establishment of the International Security Zone and concluding with the creation of the multilateral peacekeeping force.

Technically speaking, this book has little to say about how interventions unfold once a state makes an initial decision to pursue regime change openly or secretly. In this case, however, separating the justification used to deploy the first batch of troops to the Dominican Republic from the justification for staying and expanding the mission would paint a misleading picture of what transpired. While the presence of endangered nationals gave the administration cover early on, there was a widespread belief that it provided an insufficient legal basis on its own for keeping troops in the country much beyond the evacuation period to ensure that the rebels did not consolidate power. OAS involvement was therefore integral in their ability to pursue full-scale, overt regime change. From the standpoint of the theory presented here, these two exemptions are inextricably linked.

[54] "Cable [from General Palmer, May 3, 1965]," *National Security File, Country File—Dominican Republic, Volume 1, Memos and Miscellaneous, 6/64-4/65 [Folder]; National Security File—Country File, Latin America-Dominican Republic, Box 38 (1 of 2) [Collection]* (LBJ Library, 1965), 1.

[55] "The Dominican Conflict," 31.

[56] Crandall, *Gunboat Democracy: U.S. Intervention in the Dominican Republic, Grenada, and Panama*, 69.

[57] "Military Operations in the Dominican Republic," 7.

[58] Papermaster, "A Case Study of the Effect of International Law on Foreign Policy Decisionmaking: The United States Intervention in the Dominican Republic in 1965," 486–488.

Saving Endangered Americans

The Johnson administration's initial justification for deploying troops was the threat posed to American nationals by the civil war. The rescue motive was genuine.[59] But decision makers also hoped these troops could serve broader political ends.[60] A memo drafted by Assistant Secretary Mann two days before the first Marines arrived is informative. He asked the embassy to alert the warring factions that American nationals had asked for safe passage out of the country and that the U.S. government was "therefore request[ing] immediate cease-fire and cooperation on both sides in permitting orderly and safe evacuation of those Americans desiring to leave." Mann included a separate note to his counterparts labeled STRICTLY FYI wherein he pointed out that a temporary cessation in fighting brought on by the evacuation might make it possible "to obtain some kind of provisional government which presumably would be committed to fair and impartial elections at the earliest practicable date."[61]

When U.S. troops landed on April 28, Mann was keen on keeping the narrative focused on the evacuation, "avoid[ing] any suggestion that US is supporting or opposing any particular political faction or group" and refraining from "speculat[ing] on [the] length of time that it will take to carry out evacuation."[62] In a conversation with Johnson just before midnight, however, he again expressed hope that U.S. troops could help bring about a favorable end to the crisis. "The consensus," he said, "was that the presence of the Marines would calm everyone down," and that "if it all quiets down the anti-communist

[59] "Incoming Telegram [Joint State/Defense Message, April 28, 1965, 7:29 p.m.]," *National Security File, Country File—Dominican Republic, Volume 1, Cables—6/64-4/65 (3 of 3) [Folder]; National Security File—Country File, Latin America-Dominican Republic, Box 38 (1 of 2) [Collection]* (LBJ Library, 1965), 1; "Statement by the President [April 28, 1965]," *National Security File, Country File—Dominican Republic, Volume 1, Memos and Miscellaneous, 6/64-4/65 [Folder]; National Security File—Country File, Latin America-Dominican Republic, Box 38 (1 of 2) [Collection]* (LBJ Library, 1965). Johnson also makes clear in his memoirs that some OAS member nations requested U.S. assistance in evacuating their own nationals, lending credence to the seriousness of the threat. See Johnson, *The Vantage Point: Perspectives of the Presidency, 1963–1969*, 196.

[60] Robert Dallek, *Lyndon B. Johnson: Portrait of a President* (Oxford and New York: Oxford University Press, 2004), 216; Lowenthal, *The Dominican Intervention*, 137–138; Slater, *Intervention and Negotiation: The United States and the Dominican Revolution*, 32–33.

[61] "Outgoing Telegram [from Thomas Mann, April 26, 1965, 2:28 p.m.]," *National Security File, Country File—Dominican Republic, Volume 1, Cables—6/64-4/65 (1 of 3) [Folder]; National Security File—Country File, Latin America-Dominican Republic, Box 38 (1 of 2) [Collection]* (LBJ Library, 1965), 1.

[62] "Outgoing Telegram [from Thomas Mann, April 28, 1965, 11:20 p.m.]," *National Security File, Country File—Dominican Republic, Volume 1, Cables—6/64-4/65 (3 of 3) [Folder]; National Security File—Country File, Latin America-Dominican Republic, Box 38 (1 of 2) [Collection]* (LBJ Library, 1965), 1.

forces will get control and we can guide it." While optimistic, Mann was not naive: "If . . . we have to fight or go in and clean up it is possible that we will be in trouble, in terms of international organizations." He also knew that the political cover afforded by the evacuation fig leaf had an expiration date: "The real trouble would come when we are finished with the evacuation—when we have to find a reason to stay on. . . . [W]e would probably have to say that there are 2,000 Americans in the country—outside of Santo Domingo, and begin to stall a bit some time tomorrow."[63]

Decision makers continued to discuss the issue of directing U.S. military forces to engage in actual fighting under the auspices of the evacuation pretext into the following day. In a call with his CIA Director at 8:47 A.M. on April 29, Johnson responded to a comment that the United States should "clean the rebels out" or else face a communist takeover by asking: "That will put us in pretty much trouble internationally with the international organizations, OAS and United Nations, won't it?"[64] A memo from Richard Goodwin, LBJ's Special Assistant, took these concerns to heart, reiterating the importance of keeping the narrative focused on endangered nationals for the time being. Although Goodwin agreed that "anything, including military intervention, should be done if essential to prevent another Castro-type takeover in the Caribbean," he also appreciated the liabilities of this enterprise:

> I think it is very important that we strictly adhere to the story that this is for the protection of American lives. Also everything done by the Marines should be consistent with that story unless it is absolutely essential for them to act otherwise. This action is as filled with possible costs to us as was the Bay of Pigs invasion itself. First, it is as far as I remember, the first Marine intervention since Franklin Roosevelt renounced the right of unilateral intervention in the 1930s. Therefore it is an historic event. . . . Second, we should not, if possible, be in a position of suppressing a popular revolution against military rule. It is not just a matter of hurting us in Latin America—although it will. It will also have an effect on our position in Vietnam and elsewhere. Hostile people will

[63] FRUS, "38. Memorandum of Telephone Conversation Between the Under Secretary of State for Economic Affairs (Mann) and President Johnson," in *Foreign Relations of the United States, 1964–1968, Volume XXXII, Dominican Republic; Cuba; Haiti; Guyana*, ed. Daniel Lawler and Carolyn Yee (Washington, D.C.: United States Government Printing Office, 2005), https://history.state.gov/historicaldocuments/frus1964-68v32/d38.

[64] "President Johnson's Notes on His Telephone Conversation with Admiral Raborn on April 29, 1965 at 8:47AM," *April 1965, Chrono File—Citations (7301-7452)—Service Set II [Folder]; Recordings and Transcripts of Telephone Conversations and Meetings, WH Series/SR Series, Box 6—Sept 64-May 65 [Collection]* (LBJ Library, 1965), 2.

> use it as evidence that we are doing the same thing there. *It will cut the ground out from under our argument that we stand for the principle that no country has the right to interfere in the affairs of its neighbors.* Third, if we do put down the rebellion . . . we must think about what follows. We should not be in the position of having to occupy the country.[65]

General Earle Wheeler, the Chairman of the Joint Chiefs of Staff, summed up this delicate balancing act in his marching orders to General Palmer: "Your announced mission is to save US lives. Your unannounced mission is to prevent the Dominican Republic from going Communist."[66]

Cue the OAS

The evacuation narrative continued to play an important part in the administration's justification for the presence of U.S. troops in the Dominican Republic into late April and early May. But there was a nagging sense that regional approval was integral to expanding the size and scope of the operation.[67] Romulo Betancourt, the former President of Venezuela, told Ambassador C. Allan Stewart on April 30 that "[t]he United States has a certain amount of breathing time now in view of the fact it is actively evacuating Americans from the Dominican Republic. However, when time comes when there are no Americans to evacuate, or a very few of them, then the pressure and criticism from Latin American countries will become very severe. . . . [T]he United States must induce the OAS to move fast in order to set up a situation which will remove the United States from this embarrassing pose."[68]

[65] "Memorandum for the President [from Richard Goodwin to Lyndon Johnson, April 29, 1965]," *National Security File, Name File—Valenti File Re: Dominican Republic (1 of 2) [Folder]; National Security File, Name File, Box 8 [Collection]* (LBJ Library, 1965), 1, emphasis added.

[66] FRUS, "43. Editorial Note," in *Foreign Relations of the United States, 1964–1968, Volume XXXII, Dominican Republic; Cuba; Haiti; Guyana*, ed. Daniel Lawler and Carolyn Yee (Washington, D.C.: United States Government Printing Office, 2005), https://history.state.gov/historicaldocuments/frus1964-68v32/d43. Although Wheeler made these remarks on the morning of May 1, the administration had already begun to rely on a broader narrative as described in the next section.

[67] Crandall, *Gunboat Democracy: U.S. Intervention in the Dominican Republic, Grenada, and Panama*, 77. In some telephone conversations, Johnson does seem to voice frustration about the OAS and indicates that he would contemplate moving without them so long as there was a paper trail that he had sought their assistance. See "President Johnson's Notes on Conversation with McGeorge Bundy April 30, 1965 at 1:45 PM," *April 1965, Chrono File—Citations (7301-7452)—Service Set II [Folder]; Recordings and Transcripts of Telephone Conversations and Meetings, WH Series/SR Series, Box 6—Sept 64-May 65 [Collection]* (LBJ Library, 1965), 1–2.

[68] "Betancourt's Views on Dominican Situation [April 30, 1965]," *National Security File, National Security Council History—Dominican Crisis, 1965—1965 Background Documents (2 of 6) [Folder];*

Senior officials convened that same day to discuss these issues following an OAS meeting held the evening before. At first, Johnson expressed skepticism. "I am not willing to let this island go to Castro," he said. "OAS is a phantom—they are taking a siesta while this is on fire. How can we send troops 10,000 miles away and let Castro take over right under our nose. Let's just analyze—we have resisted Communists all over the world: Vietnam, Lebanon, and Greece. What are we doing under our doorstep. We know the rebel leaders are Communist, and we are sitting here waiting on OAS."[69] This thinking was consistent with Johnson's disdain for the regional body. In his notoriously colorful language, he is alleged to have said at one point that the OAS "couldn't pour piss out of a boot if the instructions were written on the heel."[70] Regardless, advisors pressed him to multilateralize the mission. "We can move through the OAS and achieve what you want," Secretary of State Dean Rusk told him. Johnson, seemingly internalizing these concerns, asked, "why don't you determine what it takes to make this take on the right color[?]" Although Under Secretary of State George Ball pointed out that U.S. forces had done a "considerable" amount so far "without [any] real angry response," some, including Bundy, worried that, "We have no international cover. We have no real legitimacy."[71]

Toward the end of the meeting, Johnson told McNamara he should "get ready so that Castro cannot take over." McNamara wanted to find "irrefutable" evidence of a "Castro takeover" as a means of pushing Latin American countries to sign on. LBJ subsequently gave the following instructions to those present: "I want US to feverishly try to cloak this with legitimacy. We cannot stand with our hand in our pocket and let Castro win. Military get ducks in a row. Diplomats see if we can do anything to get observers in here or troops from other Latin American countries. We are willing to do whatever is necessary to put the pistols down. We will have one of 3 dictators: 1) U.S., 2) Moderate dictator, 3) Castro dictator." In closing, Bundy pointed out that letting the Dominican Republic be overrun by Castro "would [be] the worst domestic political disaster we could possibly suffer. But," he cautioned, "in order to quash Castro in D.R. we need above all else to get hemispheric public opinion on our side. . . . Give the choice: stand

National Security Council Histories, Dominican Crisis 1965, Box 7 (1 of 2) [Collection] (LBJ Library, 1965), 1.

[69] FRUS, "42. Editorial Note," in *Foreign Relations of the United States, 1964–1968, Volume XXXII, Dominican Republic; Cuba; Haiti; Guyana*, ed. Daniel Lawler and Carolyn Yee (Washington, D.C.: United States Government Printing Office, 2005), https://history.state.gov/historicaldocuments/frus1964-68v32/d42.

[70] H.W. Brands, "Decisions on American Armed Intervention: Lebanon, Dominican Republic, and Grenada," *Political Science Quarterly* 102, no. 4 (1987): 614.

[71] FRUS, "42. Editorial Note."

by [and] do nothing, let Castro take over or with the OAS and local entreaties move in to quell the Castro people and save this island from black darkness."[72]

In the early hours of the morning on April 30, Ellsworth Bunker, the U.S. Ambassador to the OAS, made a statement to the regional body's Council in which he described the evacuation efforts to date, noted the continuing problem of chaos and lawlessness in the country, and urged them to adopt a ceasefire which the U.S. government "will heartily join." He made clear that if the OAS did not act, the United States would still protect its own citizens. There were "many precedents for this kind of situation," Bunker argued. "None of these is inconsistent with inter-American obligations. We wholeheartedly subscribe to these obligations, including the doctrine of non-intervention and self-determination. We are not now talking about intruding in the domestic affairs of other countries; we are talking about the elementary duty to save lives in a situation where there is no authority able to accept responsibility for primary law and order."[73] He concluded by reiterating that the United States would gladly turn authority over to the regional body for the purpose of restoring order to the island.

As noted above, the Council did ultimately pass a resolution calling for a ceasefire between the warring factions and establish an International Security Zone.[74] According to a memo from the time, the United States was authorized to "use necessary forces from Marine and/or airborne contingents to establish international neutral zone enclosing area to include Embajador Hotel and Embassy. . . . Establishment of this zone is for purpose of protecting lives of US citizens and nationals of other countries." Per Article 54 of the UN Charter, the Security Council was to be informed.[75] McGeorge Bundy relayed the news to Johnson. Sixteen nations had voted in favor of the ISZ, four abstained, and none voted against.[76]

[72] Ibid.

[73] "Statement of Ambassador Bunker During OAS Council Meeting Early a.m. April 30, 1965," *National Security File, National Security Council History—Dominican Crisis, 1965, State-DOD-OAS—Chronologies and Narratives (2 of 5) [Folder]; National Security Council Histories, Dominican Crisis 1965, Box 7 (2 of 2) [Collection]* (LBJ Library, 1965), 1–2.

[74] Lowenthal, *The Dominican Intervention*, 114–115.

[75] "Outgoing Telegram [April 30, 1965, 3:30 a.m.]," *National Security File, National Security Council Histories—Dominican Crisis, 1965—Outgoing State Cables, April 25-May 14, 1965 (1 of 5) [Folder]; National Security Council Histories, Dominican Crisis 1965, Box 5 [Collection]* (LBJ Library, 1965), 1–2.

[76] "Memorandum for the President [from McGeorge Bundy to Lyndon Johnson, April 30, 1965]," *National Security File, Name File—Valenti File Re: Dominican Republic (1 of 2) [Folder]; National Security File, Name File, Box 8 [Collection]* (LBJ Library, 1965), 1.

The announcement of the ceasefire altered how decision makers thought and talked about the presence of U.S. troops in the Dominican Republic. In addition to the narrow evacuation narrative, it was now possible for them to claim they were enforcing the ISZ called for by the OAS.[77] Mann issued updated guidance to diplomatic posts in the region that echoed these twin themes. Officials were to point out that U.S. forces were first deployed "only when there was a complete breakdown in public order." The United States then "gave immediate support at the first opportunity to initiatives for collective action under Article 39 of OAS Charter and it took the lead in urging the OAS to attempt to bring about an immediate and effective cease fire."[78] Mann's memo also included pointed language about the dangers of communism as it related to inter-American security and solidarity: "It will be no service to the cause of democracy if the ultimate outcome of the present Dominican crisis is the emergence of another communist dictator. It will be no service to the cause of non-intervention if, out of the present crisis, a communist regime should emerge which, like Cuba, constitutes itself as a beachhead for communist intervention by subversion and terror throughout the hemisphere."[79]

In a conversation with McNamara and Rusk on May 2, Johnson contemplated whether he should announce his decision to send four additional battalions to the Dominican Republic given the optics: "Why don't we say we have authorized it and we do not have to say where they are going? Does that look too big?" McNamara replied, "No, I think you could do it. Dean [Rusk] is on the other line. Dean, do you see any reason why we shouldn't announce the 4 additional battalions?" Although Rusk basically agreed, he recommended that the military "indicate the variety of the missions that they have in front of them. It is security for the zone, it is distribution of civil relief, food and medicine, assistance to the OAS Committee. In other words it is a big job to be done and it just takes more people."[80] Here we see the ceasefire and the ISZ as important to the administration's public posture. On May 2, the Papal Nuncio and the Secretary

[77] Johnson, *The Vantage Point: Perspectives of the Presidency, 1963–1969*, 201; Lowenthal, *The Dominican Intervention*, 124–125.

[78] "Outgoing Telegram [from Thomas Mann, April 30, 1965, 3:57 p.m.]," *National Security File, Country File—Dominican Republic, Volume 1, Cables—6/64-4/65 (3 of 3) [Folder]; National Security File—Country File, Latin America-Dominican Republic, Box 38 (1 of 2) [Collection]* (LBJ Library, 1965), 1–2.

[79] "Outgoing Telegram [from Thomas Mann, April 30, 1965, 3:57 p.m.]," 8.

[80] "President Johnson's Notes on Conversation with Secretary McNamara and Secretary Rusk—May 2, 1965," *May 1965, Chrono File, Situation Room Series—Citations (7901-8047)—Service Set II [Folder]; Recordings and Transcripts of Telephone Conversations and Meetings, WH Series/SR Series, Box 6—Sept 64-May 65 [Collection]* (LBJ Library, 1965), 1.

General of the OAS, José Antonio Mora, thanked Johnson for helping establish the ISZ "in accord with provisions of [the] OAS resolution."[81]

The final milestone in the OAS's involvement, also mentioned above, was the creation of a multilateral peacekeeping force made up of states from across Latin America.[82] When the idea was first floated to Johnson on May 3, there were questions about which countries which would participate, what the command structure would be, and the like. With regard to its role, Bundy told Johnson "it would run Armed Forces in the American States in the area. The President said: 'In other words, it would be the occupying forces until you got a Government' and Bundy said that was correct." Bundy told Johnson that the creation of such a force "would give us the kind of international umbrella that would help us with everybody concerned."[83] In a meeting with Vice President Hubert Humphrey on May 4, several former presidents from the region relayed their support for this initiative. During a break in the conversation, Humphrey talked on the phone with Ambassador Bunker, who indicated that if countries in the region sent forces through "an inter-American force commanded by the OAS" they "could not be accused of intervention."[84]

Movement toward a formal resolution establishing the Inter-American Peace Force, or IAPF, kicked off in the OAS in the evening on May 4. By the following day, twelve members backed the resolution.[85] On May 6, the OAS officially adopted it.[86] Fourteen nations voted in favor, five voted against, and one abstained. The resolution called for willing nations to lend "land, naval, air, or police forces" with the aim of "cooperating in the restoration of normal conditions in the Dominican Republic, in maintaining the security of its inhabitants and the inviolability of human rights, and in the establishment of an atmosphere of peace

[81] "Incoming Telegram [from W. Tapley Bennett, May 2, 1965, 12:06 p.m.]," *National Security File, National Security Council History—Dominican Crisis, 1965—Incoming State Cables, April 24-May 4, 1965 (4 of 4) [Folder]; National Security Council Histories, Dominican Crisis 1965, Box 4 (1 of 2) [Collection]* (LBJ Library, 1965), 1.

[82] Fazal, *State Death: The Politics and Geography of Conquest, Occupation, and Annexation*, 205.

[83] "President Johnson's Notes on Conversation with McGeorge Bundy, May 3, 1965—4:56 p.m.," *May 1965, Chrono File, Situation Room Series—Citations (7901-8047)—Service Set II [Folder]; Recordings and Transcripts of Telephone Conversations and Meetings, WH Series/SR Series, Box 6—Sept 64-May 65 [Collection]* (LBJ Library, 1965), 1–2.

[84] "Memorandum of Conversation [May 4, 1965]," *National Security File, Country File—Dominican Republic, Memorandum of Conversation [Folder]; National Security File—Country File, Latin America-Dominican Republic, Box 49 [Collection]* (LBJ Library, 1965), 5.

[85] "Situation Report Dominican Republic [May 5, 1965, 7:23 p.m.]," *National Security File, Country File—Dominican Republic, Volume 2, 1/64-4/65 (2 of 4) [Folder]; National Security File—Country File, Latin America-Dominican Republic, Box 38 (1 of 2) [Collection]* (LBJ Library, 1965), 1–2.

[86] Atkins and Wilson, *The Dominican Republic and the United States: From Imperialism to Transnationalism*, 138.

and conciliation that will permit the functioning of democratic institutions."[87] That same day, McNamara was already talking about "opportunities to withdraw some of our forces," which "will considerably help our public relations problem." McNamara said that "[a]s an excuse, we can say that the effectiveness of the cease fire makes this possible; later on we can say that we are withdrawing because it is clear that the Latin Americans are coming in." All senior decision makers present at the meeting "heartily endorsed the McNamara view."[88]

Pushing the Narrative

On May 7, Leonard Meeker, the State Department Legal Advisor, outlined the rationale for U.S. intervention in a memo.[89] Unsurprisingly, legal exemptions were front and center: "The United States initially landed troops in the Dominican Republic under conditions in which immediate action was essential to preserve the lives of foreign nationals. . . . This kind action is justified both on humanitarian and legal grounds. The United States continued its presence in the Dominican Republic for the additional purpose of preserving the capacity of the OAS to function in the manner intended by its Charter—to achieve peace and justice by securing a cease-fire and by reestablishing orderly processes within which Dominicans can choose their own government, free from outside interference." He then looped in language from the UN Charter, arguing that "[t]he propriety of a regional agency 'dealing with such matters relating to the maintenance of international peace and security as are appropriate for regional action' is expressly recognized by Article 52 of the Charter of the United Nations."[90]

[87] Organization of American States, "Organization of American States: Resolution Establishing Inter-American Force in the Dominican Republic," *International Legal Materials* 4, no. 3 (1965): 594–596. The nations voting in favor were Argentina, Bolivia, Brazil, Colombia, Costa Rica, Dominican Republic, El Salvador, Guatemala, Haiti, Honduras, Nicaragua, Panama, Paraguay, and the United States. Those voting against were Chile, Ecuador, Mexico, Peru, and Uruguay. Venezuela abstained.

[88] FRUS, "58. Memorandum for the Record," in *Foreign Relations of the United States, 1964–1968, Volume XXXII, Dominican Republic; Cuba; Haiti; Guyana*, ed. Daniel Lawler and Carolyn Yee (Washington, D.C.: United States Government Printing Office, 2005), https://history.state.gov/historicaldocuments/frus1964-68v32/d58.

[89] There were two earlier drafts of this memo, one on May 3 and one on May 5, both of which also alluded to the legal relevance of OAS involvement in the Dominican Crisis.

[90] "Legal Basis for United States Actions in the Dominican Republic [May 7, 1965]," *National Security File, Country File—Dominican Republic, Volume 3, Memos and Miscellaneous—4/28/65-5/7/65 (3 of 4) [Folder]; National Security File, Country File, Latin America-Dominican Republic, Box 39 [Collection]* (LBJ Library, 1965), 1–2. Adlai Stevenson, the U.S. Ambassador to the UN, made similar points when responding to Soviet critiques of U.S. action as a violation of nonintervention. See Papermaster, "A Case Study of the Effect of International Law on Foreign Policy Decisionmaking: The United States Intervention in the Dominican Republic in 1965," 489–90.

Meeker's memo also sought to show that the United States was interested in more than just "the form of legalistic procedures" and cared about the "fundamental rights of a nation under the OAS Charter." His goal was to highlight that the United States was not willing to merely advance a convenient pretext; the perceived credibility of the justifications used for intervention mattered. To demonstrate this, Meeker pointed out that the administration rejected a request by the military junta for "the United States to send in armed forces and crush the rebels. The United States could have recognized this group as the government of the Dominican Republic, and could have responded to their request." They declined this invitation since it "would have amounted to taking sides in the internal struggle and would, therefore, have resulted in actual interference with the freedom of the Dominican people to choose their own government. Such a course of action would have been inconsistent with the principles that govern the Inter-American System."[91]

Also on May 7, Dean Rusk gave an interview to John Hightower of the *Associated Press* in which he fielded numerous questions about Operation Power Pack. The details of their conversation echo many of the themes contained in the Legal Advisor's memo. "When the decision was being made to send U.S. marines into the Dominican Republic last week," Hightower asked, "was consideration given to the fact that this would break a precedent dating back about half a century?" Rusk pushed back, arguing that, "[u]nder similar circumstances governments from time immemorial have been recognized to have not merely the right but the obligation to take whatever action is necessary to save the lives of their nationals. It had nothing to do with 19th century types of intervention." Hightower followed up: "What elements of the situation . . . could justify such a departure from long-established policy?" The Secretary claimed that the reason the United States had not openly intervened in such a long while "simply reflects the fact that American nationals have not been in similar jeopardy for many years. The situation in the Dominican Republic contains unique elements which in a time of revolution contributed to chaos."[92] These responses closely follow the justifications explored in the first phase of the intervention, when saving lives was the primary rationale decision makers relied on.

Echoing the discussion from earlier in this section, Hightower pressed Rusk on the operation's timeline. "Is it correct," he asked, "to say there were two phases in the intervention covering (1) a rescue operation and (2) a move to

[91] "Legal Basis for United States Actions in the Dominican Republic [May 7, 1965]," 2–3.

[92] "Secretary's Interview with John Hightower, Associated Press [May 7, 1965]," *National Security File, Country File—Dominican Republic, Volume 3, Memos and Miscellaneous—4/28/65-5/7/65 (1 of 4) [Folder]; National Security File, Country File, Latin America-Dominican Republic, Box 39 [Collection]* (LBJ Library, 1965), 1–3.

prevent a communist takeover? If so, when did the U.S. purpose change; and did the change affect the number of troops required?" Rusk replied: "The first action taken by the United States was indeed a rescue operation, and there is voluminous evidence to indicate that the Marines arrived just in time to avoid a major calamity. The mission of the U.S. forces did expand in keeping with the necessities of the changing situation and to support the decisions of the OAS."[93] Hightower then posed a question about whether the United States was "returning to some elements of the policy of intervention employed in the 19th century and first two decades of this century when Marines were sent into various countries of this hemisphere for political purposes." Rusk retorted, "recent U.S. actions in the Dominican Republic have had nothing to do with 19th century forms of intervention for the purpose of collecting revenues, protecting concessions, or changing governments. We went in to save lives. We are there in support of the OAS and the Inter-American system."[94]

Efforts to publicize this version of events continued in the following days. At a high-level meeting on May 8, Johnson told subordinates, "we must constantly emphasize publically the gravity of the situation on April 27/28, the country team's recommendations, and our contacts with the OAS. He noted that, after the OAS had adjourned, it was the United States which urged it to reconvene; we are still encouraging and pleading with the OAS."[95] In other words, he wanted to make clear that the United States had been pushing the regional body to take the lead in handling the situation, thereby proving that his intention was not to act unilaterally. Efforts toward this end were articulated in another memo summarizing a White House meeting on May 19. "We must," it notes, "prepare a fully creditable and highly persuasive presentation of our side of the story. This is to include our position and how it has been arrived at."[96]

The argument was catching on. In a cable to Johnson on May 24, Ambassador Bennett and Deputy Secretary of Defense Cyrus Vance described a meeting with Imbert of the Government of National Reconciliation and members of the OAS, including Secretary General Mora, about the "juridical basis" of America's decision.[97] As one of Imbert's counterparts put it, "everyone [was] grateful for

[93] "Secretary's Interview with John Hightower, Associated Press [May 7, 1965]," 3.

[94] Ibid., 8.

[95] "Meeting with the President—2:00 p.m. on May 8, 1965 [June 1, 1965]," *National Security File, Country File—Dominican Republic, Volume 6—5/25/65-6/65 (5 of 5) [Folder]; National Security File, Country File—Latin America-Dominican Republic, Box 41 (1 of 2) [Collection]* (LBJ Library, 1965), 4.

[96] "Decisions Reached at May 19 White House Meeting [May 20, 1965]," *National Security File, Country File—Dominican Republic, Volume 5—5/19/65-5/31/65 (5 of 5) [Folder]; National Security File, Country File—Latin America-Dominican Republic, Box 40 [Collection]* (LBJ Library, 1965), 1, underline in original.

[97] Mora's participation was seen as crucial for demonstrating that the U.S. was not acting unilaterally; see "For the Secretary from Bundy [May 22, 1965]," *National Security File, Country*

our original landing which had undoubtedly saved country, but now we were taking action to prevent [a] solution [to an] internal political problem. He wanted to know if we considered our new position US occupation or US intervention." Mora interjected, proclaiming "that [the] Dominican problem [is] no longer merely an internal political one . . . [and] that OAS membership was committed to keeping the cease-fire for humanitarian reasons." Ferrer, the OAS lawyer, added "that [the] request of Dominican authorities for US assistance was [the] juridical base of IAF [Inter-American Force]. IAF [is] here only for peace and restoration [of] order for all elements of [the] population under OAS aegis." U.S. officials present at the meeting mused that "[Ferrer] out-lawyered local lawyers."[98] Here, we see non-U.S. officials connecting the legal dots between the initial request for U.S. intervention to the creation of the multilateral force. We also see, per the text establishing the IAPF on May 24, attempts to show that such a move was "not one of intervention, but rather one of rendering assistance to the people of a sister nation" and that "the objectives for which the inter-American force was created fall within those broad provisions of the Charter which are concerned with matters affecting the peace and security of the hemisphere."[99]

Staying Inside the Lines

As noted in Chapter 3, an observable implication of my argument is that decision makers should calibrate their words and actions so that they are consistent with the parameters of the legal exemptions they are invoking. Since one of the legal exemptions used to justify intervention was participation in a multilateral peacekeeping force authorized by the OAS, decision makers should have refrained from taking actions that seemed to favor one side or that signaled the United States would stay indefinitely. Such restraint would avoid undermining claims of impartiality and jeopardizing the operation's legality.[100] That is indeed what we see.

File—Dominican Republic, 5/65—Davidson (2 of 2) [Folder]; National Security File, Country File—Latin America-Dominican Republic, Box 51 [Collection] (LBJ Library, 1965).

[98] "Incoming Telegram [from W. Tapley Bennett, May 24, 1965, 6:23 p.m.]," *National Security File, Country File—Dominican Republic, Volume 5—5/19/65-5/31/65 (1 of 5) [Folder]; National Security File, Country File—Latin America-Dominican Republic, Box 40 [Collection]* (LBJ Library, 1965), 1–3.

[99] "Incoming Telegram [from W. Tapley Bennett, May 24, 1965, 12:18 a.m.]," *National Security File, Country File—Dominican Republic, Volume 5—5/19/65-5/31/65 (1 of 5) [Folder]; National Security File, Country File—Latin America-Dominican Republic, Box 40 [Collection]* (LBJ Library, 1965), 1.

[100] Fazal, *State Death: The Politics and Geography of Conquest, Occupation, and Annexation*, 206–209.

A memo from Mann to Bennett expressed concern "about reports US forces in DR are, by some of their actions, giving [the] impression of being [an] occupation force. While it is, of course, impossible to destroy this impression completely, we consider it highly important that US military avoid all action which would strengthen this impression." The memo then outlines various activities the armed forces should avoid wherever feasible, including "taking over buildings, both private residence and government or office buildings." It goes so far as to claim that if the military has to occupy a building, they should make every effort to do so with the consent of the current occupant and to ensure that they are providing compensation commensurate with rent. Mann concluded by pointing out that the Defense Department "agrees that this issue is sensitive political matter, not primarily military matter," and that "General Palmer will be responsive to your guidance on this issue."[101]

One week later on May 19, a memo from Bundy, Vance, Palmer, Bennett, and special envoy John B. Martin highlighted the difficulties of reaching a political settlement in the Dominican Republic. One proposed solution was to "physically interpose [U.S.] mil[itary] forces between the contending Dom[inican] mil[itary] forces" in coordination with Secretary General Mora. The advantages of this approach were manifold: "It would show the world we are truly neutral, truly humanitarian, t[ru]ly desirous of stopping the killing . . . . If taken with OAS Comm[ittee] endorsement, it will serve to demonstrate that [the] OAS is acting effectively to enforce a cease fire and this will reduce pressure in UNSC for further UN involvement."[102]

These documents demonstrate that decision makers sought to limit their actions to what was justifiable within the confines of the legal exemptions used to defend the intervention. As scholars have previously pointed out, this balancing act was anything but convenient. According to Slater, "even when it later became clear that the constitutionalists were [the] primary beneficiary [of the ceasefire], the United States could not blatantly violate it without enormous political costs, particularly in light of the frequent public warnings from the council . . . against U.S. support for, or acquiescence in, military action."[103] Tanisha Fazal similarly writes, "[t]he need to preserve the illusion that the region was acting as one

[101] "Outgoing Telegram [from Thomas Mann to W. Tapley Bennett, May 12, 1965, 11:13 p.m.]," *National Security File, Country File—Dominican Republic, Volume 5—5/19/65-5/31/65 (5 of 5) [Folder]; National Security File, Country File—Latin America-Dominican Republic, Box 40 [Collection]* (LBJ Library, 1965), 1–2.

[102] "Incoming Telegram [from McGeorge Bundy et Al., May 19, 1965, 3:23 p.m.]," *National Security File, Country File—Dominican Republic, Volume 4, 5/1/65-5/19/65 (1 of 5) [Folder]; National Security File, Country File, Latin America-Dominican Republic, Box 39 [Collection]* (LBJ Library, 1965), 1.

[103] Slater, *Intervention and Negotiation: The United States and the Dominican Revolution*, 74.

during the crisis also constrained US military actions, for example by forcing the US Marines on the ground to behave neutrally toward both sides in the civil war, as well as by having a Brazilian general command the operation. It is not clear why the United States would expend this kind of effort," Fazal argues, "if not to project the impression that it were behaving as it ought."[104]

Beyond simply calibrating their behavior, we might also expect decision makers to tailor their rhetoric accordingly if my argument is correct. This might include refraining from invoking extralegal justifications or explanations for intervention that are unrelated to particular legal exemptions. According to some accounts of this episode, Lyndon Johnson did the opposite when he switched from strictly emphasizing endangered nationals in the first few days to a broader narrative that included the threat of communism.[105] On April 30, he "warned that there were 'signs that people trained outside the Dominican Republic are seeking to gain control.' "[106] On May 2, he invoked the communist threat more explicitly.[107] There is, however, an underappreciated rationale behind this strategy that involves more than the United States simply dispensing with pretense and showing its true colors. It was part of a broader effort to secure regional backing for the intervention. Where senior officials tended to diverge from the president was in their desire to gain robust evidence of communist infiltration before making the case publicly or, in the interim, to push the message behind the scenes.[108]

An OAS meeting held at Punta del Este three years before the Dominican Crisis provides valuable context. That meeting produced a resolution declaring communism a threat to the hemisphere. It also pointed out that the actions and ideology of the Castro regime placed his country "outside the inter-American system."[109] Cuba was excluded from the regional body as a result. Latin American nations thus recognized communism as a threat to the region in the recent past.

Decision makers' efforts to highlight the communist threat in the Dominican Republic takes on new meaning against the backdrop of the 1962 Punta del Este resolution.[110] The main obstacle in late April and early May was that tangible

[104] Fazal, *State Death: The Politics and Geography of Conquest, Occupation, and Annexation*, 206.

[105] Atkins and Wilson, *The Dominican Republic and the United States: From Imperialism to Transnationalism*, 135; Crandall, *Gunboat Democracy: U.S. Intervention in the Dominican Republic, Grenada, and Panama*, 38; Lowenthal, *The Dominican Intervention*, 1–2.

[106] Crandall, *Gunboat Democracy: U.S. Intervention in the Dominican Republic, Grenada, and Panama*, 70.

[107] Ibid., 70–71.

[108] Johnson's advisors were frustrated at times with his seemingly singular focus on the communist threat. See Saunders, *Leaders at War: How Presidents Shape Military Interventions*, 161.

[109] http://avalon.law.yale.edu/20th_century/intam17.asp.

[110] In fact, some documents mention it explicitly. See "Legal Basis for United States Actions in the Dominican Republic [May 7, 1965]," 5.

evidence was hard to come by. In a conversation with Secretary McNamara in the evening of April 29, Johnson asked why he should not declare that "powers outside the republic are trying to gain control[.] We all know they are. What is wrong with my saying it?" McNamara cautioned him, "Well, I think you have got a pretty tough job to prove that, Mr. President,—as President. The rest of us can say things like that and we don't have to prove it, but you have got a handful of people there but you don't know that Castro is trying to do anything."[111] This exchange helps explain Bundy and McNamara's desire, conveyed at the April 30 meeting referenced earlier, to garner tangible evidence that Castro and the communists had infiltrated the constitutionalists as a way of getting the hemisphere to get behind an expanded operation, providing legal cover in the process.[112]

Additional decision makers emphasized the value of carefully building a case of communist infiltration among the rebels in Santo Domingo. In a memo to Johnson on May 1, Carl T. Rowan, the head of the U.S. Information Agency, suggested they "exploit as shrewdly as possible, without overdoing it, the Communist and Castroite leadership of the rebels. This is indicated in the fact that almost all the editorials supporting us in Latin America base their support on the fear that the Dominican Republic might become another Cuba, and thus a menace to the entire hemisphere." Pursuing this strategy, Rowan claimed, would "mute the cries of 'United States aggression' and 'gunboat diplomacy' and perhaps preclude attacks on USIS libraries, embassies and other American installations, with attendant Communist exploitation through Latin America and the world."[113]

Thomas Mann, who supported intervention and even invoked the communist threat himself at various points, appreciated that this approach was not without risks. In a meeting on May 3, he pointed out that the United States and Latin American nations, "in a number of documents and in a variety of forums, have expressed a general belief in the principle of non-intervention. At the same time, the Latin Americans, for many years, have recognized the necessity for collective defense against attacks on the Hemisphere." The problem was

[111] "President Johnson's Notes on Conversation with Secretary McNamara on April 29, 1965 at 5:05 PM," *April 1965, Chrono File—Citations (7301-7452)—Service Set II [Folder]; Recordings and Transcripts of Telephone Conversations and Meetings, WH Series/SR Series, Box 6—Sept 64-May 65 [Collection]* (LBJ Library, 1965), 2. See also Crandall, *Gunboat Democracy: U.S. Intervention in the Dominican Republic, Grenada, and Panama*, 65; Lowenthal, *The Dominican Intervention*, 105.

[112] FRUS, "42. Editorial Note."

[113] "Memorandum for the President [from Carl T. Rowan to Lyndon Johnson, May 1, 1965]," *National Security File, Country File—Dominican Republic, Volume 3, Memos and Miscellaneous—4/28/65-5/7/65 (4 of 4) [Folder]; National Security File, Country File, Latin America-Dominican Republic, Box 39 [Collection]* (LBJ Library, 1965), 1–2.

that they did not all view subversion from elements inside a country as synonymous with an external attack requiring a third-party response. As such, "the Latin Americans tend to adhere to the traditional line on intervention and think that we are engaged again in gunboat diplomacy." Mann complained that while some privately applauded U.S. efforts, "secret support does us no damn good," and he worried that "the sophisticated Latin Americans, who wish us well, probably did not like to see us dilute our evacuation fig leaf and switch emphasis to the anti-Communist argument." In the end he still believed the United States should make clear to the OAS "that the Communists, in trying to subvert the Dominican Republic, are the ones who are intervening."[114]

In sum, decision makers recognized the potential benefits but also the pitfalls of leaning too heavily on the communist threat in the Dominican Republic. Although there was a chance it would bring the hemisphere on board, thereby providing legal cover for U.S. forces to remain in the Dominican Republic, there was a risk that if they pushed the narrative too hard without proof it would call into question their only existing pretext at that point in time. This delicate balance makes even more sense in light of the fact that the OAS was not entirely a rubber stamp for U.S. policy. Some states who ended up vetoing the proposal for a peacekeeping force, most notably Chile, were close U.S. allies who received large sums of covert and overt support.[115]

A Dissenter

An interesting aspect of the Power Pack saga is an indirect exchange about its legality between Abe Fortas, a lawyer and confidant of Johnson's who later became a Supreme Court Justice, and Bundy. The issues highlighted in the correspondences speak to those at the heart of this book.

[114] "Meeting on the Dominican Republic—May 3, 1965 [May 4, 1965]," *National Security File, Country File—Dominican Republic, Volume 3, Memos and Miscellaneous—4/28/65-5/7/65 (3 of 4) [Folder]; National Security File, Country File, Latin America-Dominican Republic, Box 39 [Collection]* (LBJ Library, 1965), 1–2.

[115] The reasons why countries like Chile could not support the U.S., although beyond the scope of this book, are interesting. In one conversation, Frei told U.S. officials that the large communist presence in the country prevented him from supporting the U.S. resolution. See "Incoming Telegram [from W. Averell Harriman to Dean Rusk, May 7, 1965, 9:05 p.m.]," *National Security File, Country File—Dominican Republic, Bennett "HELP", 4/65 [Folder]; National Security File, Country File—Latin America-Dominican Republic, Box 48 [Collection]* (LBJ Library, 1965), 2. In another conversation, Uruguay—who also voted against the proposal—said something similar while expressing appreciation for U.S. efforts at multilateralism. See "From American Embassy, Montevideo, Uruguay Dated May 6 [from W. Averell Harriman]," *National Security File, Country File—Dominican Republic, Bennett "HELP", 4/65 [Folder]; National Security File, Country File—Latin America-Dominican Republic, Box 48 [Collection]* (LBJ Library, 1965).

On May 6, Fortas sent a lengthy note to Bundy regarding Leonard Meeker's memo.[116] He challenged the administration's legal rationale, warning they could set precedents they might not want to set. The first issue he tackled was the mission to protect Americans and other foreigners on the island. "The argument that armed intervention by a state to preserve the lives of its nationals in another state has some support in international law," Fortas wrote. "But even this limited concept is no longer uniformly accepted or in favor . . . . In any event, I should be afraid that if the United States should now assert that intervention for this purpose is a matter of legal right on the part of states, it could and would be used in the future by Communist nations to justify action which we should strongly oppose."[117]

The second justification had to do with "find[ing] a legal basis for our continued military presence in the Dominican Republic in the fact that we are acting to preserve the capability of the OAS to function in accordance with its charter, that is, to achieve peace and reestablish orderly processes of government." Fortas stated, "I know of no basis in law for such a doctrine. It would be quite a different matter if our military presence were requested by the OAS and we were, in effect, acting upon request as an instrument of the OAS, pursuant to its collective peace-keeping function."[118]

Fortas instead wanted to emphasize that the United States regretted acting unilaterally and did so only because "action had to be taken immediately and urgently, and because the OAS machinery was not available which could have acted with the necessary speed." Moreover, he wished to point out that given the humanitarian mission, leaving prematurely would have been irresponsible. Nevertheless, the United States should still make clear that it "has not changed in the slightest degree its historic position that situations like those which existed in the Dominican Republic should be handled by collective organizations—in this instance, the OAS," and that the United States sought at the earliest opportunity to involve this body and would wholeheartedly support their efforts to bring this crisis to a close.[119]

[116] Papermaster, "A Case Study of the Effect of International Law on Foreign Policy Decisionmaking: The United States Intervention in the Dominican Republic in 1965," 490–491.

[117] "Memorandum Dated May 6, 1965 Headed 'Legal Basis for United States Actions in the Dominican Republic' [from Abe Fortas to McGeorge Bundy, May 6, 1965]," *National Security File, Country File—Dominican Republic, Volume 3, Memos and Miscellaneous—4/28/65-5/7/65 (2 of 4) [Folder]; National Security File, Country File, Latin America-Dominican Republic, Box 39 [Collection]* (LBJ Library, 1965), 1–2, underline in original.

[118] "Memorandum Dated May 6, 1965 Headed 'Legal Basis for United States Actions in the Dominican Republic' [from Abe Fortas to McGeorge Bundy, May 6, 1965]," 2, underline in original.

[119] "Memorandum Dated May 6, 1965 Headed 'Legal Basis for United States Actions in the Dominican Republic' [from Abe Fortas to McGeorge Bundy, May 6, 1965]," 3–4.

Fortas concluded with a summary of his position, "recommend[ing] against use of a technical 'legal' explanation. If one were to be sought, the only possibility is as follows: Intervention is justified if an American state is the subject of aggression by another state; a 'communist' revolution is an aggression by another state: Therefore, intervention is justified in the case of a 'communist' revolution."[120] In writing this memo, Fortas is inadvertently confirming that the Johnson administration was indeed using a technical legal explanation to justify a military intervention.

In a letter to Johnson on May 8, Bundy addressed Fortas' concerns: "[W]e really cannot have it both ways. *Either we think we have a legal case or we do not, and it seems to me better for us to have one than not to have one.* This is the strong opinion of Acheson, Fisher, and Meeker himself. So with great respect to Abe, I think we have no choice on this one, and have told Meeker to go ahead. I have also asked for a final copy of the document, and it should be in your night reading."[121] Not only did Bundy want the administration to use a legal rationale, but he felt strongly enough to include a report to this effect in the President's list of things to read before bed. Moreover, the fact that Meeker as well as Dean Acheson, an informal advisor, and Adrien Fisher, the State Department Legal Advisor when Acheson was Secretary of State, all concurred is notable in and of itself. It suggests that Fortas' dissent was not widely shared among those with significant international (legal) experience in government. At the very least, Meeker, Acheson, and Fisher appear to believe that the stated legal rationale was reasonable.

Exploring the Counterfactual

The argument that the presence of several legal exemptions made possible the Johnson administration's decision to overtly intervene in the Dominican Republic implies that things would have gone differently if they were unavailable. Although it is impossible to prove any counterfactual conclusively, there are several reasons to believe that legal exemptions enabled overt action in this case

To begin with, before the OAS got involved in the crisis some in the Johnson administration contemplated ways of quietly expanding the scope of the operation

[120] "Memorandum Dated May 6, 1965 Headed 'Legal Basis for United States Actions in the Dominican Republic' [from Abe Fortas to McGeorge Bundy, May 6, 1965]," 4.

[121] "Memorandum to the President [from McGeorge Bundy to Lyndon Johnson, May 8, 1965]," *National Security File, Country File—Dominican Republic, Volume 3, Memos and Miscellaneous—4/28/65-5/7/65 (3 of 4) [Folder]; National Security File, Country File, Latin America-Dominican Republic, Box 39 [Collection]* (LBJ Library, 1965), emphasis added.

without undermining the credibility of the evacuation narrative. A top-secret postmortem of Power Pack, now declassified, summarizes a note Mann sent to Bennett on April 29 directing him to tell U.S. troops to "hold, but not expand the areas they had secured." Engaging in "offensive fighting against extremists is a major policy decision which should be made by highest authority here." What follows next is informative: "Request you give urgent considerations to development of operational plans by Alliance [i.e., the junta] *with quiet assistance of few United States officers for the deliberate and systematic reduction of insurgent-held parts of city.*"[122] Bennett's response was to propose "if not a broader role, at least a more extensive area of operations for the Marines" which might prevent the loyalists and constitutionalists from firing at one another and create space for a political solution.[123] The establishment of the ISZ on April 30 provided cover for such a mission, rendering Mann's proposal to discreetly support the ousted junta unnecessary.

There is also evidence from before and after the Dominican Crisis that lends additional support to the counterfactual, namely the use of covert action to meddle in the internal affairs of the regime in the absence of legal exemptions. Although evidence is harder to come by—and the context of intervention is somewhat different—these two episodes are still useful to explore in that they offer some semblance of within-case variation.

First, U.S. decision makers' efforts to covertly support dissidents in their quest to overthrow Trujillo in the early 1960s shows the appeal of plausible deniability when legal exemptions to nonintervention are unavailable. Much like the Bay of Pigs, plans to topple Trujillo began under Eisenhower and ramped up under Kennedy.[124] While the declassified record is sparse, "the plan's remarkable similarity to the plan being developed for removing Castro from power in Cuba suggests that it was shaped by similar concerns regarding arguably illegal US military intervention."[125] The evidence that does exist suggests that those in the Eisenhower administration were willing to intervene openly if they had

122 "The Response of the Department of State to the Dominican Crisis of April-May 1965 [July 1968]," *National Security File, National Security Council History—Dominican Crisis, 1965, State-DOD-OAS—Chronologies and Narratives (4 of 5) [Folder]; National Security Council Histories, Dominican Crisis 1965, Box 7 (2 of 2) [Collection]* (LBJ Library, 1965), 23, emphasis added. Early on in the crisis, Mann also sought to restrict even limited aid to the junta, including the provision of walkie-talkies, to decrease the visibility of the U.S. role in the actual civil war. See Gleijeses, *The Dominican Crisis: The 1965 Constitutionalist Revolt and American Intervention*, 253.

123 "The Response of the Department of State to the Dominican Crisis of April-May 1965 [July 1968]," 25.

124 O'Rourke, *Covert Regime Change: America's Secret Cold War*, 201–207.

125 Joel H. Westra, *International Law and the Use of Armed Force: The UN Charter and the Major Powers* (London and New York: Routledge, 2007), 78.

approval from the OAS. Because such support never materialized, they settled for covert action.[126] "Assistant Secretary of State Mann explained in a memorandum dated October 10, insofar as US policy was 'limited by . . . nonintervention commitments,' the absence of a permissive OAS resolution had made '[t]he problem of dealing with Trujillo . . . more difficult.' "[127]

Decision makers in the Kennedy administration faced these same constraints. The CIA's Consul General, Henry Dearborn, sent a memo to the Department of State on February 24, 1961 recommending that Kennedy "do all possible within non-interventionist commitments to hasten turnover of [the Dominican Republic] to elements which will respect guiding principles of OAS."[128] A little less than one month after the Bay of Pigs, the Cuban Task Force of the NSC penned a memo to McGeorge Bundy noting similar constraints: "While it is highly desirable in the present Dominican situation for the U.S. to be identified with and to support democratic elements seeking to overthrow Trujillo, we necessarily run some risks in doing so. If Trujillo is overthrown with U.S. support, we may well be criticized by world opinion for subverting an existing government, albeit a highly unpopular one."

In this same memo, the Task Force discussed various contingencies that shed light on the significance of legal exemptions as fig leaves for action. If the dissidents succeeded and established a pro-American government, the United States might still have to use force to help restore order. As they put it, "[f]rom the point of view of US posture in Latin America and the world, military intervention in the Dominican Republic should to the extent possible be taken through the OAS or at the request of a provisional government in conjunction with selected Latin American countries rather than by the US alone."[129] Things would be harder if the dissidents toppled Trujillo but hostile elements took over. Like in Chapter 4 with the Bay of Pigs episode, decision makers assessed the feasibility of securing an invitation for intervention from a viable

[126] O'Rourke, *Covert Regime Change: America's Secret Cold War*, 201.

[127] Westra, *International Law and the Use of Armed Force: The UN Charter and the Major Powers*, 79.

[128] FRUS, "303. Telegram From the Consulate General in the Dominican Republic to the Department of State," in *Foreign Relations of the United States, 1961–1963, Volume XII, American Republics*, ed. Edward C. Keefer, Harriet D. Schwar, and Taylor W. Fain III (Washington, D.C.: United States Government Printing Office, 1996), https://history.state.gov/historicaldocuments/frus1961-63v12/d303.

[129] FRUS, "307. Memorandum From the Cuban Task Force of the National Security Council to the President's Special Assistant for National Security Affairs (Bundy)," in *Foreign Relations of the United States, 1961–1963, Volume XII, American Republics*, ed. Edward C. Keefer, Harriet D. Schwar, and Taylor W. Fain III (Washington, D.C.: United States Government Printing Office, 1996), https://history.state.gov/historicaldocuments/frus1961-63v12/d307.

provisional government and working with the OAS to legally and legitimately restore order.[130]

Johnson's reversion to covert action *after* U.S. forces withdrew in 1966 is similarly revealing.[131] An observable implication of my argument mentioned in Chapter 3 is that once decision makers accomplish their stated objectives, any further efforts to alter domestic authority structures should be covert unless they are able to secure additional legal cover. This is precisely what happened once the military operation officially ended. On January 11, 1966, the NSC outlined a covert plan to help Joaquín Balaguer prevail over Bosch in elections that summer. The NSC memo made clear "that the operation be carried out in such a way that United States sponsorship cannot be proven in any way."[132] The CIA provided Balaguer with cash as well as campaign guidance and friendly propaganda. Armed with secret support, the U.S.-backed candidate eventually came out victorious.

Competing Explanations

This section evaluates several competing arguments to the one I advanced in this chapter. One alternative is the escalation thesis. In this view, Johnson's decision to openly invade the Dominican Republic was facilitated by the absence of serious concerns that such an action would invite a retaliatory response by rival powers like the Soviet Union or Cuba. Based on the available evidence, escalation concerns did not figure prominently in deliberations among senior decision makers about the costs and benefits of overt intervention. The bulk of the administration's attention was devoted to figuring out the implications of intervention for America's moral authority and credibility. Although it is always challenging to disprove a negative, the absence of clear expressions of escalation concerns one way or the other implies that it may not have been salient in this case. If anything, the fact that decision makers believed constitutionalist forces were trained (in)directly by Castro would seem to suggest that senior officials

[130] In a subsequent memo, Under Secretary of State Chester Bowles registered his concerns about relying on an invitation from a provisional government, referencing America's commitments to treaties and the like. See FRUS, "310. Memorandum by the Under Secretary of State (Bowles)," in *Foreign Relations of the United States, 1961–1963, Volume XII, American Republics*, ed. Edward C. Keefer, Harriet D. Schwar, and Taylor W. Fain III (Washington, D.C.: United States Government Printing Office, 1996), https://history.state.gov/historicaldocuments/frus1961-63v12/d310.

[131] According to one account, Balaguer and Bosch unsuccessfully requested that the IAPF stay through the elections. See Fazal, *State Death: The Politics and Geography of Conquest, Occupation, and Annexation*, 209.

[132] Quoted in O'Rourke, *Covert Regime Change: America's Secret Cold War*, 220.

might have expected some form of a counter-intervention, or at least an increase in Cuban involvement, in response to a U.S. invasion. Again, though, evidence is limited.

A second set of competing explanations are rooted in domestic politics. One variant, democratic peace theory, predicts that Johnson was encouraged to openly invade the Dominican Republic because it was not a liberal democracy at the time. This argument would also hold that Johnson wanted to promote democracy. It is certainly true when the United States intervened in April 1965, the Dominican Republic was not democratic.[133] It is also the case that after the invasion, the Johnson administration, along with the OAS, helped oversee new elections. Nevertheless, Johnson's quip that "[w]e will have one of 3 dictators" suggests that his chief concern was simply to gain a compliant regime out of the intervention, even if that meant an autocracy.

Another alternative related to domestic politics posits that Johnson intervened openly in the Dominican Republic because he enjoyed public support. If he did not, so the argument goes, the intervention would have been covert. The evidence in this regard is mixed. On the one hand, Johnson was certainly worried about incurring the public's wrath if he allowed a second Cuba to emerge in the hemisphere. On April 30, he told Congressional leaders: "It looks to me like I'm in a hell of a shape either way. If I take over, I can't live in the world. If I let them take over, I can't live here."[134] On the other hand, key members of Congress disapproved of invading the Dominican Republic. To take one example, Power Pack invited a stinging rebuke from one of the President's closest allies, Senator William J. Fulbright.[135] Johnson's willingness to ignore him and incur the ensuing harsh criticism is telling.

In the previous two chapters, I argued that one consideration contributing to the decision to pursue regime change covertly turned on fears of inciting nationalism in the target state. It is reasonable to ask whether the absence of such concerns contributed to Johnson's decision to openly intervene. One author makes essentially this point, arguing that nationalistic sentiments among the Dominican people were less potent than in other countries owing to the repressive Trujillo years.[136] A note of caution is in order here. For one thing, that same author argues that this point "should certainly not be overstated." He also

[133] Monty G. Marshall, Ted Robert Gurr, and Keith Jaggers, "Polity IV Project: Political Regime Characteristics and Transitions, 1800–2009. Dataset Users' Manual," *Center for Systemic Peace,* 2010.

[134] Alan McPherson, "Misled by Himself: What the Johnson Tapes Reveal About the Dominican Intervention of 1965," *Latin American Research Review* 38, no. 2 (2003): 136–137.

[135] Crandall, *Gunboat Democracy: U.S. Intervention in the Dominican Republic, Grenada, and Panama,* 89.

[136] Slater, *Intervention and Negotiation: The United States and the Dominican Revolution,* 209–210.

writes that "[m]any moderate Dominicans to whom I spoke, even those who were very dubious about the constitutionalists, were angrily opposed to the intervention, preferring by far to run the risks of a continuation of the revolutionary process."[137] The head of the loyalist junta that had been ousted by the rebels made a similar argument to U.S. officials. According to one report, "he hoped Americans would not have to shoot. He pointed out that if Americans had to fight in [the Dominican Republic], this would have long-range effect in promoting growth of nationalism and anti-Americanism, which, in turn, would play into hands of communists."[138]

Based on this evidence, it is reasonable to conclude that there was nothing approximating agreement that a short U.S. intervention was a necessary response to some shared threat, as the tainted victory thesis would predict.[139] Moreover, although it is true that U.S. officials sought to avoid the appearance that they were an occupying force—which the tainted victory thesis might also expect—the evidence presented here revealed that the primary purpose of those efforts was to bolster the legitimacy of the OAS venture and to serve as a sign of neutrality more than anything else. According to Fazal, "US policy makers were far more concerned about the reaction of their Latin American neighbors to the intervention than they were about the reaction of the Dominicans themselves."[140]

Before concluding, a word is in order about the argument that leaders will turn to overt action when there is significant time pressure to act and a perceived need to signal resolve. It is undoubtedly true that decision makers believed the window for action was closing and that allowing another communist regime to sprout up in the Western Hemisphere would damage American resolve.[141] The problem is that these factors were also present in the cases of covert regime change examined in the previous two chapters. In both Cuba and Chile, decision makers were under severe time constraints and understood that inaction could signal weakness. But they opted for secrecy anyway, knowing it was less likely to succeed, due to the lack of legal exemptions and the desire to avoid suffering hypocrisy and credibility costs. The presence of time constraints and concerns about resolve across cases of both covert and overt action diminishes the

[137] Ibid., 210.

[138] "Incoming Telegram [from W. Tapley Bennett, April 30, 1965, 3:08 p.m.]," *National Security File, Country File—Dominican Republic, Volume 1, Cables, 6/64-4/65 (1 of 3) [Folder]; National Security File—Country File, Latin America-Dominican Republic, Box 38 (1 of 2) [Collection]* (LBJ Library, 1965), 1.

[139] One book notes that the intervention did indeed antagonize the population. See Atkins and Wilson, *The Dominican Republic and the United States: From Imperialism to Transnationalism,* 147–148.

[140] Fazal, *State Death: The Politics and Geography of Conquest, Occupation, and Annexation,* 210.

[141] O'Rourke, *Covert Regime Change: America's Secret Cold War,* 223–224.

explanatory power of these variables. It is interesting to note as well that time *did* play a role in this case, albeit in a surprising way. In short, decision makers worried that if they waited too long before acting, the excuse used to justify the first deployment of troops would evaporate. Appealing to endangered Americans at the start of a civil war would have more credibility.[142]

Conclusion

Lyndon Johnson's decision to openly intervene in the Dominican Civil War in 1965 was facilitated by the presence of multiple legal exemptions. The initial deployment of troops was justified as a necessary measure to protect endangered Americans and a stopgap that would provide the OAS time to act. As the crisis wore on, U.S. decision makers lent support to a multilateral peacekeeping force under the auspices of the OAS, as my argument would predict. Decision makers also worked to ensure that they were acting within the confines of what was considered acceptable according to their stated legal rationale. This included avoiding any appearance that they were a de facto occupying power. I also brought to bear additional evidence intended to get at the counterfactual, namely that Johnson might have pursued a different approach had the OAS not ultimately authorized the mission.

The legal theory of covert action performed better than alternative arguments. Concerns about escalation did not feature strongly one way or the other. Arguments rooted in domestic politics enjoyed mixed support. Although the United States helped facilitate elections following the invasion, decision makers were only willing to throw their support behind democracy if a pro-U.S. leader was elected. Moreover, while Johnson worried about the American public's reaction to a second Cuba, he intervened over the objections of key figures in his own party. The tainted victory thesis did not perform particularly well. Although some argue that nationalism was muted in the Dominican Republic, there is evidence that the Dominican people did not embrace U.S. intervention. While decision makers did do their best to avoid the appearance of an occupation, this was done primarily to bolster the legal defense of the operation.

[142] Gleijeses, *The Dominican Crisis: The 1965 Constitutionalist Revolt and American Intervention*, 293.

7

Operation Urgent Fury: Grenada

Ronald Reagan's decision to send troops to Grenada in October of 1983, codenamed Operation Urgent Fury, stands next to Lyndon Johnson's invasion of the Dominican Republic as one of the rare instances during the Cold War in which the United States openly used force to pursue regime change abroad. At the time happened, it was also the first large-scale deployment of the American military since the Vietnam War. The operation, which began on October 25, was over in under a week. This chapter explains the factors that enabled U.S. decision makers to opt for overt intervention.

As with the last three chapters, it will be useful to start by identifying the kind of evidence we would expect to see if my argument is correct. Most obviously, we would expect decision makers to invoke one or more legal exemptions to non-intervention to justify openly toppling a sovereign regime. This would include a credible self-defense claim, whether in the form of a direct attack or the presence of American nationals in clear and present danger. It would also include an invitation for intervention by the UN Security Council or a regional body. Even better for my argument would be statements about how these exemptions conform to existing international legal standards.

Similar to Chapter 6, it is difficult to definitively prove that Reagan would have intervened covertly in Grenada if legal exemptions had been unavailable. The crisis that precipitated intervention unfolded rapidly. Exemptions were available from the start. As such, discussions were dominated by how best to present them. Despite these challenges, I bring several pieces of evidence to bear to get at the counterfactual. First, I use recently declassified documents to demonstrate that Jimmy Carter authorized covert action in 1979 in support of opposition elements in Grenada. Second, I show that officials in the Reagan administration perceived the New Jewel Movement as a threat for years prior to Urgent Fury but were reluctant to pursue overtly hardline policies against them, including actions short of force. What all of this suggests is that before mid-October 1983, which presented the United States with a unique opportunity to intervene under the auspices of legal exemptions, overt regime change was deemed too risky.

In the Shadow of International Law. Michael Poznansky, Oxford University Press (2020). © Oxford University Press.
DOI: 10.1093/oso/9780190096595.001.0001

Historical Background

Grenada was a British colony for several centuries dating back to the 1760s.[1] The United Kingdom granted the island-nation partial autonomy in 1967. Seven years later, it became fully independent.[2] Eric Gairy, the first prime minister of a sovereign Grenada, ruled through fear, brutality, and corruption.[3] Owing to his repressive policies, Gairy was overthrown in a bloodless coup on March 13, 1979 by Maurice Bishop and his Marxist-Leninist party known as the New Jewel Movement (NJM).[4]

The NJM quickly established the People's Revolutionary Government (PRG), introducing socialism to Grenada and strengthening relations with communist bloc countries. Although the PRG was initially met with enthusiasm by the public, the gradual turn toward authoritarianism and corruption alienated many of their early supporters.[5] According to declassified U.S. reports written a few days after the invasion, "[t]he Bishop regime suspended the country's constitution, refused to call early elections, ridiculed English-style democracy as 'Westminster hypocrisy' and turned instead to the Cuban model of 'revolutionary democracy,' which it tried to implement with Cuban aid."[6]

Grenada's foreign policy under Bishop reflected an effort to court left-leaning regimes while also remaining on good terms with the West.[7] Bishop wrote letters to Reagan "attempt[ing] to portray himself as the head of a small, impoverished country who desired to live in harmony with his neighbors, including the United States, and to receive assistance in his efforts to promote the welfare of the Grenadian people." But "[i]n other circles," U.S. officials observed that "Bishop stressed his determination to combat imperialism and lend all possible aid to

[1] Richard B. Sheridan, "The British Credit Crisis of 1772 and The American Colonies," *The Journal of Economic History* 20, no. 2 (1960): 165.

[2] "Grenada Papers: No. 2 Outline History [October 29, 1983]," *Grenada, 10/29/1983 (1 of 4)—Box 43—Executive Secretariat, NSC Cable File [Folder]; Executive Secretariat, NSC: Cable File: Records—Box 43, 44, 45—Box 15 [Collection]* (Ronald Reagan Library, 1983), 1.

[3] Russell Crandall, *Gunboat Democracy: U.S. Intervention in the Dominican Republic, Grenada, and Panama* (Lanham, MD: Rowman and Littlefield, 2006), 111–112.

[4] Robert Pastor, "The United States and the Grenada Revolution: Who Pushed First and Why?," in *A Revolution Aborted: The Lessons of Grenada*, ed. Jorge Heine (Pittsburgh, PA: University of Pittsburgh Press, 1990), 186.

[5] Jon Western, *Selling Intervention and War: The Presidency, the Media, and the American Public* (Baltimore and London: The Johns Hopkins University Press, 2005), 97–99. See also "Grenada IG," *Grenada, 4/1/1981-4/15/1981—Box 8—Fontaine, Roger: Files [Folder]; Fontaine, Roger: Files, Series I: Subject File—RAC Box 8—Box 8 [Collection]* (Ronald Reagan Library, n.d.), 2–3.

[6] "Grenada Papers: No. 2 Outline History [October 29, 1983]," 1–2.

[7] For a summary of the U.S.–Grenada relationship, see Pastor, "The United States and the Grenada Revolution: Who Pushed First and Why?"

such movements of 'national liberation' as the Sandinistas in Nicaragua and the Revolutionary Democratic Front in El Salvador."[8]

In late 1983, factional strife broke out in the New Jewel Movement, pitting Bishop against the more extreme wing of the party.[9] On October 12, Bernard Coard, the Deputy Prime Minister, spearheaded a coup.[10] Bishop was placed under house arrest. On October 19, he, along with several other political leaders, were murdered. A Revolutionary Military Council (RMC) headed by General Hudson Austin subsequently took control of the central government.[11] Less than a week afterward, the RMC was ousted by a U.S.-led coalition composed primarily of members of the Organization of Eastern Caribbean States (OECS). Grenada held democratic elections the following year in 1984, bolstered by millions of dollars in financial aid.[12]

Why Intervene in Grenada?

The Reagan administration's central motivation for intervening in Grenada was to prevent the New Jewel Movement from turning the country into a Cuban and Soviet client state.[13] A declassified memo from the time stated that "Grenada's importance is political, strategic and symbolic." In particular, decision makers

[8] "Grenada: The Ideology of Maurice Bishop, Part II—Bishop's World Outlook [September 18, 1984]," *Grenada (12)—Box 8—Crisis Management Center (CMC), NSC: Records [Folder]; Crisis Management Center (CMC), NSC: Records, 1981-1985—RAC Box 8—Box 7 [Collection]* (Ronald Reagan Library, 1984), i.

[9] George Shultz, *Turmoil and Triumph: My Years as Secretary of State* (New York: Charles Scribner's Sons, 1993), 325. Hints of turmoil among the senior leadership, especially between Maurice Bishop and Bernard Coard were evident some years earlier. See Mark Adkin, *Urgent Fury: The Battle for Grenada* (Lexington, MA: Lexington Books, 1989), 27–45.

[10] "Statement by the Honorable Kenneth W. Dam, Deputy Secretary of State, Before the Committee on Foreign Affairs, U.S. House of Representatives [November 2, 1983]," *War Powers—Grenada/Legal and Political Rationale (1 of 3)—CFOA 1175—Counsel to the President, White House, Office of: Records [Folder]; Counsel to the President, Other: Records—CFOA's 1175, 1176—Box 12 [Collection]* (Ronald Reagan Library, 1983), 2.

[11] "Chronology of Cuban Statements and Actions in Grenada [Tab F, October 30, 1983]," *Grenada (2 of 2)—RAC Box 1—Intelligence Directorate, NSC: Records [Folder]; Intelligence Directorate, NSC—RAC Box 1—Box 1 [Collection]* (Ronald Reagan Library, 1983), 1.

[12] Crandall, *Gunboat Democracy: U.S. Intervention in the Dominican Republic, Grenada, and Panama*, 135–148, 161.

[13] Robert J. Beck, *The Grenada Invasion: Politics, Law, and Foreign Policy Decisionmaking* (Boulder, CO: Westview Press, 1993), 11–12; Constantine Menges, *Inside the National Security Council: The True Story of the Making and Unmaking of Reagan's Foreign Policy* (New York: Touchstone, 1988), 59–60; Western, *Selling Intervention and War: The Presidency, the Media, and the American Public*, 97–98.

believed the NJM-led government "plays a radicalizing role in the Eastern Caribbean and could become a base for subversion."[14]

The construction of a 10,000-foot airstrip at Point Salines embodied these concerns.[15] Despite Bishop's assurances that it was for tourism, officials worried that the airstrip could be "use[d] by Cuban and Soviet long-range military aircraft," thereby presenting a direct threat to U.S. interests in the region.[16] Bishop's claims to the contrary were "essentially a nonargument; clearly an airport large enough to accept jumbo jets," officials argued, "could also be used for military purposes."[17] A report from the Directorate of Intelligence on April 21, 1983, affirmed this thinking: "The trend toward closer relations between the USSR and Grenada has accelerated in the past year. These growing bilateral links underscore Moscow's broad strategic interest in undermining the US position in the hemisphere. The ongoing airfield construction project in Grenada will improve the island's capability to support Soviet forces and can be used to sustain Cuban interventionism in the hemisphere and in Africa."[18]

In the course of the invasion, the U.S. military captured troves of documents detailing Grenada's various communist connections.[19] Deputy Secretary of State Kenneth Dam outlined the evidence in a speech before the House Committee on Foreign Affairs on November 2: "We know that the Soviets, Cubans and North Koreans had a military relationship with Grenada which led to signed agreements to donate $37.7 million in military equipment. Artillery, anti-aircraft weapons, armored personnel carriers, small arms, and abundant ammunition were to be furnished to an island touted by its suppliers as a tourist haven. The signed secret agreements also called for 40 Cuban military advisors—27 on a 'permanent' basis, the others for 'short periods.' "[20] In an address to the *Associated Press* two days later, Dam leveraged these documents to push back against the

[14] "Grenada IG," 1.

[15] "Grenada Policy Review [February 9, 1982]," *Grenada 1982—Box 8—Fontaine, Roger: Files [Folder]; Fontaine, Roger: Files, Series I: Subject File—RAC Box 8—Box 8 [Collection]* (Ronald Reagan Library, 1982), 1.

[16] Beck, *The Grenada Invasion: Politics, Law, and Foreign Policy Decisionmaking*, 25.

[17] "Grenada: The Ideology of Maurice Bishop, Part II—Bishop's World Outlook [September 18, 1984]," 3.

[18] "Soviet Geopolitical and Military Interests in Grenada and Suriname [April 21, 1983]," *Grenada—1983 (1)—Rac Box 8—Fontaine, Roger W.: Files [Folder]; Fontaine, Roger: Files, Series I: Subject File—RAC Box 8—Box 8 [Collection]* (Ronald Reagan Library, 1983), 1.

[19] "Preliminary Assessment of Cuban and Soviet Involvement in Grenada [October 30, 1983]," *Grenada (2 of 2)—RAC Box 1—Intelligence Directorate, NSC: Records [Folder]; Intelligence Directorate, NSC—RAC Box 1—Box 1 [Collection]* (Ronald Reagan Library, 1983), 1–9.

[20] "Statement by the Honorable Kenneth W. Dam, Deputy Secretary of State, Before the Committee on Foreign Affairs, U.S. House of Representatives [November 2, 1983]," 13–14. See also Adkin, *Urgent Fury: The Battle for Grenada*, 22–24.

notion that the administration was exaggerating the threat. "[W]hat we found in Grenada," he argued, "suggests that, if anything, we were guilty of *understating* the dangers. We now know that we had underestimated Soviet use of Cuba as a surrogate for the projection of military power in the Caribbean."[21]

Grenada's drift toward the communist bloc was also concerning to decision makers for economic reasons. These were not parochial concerns tied to corporate interests but rather had to do with the stability of global commerce writ large. A report written for Secretary of State George Shultz shortly after the invasion observed that "Grenada's position places it close to numerous key sea lanes of communication, including those from both the Panama Canal and the Venezuelan oil fields. This places Grenada astride one of the busiest sea lanes of the hemisphere through which passes at least 40 percent of all US oil imports. . . . If Cuba had aircraft based both in Cuba and Grenada, it could threaten vessels passing through these points to the Atlantic. The airfields being built on the island could have supported an air force capable of interdicting those key sea lanes."[22]

The Logistics of Urgent Fury

The plans for Operation Urgent Fury were hammered out in the span of a few days. Reagan officially authorized the operation on Saturday, October 22; it began on Tuesday, October 25.[23] The U.S. military was tasked with several objectives. The first order of business was to seize control of strategically important locations across the island, including various airfields as well as Radio Free Grenada radio, which was pumping out regime propaganda.[24] U.S. forces were also tasked with evacuating American medical students enrolled in St. George's Medical School on the island, other designated nationals, and Governor-General Sir Paul Scoon, the official representative of the Queen of England who was under house arrest at the time. Finally, they were charged with capturing the senior leadership of the People's Revolutionary Government.[25]

[21] "The Larger Importance of Grenada [November 4, 1983]," *Grenada/Public Diplomacy (November 1983) (2)—Box 5—Raymond, Walter: File [Folder]; Raymond, Walter: File—Series I, Subject—RAC Box 5—Box 6 [Collection]* (Ronald Reagan Library, 1983), 3, emphasis in original.

[22] "The Strategic Importance of Cuban Activities on Grenada [from Jonathan T. Howe to George Shultz, October 29, 1983]," *Grenada 1/20/81-10/31/83 (3)—Box 30—Executive Secretariat, National Security Council: Country File Records [Folder]; Executive Secretariat, NSC: Country File, Latin America—Falklands War, Grenada, Box 30—Box 60 [Collection]* (Ronald Reagan Library, 1983), 2, underline in original.

[23] Shultz, *Turmoil and Triumph: My Years as Secretary of State*, 329, 335.

[24] Adkin, *Urgent Fury: The Battle for Grenada*, 136–137.

[25] Beck, *The Grenada Invasion: Politics, Law, and Foreign Policy Decisionmaking*, 18.

The Joint of Chiefs of Staff was given complete autonomy. General John W. Vessey approved a combined service operation three days before the invasion was set to take place.[26] Vice Admiral Joseph Metcalf III and Major General H. Norman Schwarzkopf were placed in charge of the Joint Task Force. The Army assumed responsibility over the southern half of the island; the Marines took the northern half.[27] Before these forces arrived, "Marines from the I-84 Amphibious Readiness Group and two battalions of Army Rangers would seize the Grenadian airheads and other key objectives. These troops would then be reinforced by the Army's 82nd Airborne Division, airlifted from Fort Bragg, North Carolina. Even before the formal start of the operation, Delta Force and Navy SEAL commandos would undertake a variety of 'special operations.' "[28] In total, "approximately 8,000 American soldiers and 353 troops from Caribbean forces participated in the operation."[29]

As might be expected from a mission planned on such short notice, there were challenges and mistakes along the way. On the first day of the invasion, Army Rangers rescued a handful of medical students at the True Blue campus of St. George's only to discover that there was a second campus at Grand Anse which they had not accounted for.[30] This was "an egregious delay that could have easily opened [the students] up to being taken hostage, one of the very concerns that the invasion was supposed to eliminate."[31] Some of the mistakes entailed grave consequences. A Navy attack plane accidentally bombing a mental hospital next to RMC command posts was one such example.[32] Despite these obstacles, the intervention was over soon after it began. Most forces were home by Halloween.[33]

[26] Ibid.

[27] Crandall, *Gunboat Democracy: U.S. Intervention in the Dominican Republic, Grenada, and Panama*, 142.

[28] Beck, *The Grenada Invasion: Politics, Law, and Foreign Policy Decisionmaking*, 18.

[29] Crandall, *Gunboat Democracy: U.S. Intervention in the Dominican Republic, Grenada, and Panama*, 144.

[30] Ronald H. Cole, *Operation Urgent Fury: The Planning and Execution of Joint Operations in Grenada, 12 October—2 November 1983* (Washington, D.C.: Joint History Office: Office of the Chairman of the Joint Chiefs of Staff, 1997), 4, http://www.jcs.mil/Portals/36/Documents/History/Monographs/Urgent_Fury.pdf.

[31] Crandall, *Gunboat Democracy: U.S. Intervention in the Dominican Republic, Grenada, and Panama*, 146.

[32] Cole, *Operation Urgent Fury: The Planning and Execution of Joint Operations in Grenada, 12 October–2 November 1983*, 4.

[33] Crandall, *Gunboat Democracy: U.S. Intervention in the Dominican Republic, Grenada, and Panama*, 147.

Legal Evaluation

The Reagan administration used two legal exemptions to justify overt intervention in Grenada. First was the threat facing American students enrolled in St. George's Medical School following Bishop's murder. Second was an OECS invitation for the United States to join a collective force to restore peace and stability on the island along with a concurrent request from the Governor-General. After describing each of these exemptions separately, I will discuss how decision makers sold the legal package.

Rescuing Medical Students

The presence of large numbers of American nationals in Grenada during the outbreak of political violence provided Reagan partial legal cover for deploying forces. My intention is not to cast doubt on the administration's genuine concern for the safety of the medical students enrolled in school there. But evidence from the declassified record shows that they saw opportunity in the chaos.

On October 17, Milan Bish, the ambassador to several Caribbean states, wrote a memo to National Security Advisor Robert McFarlane and Assistant Secretary of State for Western Hemisphere Affairs Langhorne Motley foreshadowing events to come. There was not "an immediate threat to American citizen interests," Bish wrote, "[b]ut the situation could change, and we should be prepared to evacuate a maximum of 800–1000 citizens, 600 of them at the St. George's University School of Medicine campuses." He proclaimed that "[it] occurs to me . . . that the political turmoil on Grenada [may] pose an opportunity as well as a problem. The political power seems to be solidifying in Coard's favor, but things will never be the same again . . . . The confused situation of divided loyalties poses an opportunity for a third force representing democracy and freedom. If we ever entertained the option of supporting, covertly or otherwise, such a force, now would seem to be the time to act."[34]

Concern for student safety grew in subsequent days.[35] By October 20, things were looking direr. Bish warned that students could be taken hostage.

[34] "Message from the Ambassador: Situation on Grenada [from Milan Bish, October 17, 1983]," *Grenada (6/17/1983—10/25/1983) (Too Late to File)—Box 30—Executive Secretariat, NSC: Country File [Folder]; Executive Secretariat, NSC: Country File, Latin America—Grenada Box 30—Box 61 [Collection]* (Ronald Reagan Library, 1983), 1. Constantine Menges, a senior NSC staffer, felt the same way. See Menges, *Inside the National Security Council: The True Story of the Making and Unmaking of Reagan's Foreign Policy*, 60.

[35] Shultz, *Turmoil and Triumph: My Years as Secretary of State*, 325–326. Governor-General Sir Paul Scoon had also relayed reports to the U.S., who had limited intelligence capabilities on the

"[W]hatever we have to do to assure the safety of American citizens," he said, "I urge that we set it in motion now." What Bish had in mind went beyond an evacuation: "In the process we could well rid the hemisphere of an obnoxious unwanted regime. . . . I do not believe the region can carry the burden alone. Help from us will be necessary. How and in what form to provide it will soon become obvious. A military solution seems to me to be a conceivable possibility. We should be prepared for it." He also made clear that there would likely be regional support for an intervention to restore order on the island. "I am not competent to assess the military situation," Bish proclaimed. "I can only offer my strong conviction that if we must, and we may have to, we should: (1) evacuate American citizens, by force if necessary and (2) depose the thugs who have taken over, and (3) restore Grenada as a free society. If it comes to it, in my judgment, such action would meet overwhelming approval in the commonwealth Caribbean."[36] As we will see in the next section, the ambassador's prediction of regional support proved prescient.

Bish was not the only senior official who saw the presence of medical students on the island during the turmoil as presenting an opportunity to pursue broader political objectives in the process of a rescue mission. After receiving the ambassador's cables, Assistant Secretary Motley convened a meeting of the Restricted Interagency Group, a collection of senior decision makers from across the State Department, Defense Department, and the CIA, to discuss U.S. policy toward Grenada. According to a secondary account, "[g]iven such uncertain circumstances, Motley and his RIG colleagues had cause for genuine concern about the welfare of the Americans. They must also have recognized that the unstable conditions on Grenada presented attractive opportunities: to remove a Marxist regime disliked both by Grenada's neighbors and Washington; and to expel Cuban and Soviet influence."[37]

National Security Decision Directive (NSDD) 110, which Reagan signed on October 21, formalized contingency plans for the brewing crisis. The threat confronting medical students was discussed alongside more expansive objectives: "All prudent measures should be taken to protect the lives and safety of American citizens on Grenada, should the situation so require. The United States should also be prepared to participate in a multi-lateral effort to restore

island, that students might be taken hostage. See Western, *Selling Intervention and War: The Presidency, the Media, and the American Public*, 114.

[36] "Ambassador's Assessment of the Situation on Grenada [from Milan Bish, October 20, 1983]," *Grenada Cables (October 20, 1983)—Box 42—Executive Secretariat, NSC: Cable File [Folder]; Executive Secretariat, NSC: Cable File: Records, 1982-1985—Box 42—Box 13 [Collection]* (Ronald Reagan Library, 1983), 1–2.

[37] Beck, *The Grenada Invasion: Politics, Law, and Foreign Policy Decisionmaking*, 103.

order on Grenada and prevent further Cuban/Soviet intervention/involvement on the island."[38] Robert Kimmitt, the Executive Secretary of the NSC at the time, draws these connections explicitly. He stated in an interview that "as the situation on the island got more unsettled, with the U.S. medical students at St. George's college, I think you had an intersection between strategic concerns intersecting with American citizens' safety, that led to the decision to take action. If there had been no medical institution on the island, I don't know whether the U.S. would have taken any form of military action."[39]

The prospect that the United States might use endangered medical students as a fig leaf for intervention was not lost on Grenadian elites. The Chancellor of St. George's told Secretary Shultz on October 20 that he believed the RMC "would not harm Americans, so as to avoid giving the USG a pretext for intervention."[40] The regime communicated similar sentiments via Radio Free Grenada. A cable from October 21 relayed these messages: "[T]he Revolutionary Military Council advises that it will not allow 'lies' about U.S. citizens being in danger to be used as a pretext for foreign intervention in Grenada and that the PRA and peoples' militia will be used to resist any foreign intervention."[41]

U.S. officials were unpersuaded by these assurances. In a cable to Washington on October 21 assessing the regime's propaganda, Bish commented that "statements from the Grenadian RMC must be taken with a large grain of salt. It is obvious that the Caribbean leftist camp is talking a very well defined party line of psyops in an attempt to obviate the need for a foreign intervention. It is also very evident that there are in fact life-threatening situations in Grenada. The earlier reports of a lack of electrical power on the island could have resulted in

[38] "Grenada: Contingency Planning [National Security Decision Directive 110, October 21, 1983]," *National Security Decision Directive 110—Box 91291—Executive Secretariat, NSC: NSDD's [Folder]; Executive Secretariat, NSC: NSDD's—NSDD's 109-126—Box 10 [Collection]* (Ronald Reagan Library, 1983).

[39] Interview with author, August 16, 2017. Undersecretary of State Lawrence Eagleburger noted something similar. See Beck, *The Grenada Invasion: Politics, Law, and Foreign Policy Decisionmaking*, 227.

[40] "Grenada: Attitudes of the Grenada Medical School Toward Possible Evacuation of Their Students/Staff [October 20, 1983]," *Grenada 1/20/81-10/31/83 (1)—Box 30—Executive Secretariat, National Security Council: Country File Records [Folder]; Executive Secretariat, NSC: Country File, Latin America—Falklands War, Grenada, Box 30—Box 60 [Collection]* (Ronald Reagan Library, 1983), 1. He did warn, however, that they could be caught in the middle of the violence.

[41] "More on Am Citizen Welfare in Grenada [October 21, 1983]," *Grenada Invasion—Oct. 1983 (1)—Box 30—Executive Secretariat, NSC: Records—Country File [Folder]; Executive Secretariat, NSC: Country File, Latin America—Falklands War, Grenada, Box 30—Box 60 [Collection]* (Ronald Reagan Library, 1983), 2.

the loss of refrigeration and attendant loss of refrigerated medical supplies."[42] A 24-hour shoot-on-sight curfew contributed to these concerns.[43]

Invitation for Intervention

It is hard to say for certain whether Reagan would have pursued full-scale regime change in Grenada had endangered medical students been the only available legal rationale for deploying forces. If Power Pack is any guide, the answer is that they probably would not have.[44] The administration might have still deployed the military for the sole purpose of a rescue mission. There is precedent for these kinds of actions. The Israeli raid on Entebbe in 1976 and Jimmy Carter's failed hostage rescue mission in Iran in 1979 are two prominent examples. But the presence of Americans in danger alone would likely not have led to a more expansive operation.

Fortunately for the administration, they were able to secure an additional legal exemption prior to the start of the invasion in the form of an invitation for intervention by the Organization of Eastern Caribbean States, a regional body created in 1981.[45] Decision makers believed that this rendered a more expansive intervention consistent with international law.[46] The OECS invitation was bolstered by a similar request from Governor-General Scoon.[47] This section details how these events came about.

[42] "More on Am Citizen Welfare in Grenada [October 21, 1983]," 3. See also Crandall, *Gunboat Democracy: U.S. Intervention in the Dominican Republic, Grenada, and Panama*, 135–136.

[43] The curfew was intended to terrorize the population; see Beck, *The Grenada Invasion: Politics, Law, and Foreign Policy Decisionmaking*, 16–17.

[44] Secondary accounts of this crisis make similar points. See Adkin, *Urgent Fury: The Battle for Grenada*, 112–113; Beck, *The Grenada Invasion: Politics, Law, and Foreign Policy Decisionmaking*, 107, 111, 199–203. There are also declassified documents which suggest that some decision makers were wary of focusing too heavily on the evacuation as justification for regime change. See "International Law Ramifications of United States Actions in Grenada [from Theodore Olson to Edwin Meese, November 2, 1983]," *War Powers—Grenada/Legal and Political Rationale (1 of 3)—CFOA 1175—Counsel to the President, White House, Office of: Records [Folder]; Counsel to the President, Other: Records—CFOA's 1175, 1176—Box 12 [Collection]* (Ronald Reagan Library, 1983), 4–5.

[45] Menges, *Inside the National Security Council: The True Story of the Making and Unmaking of Reagan's Foreign Policy*, 60. For more on how the OECS invitation legitimized intervention through its legal implications, see Cynthia Weber, *Simulating Sovereignty: Intervention, the State, and Symbolic Exchange* (New York: Cambridge University Press, 1995), 93–99. Contrary to Weber, though, my argument suggests that the OECS was not the interpretive community the U.S. was trying to persuade. Rather, the OECS's blessing was used to justify intervention to a broader interpretive community in Latin America and the world.

[46] Shultz, *Turmoil and Triumph: My Years as Secretary of State*, 326; Western, *Selling Intervention and War: The Presidency, the Media, and the American Public*, 119.

[47] "Background on Legal/Political Rationale for U.S. Action," *War Powers—Grenada/Legal and Political Rationale (1 of 3)—CFOA 1175—Counsel to the President, White House, Office of: Records*

As noted above, there were indications as early as October 19 that Grenada's neighbors might support a U.S.-led intervention.[48] These discussions gained steam on October 21. Edward Seaga, Jamaica's Prime Minister, indicated that "concerned Caribbean leaders would call for collective action to reestablish representative government in Grenada, including the use of a Caribbean peace keeping force and a joint naval blockade involving several countries."[49] Seaga noted, however, that this was likely contingent on Sir Paul Scoon supporting such an enterprise: "The Governor General represents the only existing constitutional authority and he would be the only appropriate official to call for regional assistance to restore order, establish a bona fide government, and protect the populace." Seaga was careful to emphasize, though, "that the Governor General is willing to do this and the UK and Canada are capable of protecting him. . . . [A]ll of the East Caribbean is in a tough-minded mood."[50]

On October 22, Tom Adams, the Prime Minister of Barbados, and Eugenia Charles, the Prime Minister of Dominica, told Bish "they had been authorized

[Folder]; Counsel to the President, Other: Records—CFOA's 1175, 1176—Box 12 [Collection] (Ronald Reagan Library, n.d.), 2. Some scholars argue that "the Governor-General's invitation could have exerted virtually no influence on the U.S. decision" because it had officially come on October 24, days after Reagan had decided to invade Grenada. See Beck, *The Grenada Invasion: Politics, Law, and Foreign Policy Decisionmaking*, 205–206. But this obscures key facts. As will be described below, as early as October 21 during the initial deliberations regarding an OECS invitation there was word that Scoon would be willing to issue a formal invitation for intervention. Thus, even if his invitation was not formally received until days later, it is clear that this factored into the decision-making process. Moreover, NSC Staffer Constantine Menges' notes from October 22, 1983 indicate that Scoon had "smuggled out a request for external help in restoring law and order" in Grenada, lending further credence to the notion that U.S. decision makers factored this into their decision. See Menges, *Inside the National Security Council: The True Story of the Making and Unmaking of Reagan's Foreign Policy*, 78.

[48] In fact, some scholars note that the OECS countries expressed interest in a joint intervention as early as October 15, four days before Bishop was killed. See Crandall, *Gunboat Democracy: U.S. Intervention in the Dominican Republic, Grenada, and Panama*, 138. Secretary Shultz dates the first oral overtures to the U.S. as happening a few days after this on October 17. See Shultz, *Turmoil and Triumph: My Years as Secretary of State*, 326.

[49] "Grenada—Seaga Proposes Joint Caribbean Action and Naval Blockade of Grenada [from William A. Hewitt, October 21, 1983]," *Grenada Invasion—Oct. 1983 (1)—Box 30—Executive Secretariat, NSC: Records—Country File [Folder]; Executive Secretariat, NSC: Country File, Latin America—Falklands War, Grenada, Box 30—Box 60 [Collection]* (Ronald Reagan Library, 1983), 1. Although Jamaica was not a member of the OECS, they were coordinating closely with the organization's members on the need for action. See Adkin, *Urgent Fury: The Battle for Grenada*, 98.

[50] "Grenada—Seaga Proposes Joint Caribbean Action and Naval Blockade of Grenada [from William A. Hewitt, October 21, 1983]," 3–4. He reconfirmed the Governor-General's invitation three days later on October 24. See "Grenada: Meeting with Seaga and Adams [from Milan Bish, October 24, 1983]," *Grenada Invasion—Oct. 1983 (1)—Box 30—Executive Secretariat, NSC: Records—Country File [Folder]; Executive Secretariat, NSC: Country File, Latin America—Falklands War, Grenada, Box 30—Box 60 [Collection]* (Ronald Reagan Library, 1983), 1–2.

by the heads of government of all OECS member states . . . to inform the U.S. officially that the OECS had formally resolved to form a multinational Caribbean force to undertake to depose the outlaw regime on Grenada by any means, including intervention by force of arms, and secondly, to ask the United States and other friendly countries for the necessary assistance and means to do this." They stated that "the Charter of the OECS provides for this eventuality. Article 8 spells out that the heads of government may collectively agree to take whatever measures are necessary to defend the region and preserve peace." The two of them, plus Seaga, were "convinced that the Charter provides the legal basis for such an intervention."[51]

On October 23, decision makers articulated talking points related to the OECS invitation. They hoped to convey that the United States was considering acceding but wanted the regional body to "carefully record its invitation and the role of the United States."[52] Officials also wanted "OECS members [to] take the initiative to request [an] emergency meeting of the permanent council [of the OAS] in order to pre-empt a possible hostile invocation of OAS machinery by others." Although they were "dubious that [an] OAS permanent council meeting would produce a very strong endorsement of OECS actions and there are risks," they believed that "with vigorous diplomacy by OECS members, Jamaica, Barbados, and others, a positive outcome should be possible. The U.S. would provide support, but in a low-key manner so as to avoid jeopardizing result." The reasons decision makers gave for wanting to play a backseat role speak directly to this book's argument: "Given traditional Latin sensitivities over issues of nonintervention, if an acceptable outcome is to be secured, Caribbean countries must take lead."[53]

Reagan issued NSDD 110A that same day. It described the events leading to Bishop's murder and the OECS meeting on October 22, where members "unanimously and formally resolved to form a multi-national Caribbean force

[51] "The Organization of Eastern Caribbean States Officially, Formally Resolves Unanimously to Intervene by Force If Necessary on Grenada and Pleads for U.S. Assistance [from Milan Bish, October 22, 1983]," *Grenada Invasion—Oct. 1983 (1)—Box 30—Executive Secretariat, NSC: Records—Country File [Folder]; Executive Secretariat, NSC: Country File, Latin America—Falklands War, Grenada, Box 30—Box 60 [Collection]* (Ronald Reagan Library, 1983), 2. Elsewhere, there was some concern by decision makers that Article 8, which allowed for collective action in response to *external aggression*, might be viewed as a stretch in this particular case. See "Background on Legal/Political Rationale for U.S. Action," 3.

[52] "Instructions for Dealing with Caribbean Friends [from George Shultz, October 23, 1983]," *Grenada Invasion—Oct. 1983 (8)—Box 30—Executive Secretariat, NSC: Records—Country File [Folder]; Executive Secretariat, NSC: Country File, Latin America—Falklands War, Grenada, Box 30—Box 60 [Collection]* (Ronald Reagan Library, 1983), 1–2.

[53] "Instructions for Dealing with Caribbean Friends [from George Shultz, October 23, 1983]," 5–6.

to remove 'the outlaw regime on Grenada' and restore democracy by any means, including force of arms. They have formally requested that the U.S., along with other friendly countries, provide help in accomplishing this objective." The document also reiterated language from NSDD 110: "The recent violence and instability have also created a situation which could seriously jeopardize the lives and safety of American citizens." It then notes that the Special Situations Group called for "U.S. and allied Caribbean military forces . . . to take control of Grenada, no later than dawn Tuesday, October 25, 1983." Publicly, officials were to emphasize "[t]he multi-lateral character of [U.S. actions]," draw attention to "[t]he human rights abuses . . . of the current regime and the recent violence which potentially endangers U.S. lives," and highlight "[t]he democratic nature of the new government being installed."[54]

Selling The Legal Package

Decision makers emphasized these legal exemptions in various settings from the start of the invasion.[55] A draft of Reagan's speech to be delivered after the operation commenced declared the following: "But when I received reports that a large number of our citizens were seeking to escape the island, thereby exposing themselves to great danger, and after receiving a formal request for help from neighboring states, I concluded the United States had no choice but to act strongly and decisively. I thus agreed to the urgent requests from Grenada's neighbors to participate in the joint effort now underway."[56]

Secretary Shultz echoed these points during a press conference at 3:00 p.m. on October 25. "There are two basic reasons that determined the President's decision," he stated. "First was his concern for the welfare of American citizens living on Grenada. There are roughly a thousand of them. And what we saw was an atmosphere of violent uncertainty . . . that certainly caused anxiety

[54] Ronald Reagan, *National Security Decision Directive 110A* (Ronald Reagan Library, 1983), 1–2, https://www.reaganlibrary.gov/sites/default/files/archives/reference/scanned-nsdds/nsdd110a.pdf.

[55] "International Law Ramifications of United States Actions in Grenada [from Theodore Olson to Edwin Meese, November 2, 1983]," 1–16.

[56] "Public Statement for the President After the Operation Has Begun [Draft, 0500, October 25, 1983]," *Grenada Invasion—Oct. 1983 (3)—Box 30—Executive Secretariat, NSC: Records—Country File [Folder]; Executive Secretariat, NSC: Country File, Latin America—Falklands War, Grenada, Box 30—Box 60 [Collection]* (Ronald Reagan Library, 1983), 3. In his final remarks, Reagan also made clear that there were several members of the coalition who were not part of the OECS—including Barbados and Jamaica—who "were first approached, *as we later were*, by the OECS and asked to join in that undertaking" (quoted in Western, *Selling Intervention and War: The Presidency, the Media, and the American Public*, 94, emphasis in original).

among U.S. citizens and caused the President to be very concerned about their safety and welfare. He felt that it is better under the circumstances to act before they might be hurt or be hostage than to take any chance, given the great uncertainty clearly present in the situation." Shultz then turned to the OECS invitation, noting that "the President received an urgent request from the countries closest to the area, the Organization of Eastern Caribbean States, who of course followed these developments very closely over a long period of time, and intensively in recent days, and who determined for themselves that there were developments of grave concern to their safety and peace taking place."[57]

The question-and-answer session of the press conference is particularly revealing. Shultz was asked at one point about the complicated historical relationship between the United States and Latin American countries, specifically as it related to intervention: "Traditionally, in this part of the world, there's been a great concern about Yankee force, Yankee imperialism, Yankee aggression, et cetera. How do you . . . intend to counter the impression that the United States is once again using its overwhelming military superiority in this part of the world to achieve a specific, political objective?" Shultz responded: "[T]he principal point here is that the concerns and the requests for help came from the states in the region, and they have put their own forces into this picture. The fact that their forces are small in comparison with ours is only a reflection of the fact that they don't invest very much in the way of resources into military capability . . . . And as law and order returns, they will basically be in charge; not us. So it is no effort on our part to gain control of any other country."[58] Ambassador Bish concurrently cabled to Washington that regional leaders would echo this point in the following days.[59]

A memo dated October 26, entitled "Legal Authority for U.S. Action in Grenada," spelled out these arguments in greater detail.[60] "One purpose of U.S. participation in this force," it noted, "is to ensure the safety of U.S. citizens.

[57] "Department of State Press Conference by Honorable George P. Shultz, Secretary of State, U.S. Department of State, Tuesday, October 25, 1983, 3:00 p.m.," *Grenada Invasion—Oct. 1983 (5)—Box 30—Executive Secretariat, NSC: Records—Country File [Folder]; Executive Secretariat, NSC: Country File, Latin America—Falklands War, Grenada, Box 30—Box 60 [Collection]* (Ronald Reagan Library, 1983), 1–2.

[58] "Department of State Press Conference by Honorable George P. Shultz, Secretary of State, U.S. Department of State, Tuesday, October 25, 1983, 3:00 p.m.," 10.

[59] "Ambassador Informs Tom Adams of President's Decision [October 25, 1983]," *Grenada Cables (October 25, 1983) (1)—Box 42—Executive Secretariat, NSC: Cable File [Folder]; Executive Secretariat, NSC: Cable File: Records, 1982-1985—Box 42—Box 13 [Collection]* (Ronald Reagan Library, 1983), 1–2.

[60] The memo was written by the Legal Advisor at the Department of State. See "International Law Ramifications of United States Actions in Grenada [from Theodore Olson to Edwin Meese, November 2, 1983]," 2.

Such humanitarian action is justified under well-established principles of international law." The memo then turned to the legal basis of the OECS request: "Further, the collective actions of the United States, Jamaica, Barbados, and the OECS states are consistent with the OAS Charter. The Charter specifically allows OAS members to take collective action pursuant to regional security treaties in response to threats to peace and security. The Rio Treaty is one such treaty. The OECS states are not parties to the Rio Treaty, and the OECS Treaty is their regional security arrangement. . . . Measures taken pursuant to collective security agreements are not violations of the OAS Charter's provisions prohibiting interventions or the use of force." The discussion was also broadened to include the UN. It argued that "[r]egional collective security measures are expressly contemplated by Article 52 of the UN Charter." The memo thus concluded that "[t]he actions and objectives of the collective security force . . . are consistent with the purposes and principles of the UN Charter."[61]

On October 27, Davis R. Robinson, the Legal Advisor at the State Department, drafted "contingency guidance to be used on an if-asked basis only" regarding the invasion.[62] The first question it anticipated turned on how U.S. actions squared with the OAS and UN Charters. Robinson's suggested answer, mirroring what we saw in the preceding paragraph, pointed to Articles 22 and 53 of the OAS and UN Charters, respectively, as "recogniz[ing] the importance of regional security bodies in ensuring peace and stability." He also spoke about why the Security Council—which is supposed to be brought into the loop when regional bodies pursue enforcement actions—was not consulted beforehand. After appealing to the complexity of the issue, Robinson wrote that "not every collective measure, even one involving the use of force, is an 'enforcement action' for which Security Council approval must be sought." In this instance, the United States did not view the invasion in these terms since it was "not intended to enforce a decision

[61] "Legal Authority for U.S. Action in Grenada [October 26, 1983]," *War Powers—Grenada/Legal and Political Rationale (1 of 3)—CFOA 1175—Counsel to the President, White House, Office of: Records [Folder]; Counsel to the President, Other: Records—CFOA's 1175, 1176—Box 12 [Collection]* (Ronald Reagan Library, 1983), 1–2. See also "Grenada: A Preliminary Report [December 10, 1983]," *Grenada, 12/10/1983—Box 45—Executive Secretariat, NSC Cable File [Folder]; Executive Secretariat, NSC: Cable File: Records—Box 43, 44, 45—Box 15 [Collection]* (Ronald Reagan Library, 1983), 12. Officials were meant to reiterate these arguments in public. See "Grenada Papers No. 5 Public Diplomacy Themes [October 29, 1983]," *Grenada, 10/29/1983 (3 of 4)—Box 43—Executive Secretariat, NSC Cable File [Folder]; Executive Secretariat, NSC: Cable File: Records—Box 43, 44, 45—Box 15 [Collection]* (Ronald Reagan Library, 1983), 2–3.

[62] The memo was addressed to Fred F. Fielding, Counsel to President Reagan, and three senior officials were copied. The first, Robert Kimmitt, was interviewed for this book. The second two were Theodore Olson (Assistant Attorney General) and William H. Taft (General Counsel at the Department of Defense).

against or to impose sanctions upon a government. Indeed, it is important to note that there was no functioning government on Grenada."[63]

Robinson's line of reasoning reflects a point made in Chapter 2, namely that there is a healthy debate about the parameters of the UN's provisions on regional bodies. And in Chapter 3, I argued that the mere existence of a diversity of viewpoints creates some wiggle room for decision makers. But it is still worth reiterating that these provisions are not infinitely malleable. Had the OECS not issued its request—and assuming the OAS also declined—the United States would have been far more constrained. Moreover, the prioritization of regional bodies to handle regional crises became fairly routine in the years after the UN was created, in large part due to gridlock at the Security Council.[64]

Deputy Secretary Dam's speech before the House Foreign Affairs Committee on November 2 vigorously defended the legality of the invasion. Part of his speech was devoted to distinguishing U.S. actions in Grenada from "acts of intervention by our Soviet adversaries. Let me say the distinctions are clear. The U.S. participated in a genuine collective effort—the record makes clear the initiative of the Caribbean countries in proposing and defending this action. This action was justified by an existing treaty and by the express invitation of the Governor-General. Our concern for the safety of our citizens was genuine . . . . Our objectives are precise and limited—to evacuate foreign nationals and to cooperate in the restoration of order; they do not encompass the imposition on the Grenadians of any particular form of government." Dam further declared that "[t]hose who do not see—or do not choose to see—these signal distinctions have failed to analyze the facts. We have not made, and do not seek to make, any broad new precedent for international action; we think the justification of our actions is narrow, and well within accepted concepts of international law."[65]

This is similar to some of the language we came across in the Bay of Pigs episode in Chapter 4. One of Arthur Schlesinger's chief concerns about intervening

[63] "Guidance on Legal Questions [from Davis R. Robinson, October 27, 1983]," *War Powers—Grenada/Legal and Political Rationale (1 of 3)—CFOA 1175—Counsel to the President, White House, Office of: Records [Folder]; Counsel to the President, Other: Records—CFOA's 1175, 1176—Box 12 [Collection]* (Ronald Reagan Library, 1983), 2–3. See also "Background on Legal/Political Rationale for U.S. Action," 3–4.

[64] Thomas M. Franck, "Who Killed Article 2(4)? Or: Changing Norms Governing the Use of Force by States," *American Journal of International Law* 64, no. 5 (1970): 822.

[65] "Statement by the Honorable Kenneth W. Dam, Deputy Secretary of State, Before the Committee on Foreign Affairs, U.S. House of Representatives [November 2, 1983]," 11–12. Interestingly, Michael Kozak rejected the suggestion from UN Ambassador Jeane Kirkpatrick's legal advisor Allan Gerson that the U.S. invoke self-defense under Article 51 for fear that this would create a precedent for others to do the same in the future. See Beck, *The Grenada Invasion: Politics, Law, and Foreign Policy Decisionmaking*, 190–191.

against Castro without legal cover was that it would "become [America's] Hungary" and invite comparisons to the Soviet Union.[66] Like Schlesinger, Dam was bent on fending off these comparisons as well. It is important to remember, of course, that four years before Urgent Fury took place, the Soviets intervened in Afghanistan to crush an incipient rebellion against the wobbling communist regime there. Soviet officials argued, as they did in Hungary in 1956, that they had been invited. It was a flimsy fig leaf. U.S. decision makers wanted to avoid being accused of fabricating pretexts themselves, making the case that their actions fell within the confines of what the law tolerated. Incidentally, this shows how great powers battle over what is legally acceptable and try to use facially implausible pretexts as cudgels to paint their rivals as outlaws whenever possible.

Staying Inside the Lines

One observable implication of my theory is that decision makers should avoid saying and doing things that obviously fall outside the purview of the legal exemptions they are using to justify an intervention. Several pieces of evidence show that these dynamics were at work in this case.

On November 5, Secretary Shultz directed senior officials to justify the intervention in terms of international law "rather than on historical tradition." He highlighted the fact that "our legal arguments are soundly based and consistent with the above mentioned international charters," including those of the OAS and the UN. "We believe," he continued, "a very strong case has been made . . . and that it is not necessary to invoke historical analogies, the Monroe Doctrine or other precedents in these circumstances."[67] The decision to privilege legal arguments over alternative rationales predicated on the spheres of influence system suggests that the desire to project an image of a state committed to international law was accorded great importance.

Another example comes from a memo written after the invasion: "[G]iven traditional Latin American sensitivities over issues of non-intervention, a negative result from any OAS deliberations certainly cannot be ruled out." There was also concern that the United States could be charged with violating the UN

[66] FRUS, "81. Memorandum From the President's Special Assistant (Schlesinger) to President Kennedy," in *Foreign Relations of the United States, 1961–1963, Volume X, Cuba, January 1961–September 1962*, ed. Louis J. Smith (Washington, D.C.: United States Government Printing Office, 1997), https://history.state.gov/historicaldocuments/frus1961-63v10/d81.

[67] "22nd General Conference: Grenada and the Monroe Doctrine [from George Shultz, November 5, 1983]," *Grenada, 11/02/1983-11/05/1983—Box 44—Executive Secretariat, NSC Cable File [Folder]; Executive Secretariat, NSC: Cable File: Records—Box 43, 44, 45—Box 15 [Collection]* (Ronald Reagan Library, 1983), 1–2.

Charter. According to the authors, "[t]he theories upon which we will be relying have some degree of support in past practice and have been enunciated by legal academics and by governments invoking them" but had not "been 'codified' in U.N. or OAS instruments" and were "hotly contested by international lawyers, largely along north-south lines." On the other hand, they had "been embraced in varying degrees by the international law practice of our major allies." The administration was therefore advised to "be extremely careful in developing [its] rationale not to give credence to theories of preemptive self defense or of collective rights to maintain the political or constitutional structure of nations, such as those advanced by the Soviet Union in their justification of their invasions of Czechoslovakia and Afghanistan." Instead, officials should "emphasize the goal of restoring conditions of law and order, and governmental institutions (without regard to their character)," and the OECS's competency to handle a situation wherein violence created a vacuum of authority.[68]

As with Dam's November 2 statement cited in the previous section, we can see that officials were keen on ensuring they did not advance non-legal rationales or new and controversial interpretations of legal precepts by, for example, defending the authority of international bodies to impose particular types of regimes. In this vein, it was probably no accident that the majority of public statements in which officials defended the legality of the intervention, including from Shultz, Dam, and others, emphasized the restoration of law and order rather than imposing democracy. One of the most prominent instances where the restoration of democratic governance was explicitly mentioned as an objective—in NSDD 110A—was classified.

There is also evidence that decision makers thought about how their actions would reflect on the legal exemptions used to justify intervention. One interesting example comes from a memo authored by Michael G. Kozak, a Principal Deputy Assistant Secretary of State and Legal Advisor, on October 26. He addressed a query about whether the United States could deport Cuban nationals detained in the course of the invasion. In addition to "domestic legal problems," Kozak warned that such actions "would raise serious questions under international law respecting the treatment of combatants and civilians in wartime, and would undercut our legal rationale for U.S. actions in Grenada."[69] He went on to argue: "We have based our actions on (1) the invitation of a regional security organization to assist in collective measures limited to meet the threat

[68] "Background on Legal/Political Rationale for U.S. Action," 7–9.

[69] "Return of Excludable Cuban Nationals with Cubans Detained in Grenada [from Michael G. Kozak to James H. Michel, October 26, 1983]," *Grenada (10/28/1983—11/2/1983) (Too Late to File)—Box 30—Executive Secretariat, NSC: Country File [Folder]; Executive Secretariat, NSC: Country File, Latin America—Grenada Box 30—Box 61 [Collection]* (Ronald Reagan Library, 1983), 1.

to regional peace and stability; and (2) the need to ensure the safety of U.S. citizens. Exploiting the opportunity created by an otherwise justifiable use of force to accomplish an objective wholly unrelated to the stated basis and goals of our actions undercuts the rationale for our actions. Likewise, the injection of a bilateral Cuban issue undermines the multilateral character of our actions and casts doubt on our claim that we were not prompted to act by the larger issue of Cuban involvement in Grenada and in the Caribbean."[70] It is noteworthy that senior officials were concerned about undermining the administration's public narrative even on an issue as seemingly trivial as what to do with Cuban nationals detained in the course of the invasion.

Hints of Legal Constraints

Because this case contained legal exemptions from the start, validating the counterfactual—that Reagan would have intervened covertly, or perhaps not at all, had students not been endangered or if the OECS had not issued an invitation—is challenging. There is, however, evidence from the Carter and Reagan administrations suggesting that overt intervention was deemed too risky before legal exemptions arose in mid-October 1983 during the turmoil surrounding Bishop's murder.[71] Similar to the previous chapter, the paucity of evidence precludes doing full-blown case studies of either of these episodes. Nevertheless, the following does provide within-case variation that is theory-consistent.

To begin with, we know that Jimmy Carter contemplated covert action months after the NJM came to power.[72] Robert Gates describes the episode in his memoirs. According to Gates, Carter's National Security Advisor Zbigniew Brzezinski penned a letter to then–CIA Director Stansfield Turner "on May 8, 1979, expressing the President's concern about the growing Cuban presence on Grenada and suggesting a covert effort to focus international press attention

[70] Ibid., 3.

[71] Some authors have made similar arguments about the importance of the crisis in late-October 1983 in generating an opportunity to overtly intervene. See Pastor, "The United States and the Grenada Revolution: Who Pushed First and Why?," 208.

[72] FRUS, "324. Summary of Conclusions of a Special Coordination Committee Meeting," in *Foreign Relations, 1977–1980, Volume XXIII, Mexico, Cuba, and the Caribbean*, ed. Alexander O. Poster (Washington, D.C.: United States Government Printing Office, 2016), https://history.state.gov/historicaldocuments/frus1977-80v23/d324; FRUS, "325. Presidential Finding," in *Foreign Relations, 1977–1980, Volume XXIII, Mexico, Cuba, and the Caribbean*, ed. Alexander O. Poster (Washington, D.C.: United States Government Printing Office, 2016), https://history.state.gov/historicaldocuments/frus1977-80v23/d325.

on it. Turner responded on May 14 with a political action program going beyond Brzezinski's suggestion and intended to counter the Cubans on the island. Carter signed a 'finding' on July 3, 1979, that authorized a covert effort to promote the democratic process on Grenada and also to support resistance to the Marxist government there." In Gates' telling, "[a]ll hell broke loose when Carter's finding was briefed to the Senate Intelligence Committee on July 19." Given their "strong displeasure," the White House terminated the program even though "the committee had no legal authority to stop the covert action."[73] This is actually false.

Newly declassified documents reveal that the program continued in some form through the fall. On October 9, Frank Carlucci, the Deputy Director of the CIA, wrote that "[a]s a result of State Department reservations and opposition expressed by the Senate Select Committee on Intelligence, a mini-SCC meeting was held on 27 July 1979 in which the Grenada CA Project was reviewed. It was decided that the political action aspect of the project would be put in a holding pattern with minimum dispersal of funds for the time being. It was agreed that the project would be reviewed again after the return of Ambassador Philip Habib from his Caribbean trip in late August 1979." After noting that Habib subsequently presented a report in September, Carlucci declared that the Agency would pursue the covert action plan. If the Senate Intelligence Committee was opposed, they could offer updated instructions. To whom the CIA intended to provide financial support as part of these efforts remains classified.[74] Carlucci sent another update on November 23. "Since we have received no objections as solicited in the referenced Agency memorandum of 9 October 1979," he wrote, "and since the policy concerning Grenada has been reaffirmed in the 13 November 1979 Policy Review Committee meeting, this Agency plans to reactivate its proposed program as approved in the Presidential Finding on Grenada, signed 3 July 1979." He also mentioned that "[c]oncerned committees in Congress have been briefed on the outline of this proposal and further briefings are not deemed necessary."[75]

[73] Robert M. Gates, *From the Shadows: The Ultimate Insider's Story of Five Presidents and How They Won the Cold War* (New York: Simon and Schuster, 1996), 143.

[74] FRUS, "328. Memorandum From the Deputy Director of Central Intelligence (Carlucci) to the President's Deputy Assistant for National Security Affairs (Aaron), the Senior Adviser to the Secretary of State (Habib), and the Under Secretary of State for Political Aff," in *Foreign Relations, 1977–1980, Volume XXIII, Mexico, Cuba, and the Caribbean*, ed. Alexander O. Poster (Washington, D.C.: United States Government Printing Office, 2016), https://history.state.gov/historicaldocuments/frus1977-80v23/d328.

[75] FRUS, "331. Memorandum From the Deputy Director of Central Intelligence (Carlucci) to the President's Deputy Assistant for National Security Affairs (Aaron), the Senior Adviser to the Secretary of State (Habib), and the Under Secretary of State for Political Aff," in *Foreign Relations, 1977–1980, Volume XXIII, Mexico, Cuba, and the Caribbean*, ed. Alexander O. Poster

The details surrounding this episode, though in greater supply than ever before, are still sparse. We do not yet have a clear picture of why Carter opted for covert action in 1979 rather than more public alternatives. The declassified record sheds no light on this question. Memoirs from senior decision makers in the administration do not provide any guidance either. Robert Gates' *From the Shadows* devotes less than a page to the entire incident. Neither Zbigniew Brzezinski, Stansfield Turner, nor Cyrus Vance, Carter's Secretary of State, mention it in their memoirs.[76] Regardless, the basic correlation is consistent. Before the events of late October 1983, which presented Reagan with two legal exemptions that helped to justify overt intervention, his predecessor turned to the quiet option to resist the NJM. Verifying that this is not merely a spurious relationship will have to wait until further declassification. It is worth noting as well that the decision to act covertly was made amid the Carter administration's growing concerns about Grenada's ties to communist countries like Cuba.[77]

Evidence from the Reagan administration betrays a similar reluctance to take an overt, hardline position against the New Jewel Movement without legal cover.[78] On April 15, 1981, an Interdepartmental Group meeting reviewed an options paper for Grenada. The last section is most relevant. It identifies a range of possible approaches for dealing with the NJM. Most interesting was the option of "Cooperation with the Democratic Leadership" as a means of resisting Bishop. It involved "a diplomatic initiative to bolster the growing regional opposition to Grenada, particularly the efforts of Jamaica and Barbados to isolate Grenada. These efforts will be most effective if these regional countries take the lead. However, in close consultation with them and key allies, we should consider the following: a) promoting the exclusion of Grenada from regional institutions; b) developing a regional security capability to respond to the possible subversive threat from Grenada; and c) fostering an environment in which an effective

(Washington, D.C.: United States Government Printing Office, 2016), https://history.state.gov/historicaldocuments/frus1977-80v23/d331.

[76] Zbigniew Brzezinski, *Power and Principle: Memoirs of the National Security Adviser, 1977–1981* (New York: Farrar Straus & Giroux, 1983); Stansfield Turner, *Secrecy and Democracy: The CIA in Transition* (Boston, MA: Houghton Mifflin, 1985); Cyrus Vance, *Hard Choices: Critical Years in America's Foreign Policy* (New York: Simon and Schuster, 1983).

[77] FRUS, "320. Memorandum From the President's Assistant for National Security Affairs (Brzezinski) to Director of Central Intelligence Turner," in *Foreign Relations, 1977–1980, Volume XXIII, Mexico, Cuba, and the Caribbean*, ed. Alexander O. Poster (Washington, D.C.: United States Government Printing Office, 2016), https://history.state.gov/historicaldocuments/frus1977-80v23/d320.

[78] There is also evidence, although it is extremely limited, that "[i]n mid-1981 both the CIA and the Pentagon devised plans for the destabilization of and American intervention in Grenada." See Western, *Selling Intervention and War: The Presidency, the Media, and the American Public*, 109.

democratic opposition in Grenada can develop and press for reform and oppose the PRG's authoritarian tactics." At the end of this final prong, I found a handwritten comment—the word *covert*—in parentheses.[79] Obviously, an unattributed note scrawled in the margins of a declassified report leaves much to be desired. Nevertheless, it suggests that at least some officials were thinking about discreet ways to bolster the opposition to the NJM.

Another piece of evidence comes from a memo Stephen Bosworth, the Senior Deputy Assistant Secretary of State in the Bureau of Inter-American Affairs, wrote on February 9, 1982. He first pointed out that Grenada's relationship with the Soviet Union and Cuba was growing stronger. The prospect of the PRG holding elections and "return[ing] to constitutional rule" were slim. So far, the United States had pursued a "low-profile policy" with respect to the NJM.[80] Bosworth then considered the pros and cons of "[m]ore drastic measures" like economic warfare: "[I]f pursued in isolation [it] could push potential Caribbean allies into an embarrassing position. Although the Caribbean democracies are slowly moving toward more active opposition to the PRG, they perceive Grenada's isolation as resulting from its own actions and want to keep the door open to allow Bishop to return to the fold." He reasoned that things would be different if the United States was responding to "the establishment of Cuban/Soviet bases in Grenada or definitive evidence that the PRG is training Caribbean revolutionaries." Bosworth believed that harsh action in this scenario would be more acceptable. Moving prematurely would only "[embarrass] supportive Caribbean democracies . . . and [divide] the U.S. from hemispheric democracies after having developed a strong degree of consensus in the OAS on Central America."[81]

This memo is illuminating for a couple of reasons. First, it is similar to the evidence presented in Chapter 4, wherein the Nixon administration acknowledged they would have an easier time gaining regional support for hostile, overt actions if there was proof the Soviets were seeking to establish military facilities in Chile. Although Bosworth does not explicitly invoke the legal basis for action in this memo, his references to the perceptions of Caribbean nations is notable in light of the region's sensitivity to violations of nonintervention. Second, if Bosworth was this concerned about the risks of overt economic warfare against Grenada, it is reasonable to assume that the risks of overt military intervention would have been even greater. While all of this is correlational in nature, senior officials' aversion to pursuing openly hostile policies against Grenada prior to the emergence of legal exemptions in late October 1983 lends credence to the counterfactual.

[79] "Grenada IG," 22–23.

[80] "Grenada Policy Review [February 9, 1982]," 1.

[81] Ibid., 3–4.

Resolution 38/7

How audiences ultimately react to an intervention is beyond the purview of what I am after in this book. Even so, it might be useful to say a few words on this subject given the kind of backlash that transpired. On November 2, 1983, the UN General Assembly passed a resolution condemning the intervention in Grenada as a violation of international law. It reiterated the need to respect state sovereignty and territorial integrity and called for free elections to be held as soon as possible; 108 states voted in favor, 9 voted against, and 27 abstained.[82] When asked how he felt about the UNGA resolution condemning the invasion, Reagan famously said, "[it] didn't upset my breakfast at all."[83]

The theory advanced in this book predicts that leaders will use legal exemptions as a way of mitigating hypocrisy costs and preserving credibility, but there is always room for miscalculation, especially since decision makers act on the basis of what they perceive will be a credible legal exemption. It is possible that this is what happened to the Reagan administration, as evidenced by the passage of Resolution 38/7. It is also possible, however, that the reaction would have been even worse in the absence of legal exemptions. There are a number of reasons to suspect this is what happened.

First, the OAS declined to condemn the operation.[84] On October 27, "[t]he OAS Permanent Council convened a special session . . . to consider the situation in Grenada." According to Deputy Secretary Dam, "the US and other OECS task force participants successfully defended the joint action in Grenada. As a damage-limiting operation, the session was a triumph for the U.S. No resolution was offered, nor was one even suggested." In Dam's recounting, "Latin criticisms of the venture were comparatively mild. Much attention was given to

[82] Crandall, *Gunboat Democracy: U.S. Intervention in the Dominican Republic, Grenada, and Panama*, 154–156.

[83] Beck, *The Grenada Invasion: Politics, Law, and Foreign Policy Decisionmaking*, 49. Ambassador to the UN Jeane Kirkpatrick's statement at the international forum further defended U.S. actions against the vote. See "First U.S. Statement in UN Security Council Debate on Grenada [October 26, 1983]," *Grenada (10/26/1983) (3 of 11)—Box 42—Executive Secretariat, NSC: Cable File [Folder]; Executive Secretariat, NSC: Cable File: Records, 1982-1985—Box 42—Box 13 [Collection]* (Ronald Reagan Library, 1983).

[84] See John M. Goshko and Michael Isikoff, "OAS Votes to Censure U.S. for Intervention," *Washington Post* Dec. 23 (1989), https://www.washingtonpost.com/archive/politics/1989/12/23/oas-votes-to-censure-us-for-intervention/807f91f4-6f43-4b0b-8021-6bb994f83244/?noredirect=on&utm_term=.7a22e86e9966. See also Crandall, *Gunboat Democracy: U.S. Intervention in the Dominican Republic, Grenada, and Panama*, 155; Joanne Omang, "U.S. Seeks to Reassure OAS On Grenada Invasion Motive," *Washington Post* Nov. 15 (1983), https://www.washingtonpost.com/archive/politics/1983/11/15/us-seeks-to-reassure-oas-on-grenada-invasion-motive/4f7fc75e-a7b7-4d5b-b3f4-899e5da37f94/?utm_term=.ca6d5ef63ccb.

the principle of non-intervention but the United States was rarely the subject of direct criticism. Nicaragua, of course, attacked the US but in relatively mild terms. Mexico concentrated on the interpretation of OAS Charter articles. Other strong comments came from Colombia, Bolivia, and Argentina. Supportive or neutral statements were made by El Salvador, Guatemala, Honduras, Costa Rica, Paraguay, Uruguay, and Chile."[85] Given this regional body's long-standing skepticism of intervention, the decision not to condemn is significant.

Second, some states who voted against Resolution 38/7 did not do so reflexively. They had to be persuaded that the intervention was consistent with international law. Consider the case of El Salvador before the OAS vote. On October 27, Thomas Pickering, the U.S. Ambassador, relayed a message to Washington "that it has been directed by Salvadoran President Magana to obtain as quickly as possible the gist of U.S. legal argumentation at [an upcoming] OAS permanent council [meeting] in defense of [U.S.] action in Grenada." Pickering noted that the Ministry of Foreign Affairs was "eager to avoid finding itself forced to oppose U.S. intervention in Grenada as contrary to OAS Charter. Salvadorans would, if possible, find a way to agree with U.S. position, but have arrived at preliminary judgment that we may be in violation of our charter." His editorial comments centered on the importance of emphasizing legal justifications for intervention: "[A] strong legal case here and elsewhere in the hemisphere will be extremely helpful given proclivities of some Latin ministries to put heavy stress on such issues."[86] In the end, El Salvador declined to condemn the invasion in the OAS or the UN. A plausible interpretation for this is that they found the administration's justification sufficiently credible.

Competing Explanations

Before closing, I will take up several counter-arguments. One is that Reagan's decision to intervene overtly was facilitated by the absence of escalation concerns. At first blush, this argument seems to enjoy some support. Although the PRG had signed numerous treaties with and received military assistance from the

[85] "Grenada: Special Session of OAS Permanent Council [from Kenneth Dam, October 27, 1983]," *Grenada 10/28/1983 (1 of 6)—Box 43—Executive Secretariat, NSC: Cable File [Folder]; Executive Secretariat, NSC: Cable File: Records 1982-1985—Box 42, 43—Box 14 [Collection]* (Ronald Reagan Library, 1983), 1–2.

[86] "Salvadoran Concern About U.S. Legal Justification for Intervention in Grenada [from Thomas Pickering, October 27, 1983]," *Grenada 10/27/1983 (5 of 7)—Box 43—Executive Secretariat, NSC: Cable File [Folder]; Executive Secretariat, NSC: Cable File: Records 1982-1985—Box 42, 43—Box 14 [Collection]* (Ronald Reagan Library, 1983), 1–2.

Soviet Union, Cuba, Czechoslovakia, and North Korea,[87] senior officials did not believe these countries would respond to a U.S. invasion. On April 21, 1983, six months before hostilities began, a report from the Directorate of Intelligence characterized the Soviet Union's interest in Grenada (and Suriname) in the following terms: "We doubt that Moscow wants to develop either Grenada or Suriname into a major Soviet naval base . . . . Moscow has usually deployed nuclear systems to close, stable allies . . . . Furthermore, in view of Moscow's recognition of the Caribbean region's importance to the US security interests and political and military vulnerability of Grenada and Suriname, it would consider the high risk that Washington would respond with force to Soviet military use of Grenada and Suriname for strategic purposes."[88] According to a declassified memo written in early November 1983, "Moscow's handling of the Grenada crisis suggests that the Soviets were caught by surprise by the October 15 coup and less than fully prepared for the subsequent US-Caribbean military intervention."[89] Moreover, the memo states that "[t]he Soviets privately recognize that we have handled the Grenada situation precisely as they would. They recognize that the loss of their position in Grenada means their ability directly to influence events in the region is shakier than ever, and we doubt that they wish to risk a potentially serious and direct confrontation to retrieve the loss."[90]

There is, however, an obvious limitation of this argument: timing. Escalation-based arguments have difficulty explaining why the invasion took place in October 1983 rather than, say, in March 1982 or July 1981. If anything, concerns about escalation should have been lowest early in the regime's tenure starting in 1979, and grown steadily as the years went on and the relationship with Soviet Bloc countries deepened. The Able Archer military exercise that NATO conducted in early November 1983, which momentarily increased the risk of nuclear war, is testament to the tensions between the superpowers at that point in time.[91] The argument made in this book can better account for the timing of intervention. The presence of a coup in mid-October 1983 gave the United States multiple legal exemptions that paved the way for overt action. Additionally, the fact that legal rather than escalation concerns figured most prominently in declassified

[87] Crandall, *Gunboat Democracy: U.S. Intervention in the Dominican Republic, Grenada, and Panama*, 161. See also "Preliminary Assessment of Cuban and Soviet Involvement in Grenada [October 30, 1983]," 1–4.

[88] "Soviet Geopolitical and Military Interests in Grenada and Suriname [April 21, 1983]," 2.

[89] "Grenada and Moscow's Response [November 10, 1983]," *Grenada (11/10/1983-11/11/1983)—Box 44—Executive Secretariat, NSC Cable File [Folder]; Executive Secretariat, NSC: Cable File: Records—Box 43, 44, 45—Box 15 [Collection]* (Ronald Reagan Library, 1983), 1–2.

[90] Ibid., 8.

[91] Nate Jones, *Able Archer 83: The Secret History of the NATO Exercise That Almost Triggered Nuclear War* (New York: The New Press, 2016).

documents implies that the prospect of retaliation was neither an impediment nor an accelerant to overt intervention.

Whether or not the absence of concerns about large-scale retaliation by Grenada's key allies played a decisive role in this case, there was some sense after the invasion that the communist-aligned countries might respond in less extreme but still provocative ways to the invasion. A declassified memo from October 28 observed: "The Soviets and Cubans may orchestrate terrorism—or just the threat of it—against Eastern Caribbean States, Jamaica, and Barbados, to discourage tourism and punish them for cooperating with the United States." There was also the possibility that "[t]he Grenada operation could . . . be used as a justification for future aggressive actions by the Soviets in Pakistan or Poland . . . . If not a near threat, it is a way of looking at how the loss of Grenada might be otherwise useful."[92] Because this evidence comes from after the invasion took place, it cannot tell us whether decision makers anticipated such reactions beforehand. Nevertheless, it is within the realm of possibility that senior officials would have reached similar conclusions prior to the start of hostilities. If that is true, and the Reagan administration intervened despite concerns about inciting lower forms of retaliation by Cuba and the Soviet Union, it would work against the escalation thesis.

A second counterargument centers on domestic politics. One variant is rooted in democratic peace theory. It predicts that Reagan was able to intervene openly in Grenada because the regime was a dictatorship and that he might have also wanted to promote democracy there. This gets the basic correlation right. Grenada was not a democracy at the time of Urgent Fury. Grenada also held elections in 1984, selecting a moderate prime minister to lead the country.[93] The main limitation of this thesis is the same one facing the escalation argument, namely timing. From the moment Grenada achieved independence through the reign of Gairy and the subsequent takeover by the New Jewel Movement, the country was nondemocratic. Why Carter refrained from pursuing overt intervention—and why Reagan waited until the second half of October in 1983 to do so—cannot be explained by Grenada's status as a dictatorship.[94] My argument again fares better on this front.

[92] "Possible Immediate Responses from the Soviets or the Cubans to the Grenadian Operation [October 28, 1983]," *Grenada (1 of 2)—RAC Box 1—Intelligence Directorate, NSC: Records [Folder]; Intelligence Directorate, NSC—RAC Box 1—Box 1 [Collection]* (Ronald Reagan Library, 1983), 1.

[93] Crandall, *Gunboat Democracy: U.S. Intervention in the Dominican Republic, Grenada, and Panama*, 161.

[94] Although Western notes that "[w]hen the crisis erupted on October 13, the National Security Council staff saw the events as clear evidence of a dramatic shift in the geostrategic balance of power in the Caribbean," it is not evident why, given Bishop's close affinities with Cuba and the Soviet Bloc countries, his removal constituted a marked change in these assessments. See Western, *Selling Intervention and War: The Presidency, the Media, and the American Public*, 113.

Another domestic political argument holds that Reagan openly intervened in Grenada because he enjoyed support from audiences at home. The evidence does not support this. Reagan did not expect a warm reception prior to the invasion. To the contrary, "[t]he administration was well-aware of the fact that there would have been serious opposition in Congress. . . if the consideration of American military deployment to Grenada had become public knowledge and even the subject of extensive public debate."[95] This is part of the reason why Reagan later claimed, "We didn't ask anybody, we just did it."[96] Senior officials also believed that the short duration of the operation obviated the need to inform Congress beforehand. As Robert Beck notes of the War Powers Resolution—the 1973 legislation imposing new reporting and authorization requirements on presidents interested in using force—the administration thought "[t]he legislation did not appear to pose any serious difficulties . . . . With any luck the Grenada mission would be completed long before Congress could question the action's conformity with [War Powers]."[97] Western similarly concludes that "the War Powers Act would not be a domestic legal constraint because the president had the authority to act in 'emergency' situations to protect American citizens."[98]

A third alternative explanation is that the Reagan administration chose overt intervention owing to an absence of concerns about stoking nationalist sentiments. There is indeed evidence which suggests that the Grenadian public supported the invasion. According to a CBS poll, "91% of Grenadians were 'glad the United States troops came to Grenada.' "[99] This appears to support the tainted victory thesis. Assessing how directly relevant these concerns were in the actual decision is harder. A smoking gun would be evidence that senior officials anticipated a warm reception from the target state's public prior to intervening and chose overt intervention as a result. Unfortunately, the declassified record does not indicate one way or the other whether concerns about nationalism were on decision makers' minds prior to the invasion. Also, the bulk of the discussions contained in the declassified record turn on convincing regional and

[95] Ibid., 121–122. Interestingly, despite these concerns, the majority of Americans (at least according to one ABC-*Washington Post* poll taken from after the invasion) supported the Reagan administration's action. See Beck, *The Grenada Invasion: Politics, Law, and Foreign Policy Decisionmaking*, 2.

[96] Quoted in Western, *Selling Intervention and War: The Presidency, the Media, and the American Public*, 122.

[97] Beck, *The Grenada Invasion: Politics, Law, and Foreign Policy Decisionmaking*, 134. See also Menges, *Inside the National Security Council: The True Story of the Making and Unmaking of Reagan's Foreign Policy*, 78.

[98] Western, *Selling Intervention and War: The Presidency, the Media, and the American Public*, 119.

[99] Quoted in Crandall, *Gunboat Democracy: U.S. Intervention in the Dominican Republic, Grenada, and Panama*, 160.

global partners that the invasion was within legal bounds. I was unable to find discussions of decision makers deliberating whether and how to persuade the Grenadian public that a short intervention was necessary in response to a shared threat.

On its face, alternative arguments focused on the need to act quickly and the desire to send signals of resolve as an explanation for why Reagan chose an overt invasion also appear to enjoy some support in this case. Bishop's murder by hardliners in mid-October of 1983 undoubtedly reinforced decision makers' belief that regime change would be valuable. However, there are two main problems with this argument. First, and as already noted in Chapter 6, both the Cuba and Chile cases saw decision makers opting for covert action despite the presence of time constraints and recognition that American resolve could be damaged by inaction. This raises the obvious question of why such factors would have mattered here but not in those cases. Second, officials in the Reagan administration were worried about communism in Grenada from the time they took office. Even if Bishop's murder exacerbated those fears, we would need some explanation for why they did not act earlier. As mentioned in the Power Pack case, my argument provides an additional way of thinking about time here: the tumult of mid-October 1983 gave decision makers a small window to openly intervene in Grenada with legal cover.

A final possibility also relates to resolve but turns on the more general desire to demonstrate a continued capacity to use military power for reasons that have little to do with Grenada specifically. On October 23, 1983, just two days before Urgent Fury began, a suicide bomber targeted military barracks in Beirut, Lebanon, killing over 240 U.S. Marines. The pressure for a military response somewhere may thus have been strong.[100] Additionally, Reagan was a hawk in a post-Vietnam world where the use of large-scale force was often viewed skeptically.[101] Taken together, these factors may have created incentives for an overt invasion of a tiny country to reinvigorate U.S. prowess at relatively low cost.[102]

While both considerations probably weighed on the minds of decision makers, one of them—the barracks bombing—is a reinforcing factor at best. The reason is sequencing. Planning for an invasion of Grenada was underway

[100] Beck, *The Grenada Invasion: Politics, Law, and Foreign Policy Decisionmaking*, 146–151.

[101] Western, *Selling Intervention and War: The Presidency, the Media, and the American Public*, 100–102.

[102] Dov S. Zakheim, "The Grenada Operation and Superpower Relations: A Perspective from the Pentagon," in *Grenada and Soviet/Cuban Policy: Internal Crisis and U.S./OECS Intervention*, ed. Jiri Valenta and Herbert J. Ellison (Boulder and London: Westview Press, 1986), 179–180.

days before the Beirut incident. Given this, it cannot have been related to the initial decision to undertake an overt regime change operation in Grenada. More to the point, available evidence suggests that the barracks bombing episode, though it shook the Reagan administration, "neither stymied nor inspired the Grenada invasion."[103] The desire to rid the United States of Vietnam syndrome by invading a small country may partially explain why Reagan would have been attracted to overt intervention in Grenada. Simply because the United States could have intervened easily against a small country, however, does little to resolve the kinds of risks discussed here. More broadly, this argument has difficulty explaining why Reagan chose to intervene in Grenada two years after he took office rather than intervening much earlier into his term, or possibly even somewhere else.

Conclusion

Operation Urgent Fury was made possible by the availability of two legal exemptions to the nonintervention principle. First was the presence of medical students on the island, whom the administration could reasonably claim were in clear and present danger as a result of the coup against Maurice Bishop. Second was an invitation for intervention by the Organization of Eastern Caribbean States and the Governor-General in the name of peace and security. Senior officials consistently appealed to these exemptions as a way of signaling that the invasion conformed with America's international legal obligations. They went out of their way to avoid saying and doing things that conflicted with this narrative. Declassified documents from the Carter and Reagan administrations provide indirect support for the argument that U.S. decision makers would have chosen covert intervention had legal exemptions been unavailable in mid-October 1983.

My theory outperformed alternative explanations in most cases. Concerns about escalation were minimal. To the extent that such considerations mattered at all in this episode, decision makers openly intervened in spite of such risks. While Reagan's decision to promote democracy is consistent with democratic peace theory, the timing of the operation remains a puzzle for such arguments. Evidence that officials intervened despite anticipating a hostile response from

[103] Beck, *The Grenada Invasion: Politics, Law, and Foreign Policy Decisionmaking*, 225. Some senior officials, including Constantine Menges of the National Security Council, actually wondered whether the news would derail the invasion. See Menges, *Inside the National Security Council: The True Story of the Making and Unmaking of Reagan's Foreign Policy*, 54.

audiences at home cuts against broader domestic political arguments. Finally, while there is correlational support for the tainted victory thesis, the lack of declassified evidence demonstrating that decision makers were aware of these dynamics make it hard to provide a definitive answer about how much these concerns mattered.

8

The Future of Covert Regime Change

This final chapter accomplishes several tasks. First, it summarizes the book's theoretical claims and reviews the evidence in support of them. Second, it demonstrates the argument's applicability to U.S. interventions outside of Latin America and the Cold War. Finally, it outlines directions for future research and lays out implications for scholars and policymakers.

What Have We Learned?

This book began with several puzzles. First, I contrasted Eisenhower's and then Kennedy's decision to quietly intervene in Cuba with Johnson's decision to invade the Dominican Republic four years later. Both countries seemed like prime candidates for overt intervention. They were each squarely located in America's backyard where the chance of clashing with rivals was minimal. All three presidents were on record as being committed to combating communism. A public show of force would have demonstrated resolve. And yet, there was still variation across the two cases. A similar dynamic applied to the Obama administration's differing approaches to hostile dictators during the Arab Spring. In Libya, they pursued regime change overtly. In Syria, they opted for covert action. Why?

My argument looked to international law for answers. Certain states in the postwar era base their decision to topple regimes openly or secretly on whether they could locate a legal exemption to the nonintervention principle. When credible self-defense claims or invitations from international organizations were forthcoming, decision makers were more likely to pursue regime change openly. Absent at least one of these exemptions, they reached for the quiet option to avoid incurring hypocrisy costs and damaging their credibility and trustworthiness.

I tested these claims against four cases of U.S.-backed regime change in the Cold War, drawing from thousands of declassified documents I collected at presidential libraries and interviews with senior government officials involved

In the Shadow of International Law. Michael Poznansky, Oxford University Press (2020). © Oxford University Press.
DOI: 10.1093/oso/9780190096595.001.0001

in some of the decisions under study. The evidence supports the book's central argument. First, there is a clear correlation between the presence or absence of legal exemptions and decisions about secrecy. In the two cases lacking exemptions, presidents opted for covert regime change. In the two cases where they were present, presidents opted for overt regime change.

The evidence also supports the claim that the reason leaders worry about openly violating nonintervention turns on concerns about hypocrisy and credibility. In the two covert cases, decision makers worried that toppling regimes without legal exemptions would do violence to America's moral authority and call its trustworthiness into question. In the Bay of Pigs, for example, senior officials from both the Eisenhower and Kennedy administrations invoked America's pledge to the nonintervention principle, and the harm that would be done were they to brazenly violate it, as a constraint on their capacity to overtly intervene against Castro. These concerns were registered across the government, from military officers to political appointees and from hawks to doves. Analogous concerns were registered in the Chile case, including by hard-nosed realists like Henry Kissinger.

These concerns were absent in the overt cases, both of which entailed multiple exemptions to the nonintervention principle. In Power Pack, Johnson utilized the threat posed to U.S. nationals during the incipient civil war to justify an initial deployment of troops to the Dominican Republic. He then augmented America's military presence by appealing to the OAS-sanctioned ceasefire and eventually the creation of an inter-American peacekeeping force. The story of Urgent Fury was similar. Reagan justified his decision to deploy troops to Grenada by relying on the presence of endangered medical students on the island and an invitation to intervene from the Organization of Eastern Caribbean States. Decision makers in both of these episodes leaned heavily on the fact that international law was on their side.

Each of the alternative explanations considered in this book offered a different independent variable to explain the decision to intervene covertly or overtly. To reiterate a point made in Chapter 3, these can be considered coincident hypotheses.[1] Practically speaking, providing evidence in support of my theory does not tell us all that much about the veracity of these other arguments and vice versa. Additional evidence was needed to evaluate them. Table 8.1 summarizes how well the main competing explanations fared in each of the four cases compared to the legal theory of covert action.

[1] Sherry Zaks, "Relationships Among Rivals (RAR): A Framework for Analyzing Contending Hypotheses in Process Tracing," *Political Analysis* 25, no. 3 (2017): 351.

Table 8.1. **Legal Theory of Covert Action versus Alternatives**

Case	*Legal Theory*	*Escalation*	*Democratic Peace*	*Domestic Politics*	*Tainted Victory*
Cuba	No legal exemptions; concern about hypocrisy and credibility	Risks of clashing with the Soviet Union perceived as low	Cuba not a democracy at the time of intervention	Public likely would have supported intervention	Concern about nationalist backlash; willingness to intervene with legal exemptions
	+	–	–	–	+/–
Chile	No legal exemptions; concern about hypocrisy and credibility	Risks of clashing with the Soviet Union perceived as low	Chile democratic but primary concern was foreign audiences	Public likely would have supported intervention	Concern about nationalist backlash; willingness to intervene with legal exemptions
	+	-	+/-	-	+/-
Dominican Republic	Two legal exemptions: endangered nationals, OAS support	Escalation concerns do not feature prominently in documents	Correlational support: target autocratic, post-invasion elections held	Decision makers expected mixed reaction from public and Congress	Disparate accounts about nationalist sentiment; decision makers unconcerned
	+	–	+/–	+/–	+/–
Grenada	Two legal exemptions: endangered students, OECS support	Risks of major retaliation low; smaller scale retaliation possible	Correlational support: target autocratic, post-invasion elections held	Decision makers expected hostile reaction from public and Congress	Local population supported invasion; unclear if decision makers knew
	+	+/–	+/–	–	+/–

KEY: + = evidence supportive; +/– = evidence mixed; – = evidence not supportive

My argument consistently outperformed the alternatives. Escalation concerns were not determinative in any of the four case-study chapters. This was especially surprising in the Bay of Pigs in light of the events surrounding the Cuban Missile Crisis. The failed covert invasion actually strengthened relations between Cuba and the Soviet Union. Neither of the domestic political explanations performed well, either. Democratic peace theory is irrelevant in Cuba. In Chile, the fact that Nixon covertly targeted Allende, a democratically elected leader, is consistent, but the primary audiences being deceived were international, not domestic. In the Dominican Republic and Grenada, the United States promoted democracy following intervention, which again is consistent. There is little evidence, however, to support the claim that democracy promotion was the primary goal. Broader arguments about domestic politics fall short in all four chapters. In the two covert cases, decision makers pursued secrecy when the public would have supported more overtly hostile action. The opposite was mostly true in the overt cases.

The tainted victory thesis enjoyed mixed support across the four case studies. In the two covert cases, decision makers were indeed concerned about inciting a nationalist backlash. The problem is that this theory's expectations about when leaders should turn to overt regime change were not met. Decision makers did not discuss convincing Cubans or Chileans that a short intervention was necessary to address a shared threat. Rather, when they talked about the conditions under which they would intervene overtly, the discussion turned on legal exemptions. This is uniquely predicted by my theory. While the existence of nationalist sentiments in the Dominican Republic in 1965 is debatable, decision makers did not pay much attention either way. Evidence for the tainted victory thesis is strongest in Grenada given that the population welcomed the invasion. Even so, there is no clear evidence that Reagan would have refrained from intervening openly were this not the case.

A final alternative explanation dealt with in the empirical chapters turned on the role of urgency and resolve as a driver of intervention decisions. According to O'Rourke, leaders are especially likely to pursue overt intervention when time is of the essence and there is a desire to showcase strength and resolve.[2] While these two factors may have made public action more appealing in the overt cases, a similar set of concerns were present in the covert cases. This suggests that decision makers, regardless of time pressure or considerations about resolve, will be reluctant to intervene without legal exemptions. Interestingly, the overt cases—and Chapter 6 in particular—put a new spin on urgency arguments. Part of the

[2] Lindsey O'Rourke, *Covert Regime Change: America's Secret Cold War* (Ithaca: Cornell University Press, 2018), 63.

reason leaders felt compelled to act quickly was their perception that the available legal exemptions had a short shelf life and that if they waited too long before acting they might not be able to capitalize on them.

Beyond Latin America and the Cold War

This section shows that my argument travels outside the confines of Latin America and the Cold War. The discussion unfolds in two stages. I first examine U.S. interventions against Iraq from 1991 through 2003, holding constant a range of factors including the leader being targeted: Saddam Hussein. As will become clear, international legal concerns likely prevented the United States from openly pursuing regime change against Saddam throughout the 1990s. Although George W. Bush eventually broke with his predecessors by invading Iraq without adequate legal cover, the administration's months-long effort to secure UN authorization is testament to the constraining effect of international law. Moreover, the backlash against the United States afterward helps to illustrate the power of the mechanisms contained in my argument. Second, I explore the source of variation in two recent cases of U.S.-backed regime change: Libya in 2011 and Syria from 2012 to 2017. International law helps explain why Barack Obama opted for overt action in the former case but pursued a covert campaign in the latter.

The United States and Iraq, 1991–2003

The United States and Iraq have a long and storied history. Within the span of ten years, the United States went from secretly backing a Kurdish insurgency aimed at undermining the Baathist regime in the 1970s to supporting Saddam Hussein during the Iran–Iraq War in the 1980s.[3] Less than a decade later, the United States was in a shooting war with its erstwhile ally of convenience. This episode was triggered by Saddam's occupation of Kuwait on August 2, 1990. Within five days, President George H.W. Bush deployed forces to protect Saudi Arabia. The UN Security Council soon authorized sanctions and called for Iraq's withdrawal from Kuwait. On November 29 they passed Resolution 678 giving Saddam until January 15, 1991 to comply and threatening punishment including the use of force if he refused, which he eventually did. After the deadline lapsed, the United States along with 35 other nations launched a bombing campaign followed by a

[3] Hal Brands, "Making the Conspiracy Theorist a Prophet: Covert Action and the Contours of United States–Iraq Relations," *The International History Review* 33, no. 3 (2011): 381–408.

ground invasion in late February that ended with Kuwait's liberation 100 hours later.[4] Despite achieving a decisive victory during Operation Desert Storm, the U.S.-led multinational coalition stopped short of entering Iraqi territory and pursuing regime change.

The story does not end there, though. Three months after the invasion, Bush signed a Finding authorizing covert action aimed at bringing down Saddam.[5] Bill Clinton pursued a similar path once in office, although he reduced funding for these secret efforts.[6] DBACHILLES, a covert plan to stimulate a coup that began in 1994 and ended two years later when Saddam's forces arrested and executed many of the individuals involved, showcases the challenging environment in which the United States was operating.[7] Although at least one ploy almost worked, all of them eventually failed.[8] In the end, Bush and Clinton collectively spent around $100 million to quietly topple Saddam, without success.[9]

The absence of a declassified record surrounding these events precludes a complete analysis of the decision-making process.[10] It is hard to say for certain why these presidents refrained from openly pursuing regime change in Iraq and opted instead for covert action. On its face, Bush's decision is especially puzzling in light of the fact that Saddam was on his heels and vulnerable in the immediate aftermath of Desert Storm. Fortunately, memoirs from some of the senior

[4] Alastair Finlan, *The Gulf War 1991* (Elms Court, UK: Osprey, 2003); Lawrence Freedman and Efraim Karsh, "How Kuwait Was Won: Strategy in the Gulf War," *International Security* 16, no. 2 (1991): 6–9.

[5] Jim Hoagl, "How CIA's Secret War on Saddam Collapsed," *Washington Post* June 26 (1997), https://www.washingtonpost.com/archive/politics/1997/06/26/how-cias-secret-war-on-saddam-collapsed/b83592cb-0117-4c3c-a101-9550e29c94a3/?utm_term=.44737c1c03fa.

[6] R. Jeffrey Smith and David B. Ottaway, "Anti-Saddam Operation Cost CIA $100 Million," *Washington Post* Sep. 15 (1996), https://www.washingtonpost.com/archive/politics/1996/09/15/anti-saddam-operation-cost-cia-100-million/4864d228-3623-4ba6-b6d1-ca524d64cc22/?utm_term=.23de0e76e49a.

[7] David Ignatius, "The CIA And the Coup That Wasn't," *Washington Post* May 16 (2003), https://www.washingtonpost.com/archive/opinions/2003/05/16/the-cia-and-the-coup-that-wasnt/0abfb8fa-61e9-4159-a885-89b8c476b188/?noredirect=on&utm_term=.8677fc5b3b91.

[8] Chris Hedges, "Rebels Have Little to Show for Efforts to Topple Saddam Hussein," *New York Times* July 3 (1994), https://www.nytimes.com/1994/07/03/world/rebels-have-little-to-show-for-efforts-to-topple-saddam-hussein.html; George Tenet, *At the Center of the Storm: My Years at the CIA* (New York: HarperCollins, 2007), 302–303; Tim Weiner, "The Deal on Iraq: The C.I.A.; C.I.A. Drafts Covert Plan to Topple Hussein," *New York Times* Feb. 26 (1998), https://www.nytimes.com/1998/02/26/world/the-deal-on-iraq-the-cia-cia-drafts-covert-plan-to-topple-hussein.html; Robin Wright, "America's Iraq Policy: How Did It Come to This?," *The Washington Quarterly* 21, no. 3 (1998): 58.

[9] Smith and Ottaway, "Anti-Saddam Operation Cost CIA $100 Million."

[10] Elizabeth N. Saunders, *Leaders at War: How Presidents Shape Military Interventions* (Ithaca, NY: Cornell University Press, 2011), 191.

officials involved in these decisions make it possible to offer an educated guess about what happened.

A large part of why the United States decided not to march to Baghdad turned on the desire to stay in the bounds of UNSCR 678. In their joint book, *A World Restored*, George H.W. Bush and Brent Scowcroft, his National Security Advisor, write: "Building an international response led us immediately to the United Nations, which could provide a cloak of acceptability to our efforts and mobilize world opinion behind the principles we wished to project . . . . In our operations during the war itself, we were as well attempting to establish a pattern and precedent for the future. We had sought, and succeeded, to obtain the mandate of the world community to liberate Kuwait. Unilaterally going significantly beyond that mandate, we might have undermined the confidence of the United Nations to make future grants of such deadly authority."[11] The authors further argue that the decision to act in this way served as a boon to America's image and credibility and bolstered its leadership role on the world stage.[12]

Given these considerations, it is not hard to imagine why the Bush team in particular would be attracted to secrecy. The benefits of publicly showing restraint—that is, not openly exceeding the UN mandate by actively pursuing regime change—were deemed significant. Covert regime change offered decision makers a way to go beyond what the international community would tolerate without incurring the attendant costs, assuming of course that America's hand remained hidden.[13] There is also evidence to suggest that the administration's desire to project an image of moderation and restraint constrained them from pursuing a more aggressive covert operation akin to the Reagan administration's secret program in Afghanistan in the 1980s, which would have decreased the prospects of deniability.[14] Whether these considerations were the primary driver of covert action under Bush, and whether the Clinton administration was motivated to stay the course for similar reasons, will have to await the release of relevant documents. The available evidence is suggestive nonetheless.

George W. Bush's intervention in Iraq in 2003 appears more challenging for my theory.[15] The invasion to topple Saddam Hussein did not have UN authorization or backing from a regional body. Neither was there a credible self-defense

[11] George Bush and Brent Scowcroft, *A World Transformed* (New York: Alfred A. Knopf, 1998), 491.

[12] Bush and Scowcroft, 491–492.

[13] Joel H. Westra, *International Law and the Use of Armed Force: The UN Charter and the Major Powers* (London and New York: Routledge, 2007), 120–121.

[14] Smith and Ottaway, "Anti-Saddam Operation Cost CIA $100 Million."

[15] For a summary of the public argument, see Chaim Kaufmann, "Threat Inflation and the Failure of the Marketplace of Ideas: The Selling of the Iraq War," *International Security* 29, no. 1 (2004): 5–48.

claim.[16] In some respects, this case illustrates the limits of the argument made here. There might be instances in which decision makers are so committed to a foreign policy goal that they are willing to disregard the ramifications of violating international law.[17] This may be especially likely under unipolarity wherein the hegemon does not have to worry as much about allies and clients defecting to rival powers. All of that said, while my framework does not predict the eventual outcome of Operation Iraqi Freedom it does help explain several key aspects of it.

First, the administration tried, albeit unsuccessfully, to reconceptualize the right of states to intervene in anticipatory self-defense. This type of exercise would be unnecessary without some regard for international law. The controversial 2002 National Security Strategy's conflation of prevention with preemption offers a window into these efforts. "While the United States will constantly strive to enlist the support of the international community," the NSS stated, "we will not hesitate to act alone, if necessary, to exercise our right of self-defense by acting preemptively." It continues: "For centuries, international law recognized that nations need not suffer an attack before they can lawfully take action to defend themselves against forces that present an imminent danger of attack." Although "imminent" had historically referred to "visible mobilization of armies, navies, and air forces preparing to attack," so the line of thinking here went, "[the U.S.] must adapt the concept of imminent threat to the capabilities and objectives of today's adversaries."[18]

Second, administration officials went to great lengths to convince the international community writ large that intervention against Saddam Hussein was necessary and appropriate. In September 2002, President Bush went before the United Nations claiming that Iraq was in violation of a suite of UN Resolutions passed in the aftermath of the first Gulf War. Two months later, the UN unanimously approved Resolution 1441 finding that Iraq had not complied with promises to eliminate weapons of mass destruction and declaring the regime a threat to international peace and security.[19] In February 2003, a month before the invasion began, Secretary of State Colin Powell argued before the UN that Saddam had failed to eliminate his WMD program and that the use of force was a

[16] Tom J. Farer, "The Prospect for International Law and Order in the Wake of Iraq," *American Journal of International Law* 97, no. 3 (2003): 626.

[17] Andrew T. Guzman, *How International Law Works: A Rational Choice Theory* (New York: Oxford University Press, 2008), 112–113.

[18] George W. Bush, *The National Security Strategy of the United States* (Washington, D.C.: White House, 2002), 15.

[19] UN Security Council, "Resolution 1441 (2002)," UN Documents, 2002, http://www.un.org/Depts/unmovic/documents/1441.pdf.

necessary step to eliminate the threat.[20] After the military operation commenced in March, senior legal advisers in the Bush administration sought to make the case that it was consistent with international law by pointing to the fact that the United States was merely enforcing still-active UN Resolutions from the prior decade.[21]

In the end, these efforts did not convince the international community of the legality of the operation. Nevertheless, several factors stand out as relevant. For one thing, the fact that the Bush administration took their case to the UN is noteworthy. In the lead-up to the bombing of Kosovo in 1999, decision makers avoided taking their case before the UNSC or the General Assembly to prevent long and costly negotiations that were unlikely to go in their favor.[22] Bush's decision to go the opposite route suggests that senior officials deemed it important enough to try and secure authorization for an invasion that they were willing to incur reputational costs in the event that things did not go their way (which they did not). Additionally, senior officials in the Bush administration are commonly described as having little regard for multilateralism and international law. That is true to an extent. But it is telling that they spent time and political capital trying to legalize the operation.[23] Finally, the blowback from the invasion and Bush's efforts to walk back his unabashed unilateralism implies that the costs my theory identifies are salient.[24]

The Arab Spring

The broad contours of two episodes of regime change from the recent past—Libya in 2011 and Syria between 2012 and 2017—illustrate the continued relevance of the argument developed in this book. In Libya, the United States, along with NATO allies, intervened with the ostensible aim of protecting civilians from imminent violence at the hands of Muammar Qaddafi in the wake of large-scale protests that eventually turned into a civil war.[25] The UNSC provided legal cover

[20] John Yoo, "International Law and the War in Iraq," *American Journal of International Law* 97, no. 3 (2003): 566.

[21] William H. Taft and Todd F. Buchwald, "Preemption, Iraq, and International Law," *American Journal of International Law* 97, no. 3 (2003): 557–563.

[22] Fernando G. Nuñez-Mietz, "Legalization and the Legitimation of the Use of Force: Revisiting Kosovo," *International Organization*, 2018, 24–25.

[23] Vaughn P. Shannon and Jonathan W. Keller, "Leadership Style and International Norm Violation: The Case of the Iraq War," *Foreign Policy Analysis* 3, no. 1 (2007): 79–104.

[24] David Wippman, "The Nine Lives of Article 2(4)," *Minnesota Journal of International Law* 16, no. 2 (2007): 400.

[25] Robert A. Pape, "When Duty Calls: A Pragmatic Standard of Humanitarian Intervention," *International Security* 37, no. 1 (2012): 61–69.

for these actions by authorizing the venture and invoking the Responsibility to Protect doctrine.[26] The NATO-led operation created space for the rebels to overthrow the Libyan dictator.[27] Although there has been some debate about whether UNSCR 1973 was meant to be limited to a humanitarian mission or sanctioned the broader goal of regime change, many argue that it reasonably covered both.[28] According to Payandeh, "there are indications that the Security Council mandate did not categorically rule out the possibility of regime change in Libya on the basis of Resolution 1973."[29]

The Obama administration's approach to Syria differed markedly from its approach to Libya. Efforts to overthrow Bashar al-Assad, codenamed Timber Sycamore, were shrouded in secrecy.[30] One factor that played a role in pushing the United States into the covert sphere is unrelated to the legal theory developed here, namely the threat of escalation.[31] Syria was a Russian client state. The risks of stumbling into a direct conflict with Vladimir Putin were real. But this was not the only relevant factor. Reports from the time suggest that another reason the United States chose to support the Syrian rebels quietly had to do with the lack of legal exemptions.[32] According to a story in the *Washington Post*, "Obama opted to approve the program as a CIA covert action to avoid international law restrictions on military efforts to overthrow another government."[33] Another story in the *New York Times* noted: "Discussions about putting the Pentagon in

[26] Rebecca Adler-Nissen and Vincent Pouliot, "Power in Practice: Negotiating the Libyan Intervention," *European Journal of International Relations* 20, no. 4 (2014): 900.

[27] Alan J. Kuperman, "A Model Humanitarian Intervention? Reassessing NATO's Libya Campaign," *International Security* 38, no. 1 (2013): 105–136.

[28] For a summary of these debates, see Christine Gray, *International Law and the Use of Force*, 4th ed. (Oxford: Oxford University Press, 2018), 377–380.

[29] Mehrdad Payandeh, "The United Nations, Military Intervention, and Regime Change in Libya," *Virginia Journal of International Law* 52, no. 2 (2012): 387.

[30] This was separate from its overt efforts to destroy and degrade the Islamic State.

[31] Austin Carson and Michael Poznansky, "The Logic for (Shoddy) U.S. Covert Action in Syria," *War on the Rocks* July 21 (2016).

[32] Ashley Deeks, "Arming Syrian Rebels: Lethal Assistance and International Law," *Lawfare* May 1 (2013); Adam Entous, "Legal Fears Slowed Aid to Syrian Rebels," *Wall Street Journal* July 14 (2013), http://www.wsj.com/articles/SB10001424127887323848804578606100558048708; Jack L. Goldsmith, "Two Notes on Secrecy v. Transparency in the National Security World," *Lawfare* Oct. 3 (2013), https://www.lawfareblog.com/two-notes-secrecy-v-transparency-national-security-world; Ben Rhodes, *The World As It Is: A Memoir of the Obama White House* (New York: Random House, 2018), 232–233.

[33] Karen DeYoung, "Congressional Panels Approve Arms Aid to Syrian Opposition," *Washington Post* July 22 (2013), https://www.washingtonpost.com/world/national-security/congressional-panels-approve-arms-aid-to-syrian-opposition/2013/07/22/393035ce-f31a-11e2-8505-bf6f231e77b4_print.html; Jack L. Goldsmith, "The Remarkably Open Syrian Covert Action," *Lawfare* July 23 (2013), https://www.lawfareblog.com/remarkably-open-syrian-covert-action.

charge of the program—and publicly acknowledging the arming and training program—were eventually shelved when it was decided that too many legal hurdles stood in the way of the United States' openly supporting the overthrow of a sovereign government." The article then points out that, "[i]nstead, Mr. Obama decided to make the rebel training program a 'covert action' run by the C.I.A. He signed a secret finding allowing the agency to begin preparing to train and arm small groups of rebels in Jordan, a move that circumvented the legal issues and allowed the White House to officially deny it was giving the lethal aid."[34] These accounts are consistent with one senior official's recollection of Obama's reluctance to openly intervene in Syria without UN Security Council authorization, an unlikely prospect in light of the Russian veto.[35]

The cases explored in this section illustrate the applicability of the theory developed in this book to interventions outside of Latin America, thereby confirming that it travels geographically. It also showed that the argument travels beyond the confines of the Cold War. This is important given the dramatic changes to the international environment over time, from the collapse of the Soviet Union in 1991 to 9/11 ten years later. Despite these developments, international legal concerns continue to play a role in shaping how the United States pursues regime change abroad, often pushing them into the covert sphere.

Directions for Future Research

The themes and questions investigated in this book point to a number of areas for future research. Most obviously, it would be useful to assess whether the legal theory of covert action developed here explains the behavior of states other than the United States. Chapter 3 explained why focusing on the United States as a first cut made sense given America's postwar commitments to strategic restraint and its interest in preserving legitimate leadership. There is reason to suspect that liberal democracies in general may also be sensitive to the prospect of incurring credibility and hypocrisy costs. Rory Cormac's historical treatment of British covert action, for instance, offers numerous examples of decision makers opting for secrecy precisely to avoid violating norms such as the UN's prohibition on

[34] Mark Mazzetti, Robert F. Worth, and Michael R. Gordon, "Obama's Uncertain Path Amid Syria Bloodshed," *New York Times* Oct. 22 (2013), https://www.nytimes.com/2013/10/23/world/middleeast/obamas-uncertain-path-amid-syria-bloodshed.html.

[35] Michael McFaul, *From Cold War to Hot Peace: An American Ambassador in Putin's Russia* (Boston and New York: Houghton Mifflin Harcourt, 2018), 332.

the threat or use of force as a means of protecting the United Kingdom's reputation for "fair play and decency."[36]

Beyond liberal democracies, some autocracies may be constrained by international law, even if to a lesser degree. This is particularly likely for powerful states with an interest in promoting their own versions of international order. The Soviet Union in the Cold War is one possible example. At first blush, an autocratic superpower that perpetrated human rights abuses seems like an improbable candidate for a legal theory of covert action. But Soviet decision makers worried about many of the same things as their American counterparts. "Like the United States," Odd Arne Westad writes, "the Soviet state was founded on ideas and plans for the betterment of humanity, rather than on concepts of identity and nation."[37] It also saw itself as a champion of self-determination and anticolonialism.[38] Assessing whether these considerations shaped the Soviet Union's intervention behavior would be valuable. As proof of concept, Austin Carson's *Secret Wars: Covert Conflict in International Politics*, which privileges escalation-based concerns, acknowledges that part of the reason the Soviets were initially reluctant to overtly intervene in Afghanistan in 1979 was that it would paint them as foreign aggressors.[39] Declassified documents from the Soviet's Central Committee shows that a main source of these concerns was the UN Charter's prohibition on unwanted foreign interference of this kind.[40]

Another promising avenue for future research would be to apply this theoretical framework to other kinds of secret statecraft. For some, especially those with well-defined rules of the road, we might expect similar dynamics to apply. The modern use of unmanned aerial vehicles, or drones, for the purpose of targeted killing comes to mind. Assassinating known or suspected terrorists has become a mainstay of the U.S.-led war on terror since the 9/11 attacks. Drones have been an indispensable tool in these efforts. They expand geographic reach and allow decision makers to minimize casualties to civilians and U.S. service members. They also make it possible to loiter over targets for hours, days, and sometimes weeks for increased accuracy. The appeal of drones is obvious.[41]

[36] Rory Cormac, *Disrupt and Deny: Spies, Special Forces, and the Secret Pursuit of British Foreign Policy* (Oxford: Oxford University Press, 2018), 111, 131, 139, 195, 268.

[37] Odd Arne Westad, *The Global Cold War: Third World Interventions and the Making of Our Times* (Cambridge: Cambridge University Press, 2005), 39.

[38] Melvyn P. Leffler, *For the Soul of Mankind: The United States, the Soviet Union, and the Cold War* (New York: Hill and Wang, 2007), 67.

[39] Austin Carson, *Secret Wars: Covert Conflict in International Politics* (Princeton: Princeton University Press, 2018), 251–252.

[40] "Transcript of CPSU CC Politburo Discussions on Afghanistan [March 17, 1979]," *Cold War International History Project*, 1979, https://digitalarchive.wilsoncenter.org/document/113260.

[41] Michael C. Horowitz, Sarah E. Kreps, and Matthew Fuhrmann, "The Consequences of Drone Proliferation: Separating Fact from Fiction," *International Security* 41, no. 2 (2016): 7–42.

One interesting aspect of drone warfare is the fact that in some cases the CIA, under Title 50 authority, is the one responsible for conducting the attacks. In others, it is the Defense Department under Title 10 authority.[42] Consistent with their operational *modus operandi*, the former are supposed to be plausibly deniable; the latter are not. What accounts for this variation? Why are some drone strikes conducted in a way that is intended to hide U.S. complicity while others are acknowledged? The argument in this book suggests that international law may have something to do with it. When the operation in question would violate the nonintervention principle, the CIA may be more likely to carry out the mission. When the operation does not violate nonintervention standards, perhaps because the target in question was affiliated in some way with al Qaeda, which would satisfy the self-defense exemption, the Pentagon may be more likely to take the lead. There are other possible reasons why the CIA rather than the Pentagon may assume responsibility, including the domestic politics of the host country where the attack is taking place, the risks of escalation, the possibility of inciting nationalist backlash, and more. Teasing out which of these factors matters most would be valuable.

Another tool of secret statecraft ripe for further inquiry is cyber. Cybersecurity is one of the most rapidly growing sub-fields within international relations.[43] The laws and norms governing cyberspace operations, however, remain inchoate. The prospect of developing internationally binding standards of acceptable behavior may be years away, if not longer.[44] One obvious question for researchers is how this impacts not only why states turn to cyberwarfare but whether or not they will opt to keep their identity hidden in the process. On the one hand,

[42] Jack L. Goldsmith, "Questions About CIA v. DOD Drone Strikes," *Lawfare* May 13 (2014), https://www.lawfareblog.com/questions-about-cia-v-dod-drone-strikes.

[43] Ben Buchanan, *The Cybersecurity Dilemma: Hacking, Trust, and Fear Between Nations* (Oxford: Oxford University Press, 2016); Erik Gartzke, "The Myth of Cyberwar: Bringing War in Cyberspace Back Down to Earth," *International Security* 38, no. 2 (2013): 41–73; Erik Gartzke and Jon R. Lindsay, "Weaving Tangled Webs: Offense, Defense, and Deception in Cyberspace," *Security Studies* 24 (2015): 316–348; Jon R. Lindsay, "Stuxnet and the Limits of Cyber Warfare," *Security Studies* 22, no. 3 (2013): 365–404; Jon R. Lindsay, "Tipping the Scales: The Attribution Problem and the Feasibility of Deterrence Against Cyberattack," *Journal of Cybersecurity* 1, no. 1 (2015): 53–67; Joseph S. Nye, "Deterrence and Dissuasion in Cyberspace," *International Security* 41, no. 3 (2017): 44–71; Thomas Rid, "Cyber War Will Not Take Place," *Journal of Strategic Studies* 35, no. 1 (2012): 5–32; Rebecca Slayton, "What Is the Cyber Offense-Defense Balance? Conceptions, Causes, and Assessment," *International Security* 41, no. 3 (2017): 72–109.

[44] Martha Finnemore and Duncan B. Hollis, "Constructing Norms for Global Cybersecurity," *American Journal of International Law* 110, no. 3 (2016): 425–479; Oona Hathaway et al., "The Law of Cyber-Attack," *California Law Review* 100, no. 4 (2012): 817–886; Alexandra H. Perina, "Black Holes and Open Secrets: The Impact of Covert Action on International Law," *Columbia Journal of Transnational Law* 53, no. 3 (2015): 580–583.

we might expect that without clear norms or laws to violate, states will simply come clean owing to the reduced risks of incurring hypocrisy costs or harming their credibility. On the other hand, there are typically good reasons to keep cyberspace operations quiet. This includes escalation management, among other reasons.[45] It may also help states like the United States reconcile its commitment to a free, open, and reliable Internet on the one hand and the need to conduct offensive cyber operations on the other.[46]

The discussion so far called for future research applying the framework developed in this book to other countries and issue areas. But there are additional theoretical questions worth exploring as well. While this manuscript prioritizes the nonintervention principle, the normative environment is complex. Exploring whether and how other kinds of commitments—to democracy, human rights, and so forth—matter is a worthwhile enterprise. For example, do democracies incur hypocrisy costs by *refraining* from targeting brutal dictators or stopping humanitarian catastrophes?

Another fruitful avenue for future research would turn attention away from the intervener and focus instead on some of the other actors impacted by these decisions. In particular, it would be useful to know how the dynamics of legal exemptions affect the target's behavior. The evidence presented throughout suggests that entities in the state targeted with intervention were sensitive to the possibility that the United States would use certain events as pretexts and went out of their way—not always successfully—to make sure this did not happen. Equally interesting would be an exploration of whether the legitimacy and standing of regional organizations are negatively impacted by their decision to greenlight an intervention, especially by a powerful member, even if it is technically legal under international law.

Implications for Scholarship

This book has wide-ranging implications for a number of scholarly research programs. As noted in Chapter 1, contemporary debates about whether the liberal order ever really existed overlook the ways in which U.S. policymakers have used secret tools of statecraft to sustain the postwar system. The post-1945 world was not simply business as usual as critics argue. However, it was not as transformative as proponents contend. The reality is somewhere in between.

[45] Michael Poznansky and Evan Perkoski, "Rethinking Secrecy in Cyberspace: The Politics of Voluntary Attribution," *Journal of Global Security Studies* 3, no. 4 (2018): 402–416.

[46] Joshua Rovner and Tyler Moore, "Does the Internet Need a Hegemon?," *Journal of Global Security Studies* 2, no. 3 (2017): 184–203.

The liberal international order was constraining, but imperfectly so. Whereas American decision makers prior to 1945 routinely and openly toppled regimes deemed to be misbehaving, the desire to maintain an outward appearance of restraint and legitimacy after 1945 pushed many of these interventions into the covert sphere.

This suggests that scholars would benefit from shifting attention away from how compliance and noncompliance impacts the health of international order and focusing instead on how the visibility of compliance affects it. Some scholars have already made strides in this regard. Recent research on disclosure dilemmas offers a good example. According to Carnegie and Carson, complete transparency about deviant behavior is not an unalloyed good. To the contrary, they find that concealing rule violations can actually promote international order under certain circumstances.[47] Interrogating these and related insights—including whether exposed secret violations are less deleterious to international order and whether covert perpetrators anticipate this—would be fruitful.

This book also speaks to the literature on foreign intervention. On the one hand, it joins a growing body of scholarship pushing back against the popular notion that covert forms of interference should be analyzed separately from overt forms of interference.[48] Rather than treating the two as emanating from different data generating processes, covert and overt action are substitutes for one another with their own distinct benefits and costs. Importantly, though, this book differs from these works by prioritizing codified international law and the presence or absence of legal exemptions to explain covert action rather than escalation, nationalism, domestic politics, or liberal norms broadly conceived.

This framework has implications for how the rise of new rules regulating armed conflict might affect the conduct of regime change. The most prominent development in this regard is the rise of Responsibility to Protect. If this becomes a universally accepted standard for intervention, it could affect how states pursue regime change. By expanding the set of legal exemptions to nonintervention, R2P could enable states to openly topple regimes at a higher frequency under the guise of humanitarianism. On the other hand, the Security Council is still supposed to be brought into the loop when states wish to intervene under the auspices of this standard. This is one reason why some proponents are less concerned that it will serve as an easy pretext for self-interested states.[49]

[47] Allison Carnegie and Austin Carson, "The Spotlight's Harsh Glare: Rethinking Publicity and International Order," *International Organization* 72, no. 3 (2018): 627–657. See also Allison Carnegie and Austin Carson, "The Disclosure Dilemma: Nuclear Intelligence and International Organizations," *American Journal of Political Science* 63, no. 2 (2019): 269–285.

[48] See especially Carson, *Secret Wars: Covert Conflict in International Politics*; O'Rourke, *Covert Regime Change: America's Secret Cold War*.

[49] I thank Michael Doyle for pointing this out.

Third, this book sheds new light on long-standing debates surrounding the efficacy of international legal commitments. As with the liberal order discussion, my argument falls somewhere between the skeptics' and proponents' view of international law's effect on state behavior. While commitments like nonintervention do not prevent states from pursuing their self-interest, it has a meaningful effect on how they do so. This represents something distinct from the realists' notion that law is entirely endogenous, as well as liberal and constructivist claims that law can be truly binding.

This claim has direct implications for the decades-old debate in the legal literature about the efficacy of Article 2(4) of the United Nations Charter—the embodiment of a codified nonintervention principle. For many, it has become a dead letter. Thomas Franck's "Who Killed Article 2(4)? or: Changing Norms Governing the Use of Force by States"[50] and Michael Glennon's "How International Rules Die"[51] capture these sentiments.[52] However, almost none of these studies differentiate between interventions that were conducted openly and those done quietly.[53] Doing so offers new insights about the impact the UN Charter has had on state behavior since it came into existence in 1945. The fact that great powers often opted for covert action even when overt options would have been more efficacious is an unintended consequence of this system. This may not be the constraint proponents of the United Nations were hoping for, but it is a constraint nonetheless.

Fourth, this book contributes to the burgeoning literature on secrecy in international relations. Over the past few years, there has been a wave of scholarship exploring the ways states employ secrecy in a number of domains ranging from crisis bargaining to alliance politics, deception in wartime, and military intervention.[54] The primary purpose of secrecy in the vast majority of these studies is to

[50] Thomas M. Franck, "Who Killed Article 2(4)? Or: Changing Norms Governing the Use of Force by States," *American Journal of International Law* 64, no. 5 (1970): 809–837.

[51] Michael J. Glennon, "How International Rules Die," *Georgetown Law Journal* 93, no. 3 (2005): 939–991.

[52] For a defense of Article 2(4), see Louis Henkin, "The Reports of the Death of Article 2(4) Are Greaty Exaggerated," *American Journal of International Law* 65, no. 3 (1971): 544–548; Wippman, "The Nine Lives of Article 2(4)."

[53] Although he does not provide a full-fledged theory of covert action and international law, an important exception in this regard is Westra, *International Law and the Use of Armed Force: The UN Charter and the Major Powers.* I build on the insight that leaders sometimes use covert action to violate nonintervention by developing a framework for understanding when leaders will select one intervention option over another and connecting violations of the UN Charter to the liberal order.

[54] A non-exhaustive list includes Jonathan N. Brown, "The Sound of Silence: Power, Secrecy, and International Audiences in US Military Basing Negotiations," *Conflict Management and Peace Science* 31, no. 4 (2014): 406–431; Carson, *Secret Wars: Covert Conflict in International Politics*; Austin Carson and Keren Yarhi-Milo, "Covert Communication: The Intelligibility and Credibility of Signaling in Secret," *Security Studies* 26, no. 1 (2017): 124–156; Raymond Kuo, "Secrecy among Friends: Covert

deceive domestic audiences and to manage escalation with adversaries. The legal theory developed here offers a distinct causal variable to explain why states are often drawn to the covert sphere and suggests that scholars looking at other tools of secret statecraft should take such factors into account.

Finally, the framework outlined here entails new insights for scholars interested in how and why international organizations can legitimize great power actions. According to existing accounts, garnering the support of an organization like the UN Security Council can help states signal benign intentions to fellow leaders and persuade foreign publics that an action is justified. The reason why this works partially has to do with the fact that great powers are subjecting themselves to constraints.[55] My theory complements such accounts by offering an alternative means by which international organizations help legitimize intervention: providing a legal exemption to the nonintervention principle.

Implications for Policy

This book offers a number of lessons for policymakers. First, in cases when decision makers feel that the national interest calls for actions that violate existing rules of conduct, there is often value in exercising discretion. Henry Farrell and Martha Finnemore's aptly titled *Foreign Affairs* article—"Trump's No Hypocrite: And That's Bad News for the International Order"—helps explain why: "[A]rtful hypocrisy has been one of the United States' most important tools for building an international liberal order centered on the values of rule of law, free markets, free speech, and democracy. When America's behavior deviates from the liberal values that it suggests everyone else should follow, hypocrisy has provided the lubricant that prevents the gears of this order from seizing up."[56] Dispensing with pretense and justifying policies on the basis of

Military Alliances and Portfolio Consistency," *Journal of Conflict Resolution*, 2019; Roseanne McManus and Keren Yarhi-Milo, "The Logic of 'Offstage' Signaling: Domestic Politics, Regime Type, and Major Power-Protégé Relations," *International Organization* 71, no. 4 (2017): 701–733; O'Rourke, *Covert Regime Change: America's Secret Cold War*; Dan Reiter, "Democracy, Deception, and Entry into War," *Security Studies* 21, no. 4 (2012): 594–623; John M. Schuessler, "The Deception Dividend: FDR's Undeclared War," *International Security* 34, no. 4 (2010): 133–165; Keren Yarhi-Milo, "Tying Hands Behind Closed Doors: The Logic and Practice of Secret Reassurance," *Security Studies* 22 (2013): 405–435.

[55] Alexander Thompson, "Coercion Through IOs: The Security Council and the Logic of Information Transmission," *International Organization* 60, no. 1 (2006): 1–34.

[56] Henry Farrell and Martha Finnemore, "Trump's No Hypocrite: And That's Bad News for the International Order," *Foreign Affairs* Snapshot (2017), https://www.foreignaffairs.com/articles/2017-05-30/trump-s-no-hypocrite.

naked self-interest may be the honest thing to do. But it might also encourage other states to follow suit and create conflict in the process.[57] The Iraq War is a cautionary tale of what can happen when leaders openly topple foreign regimes without legal cover. As noted above, the United States paid a price for the invasion, damaging its moral authority and credibility.[58]

This balancing act was on display in the spring of 2019. Heated debates broke out regarding whether the United States should invoke the Monroe Doctrine in the context of a power struggle in Venezuela between anti-American strongman Nicolas Maduro and his opponent, Juan Guaidó. On March 3 of that year, then-National Security Advisor John Bolton went on *CNN* and declared that "[i]n this administration, we're not afraid to use the phrase 'Monroe Doctrine'. "[59] As some have pointed out, though, this language may be counterproductive.[60] For many countries in Latin America, it harkens back to the days of gunboat diplomacy. Even if the Monroe Doctrine is the true motivation for U.S. interest in the crisis, publicly adhering to the dictates of nonintervention remains valuable. Note that this would be true even if the United States wanted to covertly support Guaidó against Maduro.

Despite the potential benefits of discretion, there is a catch: covert operations rarely stay covert for long.[61] In the Bay of Pigs, for example, the *New York Times* reported on America's secret efforts before the invasion happened. On January 10, 1961, a front-page story read, "U.S. Helps Train an Anti-Castro Force At Secret Guatemalan Air-Ground Base."[62] This is not an anomaly. Newspapers reported on Reagan's secret efforts to fund the Contras in Nicaragua in the 1980s.[63] The proliferation of information and communications technology, which has

[57] Carnegie and Carson, "The Spotlight's Harsh Glare: Rethinking Publicity and International Order," 631.

[58] For a skeptical take, see Stephen G. Brooks and William C. Wohlforth, *World Out of Balance: International Relations and the Challenge of American Primacy* (Princeton, NJ: Princeton University Press, 2008), Chapter 6.

[59] Adam Taylor, "What Is the Monroe Doctrine? John Bolton's Justification for Trump's Push against Maduro," *Washington Post* March 4 (2019), https://www.washingtonpost.com/world/2019/03/04/what-is-monroe-doctrine-john-boltons-justification-trumps-push-against-maduro/?noredirect=on&utm_term=.79430b2b1098.

[60] Hal Brands, "First Rule of the Monroe Doctrine: Don't Talk About the Monroe Doctrine," *Bloomberg Opinion* April 24 (2019), https://www.bloomberg.com/opinion/articles/2019-04-24/first-rule-of-monroe-doctrine-don-t-talk-about-monroe-doctrine.

[61] Gregory F. Treverton, *Covert Action: The Limits of Intervention in the Postwar World* (New York: Basic Books, Inc., 1987), 4–5.

[62] Paul P. Kennedy, "U.S. Helps Train Anti-Castro Forces At Secret Guatemalan Air-Ground Base," *New York Times* Jan. 10 (1961), https://www.documentcloud.org/documents/1385912-u-s-helps-train-an-anti-castro-force-at-secret.html.

[63] See "U.S. Aid to the Contras: The Record Since '81," *New York Times* March 20 (1986), https://www.nytimes.com/1986/03/20/world/us-aid-to-the-contras-the-record-since-81.html.

empowered people in far-flung corners of the globe to record and transmit information, has exacerbated the risks of premature exposure.[64] During the course of the Navy SEAL's operation to capture or kill Osama bin Laden in Abbottabad, Pakistan in May of 2011, a Pakistani IT consultant unwittingly tweeted the ordeal for all the world to see.[65] Relatedly, Obama's covert efforts to topple Assad were reported in major newspaper outlets.[66]

Decision makers contemplating covert action must go into these operations with their eyes open and prepare for the possibility that they will not be able to achieve plausible deniability. Whether it will be best to abandon secret operations in such scenarios, or whether it is worth pursuing covert action anyway and running the risk of getting caught, depends on many factors, including the rationale for the underlying the operation, whether it violates domestic or international laws, and so forth.

Finally, the framework developed in this book speaks to a question of ongoing interest to policymakers and scholars alike: What if the United States simply walks away from the liberal international order it helped promote for the last seventy years? American foreign policy under Donald Trump is different in myriad ways from what we have seen in the past.[67] The decision to withdraw from the Paris Climate Accords, abandon the Trans-Pacific Partnership, and pull out of the Joint Comprehensive Plan of Action (the Iran Deal) have led many to question whether the United States can be trusted to keep its commitments and will continue to serve in the leadership role it has occupied since the end of World War II. As of this writing, it is too soon to tell what the impact of the Trump presidency will be. What is clear, though, is that if these recent moves do represent a trend—and the United States abandons the rules-based order—many of the constraints on overt action would diminish.

[64] Michael F. Joseph and Michael Poznansky, "Media Technology, Covert Action, and the Politics of Exposure," *Journal of Peace Research* 55, no. 3 (2018): 320–335.

[65] See Parmy Olson, "Man Inadvertently Live Tweets Osama Bin Laden Raid," *Forbes* May 2 (2011), https://www.forbes.com/sites/parmyolson/2011/05/02/man-inadvertently-live-tweets-osama-bin-laden-raid/#6bb5d936c774. The bin Laden raid, codenamed Operation Neptune Spear, was not actually a covert operation according to the definition offered here. Rather, because Obama announced U.S. complicity afterwards, it was a clandestine operation. Nevertheless, the general point about the difficulty of keeping secrets today remains.

[66] See Mark Mazzetti and Ali Younes, "C.I.A. Arms for Syrian Rebels Supplied Black Market, Officials Say," *New York Times* June 26 (2016), https://www.nytimes.com/2016/06/27/world/middleeast/cia-arms-for-syrian-rebels-supplied-black-market-officials-say.html?_r=0.

[67] Barry R. Posen, "The Rise of Illiberal Hegemony: Trump's Surprising Grand Strategy," *Foreign Affairs* 97, no. 2 (2018): 20–27.

SELECT BIBLIOGRAPHY

Abbott, Kenneth W., and Duncan Snidal. "Why States Act through Formal International Organizations." *Journal of Conflict Resolution* 42, no. 1 (1998): 3–32.

Adkin, Mark. *Urgent Fury: The Battle for Grenada*. Lexington, MA: Lexington Books, 1989.

Adler-Nissen, Rebecca. "Stigma Management in International Relations: Transgressive Identities, Norms, and Order in International Society." *International Organization* 68, no. 1 (2014): 143–176.

Adler-Nissen, Rebecca, and Vincent Pouliot. "Power in Practice: Negotiating the Libyan Intervention." *European Journal of International Relations* 20, no. 4 (2014): 889–911.

Allison, Graham T. "Conceptual Models and the Cuban Missile Crisis." *American Political Science Review* 63, no. 3 (1969): 689–718.

Allison, Graham T. "The Myth of the Liberal Order." *Foreign Affairs* 97, no. 4 (2018): 124–133.

Anderson, Elizabeth E. "The Security Dilemma and Covert Action: The Truman Years." *International Journal of Intelligence and Counterintelligence* 11, no. 4 (1998): 403–427.

Annan, Kofi. "Prevention, Promotion, and Protection: Our Shared Responsibility." *International Coalition for the Responsibility to Protect*, 2012. http://www.responsibilitytoprotect.org/index.php/component/content/article/136-latest-news/4145-kofi-annan-speech-preventin-promotion-and-protection-our-shared-responsibility.

Arend, Anthony Clark. "International Law and the Preemptive Use of Military Force." *The Washington Quarterly* 26, no. 2 (2003): 89–103.

Atkins, G. Pope, and Larman C. Wilson. *The Dominican Republic and the United States: From Imperialism to Transnationalism*. Athens and London: The University of Georgia Press, 1998.

Axelrod, Robert. "The Rational Timing of Surprise." *World Politics* 31, no. 2 (1979): 228–246.

Axelrod, Robert, and Robert O. Keohane. "Achieving Cooperation Under Anarchy: Strategies and Institutions." *World Politics* 38, no. 1 (1985): 226–254.

Aydin, Aysegul. *Foreign Powers and Intervention in Armed Conflicts*. Stanford, CA: Stanford University Press, 2012.

Barnes, Jamal. "Black Sites, 'Extraordinary Renditions' and the Legitimacy of the Torture Taboo." *International Politics* 53, no. 2 (2016): 198–219.

Baum, Matthew A., and Philip B.K. Potter. "The Relationships Between Mass Media, Public Opinion, and Foreign Policy: Toward a Theoretical Synthesis." *Annual Review of Political Science* 11 (2008): 39–65.

Beach, Derek, and Rasmus B. Pedersen. *Process-Tracing Methods: Foundations and Guidelines*. Ann Arbor, MI: University of Michigan Press, 2013.

Beck, Robert J. *The Grenada Invasion: Politics, Law, and Foreign Policy Decisionmaking*. Boulder, CO: Westview Press, 1993.

Beitz, Charles R. "Covert Intervention as a Moral Problem." *Ethics and International Affairs* 3, no. 94 (1989): 45–60.

Bellamy, Alex J., and Tim Dunne, eds. *The Oxford Handbook of the Responsibility to Protect*. Oxford: Oxford University Press, 2016.

Bennett, Andrew, and Jeffrey T. Checkel, eds. *Process Tracing: From Metaphor to Analytic Tool*. Cambridge, UK: Cambridge University Press, 2015.

Berkowitz, Bruce D., and Allan E. Goodman. "The Logic of Covert Action." *The National Interest* 51 (1998): 38–46.

Blight, James B., Janet M. Lang, and David A. Welch. *Virtual JFK: Vietnam If Kennedy Had Lived*. Lanham, MD: Rowman and Littlefield, 2009.

Blight, James G., and Peter Kornbluh, eds. *Politics of Illusion: The Bay of Pigs Invasion Reexamined*. Boulder, CO: Lynne Reinner, 1998.

Bok, Sissela. *Secrets: On the Ethics of Concealment and Revelation*. New York: Vintage Books, 1983.

"Bokassa Successor Says Dictator Killed Children in April Massacre." *New York Times* Sep. 24 (1979). https://www.nytimes.com/1979/09/24/archives/bokassa-successor-says-dictator-killed-children-in-april-massacre.html.

Bonsal, Philip W. "Cuba, Castro, and the United States." *Foreign Affairs* 45, no. 2 (1967): 260–276.

Bowett, D.W. *Self-Defence in International Law*. Manchester, UK: Manchester University Press, 1958.

Brands, H.W. "Decisions on American Armed Intervention: Lebanon, Dominican Republic, and Grenada." *Political Science Quarterly* 102, no. 4 (1987): 607–624.

Brands, Hal. "First Rule of the Monroe Doctrine: Don't Talk About the Monroe Doctrine." *Bloomberg Opinion* April 24 (2019). https://www.bloomberg.com/opinion/articles/2019-04-24/first-rule-of-monroe-doctrine-don-t-talk-about-monroe-doctrine.

Brands, Hal. "Making the Conspiracy Theorist a Prophet: Covert Action and the Contours of United States–Iraq Relations." *The International History Review* 33, no. 3 (2011): 381–408.

Brierly, J.L. *The Law of Nations: An Introduction to the International Law of Peace*. Oxford and New York: Oxford University Press, 1963.

Brooks, Stephen G., and William C. Wohlforth. *World Out of Balance: International Relations and the Challenge of American Primacy*. Princeton, NJ: Princeton University Press, 2008.

Brown, Jonathan N. "The Sound of Silence: Power, Secrecy, and International Audiences in US Military Basing Negotiations." *Conflict Management and Peace Science* 31, no. 4 (2014): 406–431.

Brown, Jonathan N., and Anthony S. Marcum. "Avoiding Audience Costs: Domestic Political Accountability and Concessions in Crisis Diplomacy." *Security Studies* 20, no. 2 (2011): 141–170.

Brzezinski, Zbigniew. *Power and Principle: Memoirs of the National Security Adviser, 1977–1981*. New York: Farrar Straus & Giroux, 1983.

Buchanan, Ben. *The Cybersecurity Dilemma: Hacking, Trust, and Fear Between Nations*. Oxford: Oxford University Press, 2016.

Bull, Hedley, ed. *The Anarchical Society: A Study of Order in World Politics*. New York: Palgrave Macmillan, 1977.

Bull, Hedley, ed. *Intervention in World Politics*. Oxford: Oxford University Press, 1984.

Bush, George, and Brent Scowcroft. *A World Transformed*. New York: Alfred A. Knopf, 1998.

Bush, George W. *The National Security Strategy of the United States*. Washington, D.C.: White House, 2002.

Buzas, Zoltan. "Evading International Law: How Agents Comply with the Letter of the Law but Violate Its Purpose." *European Journal of International Relations* 23, no. 4 (2017): 857–883.

Buzas, Zoltan. "Is the Good News About Law Compliance Good News About Norm Compliance? The Case of Racial Equality." *International Organization* 72, no. 2 (2018): 351–385.

Byers, Michael. "Jumping the Gun." *London Review of Books* 24, no. 14 (2002): 3–5.

Carnegie, Allison, and Austin Carson. "The Spotlight's Harsh Glare: Rethinking Publicity and International Order." *International Organization* 72, no. 3 (2018): 627–657.

Carnegie, Allison, and Austin Carson. "The Disclosure Dilemma: Nuclear Intelligence and International Organizations." *American Journal of Political Science* 63, no. 2 (2019): 269–285.

Carson, Austin. "Facing Off and Saving Face: Covert Intervention and Escalation Management in the Korean War." *International Organization* 70, no. 1 (2016): 103–131.

Carson, Austin. *Secret Wars: Covert Conflict in International Politics.* Princeton, NJ: Princeton University Press, 2018.

Carson, Austin, and Michael Poznansky. "The Logic for (Shoddy) U.S. Covert Action in Syria." *War on the Rocks* July 21 (2016).

Carson, Austin, and Keren Yarhi-Milo. "Covert Communication: The Intelligibility and Credibility of Signaling in Secret." *Security Studies* 26, no. 1 (2017): 124–156.

Chayes, Abram. *The Cuban Missile Crisis: International Crises and the Role of Law.* New York and London: Oxford University Press, 1974.

Chayes, Abram, and Antonia Handler Chayes. "On Compliance." *International Organization* 47, no. 2 (1993): 175–205.

Chayes, Abram, and Antonia Handler Chayes. *The New Sovereignty.* Cambridge, MA: Harvard University Press, 1995.

Clark, Ian. *Legitimacy in International Society.* Oxford: Oxford University Press, 2005.

Clarke, Richard A. *Against All Enemies: Inside America's War on Terror.* New York: Free Press, 2004.

Colaresi, Michael P. *Democracy Declassified: The Secrecy Dilemma in National Security.* Oxford: Oxford University Press, 2014.

Cole, Ronald H. *Operation Urgent Fury: The Planning and Execution of Joint Operations in Grenada, 12 October–2 November 1983.* Washington, D.C.: Joint History Office: Office of the Chairman of the Joint Chiefs of Staff, 1997. http://www.jcs.mil/Portals/36/Documents/History/Monographs/Urgent_Fury.pdf.

Coll, Steve. *Ghost Wars: The Secret History of the CIA, Afghanistan and Bin Laden, From the Soviet Invasion to September 10, 2001.* New York: Penguin Books, 2004.

Collier, David. "Understanding Process Tracing." *PS: Political Science & Politics* 44, no. 4 (2011): 823–830.

"Convention on Rights and Duties of States (Inter-American); December 26, 1933." The Avalon Project, 1933. http://avalon.law.yale.edu/20th_century/intam03.asp.

Copeland, Dale C. *The Origins of Major War.* Ithaca, NY: Cornell University Press, 2000.

Copeland, Dale C. *Economic Interdependence and War.* Princeton, NJ: Princeton University Press, 2015.

Cormac, Rory. *Disrupt and Deny: Spies, Special Forces, and the Secret Pursuit of British Foreign Policy.* Oxford: Oxford University Press, 2018.

Crandall, Russell. *Gunboat Democracy: U.S. Intervention in the Dominican Republic, Grenada, and Panama.* Lanham, MD: Rowman and Littlefield, 2006.

Cronin, Bruce. "The Paradox of Hegemony: America's Ambiguous Relationship with the United Nations." *European Journal of International Relations* 7, no. 1 (2001): 103–130.

Daddis, Gregory A. *Withdrawal: Reassessing America's Final Years in Vietnam.* New York: Oxford University Press, 2017.

Dai, Xinyuan. "Why Comply? The Domestic Constituency Mechanism." *International Organization* 59, no. 2 (2005): 363–398.

Dallek, Robert. *Lyndon B. Johnson: Portrait of a President.* Oxford and New York: Oxford University Press, 2004.

Daugherty, William J. *Executive Secrets: Covert Action and the Presidency.* Lexington, KY: The University Press of Kentucky, 2004.

Damrosch, Lori Fisler. "Politics Across Borders: Nonintervention and Nonforcible Influence over Domestic Affairs." *American Journal of International Law* 83, no. 1 (1989): 1–50.

Dean, Kevin W. "'We Seek Peace, But We Shall Not Surrender': JFK's Use of Juxtaposition for Rhetorical Success in the Berlin Crisis." *Presidential Studies Quarterly* 21, no. 3 (1991): 531–544.

"Declaration of Principles of Inter-American Solidarity and Cooperation; December 21, 1936." The Avalon Project, 1936. http://avalon.law.yale.edu/20th_century/intam07.asp.

Deeks, Ashley. "Arming Syrian Rebels: Lethal Assistance and International Law." *Lawfare* May 1 (2013).

Deudney, Daniel, and G. John Ikenberry. "The Nature and Sources of Liberal International Order." *Review of International Studies* 25, no. 2 (1999): 179–196.

DeYoung, Karen. "Congressional Panels Approve Arms Aid to Syrian Opposition." *Washington Post* July 22 (2013). https://www.washingtonpost.com/world/national-security/congressional-panels-approve-arms-aid-to-syrian-opposition/2013/07/22/393035ce-f31a-11e2-8505-bf6f231e77b4_print.html.

Downes, Alexander B., and Mary Lauren Lilley. "Overt Peace, Covert War?: Covert Intervention and the Democratic Peace." *Security Studies* 19, no. 2 (2010): 266–306.

Downes, Alexander B., and Jonathan Monten. "Forced to Be Free? Why Foreign-Inposed Regime Change Rarely Leads to Democratization." *International Security* 37, no. 4 (2013): 90–131.

Downes, Alexander B., and Lindsey A. O'Rourke. "You Can't Always Get What You Want: Why Foreign-Imposed Regime Change Seldom Improves Interstate Relations." *International Security* 41, no. 2 (2016): 43–89.

Downs, George W., and Michael A. Jones. "Reputation, Compliance, and International Law." *Journal of Legal Studies* 31 (2002): S95–114.

Durbin, Brent. *The CIA and the Politics of US Intelligence Reform*. New York: Cambridge University Press, 2017.

Edelstein, David M. "Occupational Hazards: Why Military Occupations Succeed or Fail." *International Security* 29, no. 1 (2004): 49–91.

Eichensehr, Kristen E. "Defending Nationals Abroad: Assessing the Lawfulness of Forcible Hostage Rescues." *Virginia Journal of International Law* 48, no. 2 (2008): 452–484.

Entous, Adam. "Legal Fears Slowed Aid to Syrian Rebels." *Wall Street Journal* July 14 (2013). http://www.wsj.com/articles/SB10001424127887323848804578606100558048708.

Evers, Miles M. "On Transgression." *International Studies Quarterly* 61, no. 4 (2017): 786–794.

Fairfield, Tasha, and Andrew E. Charman. "Explicit Bayesian Analysis for Process Tracing: Guidelines, Opportunities, and Caveats." *Political Analysis* 25, no. 3 (2017): 363–380.

Falk, Richard A. "CIA Covert Action and International Law." *Society* 12 (1975): 39–44.

Farer, Tom J. "The Prospect for International Law and Order in the Wake of Iraq." *American Journal of International Law* 97, no. 3 (2003): 621–628.

Farrell, Henry, and Martha Finnemore. "Trump's No Hypocrite: And That's Bad News for the International Order." *Foreign Affairs Snapshot* (2017). https://www.foreignaffairs.com/articles/2017-05-30/trump-s-no-hypocrite.

Fazal, Tanisha M. *State Death: The Politics and Geography of Conquest, Occupation, and Annexation*. Princeton, NJ: Princeton University Press, 2007.

Fazal, Tanisha M. *Wars of Law: Unintended Consequences in the Regulation of Armed Conflict*. Ithaca, NY: Cornell University Press, 2018.

Fenwick, Charles G. "The Inter-American Regional System." *American Journal of International Law* 50, no. 1 (1956): 18–31.

Feste, Karen A. *Intervention: Shaping the Global Order*. Westport, CT: Praeger, 2003.

Findley, Michael G., and Tze Kwang Teo. "Rethinking Third-Party Interventions into Civil Wars: An Actor-Centric Approach." *Journal of Politics* 68, no. 4 (2006): 828–837.

Finlan, Alastair. *The Gulf War 1991*. Elms Court, UK: Osprey, 2003.

Finnemore, Martha. "Legitimacy, Hypocrisy, and the Social Structure of Unipolarity: Why Being a Unipole Isn't All It's Cracked Up to Be." *World Politics* 61, no. 1 (2009): 58–85.

Finnemore, Martha. *The Purpose of Intervention: Changing Beliefs About the Use of Force*. Ithaca, NY: Cornell University Press, 2003.

Finnemore, Martha, and Duncan B. Hollis. "Constructing Norms for Global Cybersecurity." *American Journal of International Law* 110, no. 3 (2016): 425–479.

Forcese, Craig. *Destroying the Caroline: The Frontier Raid That Reshaped the Right to War*. Toronto, ON: Irwin Law, 2018.

Fordham, Benjamin O. "Power or Plenty? Economic Interests, Security Concerns, and American Intervention." *International Studies Quarterly* 52, no. 4 (2008): 737–758.

Forsythe, David P. "Democracy, War, and Covert Action." *Journal of Peace Research* 29, no. 4 (1992): 385–395.

Franck, Thomas M. "Who Killed Article 2(4)? Or: Changing Norms Governing the Use of Force by States." *American Journal of International Law* 64, no. 5 (1970): 809–837.

Franck, Thomas M. "Legitimacy in the International System." *American Journal of International Law* 82, no. 4 (1988): 705–759.

Franck, Thomas M. *Recourse to Force: State Action against Threats and Armed Attacks*. Cambridge, UK: Cambridge University Press, 2004.

Franck, Thomas M. "The Power of Legitimacy and the Legitimacy of Power: International Law in an Age of Power Disequilibrium." *American Journal of International Law* 100, no. 1 (2006): 88–106.

Freedman, Lawrence, and Efraim Karsh. "How Kuwait Was Won: Strategy in the Gulf War." *International Security* 16, no. 2 (1991): 5–41.

Friedman, Max Paul, and Tom Long. "Soft Balancing in the Americas: Latin American Opposition to U.S. Intervention, 1898–1936." *International Security* 40, no. 1 (2015): 120–156.

Friedman, Rebecca R. "Crisis Management at the Dead Center: The 1960-1961 Presidential Transition and the Bay of Pigs Fiasco." *Presidential Studies Quarterly* 41, no. 2 (2011): 307–333.

Gartzke, Erik. "The Myth of Cyberwar: Bringing War in Cyberspace Back Down to Earth." *International Security* 38, no. 2 (2013): 41–73.

Gartzke, Erik, and Jon R. Lindsay. "Weaving Tangled Webs: Offense, Defense, and Deception in Cyberspace." *Security Studies* 24, no. 2 (2015): 316–348.

Gates, Robert M. *From the Shadows: The Ultimate Insider's Story of Five Presidents and How They Won the Cold War*. New York: Simon and Schuster, 1996.

Gavin, Francis J. "Nuclear Nixon: Ironies, Puzzles, and the Triumph of Realpolitik." In *Nixon in the World : American Foreign Relations, 1969-1977*, edited by Fred Logevall and Andrew Preston, 126–145. Oxford and New York: Oxford University Press, 2008.

Gavin, Francis J. "Politics, Power, and U.S. Policy in Iran, 1950–1953." *Journal of Cold War Studies* 1, no. 1 (1999): 56–89.

Geddes, Barbara. "How the Cases You Choose Affect the Answers You Get: Selection Bias in Comparative Politics." *Political Analysis* 2 (1990): 131–150.

Gent, Stephen E. "Strange Bedfellows: The Strategic Dynamics of Major Power Military Interventions." *Journal of Politics* 69, no. 4 (2007): 1089–1102.

George, Alexander L., and Andrew Bennett. *Case Studies and Theory Development in the Social Sciences*. Cambridge, MA: Belfer Center for Science and International Affairs, 2005.

Gibbs, David N. "Secrecy and International Relations." *Journal of Peace Research* 32, no. 2 (1995): 213–228.

Girling, J.L.S. "The Guam Doctrine." *International Affairs* 46, no. 1 (1970): 48–62.

Gleijeses, Piero. *The Dominican Crisis: The 1965 Constitutionalist Revolt and American Intervention*. Baltimore and London: The Johns Hopkins University Press, 1978.

Gleijeses, Piero. "Ships in the Night: The CIA, the White House and the Bay of Pigs." *Journal of Latin American Studies* 27, no. 1 (1995): 1–42.

Glennon, Michael J. "The Fog of Law: Self-Defense, International Rules Die." Georgetown Inherence, and Incoherence in Article 51 of the United Nations Charter." *Harvard Journal of Law and Public Policy* 25, no. 2 (2002): 539–558.

Glennon, Michael J. "How International Rules Die." *Georgetown Law Journal* 93, no. 3 (2005): 939–991.

Go, Julian. *Patterns of Empire: The British and American Empires, 1688 to the Present*. Cambridge, UK: Cambridge University Press, 2011.

Goddard, Stacie. *When Right Makes Might: Rising Powers and World Order*. Ithaca, NY and London: Cornell University Press, 2018.

Goh, Evelyn. "Nixon, Kissinger, and the 'Soviet Card' in the U.S. Opening to China, 1971–1974." *Diplomatic History* 29, no. 3 (2005): 475–502.

Goldsmith, Jack L. "The Remarkably Open Syrian Covert Action." *Lawfare* July 23 (2013). https://www.lawfareblog.com/remarkably-open-syrian-covert-action.

Goldsmith, Jack L. "Two Notes on Secrecy v. Transparency in the National Security World." *Lawfare* Oct. 3 (2013). https://www.lawfareblog.com/two-notes-secrecy-v-transparency-national-security-world.

Goldsmith, Jack L. "Questions About CIA v. DOD Drone Strikes." *Lawfare* May 13 (2014). https://www.lawfareblog.com/questions-about-cia-v-dod-drone-strikes.

Goldsmith, Jack L., and Eric A. Posner. *The Limits of International Law*. Oxford and New York: Oxford University Press, 2005.

Goldstein, Judith, Miles Kahler, Robert O. Keohane, and Anne-Marie Slaughter. "Introduction: Legalization and World Politics." *International Organization* 54, no. 3 (2000): 385–399.

Goshko, John M., and Michael Isikoff. "OAS Votes to Censure U.S. for Intervention." *Washington Post* Dec. 23 (1989). https://www.washingtonpost.com/archive/politics/1989/12/23/oas-votes-to-censure-us-for-intervention/807f91f4-6f43-4b0b-8021-6bb994f83244/?noredirect=on&utm_term=.7a22e86e9966.

Graham, Mary. *Presidents' Secrets: The Use and Abuse of Hidden Power*. New Haven, CT: Yale University Press, 2017.

Gray, Christine. *International Law and the Use of Force*. 4th ed. Oxford: Oxford University Press, 2018.

Greenhill, Kelly M. *Weapons of Mass Migration: Forced Displacement, Coercion, and Foreign Policy*. Ithaca, NY: Cornell University Press, 2010.

Gross, Richard C. "Different Worlds: Unacknowledged Special Operations and Covert Action." *Strategy Research Project: U.S. Army War College*, 2009. https://fas.org/man/eprint/gross.pdf.

Gustafson, Kristian. *Hostile Intent: U.S. Covert Operations in Chile, 1964–1974*. Washington, D.C.: Potomac Books, Inc., 2007.

Gustafson, Kristian, and Christopher Andrew. "The Other Hidden Hand: Soviet and Cuban Intelligence in Allende's Chile." *Intelligence and National Security* 33, no. 3 (2018): 407–421.

Guzman, Andrew T. *How International Law Works: A Rational Choice Theory*. New York: Oxford University Press, 2008.

Halderman, John W. "Regional Enforcement Measures and the United Nations." *Georgetown Law Journal* 52, no. 1 (1963): 89–118.

Hanhimaki, Jussi M. *The Flawed Architect: Henry Kissinger and American Foreign Policy*. Oxford and New York: Oxford University Press, 2004.

Hartlyn, Jonathan. *The Struggle for Democratic Politics in the Dominican Republic*. Chapel Hill and London: The University of North Carolina Press, 1998.

Haslam, Jonathan. *The Nixon Administration and the Death of Allende's Chile: A Case of Assisted Suicide*. London and New York: Verso, 2005.

Hathaway, Oona, and Scott J. Shapiro. *The Internationalists: How a Radical Plan to Outlaw War Remade the World*. New York: Simon and Schuster, 2017.

Hathaway, Oona, Rebecca Crootof, Philip Levitz, Haley Nix, Aileen Nowlan, William Perdue, and Julia Spiegel. "The Law of Cyber-Attack." *California Law Review* 100, no. 4 (2012): 817–886.

Hedges, Chris. "Rebels Have Little to Show for Efforts to Topple Saddam Hussein." *New York Times* July 3 (1994). https://www.nytimes.com/1994/07/03/world/rebels-have-little-to-show-for-efforts-to-topple-saddam-hussein.html.

Hendrickson, David C. "Toward Universal Empire: The Dangerous Quest for Absolute Security." *World Policy Journal* 19, no. 3 (2002): 1–10.

Henkin, Louis. "The Reports of the Death of Article 2(4) Are Greatly Exaggerated." *American Journal of International Law* 65, no. 3 (1971): 544–548.

Hershey, Amos S. "The Calvo and Drago Doctrines." *American Journal of International Law* 1, no. 1 (1907): 26–45.

Higgins, Rosalyn. "Intervention and International Law." In *Intervention in World Politics*, 29–44. Oxford: Clarendon Press, 1984.

Hoagl, Jim. "How CIA's Secret War on Saddam Collapsed." *Washington Post* June 26 (1997). https://www.washingtonpost.com/archive/politics/1997/06/26/how-cias-secret-war-on-saddam-collapsed/b83592cb-0117-4c3c-a101-9550e29c94a3/?utm_term=.44737c1c03fa.

Hoffman, Stanley. "The Problem of Intervention." In *Intervention in World Politics*, 7–28. Oxford: Clarendon Press, 1984.

Horowitz, Michael C., Sarah E. Kreps, and Matthew Fuhrmann. "The Consequences of Drone Proliferation: Separating Fact from Fiction." *International Security* 41, no. 2 (2016): 7–42.

Humphreys, Macartan, and Alan M. Jacobs. "Mixing Methods: A Bayesian Approach." *American Political Science Review* 109, no. 4 (2015): 653–673.

Hurd, Ian. "Legitimacy and Authority in International Politics." *International Organization* 53, no. 2 (1999): 379–408.

Hurd, Ian. *How to Do Things with International Law*. Princeton, NJ: Princeton University Press, 2018.

Ignatius, David. "The CIA And the Coup That Wasn't." *Washington Post* May 16 (2003). https://www.washingtonpost.com/archive/opinions/2003/05/16/the-cia-and-the-coup-that-wasnt/0abfb8fa-61e9-4159-a885-89b8c476b188/?noredirect=on&utm_term=.8677fc5b3b91.

Ikenberry, G. John. *After Victory: Institutions, Strategic Restraint, and the Rebuilding of Order After Major Wars*. Princeton, NJ: Princeton University Press, 2001.

Ikenberry, G. John. *Liberal Leviathan: The Origins, Crisis, and Transformation of the American World Order*. Princeton, NJ: Princeton University Press, 2011.

Immerman, Richard H. *The CIA In Guatemala: The Foreign Policy of Intervention*. Austin, TX: University of Texas Press, 1982.

"Inter-American Treaty of Reciprocal Assistance." Department of International Law, OAS, 1947. http://www.oas.org/juridico/english/treaties/b-29.html.

Jaffe, Greg, and Adam Entous. "Trump Ends Covert CIA Program to Arm Anti-Assad Rebels in Syria, a Move Sought by Moscow." *Washington Post* July 19 (2017).

Janis, Irving L. *Victims of Groupthink: A Psychological Study of Foreign-Policy Decisions and Fiascoes*. Boston, MA: Houghton Mifflin, 1972.

Jentleson, Bruce. *The Peacemakers: Leadership Lessons from Twentieth-Century Statesmanship*. New York: W. W. Norton, 2018.

Jervis, Robert. "Cooperation Under the Security Dilemma." *World Politics* 30, no. 2 (1978): 167–214.

Johnson, Loch. *America's Secret Power: The CIA in a Democratic Society*. New York and Oxford: Oxford University Press, 1989.

Johnson, Loch. "Covert Action and Accountability: Decision-Making for America's Secret Foreign Policy." *International Studies Quarterly* 33, no. 1 (1989): 81–109.

Johnson, Lyndon B. *The Vantage Point: Perspectives of the Presidency, 1963–1969*. New York: Holt, Rinehart and Winston, 1971.

Jones, Howard. *The Bay of Pigs*. Oxford: Oxford University Press, 2008.

Jones, Nate. *Able Archer 83: The Secret History of the NATO Exercise That Almost Triggered Nuclear War*. New York: The New Press, 2016.

Joseph, Michael F., and Michael Poznansky. "Media Technology, Covert Action, and the Politics of Exposure." *Journal of Peace Research* 55, no. 3 (2018): 320–335.

Katzenstein, Peter J. *A World of Regions: Asia and Europe in the American Imperium*. Ithaca, NY: Cornell University Press, 2005.

Kaufmann, Chaim. "Threat Inflation and the Failure of the Marketplace of Ideas: The Selling of the Iraq War." *International Security* 29, no. 1 (2004): 5–48.

Keck, Margaret E., and Kathryn Sikkink. *Activists Beyond Borders: Advocacy Networks in International Politics*. Ithaca, NY: Cornell University Press, 1998.

Kelsen, Hans. "Collective Security and Collective Self-Defense Under the Charter of the United Nations." *The American Journal of International Law* 42, no. 4 (1948): 783–796.

Kennedy, John F. "Bay of Pigs Invasion." *C-Span* April 20 (1961). https://www.c-span.org/video/?192032-1/bay-pigs-invasion.

Kennedy, Paul P. "U.S. Helps Train Anti-Castro Forces At Secret Guatemalan Air-Ground Base." *New York Times* Jan. 10 (1961). https://www.documentcloud.org/documents/1385912-u-s-helps-train-an-anti-castro-force-at-secret.html.

Keohane, Robert O. *After Hegemony: Cooperation and Discord in the World Political Economy*. Princeton, NJ: Princeton University Press, 1984.

Keohane, Robert O. "International Relations and International Law: Two Optics." *Harvard International Law Journal* 38, no. 2 (1997): 487–502.

King, Gary, Robert O. Keohane, and Sydney Verba. *Designing Social Inquiry: Scientific Inference in Qualitative Research*. Princeton, NJ: Princeton University Press, 1994.

Kinzer, Stephen. *Overthrow: America's Century of Regime Change from Hawaii to Iraq*. New York: Times Books, 2006.

Kissinger, Henry. *A World Restored: Metternich, Castlereagh and the Problems of Peace, 1812–22*. Brattleboro, VT: Echo Point, 2013.

Knott, Stephen F. *Secret and Sanctioned: Covert Operations and the American Presidency*. New York: Oxford University Press, 1996.

Kornbluh, Peter, ed. *Bay of Pigs Declassified: The Secret CIA Report on the Invasion of Cuba*. New York: The New Press, 1998.

Kornbluh, Peter, ed. *The Pinochet File : A Declassified Dossier on Atrocity and Accountability*. New York: The New Press, 2003.

Krasner, Stephen D. *Sovereignty: Organized Hypocrisy*. Princeton, NJ: Princeton University Press, 1999.

Krebs, Ronald R. "Correspondence: Selling the Market Short? The Marketplace of Ideas and the Iraq War." *International Security* 29, no. 4 (2005): 196–207.

Kunig, Philip. "Intervention, Prohibition Of." *Max Planck Encyclopedia of Public International Law*, 2008.

Kunz, Josef L. "Individual and Collective Self-Defense in Article 51 of the Charter of the United Nations." *American Journal of International Law* 41, no. 4 (1947): 872–879.

Kuo, Raymond. "Secrecy among Friends: Covert Military Alliances and Portfolio Consistency." *Journal of Conflict Resolution*, 2019.

Kupchan, Charles A. *How Enemies Become Friends: The Sources of Stable Peace*. Princeton, NJ and Oxford: Princeton University Press, 2010.

Kuperman, Alan J. "A Model Humanitarian Intervention? Reassessing NATO's Libya Campaign." *International Security* 38, no. 1 (2013): 105–136.

Lake, David A. *Hierarchy in International Relations*. Ithaca, NY: Cornell University Press, 2009.

Lascurettes, Kyle M. *The Concert of Europe and Great Power Governance Today: What Can the Order of 19th-Century Europe Teach Policymakers About International Order in the 21st Century?* Santa Monica, CA: RAND Corporation, 2017.

Lascurettes, Kyle M. *Orders of Exclusion: Great Powers and the Strategic Sources of Foundational Rules in International Relations*. New York: Oxford University Press, 2020.

League of Nations. "The Covenant of the League of Nations." The Avalon Project, 1924. http://avalon.law.yale.edu/20th_century/leagcov.asp#art15.

Leeson, Peter T., and Paola A. Suarez. "An Economic Analysis of Magna Carta." *International Review of Law and Economics* 47 (2016): 40–46.

Leffler, Melvyn P. *A Preponderance of Power: National Security, the Truman Administration, and the Cold War*. Stanford, CA: Stanford University Press, 1992.

Leffler, Melvyn P. *For the Soul of Mankind: The United States, the Soviet Union, and the Cold War*. New York: Hill and Wang, 2007.

Levin, Dov H. "When the Great Power Gets a Vote: The Effects of Great Power Electoral Interventions on Election Results." *International Studies Quarterly* 60, no. 2 (2016): 189–202.

Lillich, Richard B. "Forcible Self-Help by States to Protect Human Rights." *Iowa Law Review* 53, no. 2 (1967): 325–351.

Lindsay, Jon R. "Stuxnet and the Limits of Cyber Warfare." *Security Studies* 22, no. 3 (2013): 365–404.

Lindsay, Jon R. "Tipping the Scales: The Attribution Problem and the Feasibility of Deterrence Against Cyberattack." *Journal of Cybersecurity* 1, no. 1 (2015): 53–67.

Lockhart, James. *Chile, the CIA and the Cold War: A Transatlantic Perspective*. Edinburgh: Edinburgh University Press, 2019.

Lowenthal, Abraham F. *The Dominican Intervention*. Baltimore, MD and London: Johns Hopkins University Press, 1995.

Lynch, Allen. "Woodrow Wilson and the Principle of 'National Self-Determination': A Reconsideration." *Review of International Studies* 28, no. 2 (2002): 419–436.

Mandelbaum, Michael. *The Case for Goliath: How America Acts as the World's Government in the 21st Century*. New York: PublicAffairs, 2005.

Marshall, Monty G., Ted Robert Gurr, and Keith Jaggers. "Polity IV Project: Political Regime Characteristics and Transitions, 1800–2009. Dataset Users' Manual." *Center for Systemic Peace*, 2010.

Maxwell, Kenneth. "The Other 9/11: The United States and Chile, 1973." *Foreign Affairs* 82, no. 6 (2003): 147–151.

Mazower, Mark. *No Enchanted Palace: The End of Empire and the Ideological Origins of the United Nations*. Princeton, NJ and Oxford: Princeton University Press, 2009.

Mazzetti, Mark, Robert F. Worth, and Michael R. Gordon. "Obama's Uncertain Path Amid Syria Bloodshed." *New York Times* Oct. 22 (2013). https://www.nytimes.com/2013/10/23/world/middleeast/obamas-uncertain-path-amid-syria-bloodshed.html.

Mazzetti, Mark, and Ali Younes. "C.I.A. Arms for Syrian Rebels Supplied Black Market, Officials Say." *New York Times* June 26 (2016). https://www.nytimes.com/2016/06/27/world/middleeast/cia-arms-for-syrian-rebels-supplied-black-market-officials-say.html?_r=0.

McDougal, Myres S. "The Soviet-Cuban Quarantine and Self-Defense." *The American Journal of International Law* 57, no. 3 (1963): 597–604.

McDougal, Myres S., and Richard N. Gardner. "The Veto and the Charter: An Interpretation for Survival." *Yale Law Journal* 60, no. 2 (1951): 258–292.

McFaul, Michael. *From Cold War to Hot Peace: An American Ambassador in Putin's Russia*. Boston, MA and New York: Houghton Mifflin Harcourt, 2018.

McManus, Roseanne, and Keren Yarhi-Milo. "The Logic of 'Offstage' Signaling: Domestic Politics, Regime Type, and Major Power-Protégé Relations." *International Organization* 71, no. 4 (2017): 701–733.

McPherson, Alan. "Misled by Himself: What the Johnson Tapes Reveal About the Dominican Intervention of 1965." *Latin American Research Review* 38, no. 2 (2003): 127–146.

Mearsheimer, John J. "The False Promise of International Institutions." *International Security* 19, no. 3 (1995): 5–49.

Menges, Constantine. *Inside the National Security Council: The True Story of the Making and Unmaking of Reagan's Foreign Policy*. New York: Touchstone, 1988.

Mitchener, Kris James, and Marc Weidenmier. "Empire, Public Goods, and the Roosevelt Corollary." *The Journal of Economic History* 65, no. 3 (2005): 658–692.

Mitzen, Jennifer. *Power in Concert: The Nineteenth-Century Origins of Global Governance*. Chicago, IL and London: The University of Chicago Press, 2013.

Monten, Jonathan. "The Roots of the Bush Doctrine." *International Security* 29, no. 4 (2005): 112–156.

Morgenthau, Hans J. "To Intervene or Not to Intervene." *Foreign Affairs* 45, no. 3 (1967): 425–436.

Moynihan, Daniel Patrick. *Secrecy: The American Experience.* New Haven, CT: Yale University Press, 1998.

Nasri, Reza. "McCain's UN Charter Confusion." *The National Interest* Aug. 9 (2013).

Neustadt, Richard E., and Ernest R. May. *Thinking In Time: The Uses Of History For Decision Makers.* New York: The Free Press, 1986.

North, Douglass C., and Barry R. Weingast. "Constitutions and Commitment: The Evolution of Institutions Governing Public Choice in Seventeenth-Century England." *The Journal of Economic History* 49, no. 4 (1989): 803.

Nuñez-Mietz, Fernando G. "Legalization and the Legitimation of the Use of Force: Revisiting Kosovo." *International Organization,* 2018, 1–33.

Nye, Joseph S. "Soft Power and American Foreign Policy." *Political Science Quarterly* 119, no. 2 (2004): 255–270.

Nye, Joseph S. "Deterrence and Dissuasion in Cyberspace." *International Security* 41, no. 3 (2017): 44–71.

O'Rourke, Lindsey. *Covert Regime Change: America's Secret Cold War.* Ithaca, NY: Cornell University Press, 2018.

OAS. "Charter of the Organization of American States," 1948. http://www.oas.org/en/sla/dil/inter_american_treaties_A-41_charter_OAS.asp.

Olson, Parmy. "Man Inadvertently Live Tweets Osama Bin Laden Raid." *Forbes* May 2 (2011). https://www.forbes.com/sites/parmyolson/2011/05/02/man-inadvertently-live-tweets-osama-bin-laden-raid/#6bb5d936c774.

Omang, Joanne. "U.S. Seeks to Reassure OAS On Grenada Invasion Motive." *Washington Post* Nov. 15 (1983). https://www.washingtonpost.com/archive/politics/1983/11/15/us-seeks-to-reassure-oas-on-grenada-invasion-motive/4f7fc75e-a7b7-4d5b-b3f4-899e5da37f94/?utm_term=.ca6d5ef63ccb.

Organization of American States. "Organization of American States: Resolution Establishing Inter-American Force in the Dominican Republic." *International Legal Materials* 4, no. 3 (1965): 594–596.

Owen, John M. "The Foreign Imposition of Domestic Institutions." *International Organization* 56, no. 2 (2002): 375–409.

Owen, John M. *The Clash of Ideas in World Politics: Transnational Networks, States, and Regime Change, 1510–2010.* Princeton, NJ: Princeton University Press, 2010.

Padelford, Norman J. "Regional Organization and the United Nations." *International Organization* 8, no. 2 (1954): 203–216.

Pape, Robert A. *Dying to Win: The Strategic Logic of Suicide Terrorism.* New York: Random House, 2005.

Pape, Robert A. "When Duty Calls: A Pragmatic Standard of Humanitarian Intervention." *International Security* 37, no. 1 (2012): 41–80.

Papermaster, Daniel I. "A Case Study of the Effect of International Law on Foreign Policy Decisionmaking: The United States Intervention in the Dominican Republic in 1965." *Texas International Law Journal* 24, no. 3 (1989): 463–497.

Pastor, Robert. "The United States and the Grenada Revolution: Who Pushed First and Why?" In *A Revolution Aborted: The Lessons of Grenada,* edited by Jorge Heine, 181–214. Pittsburgh, PA: University of Pittsburgh Press, 1990.

Payandeh, Mehrdad. "The United Nations, Military Intervention, and Regime Change in Libya." *Virginia Journal of International Law* 52, no. 2 (2012): 355–403.

Peceny, Mark. *Democracy at the Point of Bayonets.* University Park, PA: Pennsylvania State University Press, 1999.

Perina, Alexandra H. "Black Holes and Open Secrets: The Impact of Covert Action on International Law." *Columbia Journal of Transnational Law* 53, no. 3 (2015): 507–583.

Philpott, Daniel. *Revolutions in Sovereignty: How Ideas Shaped Modern International Relations.* Princeton, NJ and Oxford: Princeton University Press, 2001.

Porter, Patrick. "A World Imagined: Nostalgia and Liberal Order." *CATO Institute* Number 843 (2018): 21.
Posen, Barry R. "The Rise of Illiberal Hegemony: Trump's Surprising Grand Strategy." *Foreign Affairs* 97, no. 2 (2018): 20–27.
Pozen, David E. "Deep Secrecy." *Stanford Law Review* 62, no. 2 (2010): 257–340.
Poznansky, Michael. "Stasis or Decay? Reconciling Covert War and the Democratic Peace." *International Studies Quarterly* 59, no. 4 (2015): 815–826.
Poznansky, Michael, and Evan Perkoski. "Rethinking Secrecy in Cyberspace: The Politics of Voluntary Attribution." *Journal of Global Security Studies* 3, no. 4 (2018): 402–416.
Prados, John. *The Family Jewels: The CIA, Secrecy, and Presidential Power*. Austin, TX: University of Texas Press, 2013.
Press, Daryl G. *Calculating Credibility: How Leaders Assess Military Threats*. Ithaca, NY: Cornell University Press, 2005.
Rabe, Stephen G. *Eisenhower and Latin America: The Foreign Policy of Anticommunism*. Chapel Hill, NC and London: University of North Carolina Press, 1988.
Rabe, Stephen G. "The Johnson Doctrine." *Presidential Studies Quarterly* 36, no. 1 (2006): 48–58.
Raymond, Mark. *Social Practices of Rule-Making in World Politics*. New York: Oxford University Press, 2019.
Reisman, W. Michael, and James E. Baker. *Regulating Covert Action: Practices, Contexts, and Policies of Covert Coercion Abroad in International and American Law*. New Haven, CT and London: Yale University Press, 1992.
Reiter, Dan. "Democracy, Deception, and Entry into War." *Security Studies* 21, no. 4 (2012): 594–623.
Reiter, Dan, and Allan C. Stam. *Democracies at War*. Princeton, NJ and Oxford: Princeton University Press, 2002.
Reus-Smit, Christian. *American Power and World Order*. Cambridge, UK: Polity Press, 2004.
Rhodes, Ben. *The World As It Is: A Memoir of the Obama White House*. New York: Random House, 2018.
Rid, Thomas. "Cyber War Will Not Take Place." *Journal of Strategic Studies* 35, no. 1 (2012): 5–32.
Rogers, William C., Barbara Stuhler, and Donald Koenig. "A Comparison of Informed and General Public Opinion on U.S. Foreign Policy." *The Public Opinion Quarterly* 31, no. 2 (1967): 242–252.
Rogers, William D., and Kenneth Maxwell. "Fleeing the Chilean Coup: The Debate Over U.S. Complicity." *Foreign Affairs* 83, no. 1 (2004): 160–165.
Rohlfing, Ingo. "Comparative Hypothesis Testing Via Process Tracing." *Sociological Methods and Research* 43, no. 4 (2014): 606–642.
Roosevelt, Franklin Delano. "Inaugural Address, March 4, 1933." *World Affairs* 96, no. 1 (1933): 26–28.
Rosenau, James N. "Intervention as a Scientific Concept." *Journal of Conflict Resolution* 13, no. 2 (1969): 149–171.
Rovner, Joshua. *Fixing the Facts: National Security and the Politics of Intelligence*. Ithaca, NY: Cornell University Press, 2011.
Rovner, Joshua, and Tyler Moore. "Does the Internet Need a Hegemon?" *Journal of Global Security Studies* 2, no. 3 (2017): 184–203.
Rozell, Mark J. *Executive Privilege: Presidential Power, Secrecy, and Accountability*. 3rd ed. Lawrence, KS: University Press of Kansas, 2010.
Ruggie, John Gerard. *Winning the Peace: America and World Order in the New Era*. New York: Columbia University Press, 1996.
Russett, Bruce. *Grasping the Democratic Peace: Principles for a Post-Cold War World*. Princeton, NJ: Princeton University Press, 1993.
Ruys, Tom. *"Armed Attack" and Article 51 of the UN Charter : Evolutions in Customary Law and Practice*. Cambridge, UK: Cambridge University Press, 2010.

Saunders, Elizabeth N. *Leaders at War: How Presidents Shape Military Interventions*. Ithaca, NY: Cornell University Press, 2011.

Savage, Charlie. "Trump Poised to Lift Ban on C.I.A. 'Black Site' Prisons." *New York Times* Jan. 25 (2017). https://www.nytimes.com/2017/01/25/us/politics/cia-detainee-prisons.html.

Schelling, Thomas C. *Strategies of Commitment and Other Essays*. Cambridge, MA: Harvard University Press, 2006.

Schimmelfennig, Frank. "The Community Trap: Liberal Norms, Rhetorical Action, and the Eastern Enlargement of the European Union." *International Organization* 55, no. 1 (2001): 47–80.

Schlesinger, Arthur, Jr. *A Thousand Days: John F. Kennedy in the White House*. New York: Mariner Books, 1965.

Schoultz, Lars. *Beneath the United States: A History of U.S. Policy Toward Latin America*. Cambridge, MA and London: Harvard University Press, 1998.

Schuessler, John M. "The Deception Dividend: FDR's Undeclared War." *International Security* 34, no. 4 (2010): 133–165.

Schuessler, John M. *Deceit on the Road to War*. Ithaca, NY: Cornell University Press, 2015.

Schwartz, Thomas A. "Henry Kissinger: Realism, Domestic Politics, and the Struggle Against Exceptionalism in American Foreign Policy." *Diplomacy & Statecraft* 22, no. 1 (2011): 121–141.

Shannon, Vaughn P. "Norms Are What States Make of Them: The Political Psychology of Norm Violation." *International Studies Quarterly* 44, no. 2 (2000): 293–316.

Shannon, Vaughn P., and Jonathan W. Keller. "Leadership Style and International Norm Violation: The Case of the Iraq War." *Foreign Policy Analysis* 3, no. 1 (2007): 79–104.

Sheridan, Richard B. "The British Credit Crisis of 1772 and The American Colonies." *The Journal of Economic History* 20, no. 2 (1960): 161–186.

Shultz, George. *Turmoil and Triumph: My Years as Secretary of State*. New York: Charles Scribner's Sons, 1993.

Sievers, Loraine, and Sam Daws. *The Procedure of the UN Security Council*. 4th ed. Oxford: Oxford University Press, 2014.

Sigmund, Paul E. *The Overthrow of Allende and the Politics of Chile, 1964–1976*. Pittsburgh, PA: University of Pittsburgh Press, 1977.

Simmons, Beth. "International Law and State Behavior: Commitment and Compliance in International Monetary Affairs." *American Political Science Review* 94, no. 4 (2000): 819–835.

Simmons, Beth. *Mobilizing for Human Rights: International Law and Domestic Politics*. New York: Cambridge University Press, 2009.

Slantchev, Branislav L. "Feigning Weakness." *International Organization* 64, no. 3 (2010): 357–388.

Slater, Jerome. *Intervention and Negotiation: The United States and the Dominican Revolution*. New York, Evanston, IL, and London: Harper & Row, 1970.

Slayton, Rebecca. "What Is the Cyber Offense-Defense Balance? Conceptions, Causes, and Assessment." *International Security* 41, no. 3 (2017): 72–109.

Smith, Gaddis. *The Last Years of the Monroe Doctrine: 1945–1993*. New York: Hill and Wang, 1994.

Smith, Gregory L. "Secret but Constrained: The Impact of Elite Opposition on Covert Operations." *International Organization* 73, no. 3 (2019): 685–707.

Smith, R. Jeffrey, and David B. Ottaway. "Anti-Saddam Operation Cost CIA $100 Million." *Washington Post* Sep. 15 (1996). https://www.washingtonpost.com/archive/politics/1996/09/15/anti-saddam-operation-cost-cia-100-million/4864d228-3623-4ba6-b6d1-ca524d64cc22/?utm_term=.23de0e76e49a.

Smith, Tony. *America's Mission: The United States and the Worldwide Struggle for Democracy*. Princeton, NJ and Oxford: Princeton University Press, 1994.

Sofaer, Abraham. "Executive Power and the Control of Information: Practice Under the Framers." *Duke Law Journal* 1, no. 1 (1977): 1–57.

Spaniel, William, and Michael Poznansky. "Credible Commitment in Covert Affairs." *American Journal of Political Science* 62, no. 3 (2018): 668–681.

Suri, Jeremy. *Henry Kissinger and the American Century*. Cambridge, MA: The Belknap Press of Harvard University Press, 2007.

Taft, William H., and Todd F. Buchwald. "Preemption, Iraq, and International Law." *American Journal of International Law* 97, no. 3 (2003): 557–563.

Taliaferro, Jeffrey W. *Balancing Risks: Great Power Intervention in the Periphery*. Ithaca, NY: Cornell University Press, 2004.

Tannenwald, Nina. "The Nuclear Taboo: The United States and the Normative Basis of Nuclear Non-Use." *International Organization* 53, no. 3 (1999): 433–468.

Taylor, Adam. "What Is the Monroe Doctrine? John Bolton's Justification for Trump's Push against Maduro." *Washington Post* March 4 (2019). https://www.washingtonpost.com/world/2019/03/04/what-is-monroe-doctrine-john-boltons-justification-trumps-push-against-maduro/?noredirect=on&utm_term=.79430b2b1098.

Tenet, George. *At the Center of the Storm: My Years at the CIA*. New York: HarperCollins, 2007.

The Yearbook of the United Nations. United Nations, Lake Success, New York: Department of Public Information, 1947. https://www.unmultimedia.org/searchers/yearbook/page.jsp?volume=1946-47&page=39&searchType=advanced.

Thomas, A.J. Jr., and Ann Van Wynen Thomas. "The Organization of American States and Collective Security." *Southwestern Law Journal* 13, no. 2 (1959): 177–214.

Thomas, Ann Van Wynen, and A.J. Thomas, Jr. *Non-Intervention: The Law and Its Import in the Americas*. Dallas, TX: Southern Methodist University Press, 1956.

Thompson, Alexander. "Coercion Through IOs: The Security Council and the Logic of Information Transmission." *International Organization* 60, no. 1 (2006): 1–34.

Throntveit, Trygve. "The Fable of the Fourteen Points: Woodrow Wilson and National Self-Determination." *Diplomatic History* 35, no. 3 (2011): 445–481.

Treverton, Gregory F. *Covert Action: The Limits of Intervention in the Postwar World*. New York: Basic Books, Inc., 1987.

Tucker, Robert W., and David C. Hendrickson. "The Sources of American Legitimacy." *Foreign Affairs* 83, no. 6 (2004): 18–32.

Turner, Stansfield. *Secrecy and Democracy: The CIA in Transition*. Boston, MA: Houghton Mifflin, 1985.

Tyler, Tom R. "Psychological Perspectives on Legitimacy and Legitimation." *Annual Review of Psychology* 57 (2006): 375–400.

"U.S. Aid to the Contras: The Record Since '81." *New York Times* March 20 (1986). https://www.nytimes.com/1986/03/20/world/us-aid-to-the-contras-the-record-since-81.html.

UN General Assembly. "290 (IV). Essentials of Peace." UN Documents, 1949. http://www.un-documents.net/a4r290.htm.

UN General Assembly. "380(v). Peace Through Deeds." UN Documents, 1950. http://www.un.org/documents/ga/res/5/ares5.htm.

UN General Assembly. "2131 (XX). Declaration on the Inadmissibility of Intervention in the Domestic Affairs of States and the Protection of Their Independence and Sovereignty." UN Documents, 1965. http://www.un-documents.net/a20r2131.htm.

UN General Assembly. "2625 (XXV). Declaration on Principles of International Law Concerning Friendly Relations and Co-Operation among States in Accordance with the Charter of the United Nations." UN Documents, 1970. http://www.un-documents.net/a25r2625.htm.

UN General Assembly. "42/22. Declaration on the Enhancement of the Effectiveness of the Principle of Refraining from the Threat or Use of Force in International Relations." UN Documents, 1987. http://www.un.org/documents/ga/res/42/a42r022.htm.

UN Security Council. "Resolution 1441 (2002)." UN Documents, 2002. http://www.un.org/Depts/unmovic/documents/1441.pdf.

United Nations. "Charter of the United Nations," 1945. http://www.un.org/en/charter-united-nations/.

Vance, Cyrus. *Hard Choices: Critical Years in America's Foreign Policy*. New York: Simon and Schuster, 1983.

Vandenbroucke, Lucien S. "Anatomy of a Failure: The Decision to Land at the Bay of Pigs." *Political Science Quarterly* 99, no. 3 (1984): 471–491.

Vattel, Emer De. *The Law of Nations: Or, Principles of the Law of Nature Applied to the Conduct and Affairs of Nations and Sovereigns*. Edited by Bela Kapossy and Richard Whatmore. Indianapolis, IN, 2008.

Vincent, R.J. *Nonintervention and International Order*. Princeton, NJ: Princeton University Press, 1974.

Waldner, David. "What Makes Process Tracing Good? Causal Mechanisms, Causal Inference, and the Completeness Standard in Comparative Politics." In *Process Tracing: From Metaphor to Analytic Tool*, edited by Andrew Bennett and Jeffrey T. Checkel, 126–152. Cambridge, UK: Cambridge University Press, 2015.

Walt, Stephen M. *Taming American Power: The Global Response to U.S. Primacy*. New York: W.W. Norton, 2005.

Walzer, Michael. *Just and Unjust Wars: A Moral Argument with Historical Illustrations*. New York: Basic Books, 1977.

Warner, Michael. "Wanted : A Definition of Intelligence." *Studies in Intelligence* 46, no. 3 (2002): 15–22.

Weber, Cynthia. *Simulating Sovereignty: Intervention, the State, and Symbolic Exchange*. New York: Cambridge University Press, 1995.

Weiner, Tim. "The Deal on Iraq: The C.I.A.; C.I.A. Drafts Covert Plan to Topple Hussein." *New York Times* Feb. 26 (1998). https://www.nytimes.com/1998/02/26/world/the-deal-on-iraq-the-cia-cia-drafts-covert-plan-to-topple-hussein.html.

Weisiger, Alex, and Keren Yarhi-Milo. "Revisiting Reputation: How Past Actions Matter in International Politics." *International Organization* 69, no. 2 (2015): 473–495.

Weller, Marc, ed. *The Oxford Handbook of the Use of Force in International Law*. Oxford: Oxford University Press, 2015.

Westad, Odd Arne. *The Global Cold War: Third World Interventions and the Making of Our Times*. Cambridge, UK: Cambridge University Press, 2005.

Western, Jon. *Selling Intervention and War: The Presidency, the Media, and the American Public*. Baltimore and London: Johns Hopkins University Press, 2005.

Westra, Joel H. *International Law and the Use of Armed Force: The UN Charter and the Major Powers*. London and New York: Routledge, 2007.

Wheeler, Nicholas J. *Saving Strangers: Humanitarian Intervention in International Society*. Oxford: Oxford University Press, 2000.

Willard-Foster, Melissa. *Toppling Foreign Governments: The Logic of Regime Change*. Philadelphia, PA: University of Pennsylvania Press, 2019.

Wippman, David. "The Nine Lives of Article 2(4)." *Minnesota Journal of International Law* 16, no. 2 (2007): 387–406.

Wolff, Christian. *Jus Gentium Methodo Scientifica Pertractatum*. Edited by Joseph Drake. Oxford: Clarendon Press, 1934.

Wright, Robin. "America's Iraq Policy: How Did It Come to This?" *The Washington Quarterly* 21, no. 3 (1998): 53–70.

Wyden, Peter. *Bay of Pigs: The Untold Story*. New York: Simon and Schuster, 1979.

Yarhi-Milo, Keren. "Tying Hands Behind Closed Doors: The Logic and Practice of Secret Reassurance." *Security Studies* 22 (2013): 405–435.

Yglesias, Matthew. "Woodrow Wilson." *The Atlantic* Jan 4 (2007). https://www.theatlantic.com/politics/archive/2007/01/woodrow-wilson/41117/.

Yoo, John. "International Law and the War in Iraq." *American Journal of International Law* 97, no. 3 (2003): 563–576.

Yoon, Mi Yung. "Explaining U.S. Intervention in Third World Internal Wars, 1945-1989." *Journal of Conflict Resolution* 41, no. 4 (1997): 580–602.

Zakheim, Dov S. "The Grenada Operation and Superpower Relations: A Perspective from the Pentagon." In *Grenada and Soviet/Cuban Policy: Internal Crisis and U.S./OECS Intervention*, edited by Jiri Valenta and Herbert J. Ellison, 175–185. Boulder and London: Westview Press, 1986.

Zaks, Sherry. "Relationships Among Rivals (RAR): A Framework for Analyzing Contending Hypotheses in Process Tracing." *Political Analysis* 25, no. 3 (2017): 344–362.

Zarakol, Ayse. "What Made the Modern World Hang Together: Socialisation or Stigmatisation?" *International Theory* 6, no. 2 (2014): 311–332.

INDEX

Note: Tables and figures are indicated by *t* and *f* following the page number

For the benefit of digital users, indexed terms that span two pages (e.g., 52–53) may, on occasion, appear on only one of those pages.